Using ClarisWorks™ for Windows™

Laurie Miller Love

Addison-Wesley Publishing Company

Reading, Massachusetts   Menlo Park, California   New York
Don Mills, Ontario   Wokingham, England   Amsterdam   Bonn   Sydney
Singapore   Tokyo   Madrid   San Juan   Paris   Seoul   Milan   Mexico City   Taipei

The author and publishers have taken care in preparation of this book, but make no expressed or implied warranty of any kind and assume no responsibility for errors or omissions. No liability is assumed for incidental or consequential damages in connection with or arising out of the use of the information or programs contained herein.

Many of the designations used by manufacturers and sellers to distinguish their products are claimed as trademarks. Where those designations appear in this book and Addison-Wesley was aware of a trademark claim, the designations have been printed in initial capital letters.

Library of Congress Cataloging-in-Publication Data

Love, Laurie Miller, 1960–
    Using ClarisWorks for Windows / Laurie Miller Love.
        p. cm.
    Includes index.
    ISBN 0-201-62280-7
    1. Integrated software. 2. ClarisWorks for Windows. I. Title.
QA76.76.I57L69 1993
005.369—dc20   92-38362
                                                         CIP

Sponsoring Editor: Keith Wollman
Project Editor: Joanne Clapp Fullagar
Production Coordinator: Kathy Traynor
Cover photograph by Sean Sullivan
Set in 10-point New Century Schoolbook by ST Associates, Inc., Wakefield, MA

ISBN 0-201-62280-7

1 2 3 4 5 6 7 8 9—MA—9796959493
First printing, May 1993

*For Ray—my husband, my best friend,
and my life partner.*

Contents

Acknowledgments

This book would not be possible if it wasn't for the success of ClarisWorks. The ClarisWorks product team is to be commended on the excellence of their efforts. I personally would like to thank Bob Lisbonne (ClarisWorks product manager), Mohan Thomas (ClarisWorks SQA team), and Ellen Vavak (ClarisWorks support technician) for keeping me involved in ClarisWorks and for their continued support of and enthusiasm for my ClarisWorks books. I would also like to thank Shannon Ronald, Annie Marinovich, Jay Lee, Peter Heller, and my friends in Claris Publications.

Thanks to Adam Behrens for hanging in there with my manuscript through tech review. Adam, as usual, your comments were worth the wait.

At Addison-Wesley, my thanks to David Rogelberg, Joanne Clapp Fullagar, and Keith Wollman, who have all contributed greatly to this book. Thanks also to Kathy Traynor for coordinating the book's production.

A special thank-you to my friend and colleague, Dr. Warren Williams, president of the ClarisWorks Users Group (C•WUG). Warren, thanks so much for always encouraging me and for helping to make my first ClarisWorks book a tremendous success. I'm looking forward to continuing to work with you over the years.

I'd also like to thank the very helpful staff at ComputerWare in Capitola, CA (especially Eric), who have kept my computers running in top condition, and who helped me network my Macintosh, Windows machine, and Apple LaserWriter together so I could write about cross-platform configurations in the Appendix.

Last but not least, I owe a huge thank-you to my family for all they've done to make it possible for me to realize my dreams.

Introduction

About this book

Using ClarisWorks for Windows is intended to help you master one of the most innovative software products ever developed—ClarisWorks from Claris Corporation. Whether you are a brand-new ClarisWorks user or someone who has worked with ClarisWorks for some time, *Using ClarisWorks for Windows* teaches you how to accomplish everyday home and business projects quickly, easily, and more efficiently.

This book is NOT a rewrite of nor a replacement for the ClarisWorks documentation. Indeed, *Using ClarisWorks for Windows* provides you with knowledge you will not gain from reading the documentation alone. *Using ClarisWorks for Windows* is a practical, hands-on guide featuring dozens of real-world examples that you can follow to get the most out of ClarisWorks. As the writer of the online Help for ClarisWorks for the Macintosh, and as author of the best-selling *Using ClarisWorks* (Macintosh version), I have spent three years exploring and exploiting both the obvious features and hidden secrets of ClarisWorks. By writing this book, I hope to share with you the knowledge I have acquired, and to encourage you to use ClarisWorks in ways you may not have considered before. Throughout the book, you'll learn how to combine ClarisWorks integrated features to

- Create letterhead and envelopes with your logo
- Produce a professional newsletter that includes text, graphics, and spreadsheet data
- Keep track of addresses of friends and relatives, and print mailing labels
- Design an order entry form
- Generate a customer invoice
- Create a sales report
- Track household expenses
- Amortize a loan
- Analyze stock market information

Using ClarisWorks for Windows also features numerous tips, tricks, and shortcuts that will help you become a ClarisWorks master in no time at all.

ClarisWorks works

ClarisWorks for Windows is a tightly integrated software productivity product. What differentiates ClarisWorks from other integrated software products is that it is truly integrated. It *works* for you to get your job done.

You use ClarisWorks as you would use a pencil, a piece of paper, a calculator, a set of drawing tools, and a ruler. When you want to draw, you select the graphics tool; when you want to crunch numbers, you select the spreadsheet tool, and so on. No matter what kind of document you have open at any given time, selecting a tool from the powerful ClarisWorks tool palette gives you access to all of the menus, commands, and features of another application area. For example, if you have a text document open, simply select the spreadsheet tool from the tool palette and you immediately have access to all of the features available in the spreadsheet application environment. You don't need to open another document; you don't need to switch to another application; you just pick whatever tool you need. In this way, you no longer have to confine yourself to thinking about documents that contain only text, or only graphics, or only database information. ClarisWorks lets you combine all of these different elements, and more, into one single document. This concept of true, seamless integration is the focus of *Using ClarisWorks for Windows*.

Who should read this book

Using ClarisWorks for Windows is intended for beginning and intermediate users of ClarisWorks. It is assumed that you have ClarisWorks, that ClarisWorks is already installed on your PC, that you have some familiarity with basic features of ClarisWorks, and that you have a desire to learn more about ClarisWorks.

Although Chapter 1 does cover some ClarisWorks basics, the primary focus of the book is on applying ClarisWorks to solve specific problems. As such, you should know how to start up the application and open, close, save, and print documents.

Additionally, you should have read the Windows system software documentation so you are comfortable with basic Windows techniques such as

- Pointing, clicking, and dragging with the mouse
- Using the Clipboard through Cut, Copy, and Paste
- Working in the Program Manager
- Choosing commands from menus
- Using dialog boxes
- Selecting and editing text
- Working with disks

How this book is organized

This book follows certain conventions to help you get the most out of the material presented.

Conventions used in this book

Using ClarisWorks for Windows focuses on the highly integrated nature of ClarisWorks by describing how to use its different application environments together. This book features step-by-step procedures you can follow to create and enhance a variety of practical solutions. The procedures are clearly delineated, appearing in bold as a set of numbered steps, and are supported by a generous number of figures, so you can easily follow along with the steps.

In addition to procedures, the book includes many tips and tricks. When appropriate, special information about a particular feature or aspect of a procedure appears as a *note*, while a word of warning appears as *caution*. Special icons in the margin identify tips, which appear in italic style.

Other conventions used in this book include:

- Text that you type appears in boldface in the main text, or it appears in plain text in a numbered step, such as

  In the File Name area, type **Sales.CWK**.

  or

  2   In the File Name area, type Sales.CWK.

- Literal words appear in italics, such as

  Click next to the word *participant* in the third paragraph.

- Formulas and calculations appear in Courier font, such as

  `SUM("Total Sales")`

- The Enter, or Return, key is expressed as ↵, to differentiate it from the Enter key on the numeric keypad, such as

  Press ↵ twice to begin a new paragraph.

  Press Enter on the numeric keypad to select the frame.

Overview of chapters

The following is a brief description of the chapters in *Using ClarisWorks for Windows*:

Chapter 1: Understanding the ClarisWorks for Windows Environment

This chapter introduces ClarisWorks for Windows and its four application environments—word processing (text), graphics, spreadsheet, and database. It describes ClarisWorks document types and key operations within them. This chapter also covers how to use the ClarisWorks tool palette and everything you need to know about ClarisWorks frames. Included is general information about using the Microsoft Windows Terminal accessory to access communications capabilities.

Chapter 2: Creating Personal or Business Stationery

This chapter describes how to use the text and graphics environments to create a personal or business letterhead, a logo, and a template for matching envelopes. You will also create a two-page letter, which includes a header, footer, and footnotes, to use with the stationery. Spell-checking and using the thesaurus are also covered.

Chapter 3: Producing Newsletters

This chapter teaches you how to use the text, graphics, and spreadsheet environments together to design and lay out a two-page newsletter. Special attention is given to using ClarisWorks unique Frame Links feature to do page layout. In producing the newsletter, you learn how to create diagrams to graphically represent a process (such as an organizational chart), how to use tables in text, how to include a chart from a spreadsheet, and how to import clip art from various sources.

Chapter 4: Managing Personal Records

This chapter focuses on how to use the database environment to store and retrieve personal records. You also learn how to use different types of database layouts in ClarisWorks to create lists and mailing labels with graphics. Included is a complete discussion of how to merge database records with form letters, labels, and envelopes.

Chapter 5: Creating Business Reports and Forms

In this chapter, you use the database and graphics environments with text and spreadsheet frames to create a variety of reports and forms, including an order entry form, a customer invoice, and a sales report. You will also use ClarisWorks macro feature to relate two database documents to each other. In creating the reports and forms, you use some of the more advanced features of the database environment, such as finding information based on multiple criteria, using functions and formulas in calculation fields, using layout summary parts, and integrating spreadsheet data.

Chapter 6: Managing Financial Information

This chapter focuses on how to use the spreadsheet environment most effectively to manage personal and business financial information. You will create an annual budget and a payment table for amortizing a loan. You will also learn how to annotate your spreadsheet documents using text frames and how to enhance them with graphics and charts. Special attention is given to using ClarisWorks functions, including finance-related functions. Included are numerous tips for printing spreadsheet documents.

Chapter 7: Telecommunicating

This chapter provides detailed information on using the Windows Terminal accessory with ClarisWorks to connect to and exchange information with other computers. Topics include Terminal basics, starting Terminal via ClarisWorks, specifying settings, connecting to another computer, transferring data, and disconnecting. The chapter also presents step-by-step instructions on how to download stock market quotes from an online service and how to move that data into a ClarisWorks spreadsheet for financial analysis.

Appendix: Exchanging Data with Other Applications

The appendix discusses how to import data from and export data to other applications, including dBASE, Lotus 1-2-3, Microsoft Word for DOS or Word for Windows, Microsoft Excel 3.0, PC Paintbrush, WordPerfect for DOS or WordPerfect for Windows, and those applications that support the following file formats: ASCII Text, BMP, CGM, DIF, EPSF, PCT, PCX, RTF, SYLK, TIFF, and WMF. Other topics include the Claris XTND System, importing and exporting user dictionary terms, and cross-platform tips for exchanging files between ClarisWorks for Windows and ClarisWorks for the Macintosh.

What you need to begin

To use ClarisWorks for Windows, you need the following:

- IBM PC, or compatible, computer with a 80386 CPU or higher
- DOS 3.3 or higher AND Windows 3.0 or higher
- Minimum of 2 megabytes (Mb) RAM (4 Mb is recommended)
- One 3.5-inch high density floppy disk drive and a hard disk
- VGA (or better) compatible graphics adapter and monitor
- Keyboard
- Mouse or similar pointing device (optional, but recommended)

ClarisWorks with notebooks

Because of its seamless integration, breadth of features within each application area, and compact size, ClarisWorks is the perfect productivity software choice for notebook computer users. The ClarisWorks application occupies 1.2 Mb of disk space without filters and runs in less than 1 Mb RAM. So, you can get the full power of four applications in one without using up all of your notebook's or laptop's hard disk space with four separate stand-alone applications, or without eating up a great deal of RAM.

Whether you are using your notebook for business or home purposes, ClarisWorks for Windows is the ideal software solution for your needs.

Other hardware

You should also have a printer and a modem to get the full power of ClarisWorks. ClarisWorks supports all of the printers supported by Windows through the Print Manager. Refer to the Microsoft Windows *User's Guide* for information on using Print Manager to install and configure printers, connect to network printers, and control printing.

A modem, phone line, and cabling are required if you intend to use Windows Terminal with ClarisWorks. Although it is not required, I also urge you to subscribe to one of the many online services available (such as CompuServe, Dow Jones/News Retrieval, or MCI Mail). An online service lets you

- Connect to a vast variety of informational databases
- Get quick answers to your computer-related questions
- Communicate with other ClarisWorks users
- Make travel reservations and purchase airline tickets
- Check stock quotes
- Download shareware programs and utilities

You may also want to consider a *scanner*. This will let you convert a graphic on paper into a digitized image on your PC, which can then be read into any ClarisWorks document type.

Moving on

With our introductory "housekeeping" behind us, let's move on to the first chapter and examine the ClarisWorks for Windows environment.

Chapter One

Understanding the ClarisWorks for Windows Environment

About this Chapter

This chapter introduces you to the fundamentals of ClarisWorks for Windows. It describes each of the four application environments—word processing (text), graphics, spreadsheet, and database—and their document types. The chapter also covers general information about using the Microsoft Windows Terminal program through ClarisWorks to access communications capabilities. Basic features of and how you work with each document type are also covered. The chapter also describes in detail two important ClarisWorks features that are common across all document types—the ClarisWorks tool palette and ClarisWorks frames.

When you finish this chapter, you will understand the basic operations of ClarisWorks for Windows, particularly those you need to know about to work through the rest of this book.

What is ClarisWorks for Windows?

ClarisWorks for Windows is a tightly *integrated* software productivity package from Claris Corporation. The term integrated refers to the fact that ClarisWorks for Windows combines four major application areas into one product, enabling you to do a variety of tasks without using different software products for each task. For example, with ClarisWorks for Windows, you can create a document that combines drawings, spreadsheet data, and text. In this way, ClarisWorks for Windows provides you with a *compound document architecture* in which one document may consist of two or more types of data.

ClarisWorks for Windows also lets you automatically run the Microsoft Terminal program for accomplishing telecommunications tasks. (Terminal is a separate communications application that comes with Microsoft Windows.) ClarisWorks doesn't provide its own communications environment; rather, it automatically runs Terminal when you select Communications in the New dialog box (File menu).

A major characteristic that distinguishes ClarisWorks from other integrated software packages on the market is its seamless integration of the application areas. To access the features of another application area, you simply select a tool. This metaphor of choosing a tool for a specific element of your work closely resembles the way you work with a pen, a pencil, a compass, or a paintbrush and a piece of paper, making it easier to learn ClarisWorks than it is to learn other software programs. As a result, you can accomplish more in less time.

In addition to its seamless integration of application areas, ClarisWorks for Windows brings you the full power of each application area, making it a perfect choice for notebook computer users. Each of the four application areas is not merely a watered-down version of what you might find in a full-featured stand-alone product. For example, if you want to use the spreadsheet area of ClarisWorks by itself, you can accomplish the same types of advanced tasks that you can if you use a single spreadsheet program. You can analyze financial data, chart trends, and use formulas and functions for complex computations. Working in one of the four application areas at a time is certainly one way to use ClarisWorks. However, by using the different application areas together you gain full advantage of what ClarisWorks has to offer.

Another important characteristic of ClarisWorks for Windows is its compatibility with ClarisWorks for the Macintosh. In fact, ClarisWorks for the Macintosh looks and works exactly like ClarisWorks for Windows. ClarisWorks for Windows can read any file you create in ClarisWorks for the Macintosh, and vice versa. This means that ClarisWorks is an ideal, easy-to-use solution for cross-platform configurations. See the Appendix for more information about using ClarisWorks across platforms.

ClarisWorks is also compatible with FileMaker Pro for Windows (also from Claris Corporation). In fact, the database environment in ClarisWorks looks and works like FileMaker Pro.

ClarisWorks environments

The four different application components of ClarisWorks are called *environments*. Each environment has its own set of menus, which appear in the menu bar. Within each of these menus are commands you choose to use features that are specific to a given environment. For example, the Organize menu in the database environment includes the Sort Records command, which you use specifically for sorting records in a database. The environment in which you are currently working (called the *active environment*) determines the menus and commands available to you. Some menus and commands, such as the File and Window menus and their commands, are common across all ClarisWorks environments.

You can access the menus and commands of one environment from a document created in another by simply clicking a tool. For example, you can access text-related menus from a spreadsheet chart to add descriptive labels and titles to the chart. You can also add text to a database layout or a graphics document. In short, the menus and commands of all ClarisWorks environments are always available in the other ClarisWorks environments. How you actually apply this concept to your work in ClarisWorks is what this book is all about.

Before you can effectively use elements of several ClarisWorks environments together, it's important to understand each of them separately. Let's take a brief look at each ClarisWorks environment.

The word processing environment

The word processing (or text) environment is where you write and edit text, just as you would use a pen and paper or a typewriter to write letters, notes, proposals, and so on. The text environment lets you produce attractive, professional documents by using different fonts (in various sizes and styles) and color (if your configuration supports color). Figure 1-1 shows an example of what you can do in the text environment.

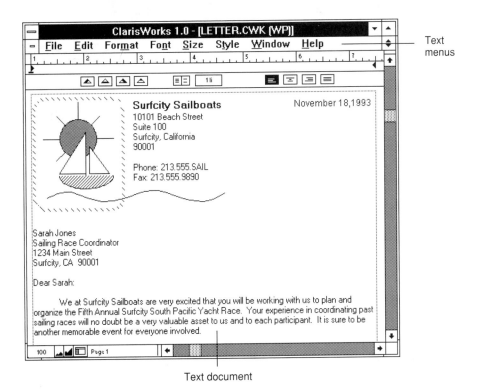

Figure 1-1 The text environment

A font, also called a *typeface,* describes a set of characters. Using different fonts in your text documents makes them more understandable and more interesting to read. For example, you can use one font for a table and another for a set of instructions. You can also use different sizes and styles of the same font to further enhance your documents. *Font sizes* are measured in *points,* such as 9-point, 12-point, 72-point, and so on. (A point is 1/72 of an inch; that is, 72 points equal one inch.) *Font styles* typically include bold, italic, underline, superscript, and subscript.

The graphics environment

Use the graphics environment to draw objects as you would use a drafting table, pens, and rulers to create drawings. Drawings can be scaled, reshaped, grouped, rotated, flipped, and locked. Enhance your drawings by applying different colors and patterns to them in any way you like. You can print your drawings separately or you can include them in other ClarisWorks document types. You can even save your drawings as .WMF files, which can be easily read and imported by other Windows applications. See the Appendix for more information on importing and exporting graphics and other types of documents.

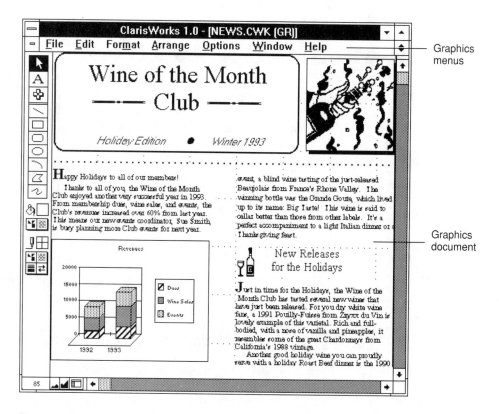

Figure 1-2 The graphics environment

In ClarisWorks, you also use the graphics environment to do page layouts in which you draw text and graphics objects in a one- or multicolumn format. Figure 1-2 shows an example of a two-column newsletter created in the graphics environment.

The spreadsheet environment

The spreadsheet environment provides you with an electronic worksheet where you can perform numeric calculations or analyze financial data. The results of numeric calculations are derived from *formulas*. A formula can be as simple as the addition of a set of numbers or as complex as determining the net present value of a financial investment. Formulas can contain numbers, text, dates, and times; they also include operators for adding, subtracting, multiplying, dividing, and so on. Formulas can also contain *functions*. Functions are built-in formulas that automatically calculate certain values for you, such as an average or the cosine of a given number. ClarisWorks for Windows includes more than 100 functions you can use in spreadsheets. By using formulas and functions, you can set up your spreadsheets to automatically solve simple or complex computations.

With the ClarisWorks spreadsheet environment, you can produce a wide variety of charts and graphs based on your spreadsheet data, as shown in Figure 1-3. This powerful feature lets you graphically view or present relationships and

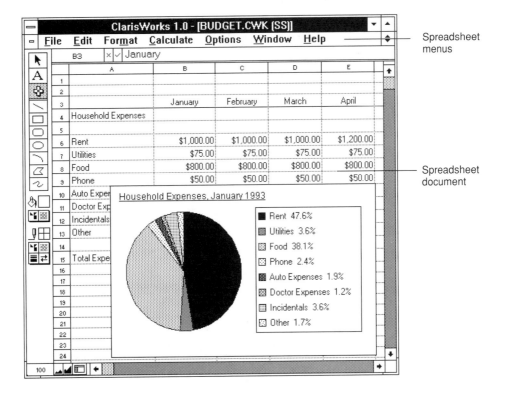

Figure 1-3 The spreadsheet environment

trends in your data. Charts are automatically updated when your data changes, making it easy for you to create up-to-date visuals for your own personal use or for professional presentations.

The database environment

You use the database environment to store and retrieve information as you would use an address book for names, addresses, and phone numbers. You may also think of it as a filing cabinet for records and business documents. The electronic nature of a database makes it easy to quickly retrieve the information you need, without searching through a stack of papers or flipping through pages in a book. The database environment also facilitates the task of storing and arranging information; you always have the flexibility to rearrange information in any way that best suits your immediate needs.

The ClarisWorks database environment includes a feature called *database layouts*. This feature makes it easy to display or print your information on the fly in a variety of different ways. For example, you can lay out your data in the form of a columnar report, as shown in Figure 1-4, or you can print your data as

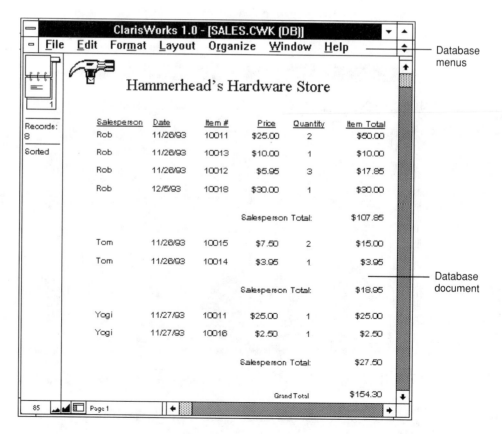

Figure 1-4 A columnar report in the database environment

mailing labels. Using elements from the graphics environment, you can enhance your database information with interesting and informative drawings, such as a business logo on a report, or a festive clip art picture on mailing labels.

One of the powerful uses for a database is the ability to summarize data. For example, a database layout of a document containing invoice data might summarize the total sales made by each salesperson. You can also copy these total sales figures to the Clipboard by choosing Copy Summaries from the Edit menu, paste them into a spreadsheet document or frame, and chart the data in a pie chart.

Many of the spreadsheet built-in functions are available in the database environment as well. By using functions in the database environment, ClarisWorks can automatically perform calculations based on any type of data in your database.

Communications

The communications capability of ClarisWorks is derived from the Windows Terminal accessory. (The communications feature is not considered a ClarisWorks environment.) When you choose New from the File menu and specify Communications as the document type, ClarisWorks automatically runs Terminal in a separate application window. This lets you access Terminal directly from ClarisWorks so you can perform communications tasks. Figure 1-5 shows Terminal running in its own application window. Notice that you can see the ClarisWorks application window behind it.

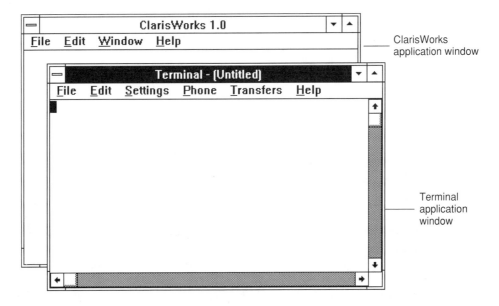

Figure 1-5 Terminal running in a separate application window

Used in conjunction with a modem, a phone line, and special cabling, Terminal lets you connect to and share information with another computer. The other computer can be across the room, in another city, or on the other side of the world. Generally, you use Terminal to connect with another computer through telephone lines. Once you are connected, you can electronically exchange information such as sending a data file to a friend or colleague, downloading stock quotes, or using an online subscription service (MCI Mail or CompuServe, for example).

Since Terminal is a separate application, you cannot seamlessly integrate its features, menus, commands, or data with the four ClarisWorks environments. For example, you cannot use communications features directly from within a spreadsheet. However, you can cut, copy, and paste information from a Terminal session window into a ClarisWorks document, just as you would cut, copy, or paste data between other Windows applications.

See Chapter 7, "Telecommunicating," for more information on using Terminal with ClarisWorks.

ClarisWorks document types

When you work in each ClarisWorks environment, you use that specific *document type;* that is, each ClarisWorks environment corresponds to its own document type. A document type simply refers to a document designed specifically for accomplishing a particular type of work. For example, a text document is designed for writing and editing text. So, as you might expect, the ClarisWorks document types are

- Text
- Graphics
- Spreadsheet
- Database

As mentioned earlier, ClarisWorks uses a compound document architecture whereby a document may contain more than one type of data. This means you start out with a specific document type and add objects from other environments using the ClarisWorks tool palette. For example, you may create a text document and add graphic objects as well as a spreadsheet to it. The resulting document is saved as the initial document type (text, in this case), even though it now also contains graphics and spreadsheet data.

One type of object you can add to documents is a *frame*, one of the most powerful features in ClarisWorks. Frames are described later in this chapter. For now, you should know that a frame is an object that acts as a view into another environment. You might think of frames as documents within documents—small versions of other document types in which you still have all of the features and commands of the other document type's environment available to you. In other words, it is through frames that you access another environment's menus and commands. It is important to understand the concept of frames in conjunction with document types because frames are key to combining features from multiple application environments into one document.

The rest of this section describes each of the four document types and their main elements and provides an overview of the basic operations specific to each document type.

Note *The file extension for all ClarisWorks document files is .CWK, regardless of document type. Stationery files have a .CWS extension.*

Text documents

Figure 1-6 shows a new, untitled ClarisWorks text document. The WP in the parentheses next to the document's name (Untitl1.CWK in this case) indicates that this is a word processing, or text, document type. The number 1 in the document's title means this is the first new, untitled document created in the current ClarisWorks session.

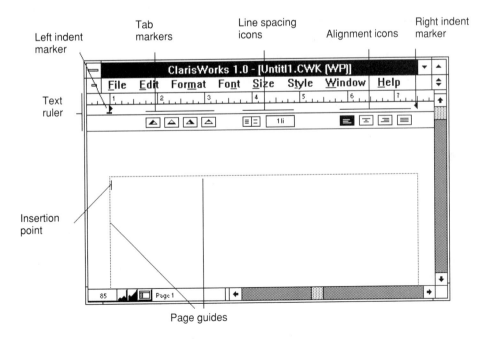

Figure 1-6 Elements of a text document

Page guides and the text ruler

When you create a new text document, you see *page guides,* which delineate page margins, and the *text ruler,* which contains various formatting icons. If your text document consists of multiple columns and includes headers and footers, the page guides also show their boundaries on the screen.

The page guides are preset to show in text documents. If you want to hide them, choose Document from the Format menu to open the Document dialog box. Uncheck (deselect) the Show Page Guides option, and click OK.

TIP

The text ruler lets you control the format of text and applies to text documents as well as text frames. There are two parts to the text ruler: the ruler itself and the formatting icons. The ruler itself shows the unit of measure set for the current paragraph(s). It also shows left and right indent markers, which correspond to your paragraph's left and right margin settings, respectively.

The real power of the text ruler lies in its formatting icons. To format text using the text ruler icons, you must first select the paragraph to be formatted. To select a paragraph, simply click anywhere in the paragraph to make it active. To select multiple paragraphs, click and drag through them (in whole or in part). Formatting changes apply to whole paragraphs at a time. So, if you change the format of a word or sentence, the paragraph containing that word or sentence is changed accordingly.

You can select a word, line, paragraph, or all text in the document using one of these techniques:

- *Double-click to select a single word*
- *Click three times quickly in succession to select a text line*
- *Click four times to select a whole paragraph*
- *Choose Select All (Ctrl+A) from the Edit menu to select the entire document*

TIP

The following is a description of the three sets of ClarisWorks icons.

Tab markers

Tab markers are used to set tab stops. You can set four types of tabs in ClarisWorks for Windows: Left (preset), Center, Right, and Align Character. You can set up to twenty tabs for each paragraph. ClarisWorks has preset, invisible tab stops at 0.5-inch intervals, which disappear when you insert your own tab stops. You set a tab stop by clicking on the appropriate tab marker and dragging it to the desired position on the ruler. To remove a tab stop, click on it and drag it off the ruler.

The type of tab you use determines how text aligns with the tab in your document. Left tab stops align text to the left of the tab, right tab stops align text to the right, and center tab stops align text in the center of the tab. Align Character tabs allow you to specify a character on which text should align. In the U.S. version, the preset tab character is a decimal separator, which aligns a column of text (such as decimal numbers) along the decimal point.

Line spacing icons

The text ruler's line spacing icons are used to change the spacing between lines within paragraphs and to *toggle,* or change, spacing measurements between the number of lines and the number of points. Line spacing can be set from 1 to 10 lines, in 0.5-line increments, or from 4 to 255 points, in 1-point increments. Line spacing is preset to 1 line, which is the equivalent of single-spaced text.

You decrease line spacing by clicking the left line spacing icon, and you increase it by clicking the right line spacing icon. Each time you click on one of these icons, the space between lines in the selected text is decreased or increased either by 0.5 lines or by 1 point. Clicking the line/points indicator toggles line spacing measurement between points and lines. Figure 1-7 shows an example of text that has line spacing set to 2.5 lines.

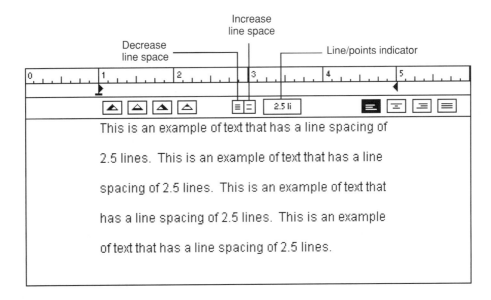

Figure 1-7 Line spacing example

If you set line spacing to points by clicking the Line/Points indicator, you can gain more precise control over the spacing between lines in a paragraph.

TIP

Alignment icons

You use the alignment icons to specify how text aligns between margins. Each icon corresponds to one of four alignment options: left (preset), center, right, or full justification.

You specify alignment by clicking once on the appropriate icon. Clicking the left or right alignment icon aligns the selected text along the left or right margin respectively and the opposite margin is ragged (uneven). Clicking the center alignment icon aligns text along the center of the page between both the left and right margins and both margins are ragged. A full justification alignment setting aligns text evenly along both margins.

You may find that the text ruler occupies too much room on your screen. You can hide the text ruler when you are not using it and see more of your document. To do this, choose Hide Rulers from the Window menu or press Shift+Ctrl+U. The Hide Rulers command changes to Show Rulers, which you can choose to show them again.

TIP

Graphics documents

Figure 1-8 shows a new, untitled graphics document. The GR in parentheses after the document's name indicates that this is a graphics document type. The number 2 in the document's title means that this is the second new document (regardless of type) created in the current ClarisWorks session.

A ClarisWorks graphics document consists of the *graphics grid,* the *graphics ruler,* and the *tool palette.* The graphics grid and the graphics ruler work together to help you precisely align objects in your document. The lines of the grid correspond to the unit of measure set for the graphics ruler. You can set the graphics grid to measure in points, picas, inches, centimeters, or millimeters by choosing Rulers from the Format menu and specifying your choice in the Rulers dialog box.

When you create a new graphics document, the graphics grid is visible but the ruler is not. To hide the graphics grid, choose Hide Graphics Grid from the Options menu. To show the graphics ruler, choose Show Rulers from the Window menu (Shift+Ctrl+U).

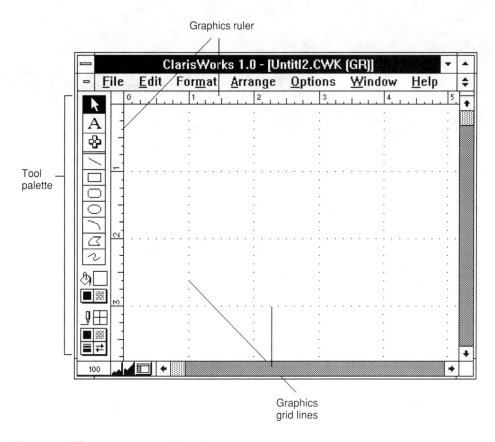

Figure 1-8 Elements of a graphics document

The tool palette appears along the left side of the window. The tool palette is available in all ClarisWorks environments, giving you the ability to add graphics and frames to text, spreadsheet, and database documents, as well as graphics documents. Graphics documents are the only ClarisWorks documents that are preset to show the tool palette. (Database documents are preset to show the status panel instead.) In other document types you can show the tool palette by clicking the Show/Hide Panel icon or by choosing Show Tools (Shift+Ctrl+T) from the Window menu. See "Using the ClarisWorks Tool Palette" later in this chapter for more information on the tool palette.

Spreadsheet documents

A spreadsheet document consists of a series of *rows* and *columns*, which intersect to form *cells*. You enter data and show the results of calculations in cells. Figure 1-9 shows a new, untitled spreadsheet document. The SS in the document's title identifies this as a spreadsheet document type.

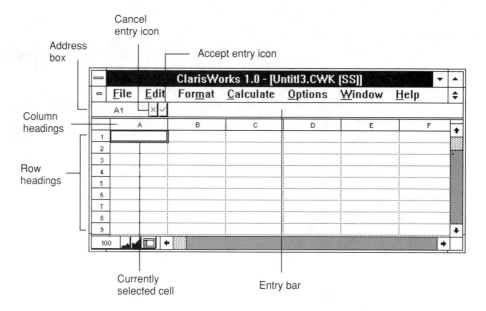

Figure 1-9 Elements of a spreadsheet document

The numbers running vertically along the left side of the spreadsheet are *row headings*; the letters running horizontally along the top are *column headings*. Together, row and column headings give each cell a unique *address*. The currently selected cell is indicated by a border around it and its address appears in the *address box* (A1 in Figure 1-9). You use cell addresses in calculations, for navigating, and for selecting cells.

For your own purposes, you can enter text *labels* in the first row or column of your spreadsheet to identify the type of data the row or column contains. For example, the budget spreadsheet shown in Figure 1-10 includes row labels like Rent, Utilities, and Food and column labels like January, February, and March. The identifying labels are not the same as row and column headings, which are inherent parts of a ClarisWorks spreadsheet.

A group of contiguous cells is called a *cell range*. Figure 1-10 shows a cell range of B6 to D8 selected. The upper-left cell (B6) and the lower-right cell (D8) are the range's *anchor points*. To select a cell range, click the upper-left anchor point (such as B6), hold down the mouse, and drag until the desired range is selected.

When a range of cells is selected, the address box shows the active cell address (the upper-left anchor point, in this case). In formulas, you indicate cell ranges by typing two periods between the anchor points, (for example, B6..D8).

The area above the column headings is called the *entry bar*. You use the entry bar to enter, view, and edit the contents of cells. Rather than entering data directly into a cell, you type it in the entry bar. ClarisWorks does not enter your data into a cell until you click the accept entry icon (√). You can also tell ClarisWorks to enter the contents of the entry bar into the selected cell by

- pressing Tab, which also selects the next cell to the right
- pressing Enter on the numeric keypad, which leaves the current cell selected (on some keyboards, you may have to press NumLock first)
- pressing ↵, which selects the next cell below the current cell
- clicking in any other cell, which selects the new cell
- pressing an arrow key (left arrow, right arrow, up arrow, or down arrow), which selects the next cell to the left, right, above, or below the current cell

This gives you a chance to confirm the cell data before it is actually entered into the cell. If you decide to cancel your entry, click the cancel entry icon (×), and nothing is entered into the cell. Whatever you have entered into a cell appears in the entry bar when that cell is selected. If the cell contains a formula, the entry bar shows the formula's text; the cell itself shows the formula's result.

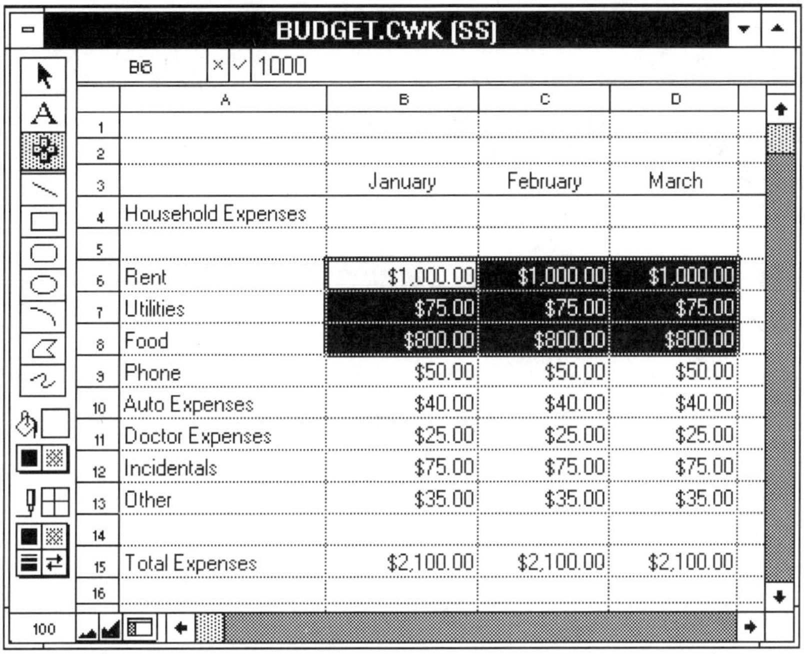

Figure 1-10 Range of cells

Note *Cells are preset to display the results of formulas. If you have checked the Formulas option in the Display dialog box (Options menu), the cell shows the formula instead.*

Besides using it to enter and view the contents of cells, you also use the entry bar to edit cell data. To edit data:

1   Select the cell containing the data to edit.

2   Make your changes in the entry bar.

3   Enter your changes into the cell using one of the techniques described earlier.

All of the standard editing operations (Cut, Copy, Paste, Clear, and Select All) are available in the entry bar. A special Edit menu command, Paste Function, is also available when you are entering or editing data in the entry bar. The Paste Function command lets you use one of the many built-in functions in your cell formulas. Using functions in your spreadsheet documents is fully described in Chapter 6, "Managing Financial Information."

Notice that the tool palette is visible in the spreadsheet document shown in Figure 1-10. As mentioned earlier, graphics documents are the only document types that are preset to show the tool palette. However, you can turn on the tool palette in any ClarisWorks document type. In the spreadsheet document shown in Figure 1-10, I chose Show Tools from the Window menu to make the tool palette visible along the left edge of the spreadsheet. When a spreadsheet cell is active and the tool palette is visible, the spreadsheet tool is selected as the active tool.

Modifying a spreadsheet's appearance

After entering data into your spreadsheet document or frame, there are numerous options available for modifying its appearance. You can

- change cell size (making it wider or taller)
- specify font type, size, style, and text color
- change alignment of data within cells
- format numeric, date, and time data
- add borders to cells
- copy cell formats

You can also use the Display dialog box to set your spreadsheet to hide the grid lines marking cells or to turn off the display of row and column headings.

Changing cell size   As you enter data, you may find that a cell's preset size is not wide enough to contain the text or data you type. You can either adjust a cell's size directly on the spreadsheet or specify exact sizes using the Row Height and Column Width dialog boxes.

To adjust the size of a single row or column at a time, change the cell size directly on the spreadsheet:

1   **Position the crossbar pointer between two row headings (to lengthen the cell) or between two column headings (to widen the cell).** For example, position the pointer between rows 3 and 4 or between columns B and C. The cursor changes to the resize pointer, as shown in Figure 1-11.

2   **Click the resize pointer, and drag to the new position.** A shadow of the grid line marking the original position follows your movements with the pointer. For example, Figure 1-11 shows the resize pointer being dragged to widen column B.

3   **Release the mouse to set the new column width.**

To set row height or column width more precisely across the entire spreadsheet, or across a selection of rows, columns, or cells:

1   **Select the cell, row, column, or range to adjust or select the entire spreadsheet.**

2   **Choose Row Height or Column Width from the Format menu.** The Row Height or Column Width dialog box opens.

3   **Type a number in the corresponding dialog box.** Row Height and Column Width dialog boxes accept entries in points. The preset row height is 15 points; the preset column width is 72 points.

4   **Click OK.**

Resize pointer

	A	B	C	D
B6		1000		
1				
2				
3		January	February	March
4	Household Expenses			
5				
6	Rent	$1,000.00	$1,000.00	$1,000.00
7	Utilities	$75.00	$75.00	$75.00
8	Food	$800.00	$800.00	$800.00

Figure 1-11 Dragging the resize pointer to change the width of column B

Expanding row height is helpful if you use a large font size to display data.

TIP

Specifying font type, size, style, and color   All of the fonts installed in your Windows system—including all of the fonts' sizes and styles—are available to you in all ClarisWorks document types. In spreadsheet documents, you specify another font and font attributes by making your choice from the appropriate *cascading menu* in the Format menu. (A cascading menu is a menu that opens when you choose a command from another menu. Any menu command that shows a right arrow next to it opens a cascading menu.) Specifically, you choose Font to change font type, Size to change font size, Style to change font style, and Text Color to change font color. If you are using a monochrome monitor, the Text Color menu shows a list of colors instead of a color palette.

Note *All installed fonts are available, but you may need to access those not appearing in the Font menu by choosing Other from the bottom of the Font menu.*

Changing data alignment   You can specify the way data aligns within cells, rows, columns, or within the entire spreadsheet. Alignment options are General (preset), Left, Right, and Center. (The General alignment option aligns text along the left cell border and aligns numbers along the right cell border.) To change data alignment, first select cells, rows, columns, or the entire spreadsheet, and then choose an alignment option from the Alignment cascading menu in the Format menu.

Formatting data   You use the Numeric dialog box to change the way numbers, dates, and times are formatted in spreadsheet cells. Choose Number from the Format menu, or press Shift+Ctrl+N to open the dialog box. Figure 1-12 shows the Numeric dialog box. In this example, the format of selected cells is set to Currency with a decimal Precision of 2, with commas to indicate thousands, millions, and so on.

Note *Number, Date, and Time options in the Numeric dialog box are mutually exclusive. If the cell contains numeric data, the dialog box shows a Number format option selected; if it contains date data, the dialog box shows a Date format option selected; or, if the cell contains time data, the dialog box shows a Time format option selected.*

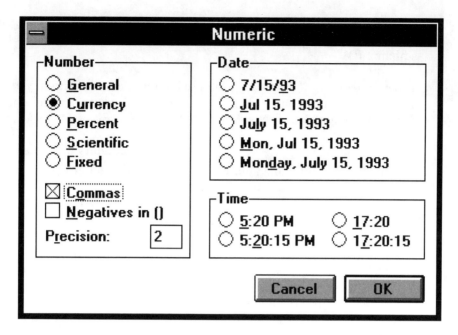

Figure 1-12 Numeric dialog box

The number format options from which you can choose and their resulting effect on the display of numeric data are summarized in Table 1-1.

Table 1-1 Numeric Dialog Box Options

Options	Description
General (preset)	Text left, numbers right; numbers display as fixed with no decimal places showing
Currency	Numbers display with a currency symbol in front of them or elsewhere as specified by the standard used in another language
Percent	Numbers are multiplied by 100 and display in fixed decimal format with a percent symbol (%) to the right
Scientific	Numbers display as exponential powers of 10
Fixed	Numbers display with a fixed number of decimal places
Commas	Numbers over 999 display with comma separators (or the separator appropriate in other international languages)
Negatives in ()	Negative numbers are enclosed in parentheses
Precision	Affects decimal display of Currency, Percent, Fixed formats, and of the mantissa in Scientific formats; can be set up to 15 (2 is preset)

The Numeric dialog box also gives you options for formatting date and time data. Dates are preset to display as MM/DD/YY, and times are preset to display as hh:mm PM.

Adding borders   Borders are useful to highlight certain data in your spreadsheet. You can add a border to an individual cell, row, or column, or add a border around a range of cells. Border options are

- Outline, which places a border around the boundary of your selection
- Left and Right, which place a border along the left or right of all cells in the selection, respectively
- Top and Bottom, which place a border along the top or bottom of all cells in the selection, respectively.

The line width of the border is fixed and cannot be changed.

Copying cell formats   ClarisWorks provides you with a convenient spreadsheet feature: the ability to copy certain cell formats from one cell, range, row, or column, to another. You can copy cell formats whether or not the cell containing the format you want to copy has data entered into it already. To do this:

1   **Specify any format options you want in a selection of cells.** For example, set number format, a border option, text color, and an alignment option.
2   **Select the cell, range, row, or column that has the format you want to copy.**
3   **Choose Copy from the Edit menu.**
4   **Select the target cell, range, row, or column.**
5   **Choose Paste from the Edit menu.**

The cell attributes that can be copied from one cell to another include number formats, font type, size, style, and color, borders, alignment options, and finally, protected status, if the cell is protected. These same cell attributes remain intact when you move data by choosing Move from the Calculate menu.

If you are copying or moving protected data (you already chose Protect Cells from the Options menu), you need to unprotect cells before you can make any changes to the copied or moved data. To do this, choose Unprotect Cells from the Options menu, or press Shift+Ctrl+H.

TIP

Enhancing spreadsheets with charts

ClarisWorks offers powerful charting capabilities in the spreadsheet environment. By charting spreadsheet data, you can easily see a visual representation of the relationships and trends among your data. You have a choice of seven different charts you can create based on data in spreadsheet documents or frames:

- Pie (regular and exploded)
- Bar
- Stacked bar
- Line
- Scatter
- X-Y
- X-Y Scatter

Within each of the chart types, you can set a variety of options, such as displaying charts in color, showing or hiding legends, creating three-dimensional charts, and specifying Y-axis minimum and maximum values. See Chapter 6, "Managing Financial Information," for more information on each chart type.

Before you can make a chart, you need to enter data into the spreadsheet. If you want the chart to include identifying text for chart elements (such as pie slices), you should enter row and/or column labels in your spreadsheet. To make a chart:

1 **With your spreadsheet document or frame active, select the cells that contain the data you want to chart. Be sure to select any row or column text labels if you want the chart's elements identified.**

2 **Choose Make Chart from the Options menu, or press Ctrl+M.** The Make Chart dialog box opens.

3 **Select a chart type from the Categories area of the dialog box.** Notice that the Options area displays different choices depending on the chart type you select.

4 **Make any changes you want in the Options area of the dialog box.**

5 **Click OK.** Your chart appears in the document's window on top of the spreadsheet data.

Figure 1-13 shows a pie chart that was created based on the data in cells A6 through B13 in the spreadsheet shown in Figure 1-10.

Notice that this chart has a title. You can enhance your chart by using the tools in the tool palette to add text or change fill and line patterns and colors, just as you would modify a graphics object. To change a chart element's fill or

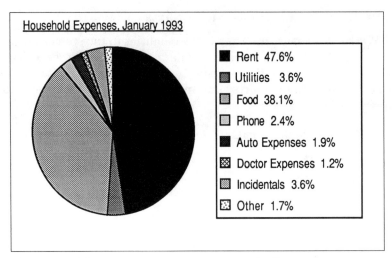

Figure 1-13 Pie chart created from data shown in Figure 1-10

line color or pattern, select its corresponding box in the legend first. ClarisWorks treats a spreadsheet chart as a graphics object after it is created. (See "Using the ClarisWorks Tool Palatte" later in this chapter for more information about using the tool palette.) You can also move the chart to another place in the document or frame, or resize the chart to make it larger or smaller. If you want to use the chart in another document or frame, you can copy it from the spreadsheet and paste it into the other document.

Your chart is dynamically linked to the spreadsheet data you used to create it. If you change related data in the spreadsheet, the chart is automatically updated to reflect that change. If you cut and paste the chart into another document, this link is broken and the chart no longer reflects changes in the spreadsheet. If you copy and paste the chart into another document, the chart in the spreadsheet document remains dynamically linked, but the copy in the other document remains static.

Database documents

Figure 1-14 shows a sample database document. The DB after the document's title identifies it as a database document type.

A database document consists of *records* and *fields*. Records contain fields, which represent categories of information. All records in one database document have the same fields. For example, all 35 records in the Friends database shown in Figure 1-14 have the fields First Name, Last Name, Street, City, State, Zip, and Birthdate. However, each record within the database document stores different information in the fields.

Database book

Status panel

Selection bar

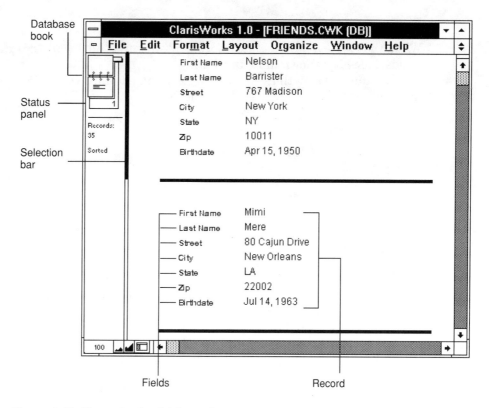

ClarisWorks 1.0 - [FRIENDS.CWK [DB]]

File   Edit   Format   Layout   Organize   Window   Help

First Name	Nelson
Last Name	Barrister
Street	767 Madison
City	New York
State	NY
Zip	10011
Birthdate	Apr 15, 1950

Records: 35

Sorted

First Name	Mimi
Last Name	Mere
Street	80 Cajun Drive
City	New Orleans
State	LA
Zip	22002
Birthdate	Jul 14, 1963

100

Fields   Record

Figure 1-14 Elements of a database document

There are three different ways you can work with and view database documents: Browse, Find, and Layout. You use Browse to enter and edit data in records, select records, copy and paste records, and view the records as a list (as shown in Figure 1-14).

You use Find to provide search criteria for finding information in the database document. You use Layout to define and modify database layouts—visual arrangements of the elements in the document. A layout determines how your database document looks on the screen or on printed output. You switch between these different views by choosing Browse, Find, or Layout from the Layout menu.

TIP

You have two options in the way you view records in Browse: List View or one record at a time. This is true no matter which layout you have in effect. ClarisWorks database documents are preset to display in List View, meaning you can view your records as a list. To view one record at a time, choose List View from the Layout menu to uncheck it in the menu. Only one record appears in the document at a time (unless Page View is turned on in the Window menu).

Defining fields

When you create a new database document, the first thing you see is the Define Fields dialog box shown in Figure 1-15.

You cannot do anything in a database document until you define the fields that will contain your data. To define fields

1 **Type a name for the field.**

2 **Choose a field type.**

3 **Click Create.**

4 **Repeat steps 1 through 3 until you have defined all of the fields you want.**

5 **Click Done.** ClarisWorks automatically switches you to Browse view, the first blank record appears, and you are ready to enter data.

Field names should be as descriptive as possible to make it easier for you to readily identify what type of information the field contains. Although field names can be up to 63 characters long, they should be as concise as possible. Lengthy field names may be difficult to work with in a layout.

The field type you use depends on the type of data the field should contain. There are six different types of fields from which you can choose:

- Text—*Text fields* contain any alphanumeric characters, including numbers that you don't intend to use in arithmetic calculations, such as phone numbers, zip codes, or invoice numbers.

- Number—*Number fields* contain any positive or negative numeric value, such as an item's price or an account balance.

- Date and Time—*Date fields* and *time fields* contain date and time type data, respectively. You are restricted in the format you use to enter date and time data. Table 1-2 lists the available formats.

- Calculation—*Calculation fields* contain the results of a calculation based on a formula; they compute the result of a formula, which can include other fields, operators, functions, and constants. For example, if your database document has a Price field and a Number of Units Sold field, you can define a calculation field that computed the total sale for each record by multiplying price by number of units sold. The formula's result, which can be text, numbers, a date, or a time, is automatically placed in the field.

- Summary—*Summary fields,* like calculation fields, also contain the results of a calculation based on a formula; they are intended for use in summary layout parts. (A *summary layout part* is an element of a database layout specifically designed to show summary calculations.) You use summary fields to compute values based on data in a field over a group of records. For example, you can define a summary field to track total sales revenue by sales region. See Chapter 5 for more information about calculation and summary fields.

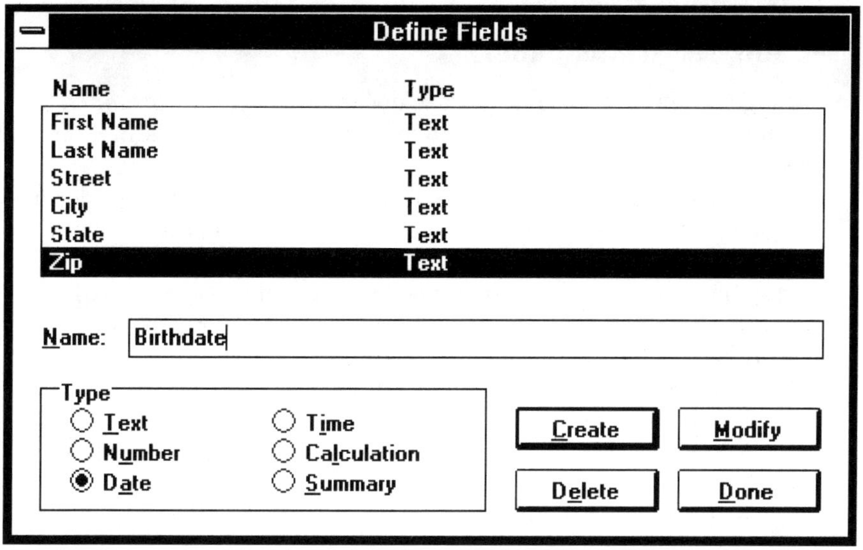

Figure 1-15 Define Fields dialog box

Table 1-2 Date and Time Data Formats

Date	Time
September 8, 1995	5:00 PM
Fri, Sep 8, 1995	5:00:30 PM
Sep 8, 1995	17:00
9/8/95	17:00:30
Friday, September 8, 1995	

Note *The date and time formats described in Table 1-2 apply to the U.S. version of Windows. Other localized English-language versions of Windows may have different date and time formats. You can also change them in any version using the International Control Panel.*

At any time, whether you are in Browse, Find, or Layout, you can modify, delete, or add fields by choosing Define Fields from the Layout menu. This gives you the flexibility to alter your document at any time.

After you define fields, you can enter data into the fields of each record, one record at a time. To add a new record, choose New Record from the Edit menu, or press Ctrl+R. The new record appears in the document immediately below the last record in the database.

Using the status panel

Along the left side of the database document is the *status panel*. The status panel shown in Figure 1-16 includes the database book and information about the status of your database document.

You use the *database book* to navigate within a database document. To move among records one at a time, click the bottom page of the book to move to the next record, or click the top page of the book to move to the previous record. To move through several records at a time, drag the bookmark up to move backward, or drag down to move forward until you reach the desired record. The record number shown below the bookmark changes as you drag it. When you release the mouse, ClarisWorks positions the document at the record corresponding to the number shown below the bookmark and makes the record active. For example, the bookmark in Figure 1-16 has been dragged to record number 19.

The type of status information that appears in the status panel includes

- Total number of records
- Find status
- Selection status
- Sort status

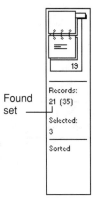

Figure 1-16 The database status panel

You can see from the status panel in Figure 1-14 that the Friends database has thirty-five records and is sorted (by zip code, in this case). The selection bar to the left of the first record indicates that it is the currently selected record. When you select one or more records, the status panel tells you how many records are selected. For example, three records are selected in Figure 1-16.

After you use Find to search for certain records given a specific criteria, the status panel tells you how many records were found that match that criteria. The set of records found based on a search criteria is called the *found set*. For example, the status panel in Figure 1-16 shows that the found set consists of twenty-one records out of thirty-five total records in the database document.

Selecting records

ClarisWorks gives you several different ways to select records in database documents. To select records, you must be in Browse. To select one record at a time, click anywhere in the record outside of the boundaries of the fields. To select more than one record:

1   **Turn on List View, if necessary, by choosing List View from the Layout menu. (Choosing Page View from the Window menu also turns on List View.)**

2   **Click in the first record to select it and drag down the document through the desired number of records.** You can also hold down the Shift or Ctrl key as you click different records. Shift-clicking selects consecutive records in the document; Ctrl-clicking selects nonconsecutive records. Selected records appear highlighted.

Once the records are selected, you can do a number of things with them, such as copying and pasting them into a spreadsheet document. You can also hide them or hide the unselected records in order to work with a part of the database. To hide selected records, choose Hide Selected [Ctrl+( ] from the Organize menu. Only those records that were not selected appear as the active set of records. To hide the unselected records (that is, to make the selected records the active set), choose Hide Unselected [Ctrl+)] from the Organize menu.

TIP

By following these steps, you can copy and paste database records into a spreadsheet document:

1   **With your database document open in Browse, turn on List View, if necessary, or choose Page View from the Window menu.** *Figure 1-17a shows the two records to be copied to a spreadsheet document.*

2   **Select the records you want to copy.**

3   **Choose Copy from the Edit menu, or press Ctrl+C.**

4   **Open a spreadsheet document and select the cell to contain the first field's data.**

5   **Choose Paste from the Edit menu, or press Ctrl+V.** *The selected records are pasted into the spreadsheet document by rows across the spreadsheet in the order specified in the Tab Order dialog box (in the database environment). Each field's data appears in a separate column. Figure 1-17b shows the results of copying and pasting the two records from the Friends database into a new, untitled spreadsheet.*

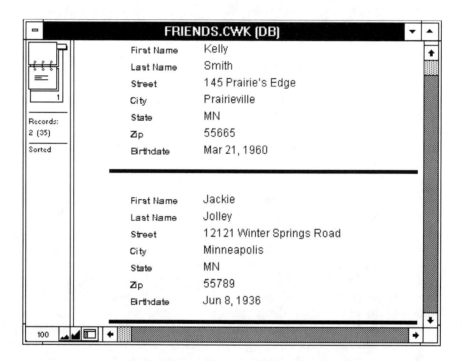

Figure 1-17a Two records copied from the database document...

Figure 1-17b ...and pasted into a spreadsheet document

The same procedure applies to copying and pasting records into any other ClarisWorks document type or pasting them into another Windows application (such as FileMaker Pro).

TIP

This gives you a very brief, and certainly not comprehensive, overview of the elements and features of each ClarisWorks document type. Throughout the rest of this book, you will have the opportunity to explore and put to practical use many more features of all document types.

Now let's examine the various ways you can view a ClarisWorks document.

Viewing documents

You view ClarisWorks documents through *windows*. In Windows lexicon, a window is an area on your screen in which you view an application or document. When you start an application in Windows, the application appears in an *application window*. An application window can't contain text or graphic objects; it can contain only other windows and application elements such as menus, tool palettes, and so on. The windows within an application window are called *document windows*. Each ClarisWorks document appears in its own document window within the ClarisWorks application window.

ClarisWorks gives you all of the standard Windows controls for opening, closing, moving, minimizing (reducing to an icon), and maximizing (enlarging to full-screen) application and document windows. (If you are unfamiliar with manipulating windows, read your Microsoft Windows *User's Guide*.) In addition, you can view your ClarisWorks documents in five different ways:

- New View
- Page View
- Working View
- View Scale
- Split Window

All of these views are available in any ClarisWorks document type. Remember that you can view database documents in Browse, Find, or Layout; spreadsheet frames can be opened up into full view by choosing Open Frame from the View menu. (Open Frame is available only when a spreadsheet frame is selected or when one of its cells is active.)

New View

New View lets you open another view of your current document. You create a new view by choosing New View from the Window menu. The new view opens in another window, which displays on top of the original window and shows the exact same contents as the original view. The title bar of the new view's window shows ":2", indicating that this is the second view of the current document, and the title bar of the original view's window shows ":1".

Opening more than one view of your document is useful in many ways. For example, if you have a multiple page document, you can open a new view for each page of your document. Then, by choosing Tile Windows from the Window menu, you can see the contents of each page simultaneously on the screen. Opening a new view is also useful in database documents when you are revising a database layout and you simultaneously want to see how the changes affect the way your data will look on screen or in print. Keep the original view in Layout, open a new view, and switch to Browse in the new view. Again, tile the two windows so you can see the contents of both windows at the same time.

Page View

Page View lets you view your document on the screen exactly as it will look when you print it. You see headers, footers, footnotes, page guides, and margins. Other applications sometimes call this Preview or WYSIWYG (what-you-see-is-what-you-get). Text documents always display in Page View; in other ClarisWorks documents, you toggle Page View on by choosing it from the Window menu. In database documents, Page View is the only way you can see summary field data without printing it. Page View does not allow you to see space closed up between fields (if Slide Objects is selected in the Layout Info dialog box) or to see merged data in database documents.

Working View

Working View, which is the opposite of Page View, is the way in which you typically work with all documents except text. Working View doesn't allow you to see headers, footers, page guides, or margins. It is usually best to work in this view because you can see more of your document in the window and because scrolling across or among pages is somewhat faster than in Page View. When Page View is not on (that is, when Page View does not have a check mark next to it in the Window menu), your document is set to Working View.

View Scale

View Scale enables you to reduce or enlarge your view of the document in the window. You set the view scale by choosing View Scale from the Window menu. When you do so, a dialog box asks you to specify the exact percentage by which you want to enlarge or reduce your view.

You can accomplish the same thing by clicking one of the zoom controls in the lower-left corner of a document window, as shown in Figure 1-18. Clicking the right control enlarges your view (or zooms in), and clicking the left control reduces it (or zooms out). The zoom percentage box shows the current level of magnification. Click the zoom percentage box to toggle between the current level of magnification and 100%. If you are working on a large spreadsheet, reducing its view lets you see more of the data. If you are working on a detailed graphics document, enlarging its view helps for fine-tuning a certain part of it.

Split Window

Split Window allows you to split the window into several panes and view different parts of your document at the same time. You split windows into panes using the pane tools. The horizontal pane tool is above the scroll bar to the right of the document; the vertical pane tool is to the left of the scroll bar below the document. Figure 1-18 shows a spreadsheet document in a window that is split into four panes.

To split a window, click on a pane tool and drag it to the desired split position. When you release the mouse, the document shows a window pane divider where you split the window. Each pane has its own scroll bars, which lets you scroll within a particular part of your document, leaving the rest of the document intact on the screen. You can split a window up to two times

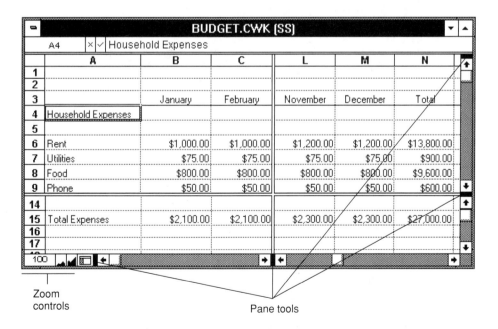

Figure 1-18 Example of a window split into four panes

horizontally and two times vertically (a total of nine panes). To remove a split, click the pane tool and drag back into its original position until the pane divider disappears.

Arranging windows

In addition to viewing the contents of document windows in different ways, you can arrange the windows themselves in tiles, in a cascade arrangement, or as icons. Arranging windows makes sense only if you have more than one document window open at a time.

Tiling windows positions all of the windows you have open so you can view them simultaneously. To tile your open windows, choose Tile from the Window menu. To cascade windows, choose Cascade from the Window menu. Cascading windows appear in a staggered fashion so they overlap one another in a stack. You can only view the contents of the active window, although the other windows' titles are visible. Figure 1-19a and 1-19b illustrate the difference between tiled and cascaded windows.

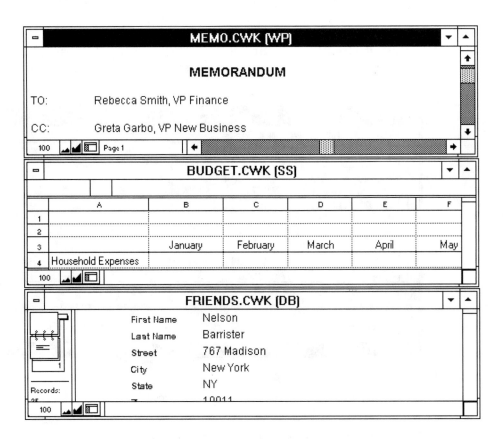

Figure 1-19a Three tiled document windows

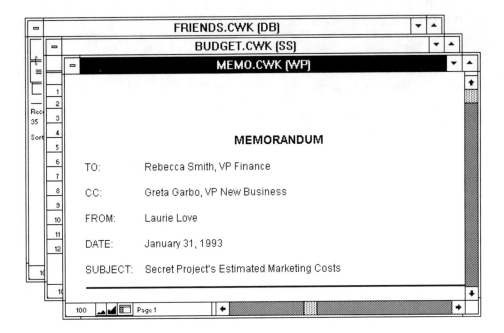

Figure 1-19b Three cascading document windows

When you choose Tile, ClarisWorks automatically tiles the windows vertically across the screen. To tile the windows horizontally down the screen (see Figure 1-19a), hold down the Ctrl key as you choose Tile.

TIP

To minimize a window to an icon, click the window's minimize button (the one with a down arrow to the right of the title bar). When you minimize document windows to icons, they are preset to appear in the lower-left corner of your screen. If you move these icons elsewhere on the screen, you can tell ClarisWorks to arrange them back to the preset position by choosing Arrange Icons from the Window menu.

You now have a general idea of the ClarisWorks document types, a sampling of their features, and how to view them onscreen. The next section describes another key element of the ClarisWorks environment—the tool palette.

Using the ClarisWorks tool palette

The tool palette shown in Figure 1-20 is what provides you with the full power of ClarisWorks integration. It contains tools for

- creating frames that contain text or spreadsheets
- making another environment active
- drawing graphics objects (such as boxes, circles, and polygons)
- changing fill patterns, fill color, and line attributes (such as pen color, pen pattern, line width, or arrowheads)

The three tools at the top of the tool palette—the graphics, text, and spreadsheet tools—correspond to the graphics, text, and spreadsheet environments, respectively. When one of these tools is selected, the menus and features associated with the given environment are available. Similarly, when a graphics, text, or spreadsheet document is created and the tool palette is visible, the associated tool is active. For example, when a spreadsheet document is active, the spreadsheet tool is selected in the tool palette, indicating that it is the active tool.

This section describes all of the tools, in the order in which they appear in the tool palette.

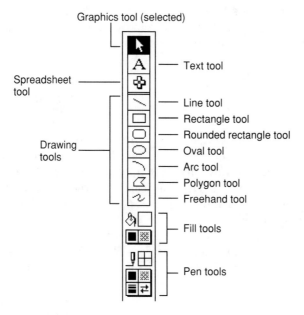

Figure 1-20 The ClarisWorks tool palette

To toggle between the two most recently selected tools in the tool palette, press Enter on the numeric keypad. For example, if the graphics tool is selected in the tool palette and you click the line tool, pressing Enter toggles between the graphics and the line tools. (You may need to press Num Lock first.)

TIP

Graphics tool

When a graphics document is active, the graphics tool is selected (highlighted) in the tool palette, as shown in Figure 1-20. The drawing, fill, and pen tools, as well as the graphics menus, are also active. In short, when the graphics tool is selected, the graphics environment is active.

In other document types, select the graphics tool to activate graphics-related menus, drawing tools, and fill and pen tools. By selecting the graphics tools in other environments, you have access to graphics-related features and are able to use them to draw graphics in your documents.

You cannot create an object with the graphics tool; you use one of the drawing tools to do that. Rather, you use the graphics tool to access the graphics environment and to select graphic objects that may already be in your document.

Graphics documents are the only document type preset to show the graphics tool selected in the tool palette. However, in two specific instances, the graphics tool is preselected in other document types.

First, a database document in Layout view shows the graphics tool preselected and graphics-related menus active. This is because each element of a database layout is treated as an object. For example, the field names are text objects, which you can resize, move, or otherwise alter, just as you would alter a graphics object. Furthermore, when you are in Layout view, ClarisWorks anticipates that you will be adding a logo, clip art, or other graphics to your database document. (You cannot add graphic elements to database documents in Browse or Find.)

Second, when you click on a chart in a spreadsheet document, the graphics tool is preselected in the tool palette, and the application switches to the graphics environment. Again, once a chart is selected, it is considered a graphics object. You will learn more about charts in Chapter 6, when you create and modify a chart based on a budget spreadsheet.

Text tool

When a text document is active, the text tool is automatically selected in the tool palette, and you are ready to type text immediately. Text-related menus and text features are active. In other document types, you select the text tool to switch to the text environment and to add text objects (called text frames) to your documents.

Remember from earlier in this chapter that frames act as views onto other environments and that frames are a type of object. You can create two types of frames in ClarisWorks: text frames and spreadsheet frames. You create text frames using the text tool. You create spreadsheet frames using the spreadsheet tool. See "Creating Text frames" (next section) and "Creating Spreadsheet Frames" later in this chapter.

Creating text frames

When you add text to graphics, spreadsheet, and database documents, you do so by creating a text frame. Figure 1-21 shows a text frame added to a spreadsheet document.

To create a text frame:

1   If the tool palette is not visible, choose Show Tools from the Window menu, or click the panel icon shown in Figure 1-22 in the bottom of the document window.

	D	E	F	
1				Spreadsheet document
2				
3	March	April	May	
4				
5				
6	$1,000.00	$1,200.00	$1,200.00	
7	$75.00	**Note:**	$75.00	
8	$800.00		$800.00	
9	$50.00	Rent will be increased to	$50.00	
10	$40.00	$1200,	$40.00	Text frame
11	$25.00	beginning in	$25.00	
12	$75.00	April 1992.	$75.00	
13	$35.00		$35.00	
14				
15	$2,100.00	$2,300.00	$2,300.00	
16				
17				

Figure 1-21 Text frame in a spreadsheet document

Panel icon

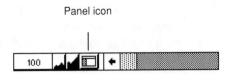

Figure 1-22 The panel icon

2   **Select the text tool.** The cursor changes to an I-beam pointer.

3   **Position the I-beam pointer in the document where you want to add text.**

4   **Click once in the document, or drag the pointer to create a text frame of a specific size.** ClarisWorks switches you to the text environment. If you click once, ClarisWorks creates a text frame with a fixed width of approximately 1.5 inches. If you drag to create the frame, you can make the frame as wide and as long as you like. In either case, as you type text, the width of the frame remains fixed, but its length expands as you type.

5   **Type the text in the frame.**

6   **Click anywhere outside the text frame to return to the main document and make it active. Press Enter on the numeric keypad to select the frame and make the graphics tool active.**

After you create a text frame and return to the main document, the frame is selected, selection handles appear around the frame, and the graphics tool is selected in the tool palette. Selection handles are small, solid squares that mark the object's boundaries. This indicates that the text frame can now be treated as any other graphics object.

Instead of typing text in a frame, you can cut or copy it from another document or application and paste it into the frame. To copy and paste text from another ClarisWorks document into a text frame:

1   **Open the document that contains the text you want to copy.**

2   **Select the text to copy.**

3   **Choose Cut (Ctrl+X) or Copy (Ctrl+C) from the Edit menu.**

4   **Open the document to which you want to add the text frame.**

5   **Select the text tool from the tool palette.**

6   **Position the I-beam pointer where you want the text frame.**

7   **Click in the document or drag to create an empty text frame.**

8   **Choose Paste from the Edit menu, or press Ctrl+V.** The text is pasted into the frame. The length of the frame expands to fit the text.

You can add a text frame to a text document type. Follow the same procedure for adding text frames to other document types, but hold down the Alt key as you click in the document or drag to create the frame. Placing text frames in text documents is a handy way to create electronic posted notes.

TIP

When you save a document containing frames, the frames, along with any other objects in the document, are saved as part of the document.

Linking text frames

One of the unique features of ClarisWorks is its ability to relate, or link, frames together in a document. This feature, known as Frame Links, enables you to do page layout in ClarisWorks.

Linking frames is actually much easier to do than it is to explain. The basic idea behind linked text frames is that you can flow text from one frame to another. Once text frames are linked, changes you make in one frame are reflected in the other frames. For example, let's say you have three text frames that are linked. You decide to add a paragraph to the first frame. ClarisWorks reflows the text in the other two linked frames to accommodate the additional text.

Linked frames also let you break a long segment of text into smaller chunks that are easier to manage. Each of these chunks can be contained in its own frame and linked to each other. Because the frames themselves are objects, you can position them anywhere in the document you want, thereby creating your own customized layout for newsletters, presentations, reports, and so on. Chapter 3, "Producing Newsletters," uses linked frames in the Wine of the Month Club newsletter.

The concepts and procedures associated with linked frames apply to both text and spreadsheet frames. This section gives you instructions for linking text frames. See "Linking Spreadsheet Frames" later in this chapter for more information on creating linked spreadsheet frames.

Since frames are a type of object and you use graphics documents primarily to work with objects, a graphics document is best suited for creating and working with linked text frames. If this doesn't make sense to you, or if you prefer to work in another document type, you can work with linked frames in text, spreadsheet, or database documents. However, you will probably find that the graphics environment gives you the tools and flexibility you need to generate page layouts most efficiently.

TIP

To create linked text frames:

1 **Choose New from the File menu, select Graphics as the document type, and click OK to create a new graphics document.**

2 **Choose Frame Links from the Options menu, or press Ctrl+L to turn the linking capability on.** Nothing appears to happen, except that the Frame Links command is checked in the Options menu.

3 **In the tool palette, click the text tool to select it.** The cursor changes to an I-beam pointer with a cross hair in it. This is the frame links pointer.

4 **Position the frame links pointer in the document where you want the first frame to appear.**

5 **Click once in the document, or drag the pointer to create a frame of a specific size.** Unlinked text frames expand in length as you type text; conversely, a linked text frame stays fixed in size as you enter text. You can go back later to resize the frame.
   The I-beam pointer appears in the text frame and text-related menus are active.

6 **Type text in the frame, or paste text from the Clipboard into the frame.** If there is more text than the frame can hold, a text overflow indicator appears in the lower-right corner inside the frame, as shown in Figure 1-23.

7 **Click once anywhere outside the frame to select it.** The cursor changes to the arrow pointer, and graphics-related menus are active. In addition to selection handles, the frame now shows little boxes, containing special icons, on the top and bottom of the frame. These are called *link indicators.*

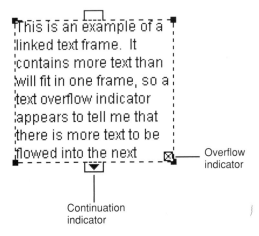

This is an example of a
linked text frame. It
contains more text than
will fit in one frame, so a
text overflow indicator
appears to tell me that
there is more text to be
flowed into the next

Overflow indicator

Continuation indicator

Figure 1-23 A linked text frame showing overflow and continuation indicators

8   **Click the continuation indicator—the one at the bottom of the frame that shows a downward pointing arrow.** The cursor changes to the cross-hair I-beam pointer.

9   **Repeat step 5.** Text overflowed from the first frame appears in the next frame.

   The overflow indicator shows if there is still more text than will fit in this frame. If this is the case, repeat steps 7, 8, and 9 until you have enough linked frames to accommodate your text. You will know when you have created enough linked frames when the overflow indicator no longer appears in the last frame you created.

You can also create empty linked frames first and add text to them later. To do this, follow the steps described earlier, skipping those steps that instruct you to type or paste text. Figure 1-24 shows four empty linked text frames and points out the different link indicators that appear around linked frames.

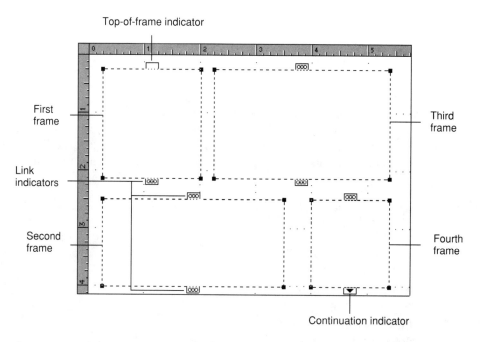

Figure 1-24 Empty linked text frames with link indicators

Note   The term link indicators *has two meanings in ClarisWorks. When two or more frames are linked, they both show a chain-link icon, which is referred to as a link indicator (see Figure 1-24). Link indicators is also used to refer collectively to all of the indicators that appear around linked frames, including the top-of-frame indicator, the continuation indicator, and link indicators (the chain-link icons).*

TIP

It's harder to work with empty linked frames than with linked frames that contain text because as soon as you click the continuation indicator, you can no longer see the border of existing frames. This makes it difficult to determine where one frame ends and another begins. So that you can see a frame's border even when the frame isn't active, increase the border's line width using the Line Width menu in the tool palette. See "Pen Tools" later in this chapter for more information about the Line Width menu.

After creating all the linked text frames you want, you can resize or reposition them to your liking. Before doing so, however, you need to select the frames. You select frames as you would any other graphics object. First select the graphics tool from the tool palette, then use one of these techniques:

- Click once on a frame to select it
- Hold down the Shift key as you click on more than one frame to select multiple frames
- Hold down the Ctrl key as you drag through multiple frames to select them
- Drag the arrow pointer around multiple frames to select them
- Choose Select All (Ctrl+A) from the Edit menu to select all frames in the document

You resize and move frames as you would other graphics objects. Follow the instructions for selecting and manipulating objects in "Drawing Tools" later in this chapter.

TIP

The easiest way to resize linked text frames is to first select all of them. This way you can see their borders and determine how changing one frame's size affects the flow of text in other frames.

If you decide later that you no longer want the text frames linked, you must first cut and paste them (either into the current document or into another one) to disable their linked status. Next, choose Frame Links in the Options menu to turn linking off. The link indicators disappear, and the text frames now act as independent, unrelated objects.

Spreadsheet tool

When a spreadsheet document is active, the spreadsheet tool is automatically selected in the tool palette, and you are ready to enter spreadsheet data immediately. Spreadsheet-related menus and features are active. In other document types, you select the spreadsheet tool to switch to the spreadsheet environment and to add spreadsheet objects, called spreadsheet frames, to your documents. I discuss spreadsheet frames in the next section.

You can add a spreadsheet to graphics, text, and database documents. Doing this creates a spreadsheet frame.

Creating spreadsheet frames

The steps for creating a spreadsheet frame are very similar to those you follow to create text frames:

1   **If the tool palette is not visible, choose Show Tools from the Window menu.**

2   **Select the spreadsheet tool.** The cursor changes to a crossbar pointer.

3   **Position the crossbar pointer in the document where you want to add the spreadsheet.**

4   **Drag the pointer to create a spreadsheet frame.** ClarisWorks switches you to the spreadsheet environment and selects the first cell in the spreadsheet (cell A1). You can make the frame as wide and as long as you like.

You cannot simply click in the document once to create a spreadsheet frame as you do when creating text frames. You must drag to create it.

5   **Enter your data in the frame.**

6   **Click anywhere outside the frame to return to the main document and make it active. Press Enter on the numeric keypad to select the frame and make the graphics tool active.**

Figure 1-25 shows a spreadsheet frame added to a text document.

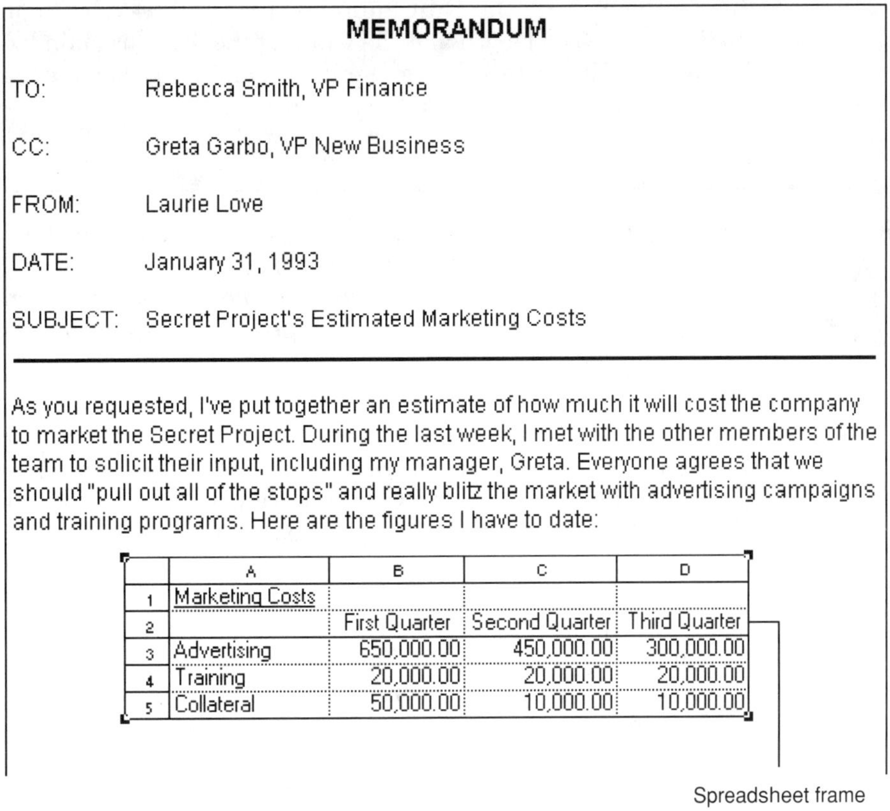

MEMORANDUM

TO: Rebecca Smith, VP Finance

CC: Greta Garbo, VP New Business

FROM: Laurie Love

DATE: January 31, 1993

SUBJECT: Secret Project's Estimated Marketing Costs

As you requested, I've put together an estimate of how much it will cost the company to market the Secret Project. During the last week, I met with the other members of the team to solicit their input, including my manager, Greta. Everyone agrees that we should "pull out all of the stops" and really blitz the market with advertising campaigns and training programs. Here are the figures I have to date:

	A	B	C	D
1	Marketing Costs			
2		First Quarter	Second Quarter	Third Quarter
3	Advertising	650,000.00	450,000.00	300,000.00
4	Training	20,000.00	20,000.00	20,000.00
5	Collateral	50,000.00	10,000.00	10,000.00

Spreadsheet frame

Figure 1-25 A spreadsheet frame within a text document

Instead of typing data in a frame, you can cut or copy it from another document or application and paste it into the frame. To cut or copy and paste data from another ClarisWorks document:

1 **Open the document (or other spreadsheet frame) that contains the data you want to copy.**

2 **Select the cells containing the data to copy.**

3 **Choose Cut (Ctrl+X) or Copy (Ctrl+C) from the Edit menu.**

4 **Open the document to which you want to add the spreadsheet frame.**

5 **Select the spreadsheet tool from the tool palette.**

6 **Position the crossbar pointer where you want the frame.**

7 **Drag to create an empty spreadsheet frame.**

8 **Select the cell(s) into which you want to paste the data.**

9   **Choose Paste from the Edit menu, or press Ctrl+V.** The data is pasted into the frame. The length and the width of the frame remain fixed at their original size. Unlike text frames, spreadsheet frames do not expand to accommodate pasted or typed data.

You can add a spreadsheet frame to a spreadsheet document. Follow the same procedure for adding spreadsheet frames to other document types, but hold down the Alt key as you drag to create the frame. The data in the spreadsheet frame cannot be linked to the data in the spreadsheet document.

TIP

After you create a spreadsheet frame, the frame is selected, selection handles appear around the frame, and the graphics tool is selected in the tool palette. This indicates that the frame can now be treated as any other graphic object. You can move it, resize it, and change other attributes such as line width, pattern, and color, and fill color.

Unlike text frames, you can open spreadsheet frames into full view. This enables you to work with the whole spreadsheet, not just that part of it that shows inside the frame. When a spreadsheet frame is open in full view, it appears in its own window. To open a spreadsheet frame:

1   **Click inside the frame to select a cell, or click outside of the frame to select the frame.**

2   **Choose Open Frame from the Window menu.**

You can also open a spreadsheet frame by selecting the graphics tool and holding down the Alt key as you double-click the frame.

TIP

An opened spreadsheet frame looks like a separate spreadsheet document but it has the same name as the document in which it was created. To close the opened frame's window and return to the frame in the main document:

- Double-click the opened frame's Control-menu box (upper-left corner of the window).
- Click the Control-menu box once and choose Close from the Control menu.
- Choose Close (Ctrl+W) from the File menu.

You can chart data in spreadsheet frames. However, there are differences between creating a chart from data in a frame and creating one from data in an *opened frame.* If you create a chart in a spreadsheet frame that's opened in full view (that is, you chose Open Frame), the chart is contained within the spreadsheet frame, as shown in Figure 1-26a. When you return to the main document containing the frame, you may have to resize the frame to see the chart.

If you create the chart from data in an *unopened frame,* the chart appears in its own frame and can be treated as a separate object, as shown in Figure 1-26b. Either way, the chart remains linked to the data in the spreadsheet frame.

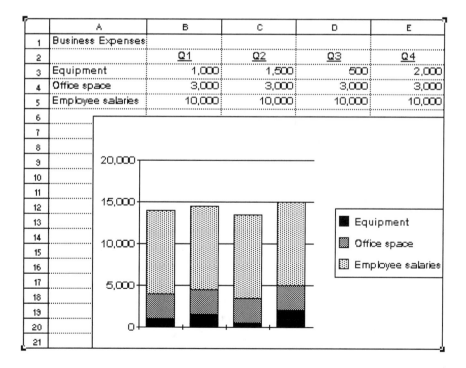

Figure 1-26a Chart created in an opened frame

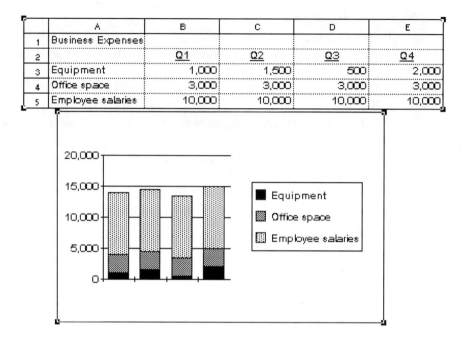

Figure 1-26b Chart created from an unopened frame

Spreadsheet frame tips and hints

Here are some suggestions for working with spreadsheet frames.

Spreadsheet frames as tables   Aside from adding spreadsheet frames to other documents for calculation purposes, spreadsheet frames work quite well for tables or schedules. Figure 1-27 shows an example of a table created with a spreadsheet frame in a text document.

To duplicate this, create a spreadsheet frame in your document, and type in the tabular data you want.

Display options   The table in Figure 1-27 shows a spreadsheet without grid lines or row and column headings. You can turn off the display of these and other spreadsheet elements in frames and spreadsheet documents. To do this:

1   **With the graphics tool, click in the spreadsheet frame to select it.**

2   **Choose Modify Frame from the Options menu, or press Shift+Ctrl+I.**
    The Display dialog box appears, as shown in Figure 1-28. You can also open the Display dialog box by holding down the Ctrl key and double-clicking the spreadsheet frame. (To open the Display dialog box when the spreadsheet environment is active, choose Display from the Options menu.)

3   Uncheck the Grid lines, Row Headings, and Column Headings options. Select or deselect any other display options you want.

4   Click OK. Your changes are made and the spreadsheet frame remains active.

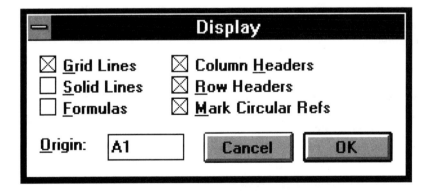

1/20/93

Dear Uncle Charlie,

      Thanks for offering to help Joe and me plan the family reunion this year. We really need your help in deciding what type of venue we should select for the great event. Should it be a strictly outdoor or indoor affair? Or should we find a place that has both indoor and outdoor facilities?

      Joe and I have done some initial research on a few places here in town. Here is what we've found out so far.

Place	Accommodates	Catering	Indoor/Outdoor
The Grand Hotel	1000	Yes	Indoor
County Park	200	No	Outdoor
Surfcity Beach	500	No	Outdoor
Elk's Lodge	200	Yes	Indoor/Outdoor

      There are still a few more places that will be sending us more information. Also, the Smith's grandmother has a nice old place in the hills that may be available. Mrs. Smith is checking it out for us.

Figure 1-27 Adding spreadsheet frames to text is a good way to create tables

Figure 1-28 Display dialog box opened from a spreadsheet frame

Other display options include

Formulas	If you check the Formulas option, spreadsheet cells that have formulas display the formulas in the cells instead of their results.
Mark Circular Refs	If you check this option, a bullet (•) appears before and after numbers in cells that result from formulas with a *circular reference.* (A circular reference means that the formula in one cell refers to itself or to another cell that contains a formula that refers back to the original cell.)
Origin	If you open the Display dialog box from a spreadsheet frame, the dialog box displays the Origin option. You use this option to set the upper-left cell you want to show in the frame. (The preset Origin is cell A1, the first cell in the spreadsheet.) This option is not available in the Display dialog box from a spreadsheet document or from an opened spreadsheet frame.

Charts in spreadsheet frames   Let's say you open a spreadsheet frame and create a chart in it. You then return to the main document, where the frame is its original size, and decide you want to modify the chart. If you click on the chart inside the spreadsheet frame, ClarisWorks selects one of the cells instead of the chart. To select the chart, click on it using the right mouse button. This technique applies to any type of object created inside of a spreadsheet frame, including text frames that may be embedded in a spreadsheet frame. By right-clicking in the frame, you select the object at the deepest level of the frame.

Other right mouse button secrets   To move a chart inside the spreadsheet frame, hold down the right mouse button as you drag the chart. To draw a graphics object inside a spreadsheet frame (such as a circle or line), select the drawing tool you want to use, and use the right mouse button as you draw inside the frame. The drawing becomes part of the frame, not part of the main document.

Linking spreadsheet frames

The process of linking spreadsheet frames is similar to that of linking text frames, but there are some differences. By linking spreadsheet frames in a document, you can

- create multiple frame objects to hold related spreadsheet data
- flow data from one frame to another
- view different parts of a spreadsheet in different frames
- resize and position the frames wherever you like in the document

The most intuitive reason for linking spreadsheet frames is so you can view different sections of a spreadsheet in separate frames within a document. For example, let's say you have a spreadsheet that contains your income and expenses for last year. One linked spreadsheet frame can show the income portion of your spreadsheet, while another frame can show expenses. Because these two frames are linked, any changes in one frame are reflected in the next. If these linked frames are in a text document, such as a letter to your accountant, the frame with the income data can follow a paragraph that highlights your key income-generating investments for the year. This is just an example. As you work with ClarisWorks, you will no doubt find many more reasons to link spreadsheet frames in your documents.

You can effectively create spreadsheet frames in any ClarisWorks document type. Although you can create linked spreadsheet frames in spreadsheet documents, this is probably not the best choice of document type. Instead, choose between a graphics, text, or database document (in Layout view).

To create linked spreadsheet frames:

1 **Open the document to which you want to add linked spreadsheet frames.**

2 **If necessary, choose Show Tools from the Window menu to make the tool palette visible.**

3 **Select the spreadsheet tool.** The cursor changes to a crossbar pointer.

4 **Choose Frame Links from the Options menu, or press Ctrl+L to turn the linking capability on.** Nothing appears to happen, except that the Frame Links command is checked in the Options menu.

5 **Position the crossbar pointer in the document where you want the first frame to appear.**

6 **Drag the crossbar pointer to create a frame of a specific size.** ClarisWorks switches to the spreadsheet environment and selects cell A1.

7 **Type your data in the cells inside the frame or paste data from the Clipboard into the frame.** Unlike linked text frames, linked spreadsheet frames do not show an overflow indicator if there is more data than the frame can show.

To determine if a linked spreadsheet frame contains more data than it can show, either size the frame so it is larger, or choose Open Frame from the Window menu to see the entire contents of the frame.

TIP

---

8 **Click once anywhere outside the frame to select it.** The cursor changes to the arrow pointer and graphics-related menus are active. In addition to selection handles, the frame shows a continuation indicator.

9 **Click the continuation indicator.** The cursor changes to the crossbar pointer.

10 **Repeat step 6 to create the next frame.** Data overflowed from the first frame appears in the next frame.

11 **Repeat steps 8, 9, and 10 until you have all of the linked spreadsheet frames you want.**

If you decide later that you no longer want the spreadsheet frames linked, delete all of them except the first linked frame. Select the remaining frame and choose Frame Links from the Options menu to turn Frame Links off. Any data you typed or pasted into the frames that you just deleted is retained in the remaining frame. You can also select, cut, and paste the frames (either in the current document or into another one) to remove their linked status.

TIP

You can also create empty linked frames first and add data to them later. To do this, follow the steps described earlier, skipping those that instruct you to type or paste data. Figure 1-29 shows four empty linked spreadsheet frames

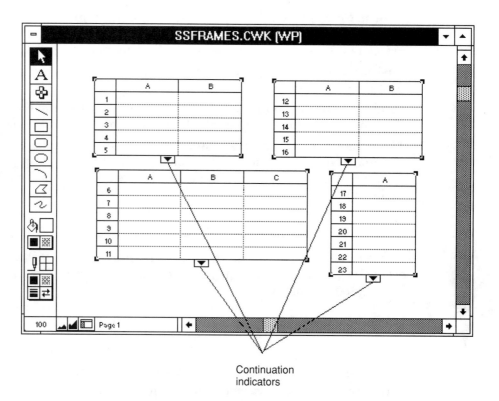

Continuation
indicators

Figure 1-29 Four empty linked spreadsheet frames in a text document

inside a text document. Notice that, unlike text frames, linked spreadsheet frames do not display the top-of-frame or link indicator; they only display the continuation indicator. Each time you click a continuation indicator and drag to create another empty linked spreadsheet frame, the row headings continue in the new frame.

The size of a spreadsheet frame determines how many rows and columns you see. The wider the frame, the more columns; the longer the frame, the more rows.

You resize and move frames as you would other graphics objects.

Drawing tools

You use the drawing tools in the tool palette to draw specific kinds of graphic objects in any ClarisWorks environment. This section first gives general instructions for drawing objects using any one of the drawing tools. Each drawing tool is then discussed in the order that it appears in the tool palette. Finally, general instructions for selecting and manipulating objects are included.

Drawing objects

To draw graphics objects in graphics, text, spreadsheet, or database documents (in Layout):

1   **Click the graphics tool to select it and select a drawing tool, or select one of the drawing tools directly.** Graphics-related menus are activated. If you select the graphics tool, the cursor changes to the arrow pointer. (If you are drawing in a graphics document, the graphics tool is already selected.) If you select one of the drawing tools directly, the cursor changes to a large plus sign (+), which is the drawing pointer.

2   **Position the drawing pointer in your document where you want to add the graphics object.**

3   **Drag to draw the object, as shown in Figure 1-30.**

4   **Release the mouse to finish your drawing.**

Figure 1-30 Drawing a graphics object using the drawing pointer

After you draw an object, the object is selected and the graphics tool becomes active again. This enables you to alter the drawing using the graphics-related menus or the fill and pen tools. For example, you can change the pattern inside the object by choosing a fill pattern from the fill pattern palette. You may also choose Rotate from the Arrange menu to rotate the object in 90-degree increments.

If you want to create multiple objects of the same type (such as a series of lines or circles), double-click the tool to lock it. Otherwise, after you finish drawing an object, the graphics tool is automatically selected again.

TIP

If you draw your object (such as a rectangle) over existing text, data, or another object, the new object is positioned over the existing text, data, or object. In other words, the new object sits in the front layer of the document. There are two ways in which you can change this: Either move the object to the back layer, or make the object transparent.

To move the object to the back layer:

1 **Select the object with the arrow pointer.**

2 **Choose Move Backward (Shift+Ctrl+minus), or Move To Back from the Arrange menu.** *Move Backward moves the object back through other objects one layer at a time. This is really only effective if you have several objects on top of one another.*

   Move To Back moves the object immediately to the back layer, which is most effective in the text or database environment. If you have one object on top of text in a text document or a database document in Layout view, use Move To Back to see the text through the object.

Moving an object to the back layer does not work in spreadsheet documents or frames. If you want to be able to see through objects (including charts) to see spreadsheet data, you need to make the object transparent. To make the object transparent:

1 **Select the border of the object with the arrow pointer.**

2 **Using the fill tool, click the fill pattern icon to open the fill pattern palette, as shown in Figure 1-31.**

3 **Choose the transparent fill pattern (see Figure 1-31).** *The object becomes transparent, which means that you can see objects or the contents of documents through them. The objects lose any fill pattern or color previously assigned to them, although line attributes remain intact.*

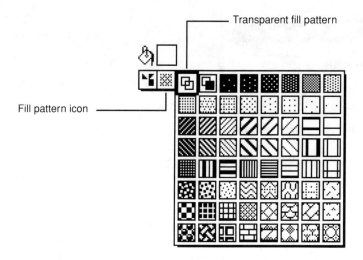

Figure 1-31 Choosing a transparent fill pattern from the fill tool

Line tool

Use the line tool to draw horizontal, vertical, or diagonal lines. ClarisWorks is preset to draw lines with a width of 1 point. You can change line width and other line attributes using the pen tools (described later in this chapter).

To constrain the line to a 0-, 45-, or 90-degree angle, hold down the Shift key as you draw the line.

Note *You change the angle of the Shift-key constraint in the Preferences dialog box from 1 to 45 degrees. This change affects the way in which lines and other objects appear when you hold down the Shift key.*

If you want to shorten a line after you've drawn it, select the line, and hold down the Alt key as you drag to shrink the length of the line.

Rectangle and rounded rectangle tools

Use the rectangle tool to draw rectangles and squares, and the rounded rectangle tool to draw them with rounded corners. These tools are preset to draw rectangles. To draw squares or rounded squares, hold down the Shift key as you draw.

Note *To draw perfect squares or rounded squares, the Shift-key constraint must be set to 45 degrees in the Preferences dialog box.*

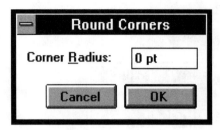

Figure 1-32 Round Corners dialog box

ClarisWorks is preset to draw rectangles and squares with a corner radius of 0 points (meaning the corners are not rounded). Rounded rectangles and squares have a preset corner radius of 18 points. You can change the corner radius by selecting the object and choosing Round Corners from the Options menu, pressing Shift+Ctrl+I, or by double-clicking a selected rectangle or square. This opens the Round Corners dialog box shown in Figure 1-32. Type the radius you want (in points), and click OK.

To convert a square into a circle (or a rectangle into an oval) without redrawing it:

TIP

1   Select the square or rectangle.

2   Choose Round Corners from the Options menu, or double-click the object.

3   In the dialog box, set the corner radius to 45 points.

4   Click OK. *This same technique can be used with rectangles and squares drawn with the rounded rectangle tool.*

Oval tool

Use the oval tool to draw ovals and circles. The oval tool is preset to draw ovals. To draw perfect circles, hold down the Shift key as you draw.

Arc tool

Use the arc tool to draw an arc, which is a line that curves between two points. To draw quarter circles, hold down the Shift key as you draw with the arc tool.

The direction in which you draw determines the curve of the arc, which is measured in degrees as the arc's start angle and arc angle. The preset start and arc angles of an arc vary depending on the direction you followed to create it. Figure 1-33 shows the preset angles of four arcs, one created in each direction you can draw (up and left, up and right, down and left, and down and right).

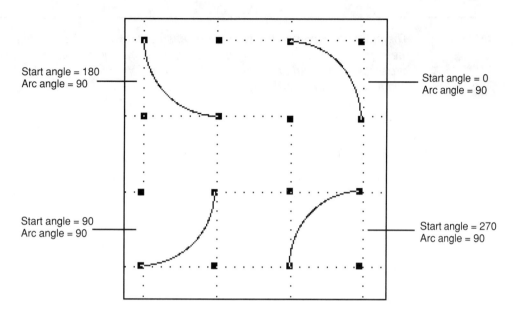

Figure 1-33 Start and Arc angles of four arcs

You can change the start and arc angles of an arc by selecting it and choosing Modify Arc (Shift+Ctrl+I) from the Options menu or by double-clicking the selected object. This opens the Arc Info dialog box shown in Figure 1-34. Type a start angle and/or an arc angle, in degrees. Either angle must be in range 0 to 359, inclusive.

Figure 1-34 Arc Info dialog box

The more you increase the arc angle measurement in the Arc Info dialog box, the more the arc begins to approximate a circle. To convert an arc object into a circle, leave the start angle measurement as it appears in the Arc Info dialog box, and type 359 for the arc angle.

TIP

Polygon tool

Use the polygon tool to draw irregular shapes that consist of angles and lines. Examples of polygons are parallelograms, octagons, triangles, and stars. To draw a polygon:

1   **Select the polygon tool.** The cursor changes to the drawing pointer.
2   **Position the pointer in the document, and click once to begin the polygon.**
3   **Move the mouse in the direction you want to create the first line of the polygon.**
4   **Click again to set the first line.**
5   **Repeat steps 3 and 4 to complete the polygon.**
6   **Double-click, or press Enter on the numeric keypad to finish.**

You can draw polygons that remain open when you finish drawing them, or you can draw polygons that close automatically. ClarisWorks is preset to draw open polygons. To set polygons to close automatically:

1   **Choose Preferences from the Edit menu.**
2   **In the Preferences dialog box, check the Automatic Polygon Closing option under Graphics.**
3   **Click OK.**

If Manual is selected in the Preferences dialog box, the polygon remains open at the point where you finished it. If Automatic is selected, the polygon automatically closes up from the point you finished to the point where you started.

There are two ways you can modify a polygon: smoothing and reshaping. (Of course, you can also modify a polygon like any other graphics object by using the fill and pen tools, which are described later in this chapter.) Polygons are preset to draw with angular corners. To smooth the corners and soften the shape of the polygon, choose Smooth from the Edit menu, or press Ctrl+(. To return to angular corners, choose Unsmooth [Ctrl+)] from the Edit menu.

Reshaping a polygon involves changing the angles that comprise it by moving the polygon's vertices. (A *vertex* is a point in the polygon where two lines meet.) To reshape a polygon:

1 **Select the polygon.**

2 **Choose Reshape from the Edit menu, or press Ctrl+R.** The cursor changes to the reshape pointer and selection handles appear in the polygon to indicate its vertices.

3 **Position the reshape pointer on a vertex.**

4 **Click and drag the vertex's handle shown in Figure 1-35.**

5 **Release the mouse to finish reshaping.**

6 **To turn reshaping off, choose Reshape from the Edit menu.**

With Reshape turned on in the Edit menu, you can add or delete a polygon vertex. To add a new vertex, position the reshape pointer on a line where you want the new vertex, and click. To delete a vertex, position the pointer over the vertex to delete, and Alt-click it.

TIP

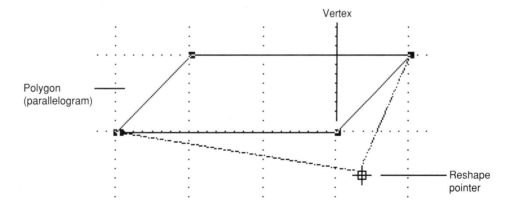

Figure 1-35 Reshaping a polygon

Freehand tool

Use the freehand tool to create freehand drawings as you would draw on paper with a pen or pencil. A freehand line can be any length and has a preset line width of 1 point. To draw a freehand shape:

1   **Select the freehand tool.** The cursor changes to the drawing pointer.
2   **Position the pointer in the document where you want to begin the drawing.**
3   **Hold down the mouse as you drag to draw the shape.**
4   **Release the mouse to finish.**

Figure 1-36 gives an example of a freehand drawing. In this example, the letter L was drawn with a line width of 3 points.

Figure 1-36 Object created with the freehand tool

ClarisWorks automatically smooths a freehand drawing. To show the drawing as an angular shape, choose Unsmooth [Ctrl+)] from the Edit menu.
Like polygons, you can reshape freehand drawings. Follow the steps for reshaping in "Polygon Tool" earlier in this chapter.

Although you cannot add a vertex to a smoothed polygon or freehand object, you can delete a vertex. Turn Reshape on in the Edit menu and Alt-click the vertex to delete.

TIP

Selecting objects

Before you can manipulate objects, you need to select them. The following steps describe how to select existing objects in any document type. These steps apply to objects created with the drawing tools, as well as to frames created with the text or spreadsheet tool. To select objects:

1 **Select the graphics tool, if necessary.** Remember that when you are working in a graphics document, the graphics tool is automatically selected in the tool palette.

2 **Position the arrow pointer over the object and click the object once to select it.**

3 **To select multiple objects, click and drag the arrow pointer around the objects.** A selection marquee tracks your movements. Objects enclosed within the selection marquee are selected. To select all objects that intersect the selection rectangle, hold down the Ctrl key as you drag.

   You can also hold down the Shift key and click each object to select them.

4 **To select all objects in the document, choose Select All (Ctrl+A) from the Edit menu.**

Once an object is selected, selection handles appear, as shown in Figure 1-37. ClarisWorks is preset to show four selection handles, one at each corner of the object. You can change this to show eight selection handles by changing the Object Selection option in the Graphics area of the Preferences dialog box.

   To deselect objects, click anywhere in the document outside of your selection. Holding down the Shift key as you drag the selection rectangle deselects objects within the rectangle. Holding down the Shift and Ctrl keys as you drag deselects those objects that intersect the selection rectangle.

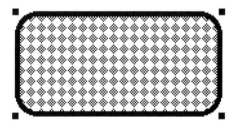

Figure 1-37 A selected object shows selection handles

Manipulating objects

When selection handles appear around an object, you can then move it to another place in the document, resize it to make it smaller or larger, or alter it in any way you choose. To move selected objects, drag them across the document to the desired position, and release the mouse. The screen automatically scrolls if you drag an object off the current screen position. To resize a selected object, click and drag one of the selection handles, and release the mouse when the object is the size you want. If you hold down the Shift key as you move or resize an object, your movements are constrained to 45-degree angles, or to the Shift-key constraint angle set in the Preferences dialog box.

ClarisWorks offers you many ways of altering the way objects appear in a document. The Arrange menu shown in Figure 1-38 contains most of the commands you use to alter and manipulate objects.

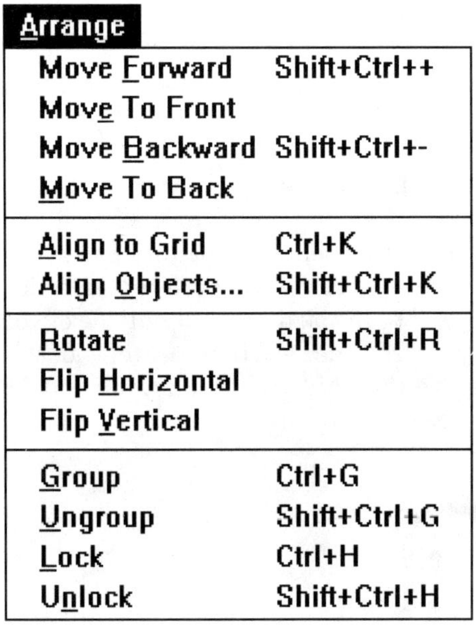

Arrange	
Move Forward	Shift+Ctrl++
Move To Front	
Move Backward	Shift+Ctrl+-
Move To Back	
Align to Grid	Ctrl+K
Align Objects...	Shift+Ctrl+K
Rotate	Shift+Ctrl+R
Flip Horizontal	
Flip Vertical	
Group	Ctrl+G
Ungroup	Shift+Ctrl+G
Lock	Ctrl+H
Unlock	Shift+Ctrl+H

Figure 1-38 The Arrange menu in the graphics environment

Here is a list of the Arrange menu commands and their effects on selected objects:

Command	Effect
Move Forward	Moves object(s) forward one layer at a time in a stack of objects
Move To Front	Moves object(s) all the way to the front of a stack of objects
Move Backward	Opposite effect of Move Forward
Move To Back	Opposite effect of Move To Front
Align to Grid	Snaps object(s) to the nearest autogrid points
Align Objects	Uses settings in the Align Objects dialog box to align objects with respect to each other
Rotate	Rotates objects in 90-degree increments
Flip Horizontal	Flips object(s) sideways
Flip Vertical	Flips object(s) upside down
Group	Groups objects together; grouped objects are treated as a single object
Ungroup	Opposite effect of Group
Lock	Locks objects so they cannot be changed
Unlock	Opposite effect of Lock

Note The autogrid, *which is preset to be turned on, is a hidden control composed of intersecting lines. It enables you to create and align objects more precisely. To turn the autogrid off, choose Turn Autogrid Off from the Options menu, or press Ctrl+Y. Also, linked frames are the only objects that cannot be rotated or flipped.*

In addition to the Arrange menu commands, you can use the Scale Selection dialog box to reduce or enlarge selected objects. Open the dialog box by choosing Scale Selection from the Options menu. You can specify a scale percentage (in the range 25 to 400, inclusive) to scale horizontally, vertically, or both.

Another method of altering objects is to add fill patterns and colors to them and to change their line attributes. You do this by using the fill and pen tools.

Fill tools

You use the fill tools to fill objects with color or patterns and to make objects transparent or opaque. Fill colors apply to any type of object, except objects that you import into a ClarisWorks document from another application. Fill patterns do not apply to frames, database fields (which are treated as objects in Layout view), or imported objects.

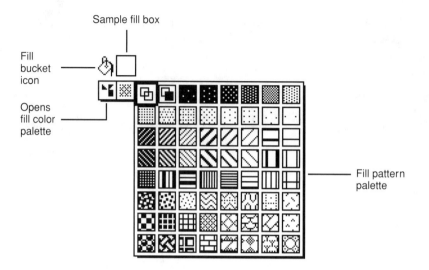

Figure 1-39 Fill tools with fill pattern palette open

The fill tools include the fill bucket icon, sample fill box, fill color palette, and fill pattern palette. Figure 1-39 shows the fill tools fill pattern palette open.

The fill bucket icon simply identifies the fill tools; you don't do anything with this icon. The sample fill box shows the current, preset fill pattern, and color. The current, preset pattern, and color are those that are in effect before you draw an object. This box does not indicate the pattern and color of a selected object whose attributes are different than the preset ones. In other words, if you select an object that has a different fill pattern and color than the presets, the sample fill box does not update to reflect them. This implies that ClarisWorks assumes you will set a fill pattern and color before drawing an object. To change the preset fill color and pattern:

1   Deselect all objects in the document.

2   Choose a new color and pattern from the appropriate fill palettes.

The sample fill box updates to reflect your changes. Your pattern and color settings remain in effect until you repeat this procedure.

On a monochrome monitor, the fill color palette displays a menu listing eight fill colors from which you can choose. On color monitors, the palette displays the number of colors supported by your monitor (up to 81 maximum). The preset fill color is white.

The fill pattern palette displays 64 patterns from which you can choose. Two of the choices in this palette let you set an object to either be transparent or *opaque* (you cannot see through it). Either of these settings is considered a fill pattern. The preset fill pattern is opaque.

TIP

You can create special effects in a text or spreadsheet frame by setting a fill color and a complementary text color. This technique is a quick and easy way to make your documents more exciting. For example, you can change the fill color in a text frame to blue and the text color to white.

TIP

The fill color and pattern palettes can be torn off *the tool palette and positioned anywhere on your screen. This is useful if you are doing frequent color and/or pattern work. To tear off a palette, click and drag it away from the tool palette. To close a torn-off palette, click the box in the upper left corner of the palette. You can also tear off the pen color and pen pattern palettes, as well as the line width and arrowhead menus (described in the next section).*

Pen tools

You use the pen tools to set or change the following line attributes:

- Color
- Pattern
- Width
- Arrowheads

Pen settings apply to all object types, including frames, database fields, and imported objects (except objects imported into a text document). Single lines you draw with the line tool, and the lines that define rectangles, squares, ovals, circles, arcs, polygons, and freehand drawings are all affected by the pen tool settings. However, arrowhead settings apply only to lines.

Note *When you import an object into a document, the object has an invisible border around it. It appears to be invisible because the pen pattern is set to transparent. To change the line settings of borders around an imported object, first select it, then use the pen tools to make your changes. Also, if you ungroup an imported object, you will lose any features that ClarisWorks doesn't support (such as dashed lines).*

The pen tools include the pen icon, sample pen box, pen color palette, pen pattern palette, Line Width menu, and Arrowhead menu. Figure 1-40 shows the pen tools with the Line Width and Arrowhead menus open.

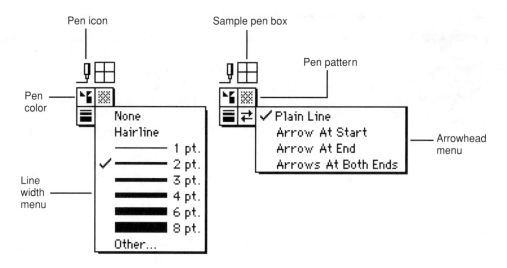

Figure 1-40 Pen tools, including the Line Width and Arrowhead menus

The pen icon simply identifies the pen tools. The sample pen box shows the current, preset line width, pattern, and color. The sample pen box works the same as the sample fill box, described in the previous section. You change the preset line attributes the same way you change preset fill attributes. To change the preset line attributes:

1   Deselect all objects in the document.

2   Use the pen tools to choose new line attributes.

The sample pen box updates to reflect your changes. Your pen settings remain in effect until you repeat this procedure.

The pen color and pen pattern palettes look the same as the fill color and pattern palettes. You can also set a line to be either transparent or opaque, just as you use the fill pattern palette to do so.

Line attributes are preset as follows:

Attribute	*Setting*
Pen color	Black
Pen pattern	Opaque
Pen width	1 point
Arrowhead	Plain line (no arrowhead)

In addition to the line widths listed in the Line Width menu, you can set a customized line width by choosing Other from the menu. This opens the Line Size dialog box shown in Figure 1-41. Type a line width in the range 0.02 to 255 points, inclusive, in 0.02-point increments.

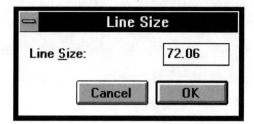

Figure 1-41 Specifying a custom line width

Summary

ClarisWorks offers you a rich environment where you can accomplish virtually any and all tasks for which you would otherwise use separate applications. Each application environment and its respective document type provides you with the full power of a stand-alone application. However, it is through the tools and frames that ClarisWorks gives you the ability to easily and seamlessly integrate different types of data in one document.

Chapter Two

Creating Personal or Business Stationery

About this chapter

This chapter describes in detail how to use the text and graphics environments to create a set of stationery—specifically, letterhead and matching envelopes. Although the examples used in this chapter pertain to business stationery, you can use the same techniques to create personal stationery.

In this chapter you will create letterhead (including a logo) and save it as stationery. You then use the stationery to write a two-page letter; format the letter; add a header, footer, and footnotes; check the letter for spelling; and use the thesaurus to find synonyms. Finally, this chapter describes how to create a template for envelopes. The envelope template uses the same logo and return address as the letterhead.

Creating the letterhead

The concept behind creating your own stationery is to give yourself a template that you can use every time you write a letter or produce another type of document, such as an income statement or a report. By creating letterhead for your business or personal stationery, you give your correspondence a unique identity—one that reflects the nature of your business or your personal interests.

In this section, you create letterhead for a fictitious business called Surfcity Sailboats. The letterhead consists of text and graphics objects. The graphics work together as a *logo*—a visual image that identifies Surfcity Sailboats. After designing the letterhead and creating the logo, you save the letterhead as stationery.

Designing the letterhead

The primary component of stationery is *letterhead*, which consists of text or graphics or a combination of both and usually appears at the top of your stationery. Other styles of stationery position the letterhead at the bottom or to one side of the stationery. Wherever it is positioned on the page, a letterhead generally includes your name or business name and address; it can also include a phone number.

Figure 2-1 shows the letterhead you will create for Surfcity Sailboats. The letterhead includes various types of graphic objects as well as text in varying font styles and sizes.

Figure 2-1 The Surfcity Sailboat letterhead

Creating a new graphics document

A graphics document is the best type of document to use in ClarisWorks for creating letterhead. You can create letterhead in another document type using the tools in the tool palette; but a graphics document gives you access to the graphics grid and rulers, which help you to position each element exactly where you want it on the page. You start the process of designing the Surfcity Sailboats letterhead by creating a new graphics document, as follows:

1   If ClarisWorks is not running, start the application by double-clicking its icon in the Program Manager. You see the New dialog box.

If you hold down the Ctrl key while you double-click the ClarisWorks icon in the Program Manager, ClarisWorks displays the Open dialog box instead of the New dialog box.

TIP

2 **Select the document type by clicking Graphics.** You can also select a document type by pressing the UpArrow or DownArrow keys to cycle through the choices in the dialog box.

3 **Click OK.** A new graphics document opens, with the graphics grid showing and the tool palette along the left side of the document.

If the graphics ruler is not visible, choose Show Rulers (Shift+Ctrl+U) from the Window menu to turn it on. The graphics ruler is preset to measure in inches, with eight divisions per inch. Because you will be working with relatively small graphic objects in this chapter, it will be easier if you change the ruler's unit of measure to a smaller unit. The other choices are picas, points, centimeters, and millimeters. If you change the measurement unit to points, you can work with the smallest unit of measure available in ClarisWorks. To change to points:

1 **Choose Rulers from the Format menu.** The Rulers dialog box opens (see Figure 2-2).

2 **In the dialog box, click Points.**

3 **Leave the Divisions setting as is, and click OK.**

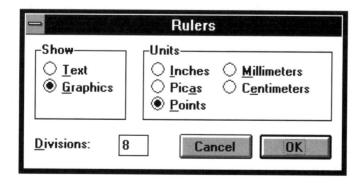

Figure 2-2 Setting the ruler units to points

The graphics ruler now shows points instead of inches, with eight divisions per unit. The unit of measurement set in the Rulers dialog box also affects the graphics grid size, which now shows a smaller interval between lines.

TIP

When the ruler units are set to points, picas, or millimeters, the ruler intervals change when you enlarge or reduce your view of a graphics document. For example, with ruler units set to points, if you set View Scale to 200%, the ruler interval changes from eight divisions per 40 points to eight divisions per 20 points. Zooming in at 400% changes the ruler interval to eight divisions per 10 points, and so on.

With ruler units set to inches, the ruler interval does not change when you reduce or enlarge your view. Rather, the divisions between inches appear to shrink or stretch with decreasing or increasing magnification, respectively.

With ruler units set to centimeters, the ruler interval changes according to zoom percentage only up to 200% magnification. After that, the ruler stretches with increasing magnification.

Creating the text frames

With your graphics document set up, you are ready to start creating the letterhead. Start by adding the company's name and address, followed by the phone and fax numbers. To do this, create two text frames. Each text block will be in a separate frame, making it easier to position them later. To create the text frames:

1 **Select the text tool.**

2 **Click and drag to create a text frame at the top of the document. Using the graphics ruler, begin the text frame at approximately 140 points, drag across to 260 points, and down to 120 points (see Figure 2-3).**

3 **Release the mouse.** Your text frame should look like the one in Figure 2-3. You see the insertion point blinking in the upper-left corner inside the frame.

4 **In the frame, type the following text, pressing ↵ after each line:**

Surfcity Sailboats
10101 Beach Street
Suite 100
Surfcity, California
90001

If you make a mistake, use the Delete or Backspace key to correct it. All standard text editing features are available to you in the text frame.

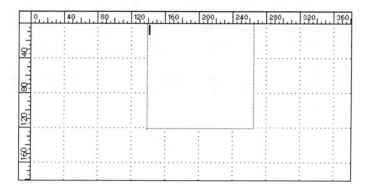

Figure 2-3 The first text frame

5   **Press Enter on the numeric keypad to complete the first frame.**

6   **Select the text tool again.**

7   **Click and drag to create the second text frame below the first.**

8   **Release the mouse.**

9   **In this frame, type the following text. Be sure to press ⏎ after the first line.**

Phone: 213.555.SAIL
Fax: 213.555.9890

10 **Press Enter on the numeric keypad when you are finished.**

The small dots that make up the graphics grid correspond to points on the ruler. Use these dots as guides for drawing graphics or frames precisely in the desired position within the document.

TIP

Your document should resemble the one shown in Figure 2-4.

Now that both of the letterhead's text frames are created, change the font to something other than the ClarisWorks default. The text shown in Figure 2-1 is set to MS Sans Serif, but you can use a different font. The font you choose for your own letterhead depends on the type of image you want to convey in your stationery. A serif font, such as Script, conveys a more elegant, traditional image; a sans serif font, such as MS Sans Serif, Arial, or Modern, gives your stationery a more contemporary look. (*Sans serif* means without *serifs,* which are the short lines stemming from the ends of the strokes of a letter, such as those you see in the font used in this paragraph.)

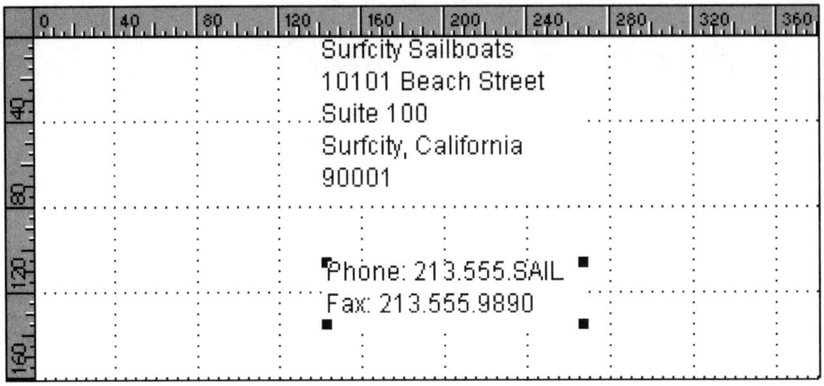

Figure 2-4 Both letterhead text frames

Note *For best results, use a font type and size that is installed in your system and installed in your printer. Font technology is beyond the scope of this book. However, you should know that your text will look jagged onscreen and on paper if you do not use a font or font size installed in your system or one that is supported by your printer.*

To change the font of the text in both text frames at the same time:

1   **Select the graphics tool if it's not already selected.**

2   **Hold down the Shift key as you click each frame to select both of them.**

3   **Choose Font from the Format menu, and select MS Sans Serif (or another font) from the Font submenu.** The text in both frames changes to the selected font type.

Now you are going to change the font size and style of the company name to emphasize it.

1   **Click the top text frame.** The insertion point appears in the text frame and text-related menus are activated.

2   **Drag across the first line to select *Surfcity Sailboats.***

3   **Choose 14 Point from the Size menu.**

4   **With the text still selected, choose Bold from the Style menu, or press Ctrl+B.**

Note *Changing the font type, size, and style may cause your text frames to expand or contract to accommodate the changes. If this occurs, you may need to resize or reposition them.*

The text frames of your letterhead design are finished for the time being. Before moving on, it's a good idea to save the work you've done so far. Choose Save from the File menu, or press Ctrl+S. In the dialog box, navigate to the disk and directory where you want this file saved. In the File Name box, type **SSLogo.CWK**, and click OK.

Adding a logo

In this section, you will add to the letterhead the graphic elements that comprise the logo. Begin by opening your graphics document (SSLogo) if it isn't already open.

The Surfcity Sailboat logo is composed of several different graphics objects, including

- 1 rounded rectangle—the logo border
- 1 circle—the sun
- 7 lines—6 for the sun's rays, 1 for the sail mast
- 2 polygons—the boat's sails
- 2 arcs—the boat's hull
- 1 freehand object—the wavy line

You will start by drawing the logo border in the letterhead. Then you will draw the elements of the sailboat and sun in a separate place in the document, group the elements into one object, and place the object inside the border.

Drawing the logo border

To draw the logo border:

1   **If the rulers are not visible, choose Show Rulers from the Window menu.** The ruler units should still be set to points.
2   **Select the rounded rectangle tool.**
3   **Click in the uppermost corner of the document immediately to the left of the text frames, and drag to create a rounded rectangle that is approximately 130 points in width and 150 points in length.**
4   **Release the mouse.**

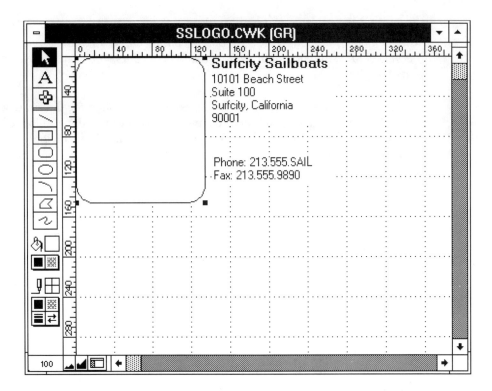

Figure 2-5 Drawing the logo border

The rounded rectangle shows selection handles and the graphics tool becomes active. Your document should resemble the one in Figure 2-5.

In order to duplicate the logo border shown in Figure 2-1, you need to change the line width and pen pattern of the rounded rectangle you just drew. To do this:

1 **With the logo border selected, click the line width icon in the tool palette, and choose 4 pt. from the Line Width menu.** The border becomes thicker.

2 **To set the pen pattern, click the pen pattern icon in the tool palette and choose the pattern shown in Figure 2-6.**

Now you will draw the elements that make up the sailboat and the sun behind it. You will work in another part of the document so you have enough room and minimize the risk of affecting the rounded rectangle and text frames that are already positioned correctly. Scroll down the document until you see a blank work area on your screen.

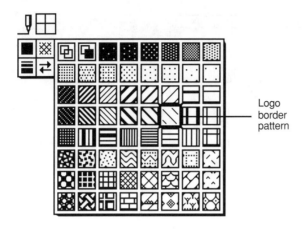

Logo
border
pattern

Figure 2-6 Choosing a pen pattern

Instead of scrolling to another place in the document, you can lock a graphic object in place so it cannot be moved or edited. To do this, select the object (such as the logo border), and choose Lock (Ctrl+H) from the Arrange menu. Now you cannot move the object or make any modifications to it unless you unlock it by selecting Unlock in the Arrange menu.

TIP

Because you will be drawing relatively small objects, you can enlarge the view of your document. This makes it easier to work in detail. Click the right zoom control to enlarge the view of your document to 200%.

Creating the sailboat

Now you will create the sailboat elements in this order: sails, hull, and mast. The sails are actually triangle objects, or polygons. To do so:

1   **Click the polygon tool to select it.**

2   **To draw the left sail, position the drawing pointer in the document, hold down the Shift key, and click and drag straight across to create the bottom line of the triangle.** Remember that holding down the Shift key constrains your movements to 45-degree angles; in this case, it constrains your movement to a straight line. The bottom line of the triangle should be about 35 points long.

3   **With the Shift key still pressed, click again to end the first line, and drag straight up to create the right line of the triangle.** The right line should be about 50 points long and should be at a right angle to the first line.

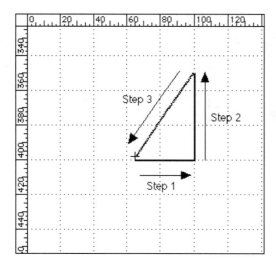

Figure 2-7 Drawing the first sail

4   Click again to end the second line, release the Shift key, and drag at an angle from the top of the second line to the beginning of the first line.

5   When the triangle appears to be closed up, double-click to finish.

These steps are illustrated in Figure 2-7. The arrows in the figure show the direction in which you drag.

You can use your completed sail (actually a right angle triangle) to create the right sail. Rather than draw another triangle, you can duplicate the first one and resize it. To do this:

1   With the triangle selected, choose Duplicate from the Edit menu, or press Ctrl+D. ClarisWorks creates an exact duplicate and places it on top of the original.

2   Click the new triangle, and drag it away from the original so it is positioned just to the right of the original.

3   Choose Flip Horizontal from the Arrange menu. The duplicate sail appears back-to-back with the first one.

4   With the duplicate still selected, click the upper-right selection handle, and drag down and to the left to make the duplicate smaller than the original. The bottom line of the duplicate triangle should be approximately 25 points and its left line should be 40 points.

5   When the duplicate is the correct size, release the mouse.

6   **Drag the duplicate across, and position it approximately 5 points to the right of the original.**

Figure 2-8 shows what your logo should look like so far.

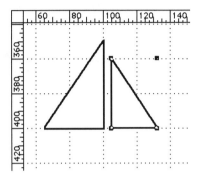

Figure 2-8 The boat's sails are complete

You've completed the two sails of the boat. Now you're going to draw the boat's hull, using the arc tool. Using a technique similar to what you used to create the sails, you will draw one arc first, duplicate it, and flip it to complete the hull. You will also use a fill pattern in the arc to give it a more interesting look.

1   **Click the arc tool to select it.**

2   **Position the drawing pointer in the document below the left sail.**

3   **Click and drag with a sweeping motion downward and to the right until you have an arc that has a start angle of 180 degrees and an arc angle of 90 degrees.**

4   **With the arc selected, choose Duplicate from the Edit menu.**

5   **Drag the duplicate arc to the right of the original.**

6   **Choose Flip Horizontal from the Arrange menu.**

7   **Drag the duplicate to position it next to the original, as shown in Figure 2-9.**

You may need to position the boat hull closer to the bottom of the sails. If so, select both arcs, and drag them into position.

Now that you have the boat's sails and hull drawn, you're going to add a pattern to the hull and a mast to the main sail. Before continuing, save your SSLogo document by pressing Ctrl+S.

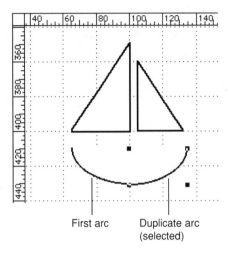

First arc   Duplicate arc
                   (selected)

Figure 2-9 The boat hull is made up of two arcs

To add a pattern to the hull:

1   **Select both arcs.**

2   **Choose a fill pattern from the palette.** The fill pattern used in the logo is
    shown in Figure 2-10.

Because the selected hull pattern is a series of diagonal lines and the two
arcs may not be completely lined up, you may have to adjust the position of
either arc so the pattern repeats correctly across both arcs. In other words,

Boat hull pattern

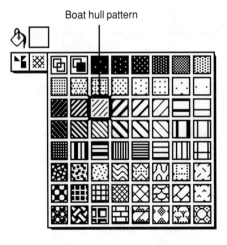

Figure 2-10 The boat hull pattern

you may have to adjust the arcs so the diagonal lines appear to be continuous, unbroken lines throughout the hull. Click the zoom percentage box to toggle between 200% and 100% magnification, and verify that the two arcs line up properly at both magnification levels.

Now add a mast to the main (left) sail.

1   **Select the line tool from the tool palette.**

2   **Position the drawing pointer at the lower-right corner of the main sail.**

3   **Hold down the Shift key as you click, and drag down to draw a short straight line between the main sail and the hull.**

4   **Release the mouse.**

Your sailboat is complete. Before you draw the elements of the sun, group the elements of the boat together so they are treated as one object. To do this, select all of the boat's elements and choose Group (Ctrl+G) from the Arrange menu. The boat is selected as one complete object, as shown in Figure 2-11.

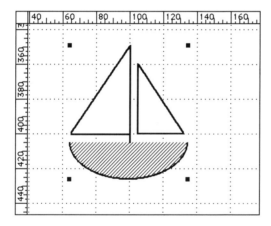

Figure 2-11 The completed sailboat, shown at 200% magnification

Adding the sun

The sun in the logo is composed of a circle, filled in with color, and six lines emanating from the circle. As before, you are going to work in a different part of the document so you do not affect any of the objects created up to this point. This time, scroll across the document until you have a clean area within which to work. Make sure the rulers are showing, ruler units are still set to points, and the view scale is set to 200% magnification.

TIP

If you have several graphics objects scattered across your document, you can reduce the view of the document to see all of them at once on your screen. This is useful for giving you an overview of your drawing and for determining the relative distances between the objects in the document. To reduce the view, set View Scale (Window menu) to 50%, or click the left zoom control until the zoom percentage box shows 50%. If you prefer, create a new view of your document by choosing New View from the Window menu, and set one view to 50% and the other view to 100% or 200%.

To draw the sun and its rays as they appear in the logo:

1   **Click the oval tool to select it.**

2   **Hold down the Shift key as you click and drag to create a circle with a diameter of about 50 points.** Remember that holding down the Shift key as you drag with the oval tool constrains the object to a perfect circle.

3   **Release the mouse.** The circle is selected.

4   **Select the line tool, and position the drawing pointer at the top of the circle.**

5   **Holding down the Shift key, click and drag upward to draw a straight line of about 25 points in length.** Now use this line as a basis for two of the other sun rays.

6   **With the line selected, choose Duplicate from the Edit menu.**

7   **Choose Rotate from the Arrange menu, or press Shift+Ctrl+R.** The duplicate line rotates at a 90-degree angle to the original.

8   **Drag the duplicated, rotated line to the left of the circle, and position it so that one end of the line is touching the circle.**

9   **Repeat step 6 and step 8 to duplicate this line and position the second duplicate to the right of the circle.**

The longer sun rays are completed. Using the same technique, draw a shorter line (about 15 points long) on a diagonal between two of the existing straight lines. (Holding down the Shift key as you draw will constrain your line to a 45-degree diagonal.) Follow steps 6 through 9, listed earlier, to create two duplicate, rotated diagonal lines, positioning them between the straight lines. Your drawing should resemble the one shown in Figure 2-12.

To complete the sun, add a fill color to the circle. First, select the circle, then choose a color from the fill color palette. The color used in the completed logo is a shade of gray.

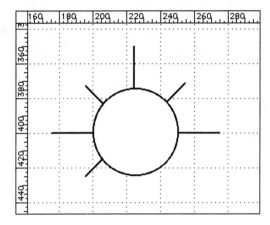

Figure 2-12 The logo's sun and sun rays

Note *If you are using a monochrome monitor, the fill color palette is actually a menu listing colors. You can use the Fill Color menu to choose a fill color but you will not be able to see the color onscreen. Likewise, if you do not have a color printer, you will not be able to see the color printed out on the page.*

Now that the sun is completed, move it into its position in the logo, behind the sailboat. To do this, you need to switch the view of the document back to 100% magnification so you can see both the sailboat and the sun at the same time. Click the left zoom control or set the View Scale to 100%. Scroll the document so you can see the boat and the sun in the window.

To position the sun behind the sailboat:

1   **Select all of the elements of the sun, including the rays.**

2   **Drag the selection on top of the sailboat.** As you drag the selected elements into position, an outline of the selection shadows your movements with the mouse, and the elements remain in their original position with selection handles around them, as shown in Figure 2-13.

    When you release the mouse, the sun moves into the position indicated by the selection outline, and all of its elements are selected.

3   **To group the sun elements into one object, choose Group from the Arrange menu.** The sun is in the proper position but it is blocking part of the boat. To correct this, you need to move the sun behind the boat.

4   **With the sun selected, choose Move To Back from the Arrange menu.** Your drawing should resemble the one shown in Figure 2-14.

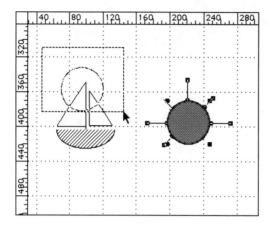

Figure 2-13 Positioning the sun

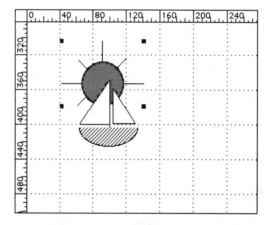

Figure 2-14 Sailboat and sun completed

With the sailboat and sun graphic elements of the logo completed, you can now group them together and move them into position inside of the border you created earlier. First, group the sailboat and sun elements by selecting both of them and choosing Group from the Arrange menu. To get a better overall picture of the document so far, reduce the view to 66.7% by clicking the left zoom control. This enables you to see both the boat/sun elements and the border on the screen at the same time. To move the boat/sun grouped object into the border, select it, then drag it until it is centered inside of the border.

The final touch to the logo is a graphic design element that works to tie the logo and the text frames of the letterhead together. This design element is a curving line resembling a wave, which you will create using the freehand tool. Before adding this final element, lock the other elements of the letterhead so you don't disturb them as you draw, and enlarge your document view to 100%.

1   **Choose Select All (Ctrl+A) from the Edit menu.**

2   **Choose Lock (Ctrl+H) from the Arrange menu.** All objects in the document are locked, as indicated by the grayed-out selection handles around each object. Now draw the wave line.

3   **Click the zoom percentage box to return to 100% magnification.**

4   **Select the freehand tool.**

5   **In the Line Width menu in the tool palette, set the line width to Hairline.**

6   **Open the pen color and pattern palettes to make sure the pen color is black and the pattern is opaque.**

7   **With the drawing pointer positioned inside the logo border below the sailboat, click and drag to the right as you draw a curving line like the one shown in Figure 2-15.**

8   **Release the mouse.**

Figure 2-15 Completed letterhead with wave line in place

If you are not satisfied with the shape of your freehand line, you can reshape it by choosing Reshape from the Edit menu and using the reshape pointer to reposition the lines' vertices. See "Polygon Tool" in Chapter 1 if you need to refer to the reshaping discussion.

Your letterhead is nearly complete. You need only fine-tune the position of the objects within it so they are properly aligned with respect to one another. Because all of the objects except the wave line are locked, you cannot align them until you unlock them. Select all of the objects, and choose Unlock from the Arrange menu. To align the left edges of the text frames with each other:

1   **Click outside the selection to deselect all of the objects.**

2   **Select the boat/sun object.**

3   **Hold down the Shift key as you select the top text frame.**

4   **Choose Align Objects (Shift+Ctrl+K) from the Arrange menu.**

5   **In the "Top to Bottom" area of the dialog box, click "Align top edges," leave "None" selected as the "Left to Right" option, and click OK.** The top ray of the sun is aligned with the top of the text frame.

6   **Deselect the boat/sun object and select both text frames.**

7   **Choose Align Objects from the Arrange menu again.**

8   **This time, click "Align left edges" in the "Left to Right" area of the dialog box, click "None" in the "Top to Bottom" options, and click OK.** The left edges of both text frames are aligned with each other.

Now you are finished with your letterhead and are ready to save it.

Saving the letterhead as a .WMF file

If you want to be able to import your letterhead into other applications, you can save it as a .WMF file, a graphics file format supported by most Windows applications. To save it as a .WMF file:

1   **Choose Save As from the File menu.**

2   **In the dialog box, click the List Files of Type drop-down menu to open it.**

3   **Choose Windows MetaFile (*.WMF) from the list, give your document a different name, and click Save.**

ClarisWorks saves the letterhead in .WMF format. When you import it into another document, the letterhead appears as one graphic element. See the Appendix for more information about importing and exporting files with ClarisWorks.

Saving the letterhead as stationery

ClarisWorks offers a feature that lets you save documents as stationery. By choosing the ClarisWorks Stationery file type in the Save As dialog box, you can create a template that you can use over and over. When you open a stationery document, ClarisWorks opens it as a new, untitled document each time. The document type used to create the stationery remains intact, so the new, untitled stationery document has the same document type as that in which it was created.

Since you will use the letterhead for writing letters, you will need to save the letterhead as stationery from a text document, rather than the graphics document that you used to create it. To move the letterhead to a text document and save it as stationery:

1　**With the graphics document containing the letterhead open, select all of the objects by pressing Ctrl+A.**

2　**Choose Group from the Arrange menu to group all of the objects together as one unit.**

3　**Choose Copy (Ctrl+C) from the Edit menu.** The letterhead is copied to the Clipboard.

4　**Open a new text document by choosing New (Ctrl+N) from the File menu, and click OK in the dialog box.** A new text document opens. The preset new document type is text, so you don't have to take an extra step to manually select it.

5　**With the text insertion point blinking in the upper-left corner of the new document, choose Paste (Ctrl+V) from the Edit menu.** The letterhead objects are pasted at the top of the document from the Clipboard.

6　**Press ↵ twice to move the text insertion point down two lines below the letterhead.**

7　**Choose Save As (Shift+Ctrl+S) from the File menu to save the text document as stationery.** The Save As dialog box opens.

8　**In the dialog box, click the List Files of Type drop-down menu to open it, as shown in Figure 2-16.** The drop-down menu lists some of the different formats available for saving text documents. See the Appendix for more information on all of the Save As options.

9　**Scroll in the list if necessary, and choose ClarisWorks Stationery (*.cws) from the drop-down menu shown in Figure 2-16.**

10　**In the File Name box, type a name for your stationery, such as Ltrhead.CWS.**

11　**Locate the folder or disk where you want the stationery saved.**

12　**Click OK.**

The Surfcity Sailboats letterhead is now saved as stationery. The text document remains open as an untitled document. Close it now without saving it by pressing Ctrl+W and by clicking No in the message box. The graphics document you used to create the letterhead (SSLogo) is still open, too. You will use some of the elements of this graphics document later in this chapter, so save it now by pressing Ctrl+S.

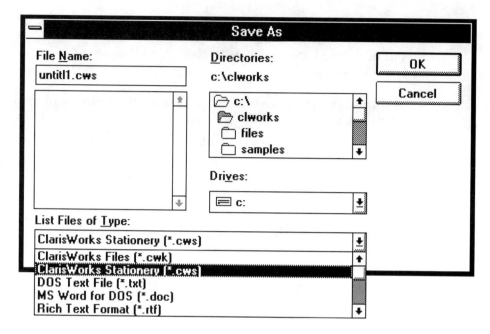

Figure 2-16 This drop-down menu lists the Save As options available for a text document, including ClarisWorks Stationery

Whenever you want to write a letter using the stationery, simply choose the stationery's name from the directory in the Open dialog box. An untitled document opens with the letterhead in place and the text insertion point in position, ready for you to begin writing the text of your letter.

Writing a letter

Now that you have your own stationery created, you can use it for all of your correspondence. In this section, you will use the Surfcity Sailboats stationery to write, format, and print a business letter. The letter is two pages in length, allowing for a description of how to treat the first page differently than the rest of the document. In addition to a header, the letter includes a footnote, which will be marked with a character other than a footnote number. When you are finished with this section, you will have applied many of ClarisWorks text-related features.

Figure 2-17 shows what your final letter will look like.

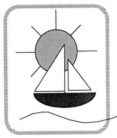

Surfcity Sailboats
10101 Beach Street
Suite 100
Surfcity, California
90001

Phone: 213.555.SAIL
Fax: 213.555.9890

November 11, 1993

Sara Jones
Sailing Race Coordinator
1234 Main Street
Surfcity, CA 90001

Dear Sara:

We at Surfcity Sailboats are very excited that you will be working with us to plan and organize the Fifth Annual Surfcity South Pacific Yacht Race. Your experience in coordinating past sailing races will no doubt be a very valuable asset to us and to each participant. It is sure to be another memorable event for everyone involved.

As I mentioned to you on the phone today, the race is a short six months away. With that in mind, we should get right down to business with the details you will need to know.

To date there are 100 boats registered for the race, but we expect more than 250 participants before the registration deadline.* The registration fee is $500 per boat. When a registrant wants to sign up for the race, you will need to get a 50% nonrefundable deposit from them. The remaining fee is due the day of the race. Upon registration, fill in a form to gather the following registration information:

Model, make, year of boat
Size of boat
Name of boat
Vessel registration number
Name, address, and phone number of owner(s)
Names and phone numbers of crew members
Previous races and awards

---

* The deadline for registering is December 10, 1993

Figure 2-17 Page 1 of a two-page business letter on Surfcity Sailboats letterhead

Sara Jones
November 11, 1993

Remember to classify the entrants into one of these categories, based on size of the boat:

30 feet and under – Category 1
31 to 40 feet – Category 2
41 to 60 feet – Category 3
Over 60 feet – Category 4

Once you've registered a participant in the race, send them a confirmation letter. In the letter, remind them of the start time for the race, based on their particular category qualification. Category 1 boats start at 6:00 AM, Category 2 starts at 7:30 AM, Category 3 starts at 9:00 AM, and Category 4 boats start at 12:00 noon.

With the confirmations, include the charts for the race and an invitation to the Surfcity South Pacific Yacht Race Party at the Papeete Sur la Mer hotel. The party is being coordinated by Maaruru Cie in Papeete, Tahiti, the final destination of the race. Although Maaruru Cie will be sending you the final details on the party, here is a tentative agenda:

4:30 PM	Cocktails and appetizers will be served in the patio garden of the hotel, and a steel band will play
6:00 PM	Five-course dinner will be served in the main dining room of the hotel
7:30 PM	Race Winners Awards Ceremony
9:00 PM	Dancing

Please give me a call if you need clarification on anything at all. And once again, I'm pleased we will be working together on this year's race.

Sincerely,

Ned Nautical
President

page 2

Figure 2-17 (continued) Page 2 of the business letter

Begin by opening a copy of the letterhead you created in the last section:

1   **Choose Open from the File menu.**

2   **In the Open dialog box, choose ClarisWorks Stationery (*.cws) from the List Files of Type pop-up menu.** This filters out the list of documents in the directory to show only those that are stationery.

3   **Select Ltrhead.CWS, and click OK. Now you are ready to set up the pages of your document.**

Setting up the document

The first step in creating any text document is to set document margins and other options that affect the entire document. In ClarisWorks, you do this by using the Document dialog box, shown in Figure 2-18.

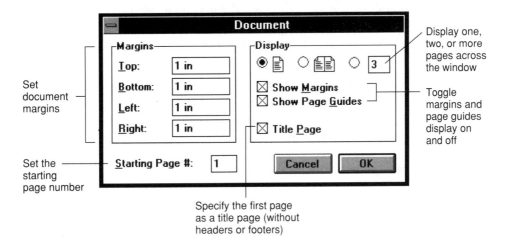

Figure 2-18 Document dialog box for setting text document options

Setting document options

A good place to begin your letter is by setting the margins in the Document dialog box. Choose Document from the Format menu to open the dialog box. All four margins are preset to 1 inch. Since you will want a little more room in the top margin, set Top to 1.25 inches.

Note *The unit of measure you have set in the Rulers dialog box for the text ruler determines the unit of measure used for margins in the Document dialog box. The preset text ruler unit of measure is inches; thus, the margin settings in the Document dialog box display in inches also. Other units of measurement are picas, points, centimeters, and millimeters (see Figure 2-2). If you set the text ruler to measure in picas, the Document dialog box shows margin settings in picas.*

Notice that the letter has a header and footer on the second page but not on the first. To get this result, you need to instruct ClarisWorks to treat the first page differently from the rest of the document. You do this by specifying the first page as a *title page*. In ClarisWorks, title pages are formatted the same way as the rest of the document, but they do not contain headers or footers. Click Title Page in the Document dialog box now to prevent headers and footers from appearing on the first page of the letter.

Your letter is going to be two pages long, and you will want to be able to get an overall view of both pages in the document window at the same time as you work with it. To do this, click the icon that shows two pages side by side in the Display area of the dialog box. When you are finished setting these options, click OK to return to your document.

When you have the page display options set to show two or more pages across the window, reduce the view of the document so you can see the pages displayed side by side. If you want to reduce your view of a document, use the View Scale command from the Window menu to set an exact percentage, or click the left zoom control in the lower-left corner of the window border.

TIP

Setting Preferences

In addition to setting page options from the Document dialog box, you can set other options using the Preferences dialog box shown in Figure 2-19.

You need to change the footnote and date format settings in the Preferences dialog box. As mentioned earlier, the letter contains a footnote that is marked with a character other than a footnote number. This means that you do not want ClarisWorks to automatically number footnotes throughout the document (the preset setting). In addition, you want the date to display in the letter in a format other than the preset date format, which displays as 7/5/93 in the Preferences dialog box. To change these preferences settings:

1   Choose Preferences from the Edit menu to open the Preferences dialog box (see Figure 2-19).

2   Deselect Auto Number Footnotes.

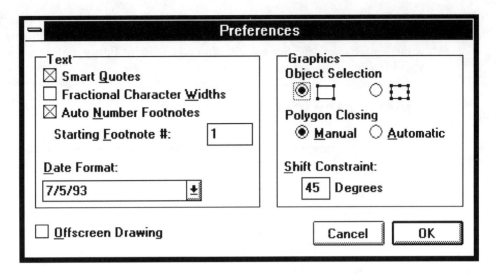

Figure 2-19 Preferences dialog box

3 **Click at the right of the Date Format box.** The Date Format drop-down menu opens, listing five different formats available for displaying the date. The choices are

7/5/93
Jul 5, 1993
July 5, 1993
Mon, Jul 5, 1993
Monday, July 5, 1993

(These date format options are available for the U.S. version of Windows. The options vary depending on your settings in the International Control Panel.)

4 **Click July 5, 1993 to select the new date format.**

5 **Click OK to return to the document.**

Now each time you add a footnote to the current document, ClarisWorks prompts you for the character to use to mark it; each time you insert the date in any document, it appears in the new format.

Using Print Setup

You can also use the Print Setup dialog box (File menu) to set up your page. This dialog box allows you to set printing options for your document. (You will actually print the document later in this chapter.) The options available in Print Setup vary by the type of printer you are using. In general, you use Print Setup to set the orientation of your document to vertical or horizontal, specify the paper size and source, reduce or enlarge the document when you print it, and to set other printer effects. Refer to your printer manual for more information on your printer's options. For information on the Print Setup dialog box, read the Windows documentation.

Entering the text

With the stationery document set up, you are now ready to enter the text of the letter, which consists of the address, the body, and the signature. Make sure your document view is set to 100%. To enter the text of the letter:

1 **Make sure the text insertion point is positioned two lines below the letterhead.**

2 **Choose Times New Roman (or any other font) from the Font menu, and set the font size to 12 Point.**

3 **Type the text of the letter shown in Figure 2-20.**

Note *The dash character used in the boat category list at the top of page 2 is actually an* en dash. *To type an en dash, press the NumLock key to turn on NumLock, and hold down the Alt key as you type **0150** on the numeric keypad. When you release the Alt key, the en dash character appears in the document.*

When you are finished, you should have two pages of text. To switch between pages, click in the horizontal scroll bar. (If you did not change the display of multiple pages in the Document dialog box, click the vertical scroll bar to move between the pages.) Scroll to the top of the first page of the letter now so the upper-right corner of the page is visible.

Now you are going to add the date to your letter. Since the letterhead occupies most of the top of the page, you cannot simply enter the date right where you want it. Try this: Position the text insertion point immediately to the right of the letterhead. The text insertion point is quite long because line spacing is set to 1 line in the text ruler (that is, one line high). If you begin typing some text, it displays along the bottom of the insertion point rather than at the top, where you want it. Figure 2-21 illustrates the problem.

To overcome this, use a text frame to hold the date, and move the frame into the desired position:

1 **If the tool palette is not visible, click the Hide/Show Panel icon (next to the zoom controls) to show it.** The text tool should already be selected in the tool palette.

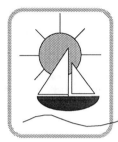

Surfcity Sailboats
10101 Beach Street
Suite 100
Surfcity, California
90001

Phone: 213.555.SAIL
Fax: 213.555.9890

Sara Jones
Sailing Race Coordinator
1234 Main Street
Surfcity, CA 90001

Dear Sara:

We at Surfcity Sailboats are very excited that you will be working with us to plan and organize the Fifth Annual Surfcity South Pacific Yacht Race. Your experience in coordinating past sailing races will no doubt be a very valuable asset to us and to each participant. It is sure to be another memorable event for everyone involved.

As I mentioned to you on the phone today, the race is a short six months away. With that in mind, we should get right down to business with the details you will need to know.

To date there are 100 boats registered for the race, but we expect more than 250 participants before the registration deadline. The registration fee is $500 per boat. When a participant wants to sign up for the race, you will need to get a 50% nonrefundable deposit from them. The remaining fee is due the day of the race. Upon registration, fill in a form to gather the following registration information:

Model, make, year of boat
Size of boat
Name of boat
Vessel registration number
Name, address, and phone number of owner(s)
Names and phone numbers of crew members
Previous races and awards

Remember to classify the entrants into one of these categories, based on size of the boat:

Figure 2-20 Text of the letter (page 1 of 2)

30 feet and under – Category 1
31 to 40 feet – Category 2
41 to 60 feet – Category 3
Over 60 feet – Category 4

Once you've registered a participant in the race, send them a confirmation letter. In the letter, remind them of the start time for the race, based on their particular category qualification. Category 1 boats start at 6:00 AM, Category 2 starts at 7:30 AM, Category 3 starts at 9:00 AM, and Category 4 boats start at 12:00 noon.

With the confirmations, include the charts for the race and an invitation to the Surfcity South Pacific Yacht Race Party at the Papeete Sur la Mer hotel. The party is being coordinated by Maararu Cie in Papeete, Tahiti, the final destination of the race. Although Maararu Cie will be sending you the final details on the party, here is a tentative agenda:

4:30 PM Cocktails and appetisers will be served in the patio garden of the hotel, and a steel band will play
6:00 PM Five-course dinner will be served in the main dining room of the hotel
7:30 PM Race Winners Awards Ceremony
9:00 PM Dancing

Please give me a call if you need clarification on anything at all. And once again, I'm pleased we will be working together on this year's race.

Sincerely,

Ned Nautical
President

Figure 2-20 (continued) Text of the letter (page 2 of 2)

Figure 2-21 Adding text following a graphic forces the text to display along the bottom of the insertion point

2   **Hold down the Alt key as you click anywhere in the document.** ClarisWorks creates a text frame and positions the text insertion point inside the frame.

Now you could simply type the date. However, using the Insert Date feature, you can enter today's date and it will be updated each time you open the document.

3   **Choose Insert Date from the Edit menu.** ClarisWorks automatically inserts the current date inside the text frame, in the format you specified in the Preferences dialog box. The date appears in the preset font, 12-point Arial. If the text of your letter is in a different font, change the font of the date to match it.

4   **If the text ruler is not visible, choose Show Rulers from the Window menu.**

5   **With the text insertion point still inside the text frame, click the right justification alignment icon in the text ruler.** The date aligns along the right edge of the text frame.

6   **Press Enter on the numeric keypad to select the frame.** Selection handles appear around the frame, and the graphics tool is selected in the tool palette.

7   **If the frame is too small to show the complete date, resize the frame by clicking the selection handles and dragging until the frame is large enough.**

8   **Click and drag the text frame into the upper-right corner of the page so it is positioned as shown in Figure 2-22.**

9   **Press Enter on the numeric keypad again to switch to the text tool.**

Surfcity Sailboats
10101 Beach Street
Suite 100
Surfcity, California
90001

Phone: 213.555.SAIL
Fax: 213.555.9890

November 11, 1993

Figure 2-22 Date of the letter in proper position

With the text of the letter entered and the current date in position, you can move on to add a header, a footer, and a footnote to the letter, but you should save your letter first. Choose Save from the File menu and name your document Ltr2Sara.CWK. Periodically saving your work makes it much easier to recover from a power surge or system crash.

Adding headers, footers, and footnotes

You can add headers and footers to any ClarisWorks document type or to text or spreadsheet frames opened in full-frame view. However, footnotes can be inserted only in text documents. Headers, footers, and footnotes are visible only when you have your document set to Page View. (Remember that text documents always appear in Page View.) When you add a header, footer, or footnote, ClarisWorks automatically switches you to Page View if your document is not in Page View already.

You can put virtually anything you want in a header, footer, or footnote, including page numbers, dates, times, any text, and graphics.

TIP

Using the Insert command from the File menu, you can insert text or graphics from another document into a header, footer, or footnote. For example, if you have a logo saved as TIFF, you can insert your logo in a header or footer. Or, you can insert text saved in a Microsoft Word for Windows document into a ClarisWorks footnote. You can't use Insert with headers or footers in database documents.

If you want to include graphics in a header or footer, and you want that graphic to repeat on every page, you must either use the Insert command or use the copy-and-paste method rather than drawing directly in the header or footer. If you draw directly inside a header or footer region, the graphic appears only on the page in which you drew. You can then copy and paste it into the header or footer region on subsequent pages.

When you first add a header, footer, or footnote, ClarisWorks opens a region in your document to contain it. This region is preset to contain one line of text. As you type or insert text or graphics, the region expands to hold the information. For example, if your header is ten lines of text, the header region expands into the main document. If the information in a header, footer, or footnote region is more than the region can contain, an overflow indicator appears in the lower-right corner of the region. (The overflow indicator is similar to the one that appears in linked text frames.)

Note *The actual size limit of a header or footer region depends on several factors, such as document margin settings, font size of text, page size, and so on. However, if you use the preset 1-inch margins for your document and you use a 12-point font, you can include approximately fourteen lines of text in a header or footer. In other words, headers and footers can each occupy up to one-third of a page. A footnote, on the other hand, can be the entire length of one document page (except for the text line containing the footnote marker).*

Headers, footers, and footnotes are treated as separate paragraphs and have their own rulers. This lets you align, tab, or space text inside of them differently than the text of the main document. You can also copy ruler settings of one or more paragraphs from the main document to header, footer, or footnote paragraphs.

Headers and footers are repeating elements, meaning they appear the same on each page of a document. The exception to this is a title page, which does not show headers or footers.

Footnotes, on the other hand, appear only at the bottom of pages that contain the corresponding footnote number or mark. If a document contains both a footer and footnotes, the footnote appears above the footer at the bottom of the page. A hairline rule displays just above the first footnote on the page to separate the footnote section from the main document.

Inserting the header and footer

This section describes how to insert a header and footer into the business letter you created earlier (Ltr2Sara). To insert a header:

1   **With the text insertion point positioned anywhere in the document, choose Insert Header from the Format menu.** ClarisWorks opens the header area of the document and positions the text insertion point inside this region. Since you designated the first page as a title page, ClarisWorks opens the header region of the page after the title page, or page 2 in your letter.

2   **Type** Sara Jones **and press ⏎.**

3   **Choose Insert Date from the Edit menu to insert the current date in the second line of the header.**

4   **Select both lines of the header.**

5   **Change the font to that used in the rest of the document by choosing the appropriate font from the Font menu.**

6   **Click the right alignment icon in the text ruler to align the header text along the right margin of the document.**

7   **Press Enter on the numeric keypad to return to the main document.**

Your header should look like the one shown in Figure 2-23.

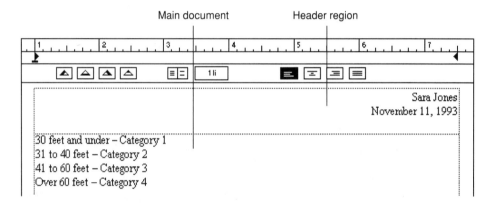

Figure 2-23 Adding the header to the letter

To insert a footer at the bottom of the second page:

1   **Choose Insert Footer from the Format menu.** ClarisWorks opens the footer area of the document and positions the text insertion point inside this region.

2   **Type** page **in the footer.** Be sure to leave a space after the word *page*.

3   **Choose Insert Page # from the Edit menu to insert the current page number in the footer after the word *page*.**

4   **Select the footer text, change the font to that used in the rest of the document if necessary, and change the font size to 10 point.**

5   **Click the center alignment icon in the text ruler to align the text in the center of the footer region.**

6   **Press Enter on the numeric keypad to return to the main document.**

Your footer should look like the one shown in Figure 2-24. Because you designated the first page of the letter as a title page in the Preferences dialog box, the header and footer appear only on the second page of the letter.

If you want to edit a header or footer, simply click inside of the region. To permanently delete a header or footer from a document, choose Remove Header or Remove Footer, respectively, from the Format menu.

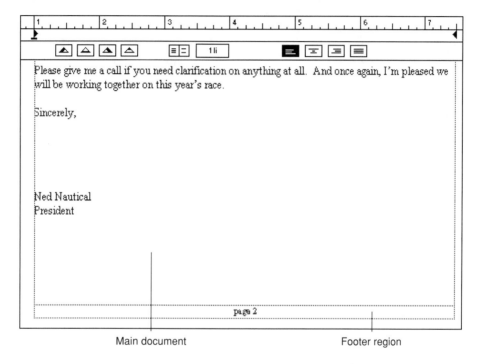

Figure 2-24 Adding a footer to the letter

Caution *Once you remove a header or footer, the deletion is permanent. You cannot undo the deletion to reinstate the header or footer.*

The letter's header and footer is now completed. The next section describes how to insert a footnote in the letter.

Inserting the footnote

Looking at the letter shown in Figure 2-17, you see that the first page includes a footnote that is marked with an asterisk rather than with a footnote number. Earlier, using the Preferences dialog box, you chose not to automatically number footnotes. As a result, you must specify a footnote mark character each time you insert a footnote. This allows you to customize the way footnotes are denoted in the current document.

TIP

Marking the footnote in the sample letter with an asterisk makes more sense than using footnote numbers because the letter contains only one footnote. Whether you use a special character or the preset automatic footnote numbering feature to mark footnotes depends on your own preference. Generally, if you plan to insert more than one footnote in a document, leave the Auto Number Footnotes option selected in the Preferences dialog box. If your document contains only one footnote, deselect that option and use a unique special character to mark the footnote.

The preset font type and size for footnotes is 10-point Arial and footnotes are preset to align along the left margin.

To add the footnote to your business letter (Ltr2Sara):

1   Position the text insertion point after the period following the word *deadline*, as shown in Figure 2-25.

Text insertion point

To date there are 100 boats registered for the race, but we expect more than 250 participants before the registration deadline| The registration fee is $500 per boat. When a participant wants

Figure 2-25 Position the text insertion point for inserting a footnote

2   Choose Insert Footnote (Shift+Ctrl+F) from the Format menu. The Mark Footnote dialog box shown in Figure 2-26 prompts for the character to use for denoting the footnote.

3   In the dialog box, type an asterisk by pressing Shift+8.

Figure 2-26 Entering a footnote mark character in the dialog box

4   **Click OK.** ClarisWorks opens the footnote region at the bottom of the page containing the footnote (page 1, in this case). The asterisk character appears in 9 point superscript in the main text and in the footnote region. The text insertion point is positioned inside the footnote region ready for you to enter footnote information.

5   **Type** The deadline for registering is December 10, 1993.

6   **Press Enter on the numeric keypad to return to the main document.**

You can use up to nine characters to mark a single footnote by typing the characters in the Mark Footnote dialog box. For example, you might choose the word note *to mark a footnote;* note *would then appear in superscript in the text and in the footnote region.*

TIP

If you later decide that you want to move the footnote to another place in the document, you can do so without having to retype it. To move the footnote:

1   **Select the footnote character (or number) in the main document.**

2   **Choose Cut from the Edit menu.**

3   **Position the text insertion point where you want the footnote moved in the main document.**

4   **Choose Paste from the Edit menu.**

The footnote in the main document and in the footnote region moves as specified. If you have more than one footnote in your document and Auto Number Footnotes on, ClarisWorks automatically renumbers the other footnotes.

To remove a footnote, select its number or character in the main document. Choose Cut or Clear from the Edit menu, or press Delete or Backspace. Any remaining footnotes are renumbered, unless you are using specific footnote marks in the document.

Note *Once you delete a footnote, you can choose Undo from the Edit menu to reinsert it. You must choose Undo immediately after the deletion and before you do anything else in your document.*

Formatting the letter

Now that all of the text, including headers, footers, and footnotes, is entered in your letter, format your letter so it looks like the one shown in Figure 2-17.

In ClarisWorks text documents, all of the lines within a paragraph are preset to align with the left margin, and the right margin is ragged. You end a paragraph by pressing ↵, and the next line begins flush with the left margin setting.

In its final format, the business letter uses a variety of paragraph formats. Most of the paragraphs have the first line indented, with remaining lines within the paragraph flush against the left margin. One of the lists (the registration information) uses an indented left margin setting, while another list (the agenda) uses a hanging indent, which starts the first line of a paragraph to the left of the remaining lines. (See "Making Hanging Indents" later in this chapter for more information about indenting.) The letter also includes a tabbed list (the boat categories) that demonstrates the use of an Align Character tab.

You change paragraph formats by selecting one or more paragraphs and by using the left margin, right margin, and first line markers in the text ruler. Formatting changes affect an entire paragraph or multiple paragraphs. That is, settings in the text ruler affect all of the lines of text within a paragraph selection. Because of this, you needn't select the whole paragraph. You can simply position the text insertion point, then select a word or a line of text within the paragraph. You can also click the mouse four times quickly in succession to select the whole paragraph. Whichever way you choose to make a paragraph active, the changes you make in the text ruler apply to all of the text within the active paragraph(s).

In this section, you will use the text ruler to format your business letter by

- changing the left and right indent settings
- indenting the first line of a paragraph
- copying ruler settings to other paragraphs
- making a hanging indent
- setting an Align Character tab
- inserting a page break

Indenting the first line of a paragraph

The main body of the letter is formatted with paragraphs that have the first line indented. To make this formatting change:

1 **With your letter open and active, position the text insertion point anywhere in the first paragraph to make it active.**

2 **If the text ruler is not visible, choose Show Rulers from the Window menu.**

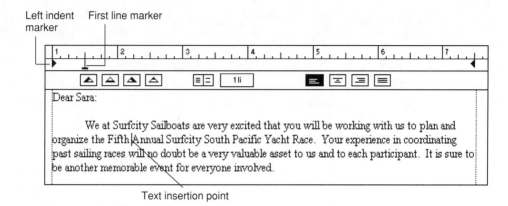

Figure 2-27 Indenting the first line of a paragraph

3   Click the first line marker and drag to the right until it is at the 1.5-inch mark on the ruler, as shown in Figure 2-27.

The first line of the paragraph is now indented 0.5 inches. Subsequent lines within the paragraph align with the left margin setting at the position indicated by the left indent marker (1 inch, in this case). At this point, if you want to indent all of the other lines in the paragraph, you can drag the left indent marker to the desired position on the text ruler. As you move the left indent marker, the first line marker moves along with it at the relative distance you specified (0.5 inches, in this case).

If you want to move the left indent marker in the ruler without disturbing the position of the first line marker, hold down the Alt key as you drag the left indent marker. The first line marker stays exactly where you originally positioned it on the text ruler.

TIP

Copying ruler settings

Instead of repeating the above steps to indent the first line of the other paragraphs, you can copy and paste the settings of the text ruler from one paragraph to one or more paragraphs. This method is particularly handy if you have changed many of the ruler settings (such as the first line indent, the text alignment, tab stops, line spacing, and so on) and want other paragraphs to have the same settings, without having to remember all of the settings you changed.

To copy ruler settings from the first paragraph of your letter to the next two paragraphs:

1   Click in the first paragraph to make it active.

2   Choose Copy Ruler from the Format menu, or press Shift+Ctrl+C.
The ruler settings of the first paragraph are copied to the Clipboard. (If the Clipboard contains anything else, copying the ruler settings to it does not cause the Clipboard to lose its previous contents.)

3   Click in the second paragraph and drag down the document to select the second and third paragraphs simultaneously. You don't have to select whole paragraphs. If your selection includes only part of the second paragraph and part of the third, ClarisWorks makes them both active.

4   Choose Apply Ruler from the Format menu, or press Shift+Ctrl+V.
The second and third paragraphs of the letter are formatted exactly like the first one. Specifically, all three paragraphs have the first line indented 0.5 inches.

The Apply Ruler command is not available until you have previously chosen the Copy Ruler command. Once you copy a ruler, its settings are stored in the Clipboard until you copy another ruler's settings. Finish indenting the first line of the remaining paragraphs by clicking in them and choosing Apply Ruler from the Format menu. The four remaining paragraphs that need to be formatted begin as follows:

- Remember to classify...
- Once you've registered...
- With the confirmations, include...
- Please give me a call...

Changing left margin indent settings

The next formatting change you will make is to change the left margin indent settings of the registration information list on the first page of the letter (see Figure 2-28). The list is actually composed of seven lines of text, each treated as a separate paragraph. (Each line ends with a ↵.) To change the settings for the entire list, you need to select each line.

1   Click anywhere in the first line of the list.

2   Drag down until all seven lines in the list are selected.

3   In the text ruler, click the left indent marker and drag to the right until it is positioned at the 2-inch mark on the ruler.

Model, make, year of boat
Size of boat
Name of boat
Vessel registration number
Name, address, and phone number of owner(s)
Names and phone numbers of crew members
Previous races and awards

Figure 2-28 The registration information list needs to be formatted

The list is now indented 2 inches from the edge of the page and 1 inch from the left margin setting. If you want, you can copy and paste the ruler settings from the first line of the list to the other six lines.

Setting an Align Character tab

In this next series of steps, you will set a different kind of tab stop on the ruler—an Align Character tab. As you may remember from Chapter 1, Align Character tabs let you align text along a specified character, such as a decimal point.

In the business letter, you will use an Align Character tab to align each line in the list of boat categories on the en dash character. (Earlier in this chapter you learned how to produce an en dash by holding down the Alt key as you type 0150 on the numeric keypad.) In Figure 2-29, the en dash appears within each line in this list to separate boat size information from the associated category.

Before you proceed through these steps, position the text insertion point at the beginning of each of the four lines in the list, and press Tab. This shifts each line of text to the right by 0.5 inch. (Recall from Chapter 1 that ClarisWorks has invisible, preset tab stops at 0.5-inch intervals.) After you have completed the following steps, the tabbed text will align on the en dash.

en dash character

30 feet and under – Category 1
31 to 40 feet – Category 2
41 to 60 feet – Category 3
Over 60 feet – Category 4

Figure 2-29 Information within the boat categories list is separated by an en dash character

1   **Make the top of the second page of the letter visible.**

2   **Select the four lines of text that comprise the boat categories list.**

3   **With the text selected, click the Align Character tab marker and drag it onto the text ruler until it is at the 3-inch mark.**

4   **Double-click the Align Character tab marker to open the dialog box shown in Figure 2-30.**

5   **In the dialog box, hold down the Alt key as you type** 0150 **on the numeric keypad to produce an en dash, and click OK.**

The boat categories list now looks like that shown in Figure 2-31. Notice that the en dash in each text line aligns with the tab marker in the text ruler.

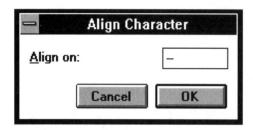

Figure 2-30 Align Character dialog box

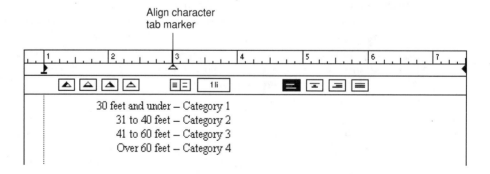

Figure 2-31 The boat categories list is aligned on the en dash character

Inserting a page break

Now you'll insert a page break at the bottom of the first page. If you look at the bottom of the first page, you see that the page automatically breaks after the paragraph that begins *Remember to classify*. Instead, you can insert a page break so the first page of text ends after the registration information list.

To insert the page break:

1   **Position the text insertion point at the end of the last line in the registration information list (the bottom of the first page).**

2   **Choose Insert Break from the Format menu, or press Enter on the numeric keypad.**

An invisible page break is inserted at the text insertion point position, the top of the second page appears on the screen, and the text insertion point is repositioned at the top of the second page. Also notice that the paragraph that begins *Remember to classify* appears on the second page, shifted down by two lines. If you later decide to remove the page break and let the pages break automatically, simply position the text insertion point at the end of the break, and press Delete or Backspace.

Note *You cannot remove automatic page breaks. Only page breaks you insert with the Insert Break command or by pressing Enter on the numeric keypad can be removed.*

You can also use the Insert Break command to force a break between columns in a multicolumn document.

TIP

Making hanging indents

The format of the business letter is nearly complete. The last formatting change is to format the agenda on the second page of the letter using *hanging indents*, in which the first line of the paragraph starts to the left of the remaining lines (that is, the first line marker is left of the left indent marker on the ruler).

The lines of text associated with each time period (4:30 PM, 6:00 PM, and so on) are treated as separate paragraphs. So again, you need to select all of these text lines to apply text ruler settings at the same time. In addition to making hanging indents, you will shorten the right margin indent setting to emphasize the agenda with more white space. Finally, you will set a tab so the first line of text for each time period aligns with the second line of text. To do this:

1   **Select all of the agenda's lines of text.**

2   **In the text ruler, click and drag the left indent marker to the right until it is at the 1.5-inch mark on the ruler.** The first line marker moves with the left indent marker. The selected lines of text are now all indented 0.5 inches from the left margin.

3   **With the text still selected, hold down the Alt key as you click and drag the left indent marker to the right until it is at the 2.5-inch mark on the ruler, as shown in Figure 2-32.** The first line of each paragraph now hangs to the left of the second line by 1 inch.

4   **To change the right indent setting of the selected text, click and drag the right indent marker to the left until it is at the 6.5-inch mark on the ruler.** This gives you more white space between the text and the right margin of the page.

5   **With the same text still selected, click the left tab marker and drag it onto the ruler at the 2.5-inch mark.**

6   **In the document, click to the right of the space between *PM* and *Cocktails* in the first line, and press Tab to separate the time from the associated text. Repeat this step for each line of text in the agenda.**

When you are finished, the agenda should be formatted as shown in Figure 2-33.

In the previous set of steps you placed a tab on the ruler. When you set hanging indents, you do not necessarily have to set a tab at the same position as the left indent marker to have the text align properly. If you skip this step, pressing Tab to separate the time from the text still causes the text to align with the left indent marker. To remove a tab, click the tab marker and drag down until it is off the ruler.

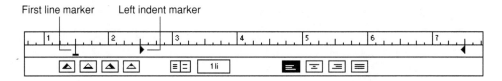

Figure 2-32 Setting a hanging indent

Left tab marker

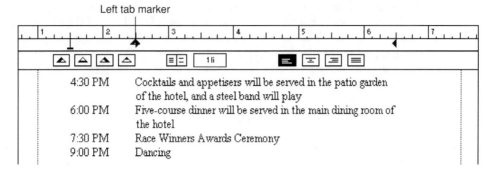

4:30 PM	Cocktails and appetisers will be served in the patio garden of the hotel, and a steel band will play
6:00 PM	Five-course dinner will be served in the main dining room of the hotel
7:30 PM	Race Winners Awards Ceremony
9:00 PM	Dancing

Figure 2-33   The final format of the agenda, including tab, hanging indent, and right margin indent settings

Your business letter should now be completely formatted so that it looks like the one shown in Figure 2-17. Press Ctrl+S to save the letter before continuing.

The next two sections describe how to check the letter for any spelling errors and how to use the thesaurus to find synonyms.

Checking the spelling

Before you print any document, it is always a good idea to check your spelling. Nothing is more unprofessional than a document containing misspelled words. ClarisWorks for Windows comes with an electronic spelling checker, making it very easy for you to catch and correct misspellings. The spelling checker works in conjunction with dictionaries. ClarisWorks comes with a 100,000-word dictionary, called the *main dictionary*. Also included in the product is one *user dictionary*, which you use to expand upon the main dictionary. You can also create more user dictionaries to store specialized vocabularies, such as scientific terms. When you install ClarisWorks onto your hard disk, the main and user dictionaries are installed in the Claris directory within the Windows directory. The main dictionary file is called USENG.NDX, and the user dictionary is called USERD.SPL. If you create other user dictionaries, they automatically have the .SPL file extension.

Note   *Claris separately offers a variety of international spelling dictionaries, such as UK (British English), French, German, Swedish, and Italian dictionaries, to name a few. Contact your local dealer or Claris Customer Assistance department for more information.*

The ClarisWorks spelling checker works by comparing the words in your document against those in the current main and user dictionaries. Any word in your document that does not exist in one of the dictionaries is considered misspelled. The word may actually be spelled correctly but may not be included in the main or user dictionary. Names of people, cities, and countries are typical examples. In these instances, you can add the word to your user dictionary. (You can only add new words to the user dictionary. The main dictionary cannot be altered.) The next time you spell-check a document that contains the new word, ClarisWorks will consider it spelled correctly.

You use the spelling checker by choosing commands from the Spelling cascading menu in the Edit menu. Although this section describes how to use the spelling checker with a text document, you can also use it with graphics, spreadsheet, and database document types.

If your business letter is not open on your screen, choose Open from the File menu to select and open it. If the business letter is open but not currently active, choose its name from the Window menu to activate it.

You may have noticed that the business letter contains one misspelled word—*appetisers*. The letter also contains several foreign words or names that ClarisWorks may consider misspelled, such as *Maaruru Cie* and *Papeete*. In the following steps, you use the spelling checker to correct the misspelled word and to add words to the user dictionary. It doesn't matter where your text insertion point is positioned in the document when you initiate a spelling check. ClarisWorks automatically starts checking the document from the beginning and continues through the entire document, including headers, footers, footnotes, and text inside of frames. To spell-check the letter to Sara Jones:

1   With the business letter open and active, choose Check Document from the Spelling cascading menu in the Edit menu, or press Ctrl+=.
The Spelling dialog box opens and displays the first suspect word in the Word box. Figure 2-34 shows *Surfcity* as a suspect word.

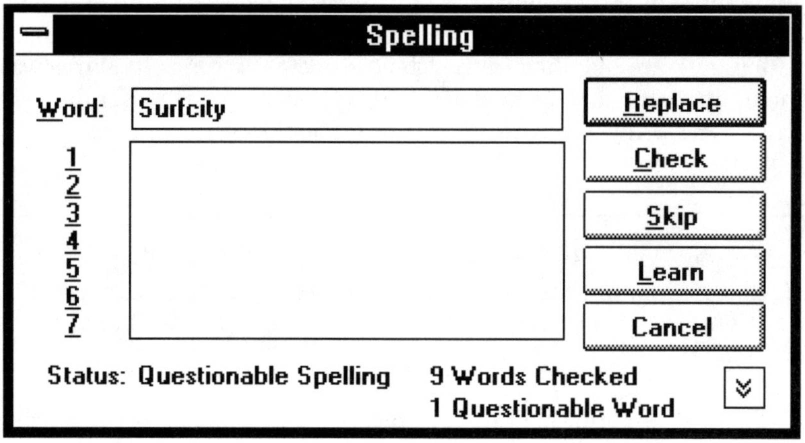

Figure 2-34 Spelling dialog box

The "9 Words Checked" statistic indicates the number of words checked in the document up to the current suspect word. The "1 Questionable Word" statistic indicates that this is the second word with questionable spelling. These statistics may differ in the dialog box you see if your dictionary already contains some of the words considered questionable.

2   **Click Learn to add the word *Surfcity* to the user dictionary.** Adding the word to your dictionary is a transparent process. ClarisWorks simply *learns* the word and continues checking the document. After you click Learn, ClarisWorks will not consider *Surfcity* to be misspelled in the current or any subsequent documents that you spell-check.

If you do not want to add *Surfcity* to your dictionary, click Skip. The next time ClarisWorks comes across *Surfcity* in the document during the current session, it will not consider it a misspelled word.

If you do not want to continue spell-checking, click Cancel. If you continue, the Word box of the Spelling dialog box displays what ClarisWorks believes is the next misspelled word (in this case, *Papeete*).

3   **With *Papeete* displayed in the Word box, click Skip.** This word is spelled correctly but you decide not to add it to the user dictionary. ClarisWorks continues checking for spelling. The Word box now shows the next suspect word.

If you do not want ClarisWorks to flag the suspect word every time you spell-check the document, add it to the user dictionary by clicking Learn. You can always go back into the user dictionary and delete or edit any words you added to it. (Editing a user dictionary is described later in this chapter.)

TIP

---

4   **Continue to click Skip until the Word box displays *appetisers*.**

5   **With the suspect word *appetisers* displayed in the Word box, click the context switch in the lower-right corner of the dialog box.** By clicking the context switch, you can view the suspect word as it is used in the context of the document, as shown in Figure 2-35. Clicking the switch again closes up this part of the dialog box.

By dragging the Spelling dialog box to another position on the screen, you can also view the suspect word directly in the context of your letter.

TIP

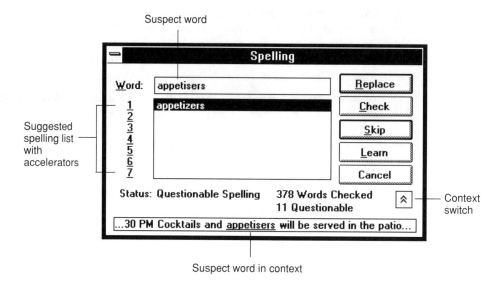

Figure 2-35 The Spelling dialog box with the suspect word in context and with suggested spelling

Notice that the Spelling dialog box lists one or more alternative spellings. Next to each suggestion is an Alt-key equivalent (or accelerators). If the correct spelling appears in the list, you can double-click it in the suggestion list, or press the appropriate Alt-key equivalent to replace the suspect word and continue checking your spelling. If none of the suggestions suit you, you can simply edit the word in the Word box, and click Replace to replace it and continue checking.

6 If necessary, scroll through the suggested spelling list until you see the word *appetizers* displayed and double-click it. Or, press the accelerator (such as Alt+1) to replace the word with the correct spelling. ClarisWorks replaces *appetisers* with *appetizers* and continues checking. When there are no more suspect words in the document, the Replace button in the dialog box changes to Done.

7 When you are finished spell-checking your letter, click Done.

TIP

In addition to checking whole documents for misspelled words, you can use the Spelling dialog box to check the spelling of a single word or phrase. To do this, press Ctrl+= to open the Spelling dialog box. Type the word or phrase you want checked in the Word box, and click Check. The suggested spelling list shows alternate spellings, just as it does when you check a whole document.

You can also paste a word or phrase into the Word box from the Clipboard, or copy text from the Word box to the Clipboard.

The Spelling dialog box shows status information as you check your document, including the number of words checked and the number of questionable words. This information appears in the lower half of the dialog box. As the spelling checker seeks your document for misspellings, the status area shows *Spelling. . . .* When a suspect word is located, the status area reads *Questionable Spelling,* as shown in Figure 2-35. When the spelling checker has reviewed the entire document, the *Finished Spelling* message appears. If you use the Spelling dialog box to check the spelling of a single word and the word is spelled correctly, the status area shows *Correct Spelling*.

TIP

Because the Spelling dialog box shows the number of words checked in the document, you can use it to count the number of words in your document. Simply run the spelling checker through your document. When the status area shows Finished Spelling, *read the* Words Checked *statistic to determine how many words are in your document. This technique allows you to check your word count when you are writing a paper, report, or article that must contain a specific number of words.*

Creating a new user dictionary

In the previous section you used the Spelling dialog box not only to check misspelling but also to add words to the user dictionary. ClarisWorks comes with one user dictionary. What if you want to create a new user dictionary just to store specialized terms to use for certain projects? For example, if you are writing a psychology research paper that contains numerous terms specific to the psychology field, you can create a separate user dictionary for these terms. Creating specialized user dictionaries gives you the advantage of more quickly spell-checking documents that contain words ClarisWorks may otherwise consider misspelled. This process is more efficient because ClarisWorks does not stop and flag special terms as misspellings.

TIP

If you are a student who is enrolled in several different courses, create a different user dictionary for each subject you are taking. For example, create a different dictionary for biology, economics, computer science, or music terms.

You can create as many user dictionaries as you want (limited only by disk space) but you can only have one user dictionary installed at a time. To create a new user dictionary:

1   **With a document open on your screen, choose Install Dictionaries from the Spelling cascading menu in the Edit menu.** The Install Dictionaries dialog box opens, as shown in Figure 2-36.

Note *The Spelling cascading menu and its commands are not available unless you have a document open. Opening any ClarisWorks document type activates the Spelling cascading menu and its commands.*

2   **Click User to select the type of dictionary you will create.**

3   **In the File Name box, type the name of the new user dictionary, such as** Psych.SPL. (Remember that user dictionaries have a .SPL file extension.) As soon as you begin typing a new name, the New button becomes available in the dialog box.

4   **If necessary, navigate to the Claris subdirectory in the Windows directory.** You should save your dictionaries in the same directory as the ClarisWorks main dictionary so ClarisWorks can find them. (The search path for dictionaries is determined by the path in the CLARIS.INI file.)

5   **Click New in the dialog box.**

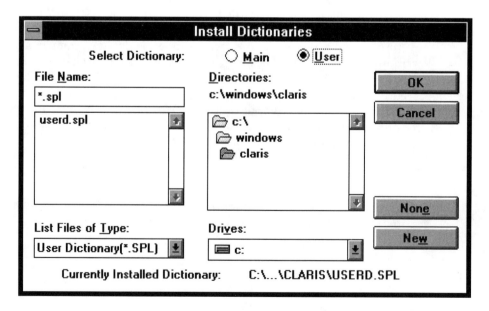

Figure 2-36 Using the Install Dictionaries dialog box to create a new user dictionary

ClarisWorks creates a new user dictionary and returns you to where you were before creating it. The newly created user dictionary becomes the currently installed one. Now, each time you spell-check a document, ClarisWorks uses the main dictionary and your new user dictionary. When a suspect word is found, such as algophobia, you can click Learn to add it to your new user dictionary.

Editing a user dictionary

At any time, you can edit the terms in a user dictionary, delete those you no longer want stored in the dictionary, or add terms to a user dictionary outside of a spell-check session. You can also import the contents of a text file into a user dictionary, or export the contents of a user dictionary to a text file. All of these tasks can be accomplished by choosing User Dictionary from the Spelling cascading menu. Doing so opens the User Dictionary dialog box shown in Figure 2-37.

The left area of the User Dictionary dialog box lists terms stored in the currently installed user dictionary (Psych.SPL, in this case). The bottom area of the dialog box shows the Import and Export buttons. Clicking Import lets you automatically add terms from a text file to the ClarisWorks user dictionary without having to add them manually. Export lets you save a user dictionary as a text file—a format that can be read by just about any Windows application. You access the Import and Export buttons by clicking the Text File switch at the lower right of the dialog box. Clicking the Text File switch again hides these options. (See the Appendix for more information on the user dictionary import and export features.)

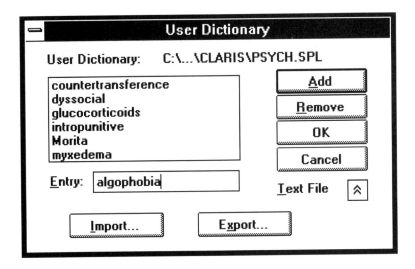

Figure 2-37 User Dictionary dialog box

To edit a word in the currently installed user dictionary:

1   **Choose User Dictionary from the Spelling cascading menu.**

2   **In the dialog box, locate the word to edit, and click once to select it.**
The selected word appears in the Entry box.

3   **Click Remove.** ClarisWorks removes the selected word from the list of
terms but leaves the word highlighted in the Entry box.

4   **Edit the word in the Entry box.** You can type or delete characters, or Cut,
Copy, and Paste text in the Entry box.

5   **When you are finished editing the word, click Add, or press ↵, to add
it to the dictionary.**

6   **When you are finished, click OK.**

To delete a word from the user dictionary, follow steps 1 through 3 listed
previously, and click OK to permanently remove it.
To add a word to the user dictionary:

1   **Choose User Dictionary from the Spelling cascading menu.** The User
Dictionary dialog box opens. The text insertion point appears in the Entry
box, which is blank.

2   **In the Entry box of the dialog box, type the word you want to add.**
For example, Figure 2-37 shows the word *algophobia* being typed in the
Entry box. Do not type any spaces, semicolons, or special characters, such
as •. If you do, an alert message appears, as shown in Figure 2-38, and you
should click OK to continue.

3   **Click Add.** ClarisWorks adds the new word to the list in the directory and
leaves the word highlighted in the Entry box, as shown in Figure 2-39. At
this point, if you change your mind, you can click Remove to delete the new
entry.

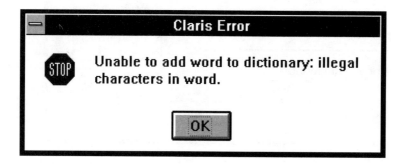

Figure 2-38   A message appears if you attempt to include illegal characters in a dictionary
entry

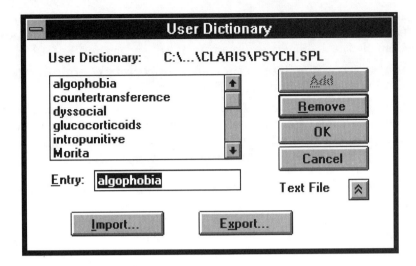

Figure 2-39 Adding a word to a user dictionary

4   If you want to add another word, begin typing in the Entry box, and click Add.

5   When you are finished adding words to the dictionary, click OK. If you do not want any of the new words added to the dictionary, click Cancel.

Now, each time you write a psychology-related document, you can install the Psych.SPL user dictionary containing the words you've added or edited using the User Dictionary dialog box and check for misspelled words.

Installing a dictionary

Installing a user dictionary is simply a matter of telling ClarisWorks where the user dictionary is located on your hard disk so the application can open it. Used in this sense, the word *install* is misleading. Normally, installing refers to the process of running an install program to move one or more files from a floppy disk to a hard disk. In the case of dictionaries, install refers to defining the location of dictionary files(s).

To install the Psych.SPL or any another user dictionary:

1   Open the document you want to spell-check.

2   Choose Install Dictionaries from the Spelling cascading menu. The Install Dictionaries dialog box opens.

3   Click User if it's not already selected in the Select Dictionary area of the dialog box.

4   **If you see that the Psych.SPL user dictionary is listed as the Currently Installed Dictionary at the bottom of the dialog box, click Cancel.** The dictionary is already installed and current.

5   **If necessary, navigate to the disk or directory containing Psych.SPL until you see it listed in the file list area.**

6   **Double-click the name of the user dictionary you want to install, such as Psych.SPL, or click the user dictionary's name once, and click OK.** ClarisWorks returns to the open document, and your user dictionary becomes the currently installed one.

You can follow the previous steps any time you want to switch the user dictionary that ClarisWorks uses during a spell-check session. You can install only one user dictionary at a time.

Following a similar procedure, you can also install a main dictionary. Installing a main dictionary becomes necessary when ClarisWorks cannot locate it on your hard disk. When you first install ClarisWorks, the main ClarisWorks dictionary is automatically installed in the Claris directory within the Windows directory; that is, the default search path, as defined in the CLARIS.INI file, is C:\WINDOWS\CLARIS. When you launch the application, ClarisWorks automatically installs (loads into memory) the main dictionary from the default search path.

Note *You can change the default search path by editing the CLARIS.INI file. CLARIS.INI is a text file that resides in the Windows directory. It stores the following information:*

- *ClarisWorks preferences*
- *Default search path for all installed Claris products*
- *Default search path for the ClarisWorks main dictionary, user dictionary, and thesaurus files*
- *Name of currently installed main dictionary, user dictionary, and thesaurus files*

To edit this file, open it in ClarisWorks as a text file. If you make changes, be sure to save the file as text with the file name CLARIS.INI, and be sure to save it in the Windows directory.

If ClarisWorks cannot find the main dictionary in the default path, you need to install it. To do so:

1   **With a document open, choose Install Dictionaries from the Spelling cascading menu in the Edit menu.**

2 **In the Install Dictionaries dialog box, click Main.** Figure 2-40 shows the Install Dictionaries dialog box with Main Dictionary selected. Compare this dialog box with the one shown in Figure 2-36 and notice that the New and None buttons are not available when Main is selected. These buttons, which are used for creating and ignoring dictionaries, respectively, are available only when User is selected in the dialog box. (Ignoring dictionaries is described later in this section.)

3 **Navigate to the disk or directory containing the main dictionary until you see it listed in the file list area. (It is called USENG.NDX, unless you have changed the name.)**

4 **Select USENG.NDX from the file list, and click OK.** The main dictionary becomes the currently installed one.

The ClarisWorks main dictionary and any user dictionaries can be used in other Claris products that use a spelling checker, such as FileMaker Pro. Conversely, you can use FileMaker Pro's dictionaries with ClarisWorks.

TIP

Install Dictionaries

Select Dictionary: ● Main   ○ User

File Name: Directories:
*.ndx   c:\windows\claris

useng.ndx   ▭ c:\
                          ▭ windows
                          ▭ claris

                                              OK
                                              Cancel

                                              None
                                              New

List Files of Type: Drives:
Main Dictionary[*.NDX]   ▭ c:

Currently Installed Dictionary: C:\...\CLARIS\USENG.NDX

Figure 2-40 The Install Dictionaries dialog box with Main selected

ClarisWorks gives you the option of using only the main dictionary during a spell-check session. That is, you can tell ClarisWorks to ignore all user dictionaries and just use the main dictionary. To do so:

1   **With a document open, choose Install Dictionaries from the Spelling cascading menu.**

2   **In the dialog box, click User.** The bottom of the dialog box shows which user dictionary is the Currently Installed Dictionary.

3   **Click None.**

The next time you open the Install Dictionaries dialog box and select User, the bottom of the dialog box shows <None> as the Currently Installed Dictionary. When you want to access a user dictionary again, follow the previous steps for installing one.

You have many options available for using or not using certain dictionaries for spell-checking in ClarisWorks. You can simply use the main and user dictionaries that come with ClarisWorks, or you can create many different user dictionaries for specialized terms and install the appropriate one when you need it. You can also choose not to use any user dictionaries and use only the main dictionary for checking your spelling.

In the next section, you will look for synonyms for words used in the business letter created earlier in this chapter.

Looking for synonyms

ClarisWorks comes with a 660,000-word thesaurus, which you use to look up synonyms (words of similar meaning) of selected words. If your document contains several occurrences of the same word, you can use the thesaurus to look for words to use in place of it, thereby expanding the vocabulary of your document. Or, use the thesaurus to locate a more descriptive term for the meaning you are trying to convey.

Note *The thesaurus file (UTHES.MTH) is installed on your hard disk in the Claris directory within the Windows directory.*

Although this section describes how to use the thesaurus in a text document, you can also look up synonyms in graphics, spreadsheet, and database documents.

The following steps describe how to look up synonyms for the word *participant*, which occurs four times in the business letter.

Note *When you look up synonyms for plural words, the ClarisWorks thesaurus displays singular synonyms. Clicking Replace in the dialog box replaces the plural word with the singular synonym. You must manually edit the synonym replaced in the text to make it plural.*

1   **If it is not already open, choose Open from the File menu to open the business letter (Ltr2Sara).**

2   **In the third paragraph, select the word *participant* in the sentence "When a participant wants to sign up..." by double-clicking the word.**

3   **Choose Thesaurus from the Spelling cascading menu (Edit menu), or press Shift+Ctrl+Y.** The Word Finder Thesaurus dialog box opens, as shown in Figure 2-41.

4   **Click Lookup.** As shown in Figure 2-41, the selected word, or lookup word, appears at the top of the dialog box and in the Find box. The Synonyms area lists words that have a similar meaning to the lookup word. This area also includes a part-of-speech label (such as noun, in the figure). If the word has different senses (or areas of meaning), a sense indicator introduces each one.

5   **Select a synonym from the list by clicking it once.** For example, select the word *registrant* from the list. The selected word appears in the Find box.

6   **Click Replace to replace the lookup word with the selected synonym and return to the document. Or click Lookup to look for synonyms of the selected word in the Synonyms area.**

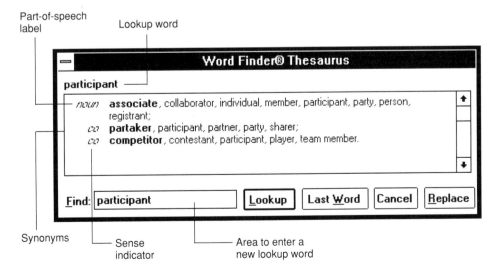

Figure 2-41 Word Finder Thesaurus dialog box

If you click Lookup in Step 6, a new set of synonyms appears in the dialog box. For example, if you look up synonyms for *registrant,* the dialog box looks like the one shown in Figure 2-42.

Notice that the Last Word button is now available in the dialog box shown in Figure 2-42. Clicking Last Word opens a list of all previous lookup words, as shown in Figure 2-43. The list includes all words you looked up since the beginning of this session with the thesaurus. To review the synonyms for one of these lookup words, select the word from the list, and click Lookup.

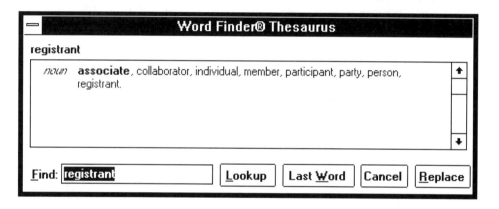

Figure 2-42 Looking up additional synonyms

You don't have to select a word in a document before you can use the thesaurus. Instead, you can open the Word Finder Thesaurus dialog box, type or paste a word into the Find box, and click Lookup to see a list of synonyms. You can also copy a word from the Find box to the Clipboard.

TIP

Figure 2-43 Reviewing previous lookup words

Now that you have checked your letter for spelling errors and replaced one of the words with a synonym, you are ready to print your letter.

Printing the letter

To print your business letter:

1   **If it is not already open, open your letter.**

2   **Choose Print from the File menu, or press Ctrl+P.** The Print dialog box opens. Figure 2-44 shows the Print dialog box for the printer I use with my Windows machine: an Apple LaserWriter II NTX. ClarisWorks automatically uses the default printer you have set for your system. The Print dialog box that you see on the screen shows your default printer.

3   **If your printer is capable of printing in color or grayscale or of printing halftones, make sure this capability is turned on. (Refer to your printer manual for information on how to turn on this feature.)** Because the sailboat logo uses shades of gray, you'll get the best results with this printing capability turned on. If your printer doesn't support color, grayscale, or halftones, your output will look acceptable, but the logo will not have the best resolution.

4   **Change any other printing options you want.**

5   **Click OK to print the letter.**

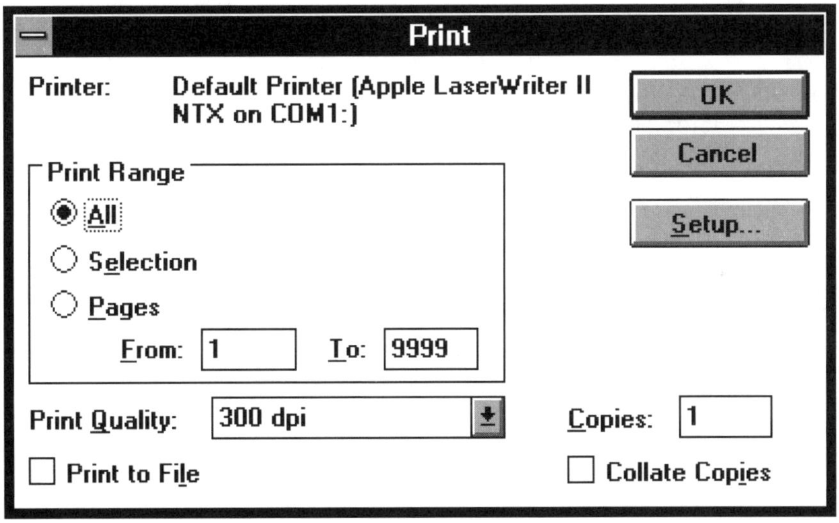

Figure 2-44 Print dialog box

With your business letter completed and printed, save the document by pressing Ctrl+S. You can close the document now if you want; you won't need it for the remainder of this chapter. To close it, choose Close from the File menu, or press Ctrl+W.

In the next section, you will complete your business stationery by creating an envelope template that includes your business logo and return address.

Creating an envelope template

When you go to a printing house and order business or personal stationery, you can also order envelopes that match your letterhead. Similarly, with ClarisWorks, you can create your own letterhead and an envelope template to match your letterhead. The envelope template places your logo and return address in the upper-left corner of your envelope when you print it, as shown in Figure 2-45. You can then print envelopes with or without a sending address.

Creating envelope templates is not a very intuitive task. In fact, it is something that many computer users think about doing but avoid because it can be a frustrating experience. It can consume many hours of trial and error to get the results you want, and you can waste lots of paper in the process. This is true no matter what application you use, even ClarisWorks. This section presents a series of straightforward steps you can follow to painlessly obtain successful results.

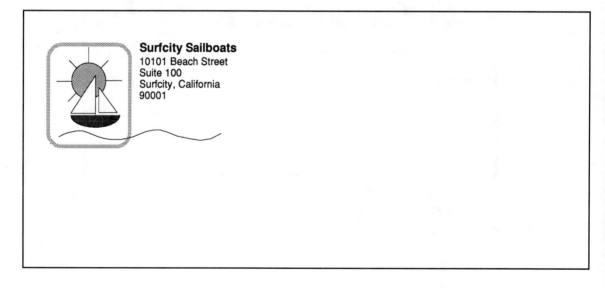

Figure 2-45 Example of an envelope template

In this section, you create an envelope template to match the Surfcity Sailboats letterhead. The envelope uses the same logo and return address that you created at the beginning of this chapter. You will then print a set of envelopes, without a sending address, to complete your set of stationery. In Chapter 4, you will use the ClarisWorks mail merge feature to merge names and addresses from a database with the envelope template created in this section.

Throughout the section, it is assumed that you do not have an envelope cassette or feeder to work with your printer and that you feed the envelope in the center of your printer rather than along either the left or right edge.

Setting up the envelope

The most important step you can take before you begin to create an envelope template is to think about the orientation of your envelope in relation to your printer. Unless you have an envelope cassette or feeder for your printer, you get the best results by manually feeding a blank envelope sideways into the printer. Figure 2-46 shows how to feed an envelope into a laser printer (top) and into a dot-matrix printer (bottom).

When you feed the envelope sideways into the printer, you must use the Print Setup dialog box to set the page orientation to landscape mode rather than portrait mode. The landscape setting instructs your printer to rotate your document 90 degrees to the right so that it prints sideways (horizontal orientation). The preset portrait mode does not rotate your document, but prints it as you see it on the screen, in a vertical orientation.

In addition to using the Print Setup dialog box, you must adjust the page margins of your document to match the size of your envelope. The preset

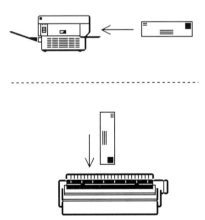

Figure 2-46 You get the best results if you feed envelopes sideways into your printer

document margins in ClarisWorks assume a standard U.S. letter page size of 8.5 inches (width) by 11 inches (height); a standard U.S. business envelope is 9.5 inches (width) by 4 inches (height).

Now, think about the relationship of your envelope to the printer and to a standard 8.5-by-11 page. Assume that your envelope is a standard business size. Imagine that the envelope itself is glued to the middle of a standard 8.5-by-11 piece of paper. Figure 2-47 illustrates the relationships you need to bear in mind as you set up your envelope template.

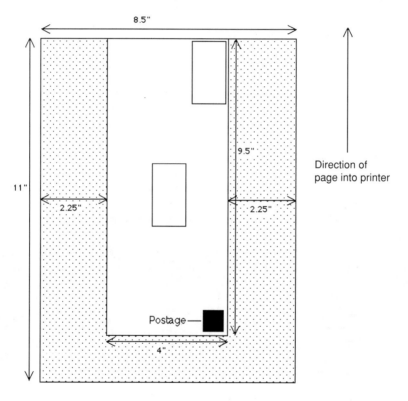

Figure 2-47 The relationship of the envelope to a standard page and to the printer

Before setting up your envelope, you need to create a new document for it. A graphics document is the best choice for your envelope template, because the envelope will contain graphics as well as text, and you will need to alter the graphics. If your envelope template does not contain graphics, you can create a text document type for it. To create the graphics document:

1   Choose New (Ctrl+N) from the File menu to create a new document.

2   In the New dialog box, click Graphics and click OK, or press Alt+G to create a new, untitled graphics document.

3   Choose Show Rulers from the Window menu to turn on the graphics rulers.

4   Choose Page View (Shift+Ctrl+P) from the Window menu to turn page view on.

Having the ruler visible makes it easier for you to determine the size and placement of objects on your envelope template. (Because you will be measuring the dimensions of the envelope in inches, leave the ruler units set to inches in the Rulers dialog box.) Turning on Page View helps you see your document exactly as it will look when you print it.

Now you are ready to set page orientation and document margins so the new document you just created supports the relationships illustrated in Figure 2-47. The following steps use the dimensions shown in Figure 2-47 to change these settings.

1   With your new graphics document open, choose Print Setup from the File menu. The Print Setup dialog box opens. Figure 2-48 shows the Print Setup dialog box for my printer. The dialog box you see differs depending on the type of printer you are using.

2   In the Orientation area of the dialog box, click the Landscape option (see Figure 2-48).

3   Click OK. ClarisWorks changes the orientation of your document onscreen.

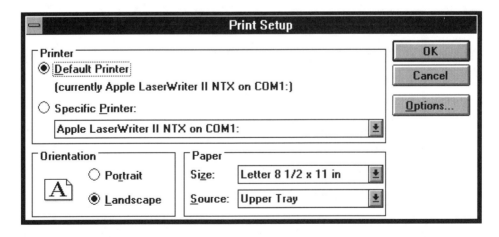

Figure 2-48 Print Setup dialog box

To see the orientation change, reduce the view of your document to 50%. The graphics ruler indicates that the page width is approximately 10.5 inches and height is 8 inches.

TIP

4   **Choose Document from the Format menu.** The Document dialog box opens.

5   **In the dialog box, change the Top, Bottom, Left, and Right margin settings to those shown in Figure 2-49.** These settings correspond to the dimensions of a standard business envelope (4 by 9.5) as if that envelope appeared sideways in the middle of an 8.5-by-11 page.

6   **Leave all the other document options as is, and click OK.** ClarisWorks changes the margins as you specified them. If you reduce the view of your document to 50%, your screen should look similar to the one shown in Figure 2-50. Notice that the graphics ruler now indicates a page width of 9.5 inches and a page height of 4 inches.

With your envelope template document set up, you are ready to add the logo and return address to the envelope.

```
┌──────────────────────────────────────────────────────┐
│ ─        Document                                       │
├──────────────────────────────────────────────────────┤
│  ┌Margins──────────────┐   ┌Size──────────────────┐   │
│  │ Top:    [2.25 in ]   │   │ Pages Across:  [1    ]│   │
│  │ Bottom: [2.25 in ]   │   │ Pages Down:    [1    ]│   │
│  │ Left:   [0.5 in  ]   │   └───────────────────────┘   │
│  │ Right:  [1 in    ]   │   ┌Display────────────────┐   │
│  └─────────────────────┘   │ ⊠ Show Margins         │   │
│                             │ ⊠ Show Page Guides     │   │
│  Starting Page #: [1 ]      └───────────────────────┘   │
│                             [ Cancel ]   [   OK   ]     │
└──────────────────────────────────────────────────────┘
```

Figure 2-49 Setting the envelope template document margins

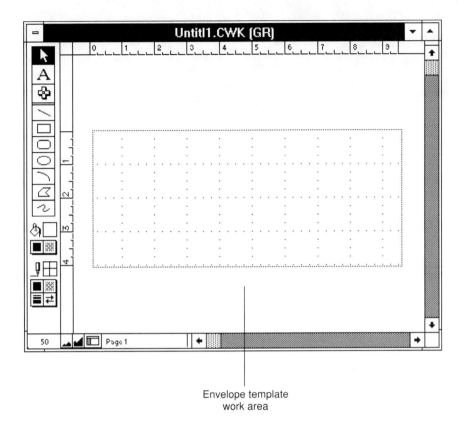

Envelope template
work area

Figure 2-50 A blank envelope template

Adding the logo and return address

In this section you will use the letterhead logo you created earlier in this chapter and add it to the envelope template you just created. When you are finished with this section, the Surfcity Sailboats logo and return address appears in the upper-left corner of the envelope in the return address area.

Before you can add the logo to the envelope, you need to make a few modifications. The sailboat logo itself is a bit too large for the envelope, and the return address does not need to include the business phone and fax numbers. To make these modifications, open the graphics document you saved earlier called SSLogo, if it is not already open.

The first modification you will make is to reduce the size of the sailboat logo graphic so it fits better on the envelope template. To do this:

1   **Click in the sailboat logo to select it.** Remember that you grouped all of the elements in this document before you saved it. By clicking in the logo, you select all of the objects as if they were one.

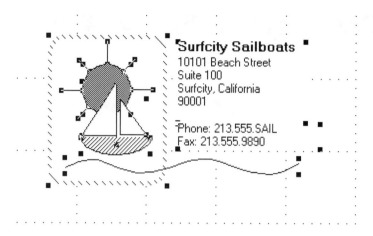

Figure 2-51 Ungrouped objects in the SSLogo document

2   **Choose Ungroup (Shift+Ctrl+G) from the Arrange menu so you can work with individual elements of the design.** ClarisWorks selects each logo element separately, as indicated by the selection handles shown in Figure 2-51. (You may need to choose Ungroup multiple times to ungroup all of the elements.)

3   **With all of the objects selected, hold down the Shift key as you click in each of the text frames, one at a time.** This deselects the text frames so you can work with the graphics elements only.

4   **Group only the graphics elements by choosing Group from the Arrange menu.**

5   **Choose Scale Selection from the Options menu.** The Scale Selection dialog box opens, as shown in Figure 2-52.

6   **To scale the graphic by 80% both vertically and horizontally, type 80 in both boxes (see Figure 2-52), and click OK.**

Everything in the SSLogo document, except the two text frames, is reduced to 80% of the original size.

To delete the phone and fax information and align the remaining text frame with the sailboat logo graphic:

1   **Click in the text frame containing the phone and fax information to select it.**

2   **Press Delete or Backspace, or choose Cut or Clear from the Edit menu.** The text frame disappears from the document, leaving the grouped graphic and the text frame containing the return address information.

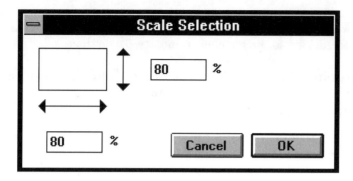

Figure 2-52 Setting the scale percentages to 80

3   Choose **Select All (Ctrl+A)** from the **Edit** menu to select both of the remaining objects.

4   Choose **Align Objects (Shift+Ctrl+K)** from the **Arrange** menu.

5   In the **Align Objects** dialog box shown in Figure 2-53, click the "Align top edges" option in the "Top to Bottom" area, leave "None" selected in the "Left to Right" area, and click OK.

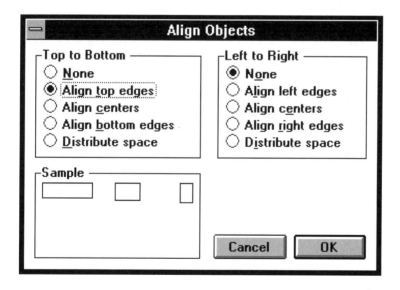

Figure 2-53 Aligning the top edges of the remaining objects in the SSLogo document

The top handles of the text frame and the reduced sailboat logo graphic are now aligned with each other. Having made these modifications to your logo, you can now add the design to the envelope template. To do this:

1   **Both the graphic and text frame objects should still be selected. If they aren't, press Ctrl+A to select them.**

2   **Choose Group from the Arrange menu.**

3   **Choose Copy from the Edit menu to copy the selection to the Clipboard.**

4   **Switch to your envelope template.**

5   **Choose Paste from the Edit menu.** The design is pasted onto the envelope template from the Clipboard.

6   **Drag the design to the upper-left corner of the envelope template document.**

Your envelope template is complete. At this point, if you want to add a sending address to the envelope, you can do so by creating a text frame, typing the address inside of it, and positioning the frame as desired on the envelope.

Since this document is a template, you save it as stationery. Follow the steps earlier in this chapter to save the envelope template, which is a graphics document, as ClarisWorks stationery. Name the template Envelope.CWS. Each time you want to print envelopes that match your letterhead, you open the template as a blank document that has margins and page orientation set correctly for the task.

Printing envelopes

As mentioned earlier, the best way to print envelopes is to feed them manually into the printer (unless you have an envelope cassette or feeder). This is true for virtually any kind of printer. Setting your printer to print manually gives you time to properly insert a blank envelope into the printer and allows you to feed each envelope individually through the printer.

No matter which printer you are using, check the following before you begin printing:

- A copy of your envelope template is open and active.
- Page orientation is set to landscape (horizontal) in the Print Setup dialog box.
- The number of blank envelopes you want to print are readily at hand.

Remember that you will be feeding envelopes sideways into the printer. Hold one of your blank envelopes face up, and turn it sideways so the flap side is underneath the right edge of the envelope. This is the direction you will feed the envelope into the printer, as shown in Figure 2-54.

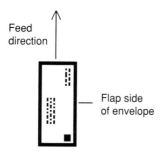

Figure 2-54 Feed direction of envelopes

Here are the general steps you should take to print envelopes from ClarisWorks for Windows. For specific printer settings, options, and instructions, refer to your printer manual.

1   **Make sure that your printer is properly connected to your computer and that the power is on.**

2   **Position the first blank envelope in the middle of the printer's paper tray or platen.**

3   **If necessary, open the Print Manager from the Program Manager and make the printer you want to use the default printer. Change any port or printer settings as needed. Omit this step if the printer you want to use is the printer named in the Print dialog box as the default printer.**

4   **If necessary, switch to ClarisWorks. With the envelope template open and active, choose Print Setup from the File menu, and set the orientation to landscape.**

5   **If your printer supports manual feeding, select Manual Feed as the Paper Source option, and click OK to close the Print Setup dialog box.**

6   **Choose Print (Ctrl+P) from the File menu, and specify the number of envelopes you want to print in the Copies entry box.**

7   **Select any other printing options you want in the dialog box.**

8   **Click OK to begin printing your envelopes.**

Because you inserted an envelope into the feeder before you began printing, ClarisWorks goes ahead and prints the first envelope. After the first envelope is printed, slide the next envelope into the center of the printer's paper tray or platen until you feel it stop. The next envelope prints. Continue doing this until all of your envelopes are printed.

Summary

In this chapter, you used the features of the text and graphics environments together to create a set of business stationery—letterhead with a logo, a two-page business letter, and envelopes to match your letterhead. You also learned the practical uses of the spelling checker and thesaurus that come with ClarisWorks.

You can apply the techniques described in this chapter to create your own personal stationery or to customize other types of documents. For example, if you frequently write reports, you can create a stationery document that contains an identifying graphic (like the logo) and is formatted appropriately for your report. You may also want to apply the concept you used to set up a custom document size for envelopes to create your own business cards.

The next chapter expands on the techniques presented in this chapter by describing how to design and lay out a newsletter that includes text, graphics, and spreadsheet data.

Chapter Three

Producing Newsletters

About this chapter

This chapter teaches you how to do page layout in ClarisWorks and demonstrates how you can create a ClarisWorks document that contains many different data types.

You will use the graphics, text, and spreadsheet environments together to produce a two-page newsletter. In producing the newsletter, you will use text frames for the newsletter articles and for other text elements. In addition, you will use spreadsheet frames to create a table in the text and to show a spreadsheet chart. The sample newsletter also includes such graphic elements as an organization chart, design elements, and clip art imported from various sources.

The techniques presented in this chapter can apply to any type of newsletter you may want to create for business, school, family events, or clubs.

Designing a newsletter

In this chapter, you produce a holiday newsletter for a fictitious club called the Wine of the Month Club. The newsletter is two pages in length and consists of articles, a chart, a diagram, and a variety of graphic elements. Figure 3-1 shows what your finished newsletter will look like.

Wine of the Month
—·— Club —·—

Holiday Edition • Winter 1993

Happy Holidays to all of our members!

Thanks to all of you, the Wine of the Month Club enjoyed another very successful year in 1993. From membership dues, wine sales, and events, the Club's revenues increased over 60% from last year. This means our new events coordinator, Sue Smith, is busy planning more Club events for next year.

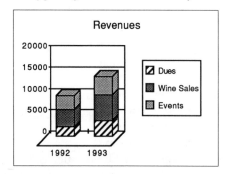

Speaking of events…The annual Harvest Ball (September 26) was a gala evening where we were fortunate to feature some of the more prized Cabernets of the Napa Valley. If the sampling we tasted is any indication of what we can expect for this vintage, it's time to start stocking those wine cellars now. We raffled off a couple of these special wines. Congratulations to Winston Winfield for winning a 1990 GrapeLeaf NV Cab, and to Ann Anonymous for winning the 1990 Haute Cab. Special thanks to Margo Mainly for coordinating the Harvest Ball, and to Bob Bubbly for doing such a fantastic job of getting the wineries to donate those fabulous reds!

Last month was our annual Beaujolais Nouveau event, a blind wine tasting of the just-released Beaujolais from France's Rhone Valley. The winning bottle was the Grande Goute, which lived up to its name: Big Taste! This wine is said to cellar better than those from other labels. It's a perfect accompaniment to a light Italian dinner or a Thanksgiving feast. ◆

New Releases for the Holidays

Just in time for the Holidays, the Wine of the Month Club has tasted several new wines that have just been released. For you dry white wine fans, a 1991 Pouilly-Fuisse from Zzyxx du Vin is a lovely example of this varietal. Rich and full-bodied, with a nose of vanilla and pineapples, it resembles some of the great Chardonnays from California's 1988 vintage.

Another good holiday wine you can proudly serve with a holiday Roast Beef dinner is the 1990 Zinfandel from Ione Wines. Its flavors are peppery, yet smooth, without being too spicy. Here are our recommendations for your holiday imbibement. ◆

Vintner	Year	Varietal	Retail Price
Bubbles	1991	Champagne	$10.00
Grand Goute	1992	Beaujolais	$15.00
Ione Wines	1990	Zinfandel	$7.00
Temptation	1990	Cabernet	$20.00
ZZyxx du Vin	1991	Pouilly-Fuisse	$18.50

Figure 3-1   The Wine of the Month Club newsletter (page 1)

Wine of the Month Club • Holiday Edition • page 2

New Club Board

Yes, friends, the Club board has undergone another reorganization. With Yvette Blanc moving to Timbuktu and Rob Romantique going abroad for two months, we were forced to replace two of our key positions on the board: Secretary and Treasurer. The search was long and hard. Thanks to the Club members who submitted recommendations and took the time to help recruit for these positions.

Eunice Inx is our new Secretary. Ms. Inx will be responsible for taking minutes at the Club's monthly meetings, gathering Club news, and editing the Wine of the Month Club newsletter (the one you're reading now). Eunice has an extensive background in managing public relations for non-profit organizations, and recently moved to our town from Chicago, Illinois. Her experience should be a great asset to the Club.

After a long search for a new treasurer, we are pleased to announce that Rich Banks has accepted the position. Rich is the chief financial officer for the MegaBucks Corporation, the largest local business by far. "I will be retiring from MegaBucks in a couple of months, and look forward to getting more involved with the Wine of the Month Club," says Mr. Banks. He will be responsible for collecting membership dues and keeping the Club's budget balanced.

It was hard saying good bye to Yvette and Rob. They each contributed a great deal of time to the Club, and brought with them extensive knowledge about wines. We all wish them well in their new endeavors.

Be sure to introduce yourself to Rich and Eunice at next month's meeting. ◆

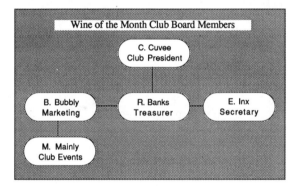

Wine of the Month Club Board Members

- C. Cuvee — Club President
- B. Bubbly — Marketing
- R. Banks — Treasurer
- E. Inx — Secretary
- M. Mainly — Club Events

WISHING YOU A VERY HAPPY HOLIDAY SEASON AND A PROSPEROUS NEW YEAR!

Figure 3-1   (continued) The Wine of the Month Club newsletter (page 2)

The process of designing a newsletter involves laying out pages. *Page layout* refers to the way you position and format elements within a newsletter or any other document. Although there are several Windows applications on the market specifically intended for page layout, with ClarisWorks you don't need to learn a separate application to do page layout. ClarisWorks powerful, flexible page layout capabilities are already built in, and they are available from any ClarisWorks environment.

Sketching your ideas

Before you sit down in front of your computer to begin your newsletter, take some time sketching out your ideas on paper. Think about what information you want to include in the newsletter and the best way to present the information. For example, if you know you want to include some financial figures, is it best to place the figures in text, or to show them in a chart or graph? Here are some general tips you can follow as you design your newsletter layout.

First, decide what articles or stories you want to include in the newsletter. Pick one or two of the more important or more interesting articles; these should appear on the front page. Decide where you want to place the remaining articles.

Next, think about how you can use graphics to enhance the meaning of the text and to attract the reader's attention. A newsletter that is long on text and short on graphics is simply less interesting to read. Aside from giving your newsletter visual interest, figures, diagrams, and other graphics can often convey meaning more directly than text can. On the other hand, using too many figures can make your newsletter look busy or distract from the meaning within the text. It is important to strike a balance between use of graphics and use of text.

When you have a pretty good idea of what articles and graphics you want to include in your newsletter, start sketching some ideas of how you want the pieces laid out on the pages. Think about how your pieces will look in a one-, two-, or three-column layout. Do you want to use a two-column layout throughout the newsletter, or one column on the first page and two on subsequent pages? Experiment on paper until you feel you have a page layout that works best with your pieces.

Figure 3-2 shows a sketch of the Wine of the Month Club newsletter you will produce in this chapter. The sketch shows a two-page, two-column layout and indicates the placement of the newsletter elements. On the first page, a chart, a table, and clip art are positioned on the page so that they balance out the text and draw the reader's eye across the page. The second page contains only one graphic element—a diagram that supports the text of the article on the page.

Elements of the newsletter

Looking at the sketch in Figure 3-2, you see that the Wine of the Month Club newsletter includes the following pieces:

Page 1

Page 2

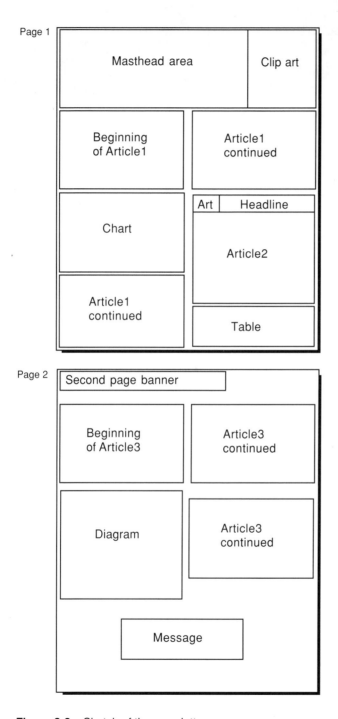

Figure 3-2   Sketch of the newsletter

- Masthead (area for the name of the newsletter)
- Clip art
- Three articles
- Chart
- Table
- Headline
- Second page banner
- Diagram
- Closing message

Each of these elements falls into one of three data type categories: text, graphics, or spreadsheet.

Text elements

The text elements of the newsletter include the three articles, the masthead area, the headline for the second article, the second-page banner, and the closing message on page 2. Each of these text pieces is contained in a text frame on the page.

If you recall from Chapter 1, you can create linked or unlinked text frames in a document. This newsletter uses linked text frames to flow the text of the first and third articles within the page layout. Using linked text frames lets you place parts of the article in different areas on the page.

The newsletter also uses unlinked text frames for the masthead, second article headline, second article text, second page banner, and closing message. Unlinked frames hold information that does not continue from one frame to the next; that is, they are independent from one another.

Each text element is enhanced in one way or another with a related graphic element.

Graphic elements

The newsletter's graphic elements consist of the following:

- Clip art
- Design elements
- Diagram

Clip art is a collection of graphic images, usually in .TIFF, .BMP, or EPSF format, that isn't protected by copyright. (See the Appendix for details on importing graphics files.) When you purchase clip art, either on disk or CD-ROM, you get pieces of finished art that you can use in newsletters or any other kind of document. In this newsletter, you will use three different clip art images: a picture of a champagne bottle being uncorked, a picture of a wine glass and wine bottle, and a design element.

Design elements are abstract images that enhance a document's design. They do not generally relate directly to the content of your document. Rather, they support the page design of your document. One of the design elements you will use in the newsletter is actually a piece of clip art that appears on either side of the word *Club* in the masthead. In addition, you will use two other design elements: dotted lines and *dingbats*, which are typographical symbols. Dotted lines help to separate the masthead from the main body of the newsletter on the first page and the third article from the closing message on the second page. Dingbats denote the end of each article.

Another graphic element in the newsletter is a diagram, which appears on the second page. In this case, the diagram is a chart showing the organization of the Club's board members. You will use ClarisWorks drawing tools to create the organization chart in the newsletter.

The newsletter contains an additional chart, which is based on spreadsheet data. A chart behaves like any other graphic object.

Spreadsheet elements

The newsletter includes two spreadsheet elements, both of which are independent (unlinked) spreadsheet frames. See Chapter 1 for details on creating frames. The first spreadsheet frame contains financial data regarding the Club's sources of revenues. This spreadsheet frame, which is hidden in the newsletter's final form, is used for the sole purpose of creating a three-dimensional stacked bar chart.

The second spreadsheet frame is used for the table at the bottom of page 1. The inherent nature of a spreadsheet frame, with its rows and columns, easily lends itself to presenting tabular information.

You can include database information in your documents as tables. For example, the data in the table on page 1 of the newsletter could have come directly from a ClarisWorks database document. To do this, you copy the records from a database document and paste them into a spreadsheet frame.

TIP

Now that you have an idea of what the newsletter will look like and what elements it will contain, you are ready to set up the newsletter in ClarisWorks.

Setting up the document

Begin by creating a new ClarisWorks graphics document. A graphics document is the best choice of document type for doing page layout because it gives you flexibility in creating, positioning, and manipulating frames and other graphics objects. Additionally, graphics documents include a graphics grid and graphics rulers, which let you position your newsletter elements precisely on the page.

Although you can use a text document to do page layout if you prefer, a text document does not give you as much flexibility as a graphics document. The major disadvantage is that multiple columns in a text document are all the same width and occupy the length of the document. (You can, however, use text frames in a text document, which allow for variable column widths and lengths.) In a graphics document, each of your columns can have a different width and length.

Note   *The following steps assume your newsletter will be set up on a standard 8.5-by-11-inch page. If you want to set up a newsletter for international distribution, the standard size of a page is 8.25 by 12 inches, also called A4 size paper. To set up for an A4 page, choose Print Setup, and select the A4 Letter option in the dialog box.*

To set up the new document for your newsletter:

1   **Make sure a new, untitled graphics document is open and active.**

2   **Choose Document from the Format menu.**

3   **In the Document dialog box, change the document margins to those shown in Figure 3-3.** Since your newsletter is going to be two pages, you need to change one of the Size options in the dialog box, either Pages Across or Pages Down (both are preset to 1).

4   **Press Tab until the Pages Down box is highlighted, and type** 2. **(Figure 3-3 reflects this change).**

5   **Leave all other settings as is, and click OK.**

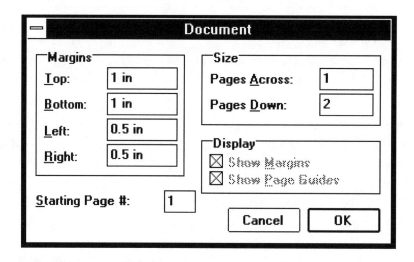

Figure 3-3   Document dialog box showing newsletter settings

Your newsletter document is now set up for a two-page newsletter with a working area of 7.5 by 9 inches for each page (7.5 by 18 inches total).

To see your changes, switch to Page View by choosing it from the Window menu, and turn on the graphics rulers by choosing Show Rulers from the Window menu.

When you set Pages Down to 2 in the Document dialog box, ClarisWorks adds another page below the first one in your document. To see the second page, scroll down the window. If you set Pages Across to 2 instead, the new page appears to the right of the first one, and you scroll across the window to see it.

Note   *You can set a maximum of 999 pages across or down with a maximum of 32,767 total pages.*

As you navigate between pages, the current page number is indicated in the lower-left corner of your document window in the Page Number box (see Figure 3-4). The Page Number box is only available in Page View.

TIP

Besides setting up a graphics document for two or more pages, you can change the Pages Across and Pages Down settings for other reasons. If you have moved a graphics object off the document and can no longer see it, increase the Pages Across or Pages Down setting to bring the object back into view. If you are working with a graphics document that has more than two pages, you can set both Pages Across and Pages Down. For example, in a four-page document, set both Pages Across and Pages Down to 2. This way, when you reduce the document's view, you can see all four pages in the window at one time.

Now you are ready to add the elements of your newsletter to the document. First you will add the text elements. It makes sense to lay out the text elements first because they comprise the main structure of your newsletter.

This is a good place to save what you've done so far. Choose Save (Ctrl+S) from the File menu, and name your document something like ClubNews.CWK.

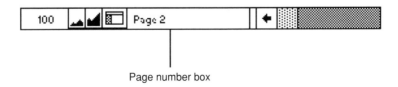

Page number box

Figure 3-4   The Page Number box shows the current page number

Note   *Although you will not be reminded to save your document throughout the rest of this chapter, be sure to periodically save your work.*

Adding text

The first text frame you create will be an unlinked text frame to contain the text of the masthead. If it is not already open, begin by opening the newsletter document you created in the previous section, and make sure Page View is on and the rulers are visible.

Creating the text frame for the masthead

The masthead area appears at the top of the first page and contains the title and date of the newsletter (see Figure 3-1). In this section, you create a text frame for the masthead, format the text, and place a border around it.

    To create the text frame for the masthead:

1   **In the tool palette, click the text tool to select it.**

2   **Click and drag to create a text frame at the top of the document.**
Using the graphics ruler, begin the text frame in the upper-left corner of the document, drag across to approximately 5 inches, and down to approximately 1.75 inches (see Figure 3-5).

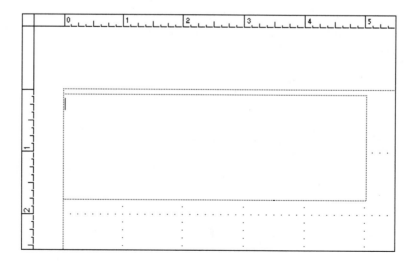

Figure 3-5   Text frame for the masthead

3   **Release the mouse.** Figure 3-5 shows the correct size and placement of the text frame.

Now enter the masthead text and change its font type and size. The name of the newsletter, *Wine of the Month Club,* has a different font type and size than the line of text containing the date.

1   **With the text insertion point in the frame, type the following text, pressing ⏎ after each line:**

> Wine of the Month
> Club
> \<blank line\>
> Holiday Edition | Winter 1993

In the last line, type five spaces after the word *Edition*, type a lowercase *L,* type five spaces after the *L,* and type the remainder of the line's text. In step 4 you will change the *L* into a bullet character.

2   **To change the font type and size of *Wine of the Month Club,* select the first two lines of text in the frame, choose Times New Roman from the Font menu, and 36 Point from the Size menu.**

3   **To change the font type and size of the last line, select the whole line, and choose MS Sans Serif from the Font menu and 18 Point from the Size menu.**

4   **Select the lowercase *L* in the last line, and choose Wingdings from the Font menu.** The *L* changes into a bullet character (•).

5   **Select the entire last line again, and choose Italic from the Style menu.**

Figure 3-6 shows the results of your font and size changes.

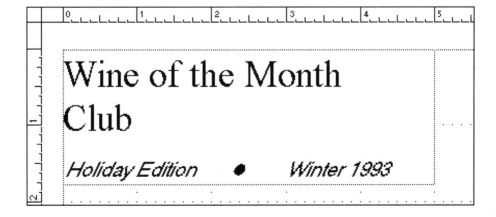

Figure 3-6   Text of the masthead with font changes made

If you do not have Times New Roman or MS Sans Serif installed in your system, choose other fonts. Whichever font you use, use a larger font size for the title than for the rest of the newsletter. If you don't have Wingdings, use the Windows Character Map accessory to help you choose a font capable of producing a bullet character. (Character Map shows what character or symbol you can produce for each key on the keyboard for a selected font. Refer to your Microsoft Windows *User's Guide* for more information.)

Now, change the alignment of the text so it is centered between the left and right edges of the frame. Before you do so, switch from the graphics ruler to the text ruler.

TIP

Throughout this chapter you will be switching between the graphics and the text rulers. The graphics ruler is useful for precisely positioning objects in the document; the text ruler is useful for formatting text, such as setting alignment and changing paragraph indents. Rather than choosing Rulers from the Format menu and selecting the ruler you want from the dialog box, you can create a macro that switches the rulers for you. To start the macro, choose Record Macro from the Macros cascading menu in the File menu, then take the steps necessary to change the type of ruler. When you are finished, choose Stop Recording from the Macros cascading menu. See Chapter 4 and Chapter 7 for more information on recording macros.

To change alignment:

1   **Press Ctrl+A to select all of the text in the frame.**
2   **Choose Rulers from the Format menu.** The Rulers dialog box appears.
3   **In the Show area of the dialog box, click Text, and click OK.** The rulers showing in the window switch from the graphics ruler to the text ruler.
4   **In the text ruler, click the center alignment icon.** The text is centered within the frame, as shown in Figure 3-7.
5   **When you are finished, press Enter on the numeric keypad.**

The frame is selected and your masthead text frame is complete. Now you can emphasize the masthead text by placing a border around it.

Another way to align text inside a text frame is to select the frame, and choose Left, Center, Right, or Justify from the Alignment cascading menu in the Format menu.

TIP

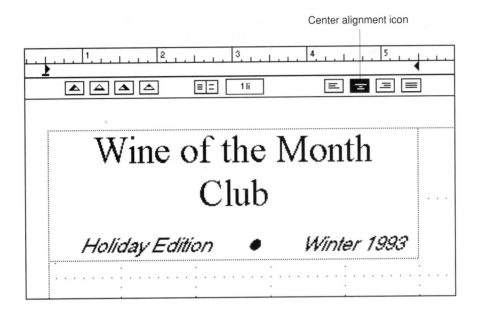

Figure 3-7   Using the text ruler to align text in the center of the frame

Drawing the masthead border

To draw a border around the masthead text:

1   **Switch to the graphics ruler using the Rulers dialog box.**
2   **In the tool palette, select the rounded rectangle tool.**
3   **Click in the upper-left corner of the document, and drag to create a rounded rectangle that is approximately 5 inches wide and 2 inches long.**
4   **Release the mouse.**

You may find it easier to turn off the autogrid when you are drawing or positioning objects. To do so, choose Turn Autogrid Off from the Options menu, or press Ctrl+Y.

TIP

The rounded rectangle appears to have hidden the masthead text frame. The text frame is still there but it is behind the rounded rectangle object. To move the rectangle behind the text frame so you can see the text, select the rounded rectangle, and choose Move To Back from the Arrange menu.

Note   *If part of the rectangle appears to be cut off, click the text frame to select it, and move it until it is in the center of the rectangle. Or, change the fill pattern of the text frame from opaque to transparent.*

To change the border line width:

1   **Select the rectangle.**
2   **Click the line width icon in the tool palette.**
3   **Choose a size (such as 2 point) from the line width menu.**

Your masthead should now look similar to the one shown in Figure 3-8. Later in this chapter, you will add design elements to the masthead, but for now, your masthead is finished. Select the masthead text frame and border together and group them by choosing Group from the Arrange menu.

Now you are ready to start adding the text of your articles to the newsletter.

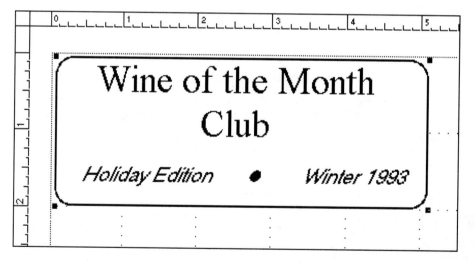

Figure 3-8   Completed masthead

Laying out the text of the articles

In this section, you use the Frame Links feature to lay out the text of the three articles. Article1 and Article2 appear on the front page; Article3 appears on the second page. Throughout this section, you use a variety of techniques to lay out the articles. These techniques demonstrate the versatility of doing page layout in ClarisWorks.

You begin by laying out Article1 (the lead article) using linked text frames and pasting text from another text document into the text frames. You create one linked frame and paste the text, then create subsequent linked frames until all of the text is laid out. Anything you paste or type in the first frame continues in the next linked frame.

To lay out Article2, you create an empty unlinked text frame. Instead of pasting text into the frame, you type Article2's text.

The procedure for laying out Article3 is similar to the one you use for Article1, except you draw all of the empty linked text frames first, then paste the text into them from another document.

Throughout this section you can adjust line spacing within the text frames to get more or less text in the frame. To do this, click the Line/Points indicator in the text ruler to work in point increments.

TIP

Laying out Article1

Let's assume that the text of the first newsletter article already exists in another ClarisWorks document—a text document. Figure 3-9 shows the article text. This text is not formatted as it will be in its final form. Later on, after you lay out all of the articles, you will make the necessary formatting changes.

Since the text in Figure 3-9 does not actually exist, you will need to create a new text document now and type in the text shown in the figure. To follow the example, the font should be set to Times New Roman 12 point. When you are done, save the document as Article1.CWK and leave the document open.

If your newsletter document is not already open, open it now. Make sure that the tool palette, graphics ruler, and graphics grid are visible.

If you look at the newsletter sketch shown in Figure 3-2, you see that Article1 starts in one frame and continues in two more frames. So, in the following steps, you create the first frame, paste in text from the Article1 document, and create the second frame. ClarisWorks automatically flows text from the first frame. When you create the third frame, ClarisWorks flows text from the second frame.

Happy Holidays to all of our members!

Thanks to all of you, the Wine of the Month Club enjoyed another very successful year in 1992. From membership dues, wine sales, and events, the Club's revenues increased over 60% from last year. This means our new events coordinator, Sue Smith, is busy planning more Club events for next year.

Speaking of events...The annual Harvest Ball (September 26) was a gala evening where we were fortunate to feature some of the more prized Cabernets of the Napa Valley. If the sampling we tasted is any indication of what we can expect for this vintage, it's time to start stocking those wine cellars now. We raffled off a couple of these special wines. Congratulations to Winston Winfield for winning a 1990 GrapeLeaf NV Cab, and to Ann Anonymous for winning the 1990 Haute Cab. Special thanks to Margo Mainly for coordinating the Harvest Ball, and to Bob Bubbly for doing such a fantastic job of getting the wineries to donate those fabulous reds!

Last month was our annual Beaujolais Nouveau event, a blind wine tasting of the just-released Beaujolais from France's Rhone Valley. The winning bottle was the Grande Goute, which lived up to its name: Big Taste! This wine is said to cellar better than those from other labels. It's a perfect accompaniment to a light Italian dinner or a Thanksgiving feast.

Figure 3-9   Article1's text

1 **Click anywhere in the newsletter document to deselect any selected objects.**

2 **Make Article1 the active document by choosing it from the Window menu, if necessary.**

3 **Press Ctrl+A to select all of the text in the document, and choose Copy (Ctrl+C) from the Edit menu.**

4 **Make the newsletter document active by choosing it from the Window menu.**

5 **Choose Frame Links from the Options menu, or press Ctrl+L to turn it on.**

6 **Select the text tool from the tool palette.**

7 **Click and drag to create a text frame below the masthead in the document.** Using the graphics ruler, begin the text frame at the left margin, at approximately 2.25 inches down, and drag across to approximately 3.5 inches and down to approximately 3.75 inches.

8 **Release the mouse.**

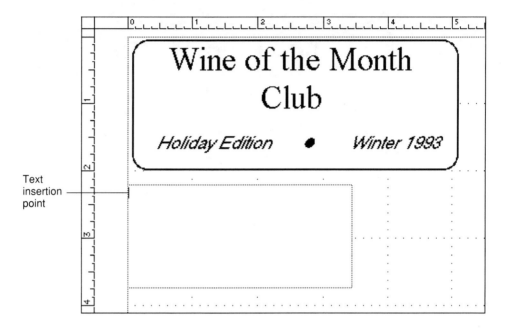

Text
insertion
point

Figure 3-10   First text frame for Article1

Your text frame should look like the one shown in Figure 3-10. Notice that the text insertion point automatically appears inside the frame as soon as you release the mouse.

Now paste the text you copied from the text document into the frame. With the text insertion point in the beginning position, choose Paste (Ctrl+V) from the Edit menu. The first paragraph appears in the text frame and the overflow indicator tells you that there is more text than will fit in the frame (see Figure 3-11).

To create the second linked frame and flow the article text into it:

1 Press Enter on the numeric keypad, or click in an empty place in the document, to exit the first frame and to select it. Selection handles and a continuation indicator appear around the frame (see Figure 3-12).

2 Click the continuation indicator. This tells ClarisWorks you want to create another text frame into which the overflow text will continue.

3 Scroll down the document, and click and drag to create the second linked text frame. Leave room for the chart, which you will create later in this chapter, and start the second frame at approximately 6.5 inches down the left margin, and drag across to 3.5 inches and down to near the bottom of the page.

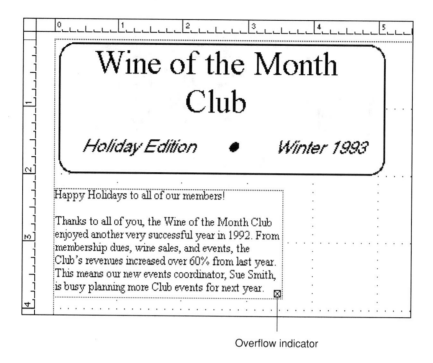

Overflow indicator

Figure 3-11   First paragraph of Article1 in the text frame

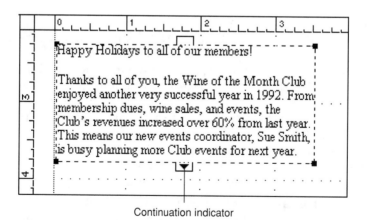

Continuation indicator

Figure 3-12   The first frame shows a continuation indicator (one of the link indicators)

4   Release the mouse. ClarisWorks automatically continues the text of the article from the first frame into the second. At the same time, selection handles and link indicators appear around the second frame (see Figure 3-13).

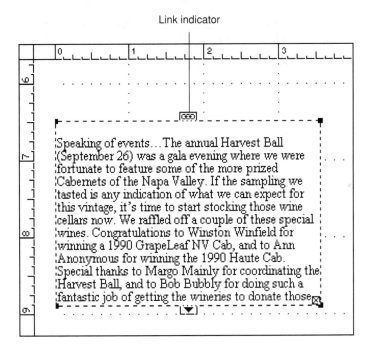

Figure 3-13   Article1 text flows into the second linked frame

With only one more linked frame to create, you are almost finished laying out the first article. The last linked frame for Article1 is positioned next to the first frame in the second column. To create it:

1 **Click the continuation indicator at the bottom of the second frame.**

2 **Scroll to the upper-right corner of your document, and click and drag to create the frame.** Begin the frame at 4 inches across and 2.25 inches down and drag across to the right margin and down to approximately 4 inches.

3 **Release the mouse.**

If all of the text you pasted in the first frame has completely flowed across all three frames, the third frame doesn't show an overflow indicator. If it does, click the lower right selection handle, and drag down slightly until the overflow indicator disappears.

To see your whole document on the screen, reduce the view by choosing View Scale from the Window menu and setting a view scale percentage such as 60%.

TIP

Laying out Article2

In this section, you create an empty unlinked text frame and type the text of Article2 into it. The text frame for Article2 is unlinked because you do not need to continue text from it to another frame. Also, the text inside this frame is not related to other text in the newsletter.

To lay out the Article2:

1   **Open your newsletter document, if necessary.**

2   **Click once anywhere in the document (except on another object) to deselect the linked text frame you just created in the previous section.**

3   **Choose Frame Links (Ctrl+L) from the Options menu.** This disables Frame Links. Subsequent text frames that you create will not be linked. However, the three frames you created for the first article maintain their linked status.

4   **Select the text tool in the tool palette.** If you reduced your document view earlier, restore it to 100% magnification before you move on.

5   **Click and drag in the second column of the document, below the last frame you created, to create the text frame.** Leaving room for Article2's headline and clip art, which you will add later in this chapter, start the frame at 4 inches across and approximately 4.75 inches down, and drag across to the right margin and down to approximately 7 inches (see Figure 3-14).

6   **Release the mouse.** The text insertion point appears inside the frame at the end of the text that is displayed.

7   **Type the text shown in Figure 3-14.**

8   **When you are finished, press Enter on the numeric keypad, or click outside the frame to select it.**

The text shown in the figure is Times New Roman 12 point. If your text appears in a different font and/or size, change it by choosing Times New Roman from the Font cascading menu, and 12 Point from the Size cascading menu in the Format menu.

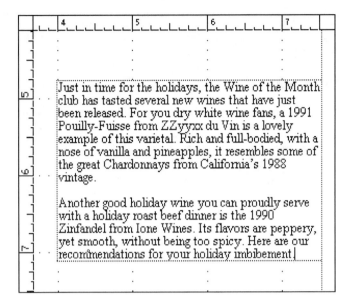

Figure 3-14   Text frame containing the second article

Note   *If the frame is not long enough for the typed text, it will expand accordingly. Alternately, if the frame is too big for the typed text, it will shrink to the size of the text block when you select the frame.*

With the second article in position in the newsletter, you are ready to lay out the third and last article.

Laying out Article3

Assume that the text of this article already exists in another text document, as you did for Article1. This time, however, let's assume the text document was created in a Windows application other than ClarisWorks, such as WordPerfect or Microsoft Word. Figure 3-15 shows the article text.

Open another word processing application, such as Microsoft Word, create a new document, and type in the text shown in Figure 3-15. To follow the example, use Times New Roman 12 point for the article and Times New Roman 18 point for the article's headline. When you are done, save the document as Article3, and quit the other word processing application.

Now launch ClarisWorks, if necessary, and open your newsletter document (ClubNews). Make sure that the tool palette, graphics rulers, and graphics grid are visible.

If you look at the newsletter sketch shown in Figure 3-2, you see that Article3 appears on the second page in three frames. In the following steps, you

New Club Board

Yes, friends, the Club board has undergone another reorganization. With Yvette Blanc moving to Timbuktu and Rob Romantique going abroad for two months, we were forced to replace two of our key positions on the board: Secretary and Treasurer. The search was long and hard. Thanks to the Club members who submitted recommendations and took the time to help recruit for these positions.

Eunice Inx is our new Secretary. Ms. Inx will be responsible for taking minutes at the Club's monthly meetings, gathering Club news, and editing the Wine of the Month Club newsletter (the one you have in your hands). Eunice has an extensive background in managing public relations for non-profit organizations, and recently moved to our town from Chicago, Illinois. Her experience should be a great asset to the Club.

After a long search for a new treasurer, we are pleased to announce that Rich Banks has accepted the position. Rich is the chief financial officer for the MegaBucks Corporation, the largest local business by far. "I will be retiring from MegaBucks in a couple of months, and look forward to getting more involved with the Wine of the Month Club," says Mr. Banks. He will be responsible for collecting membership dues and keeping the Club's budget balanced.

It was hard saying good bye to Yvette and Rob. They each contributed a great deal of time to the Club, and brought with them extensive knowledge about wines. We all wish them well in their new endeavors.

Be sure to introduce yourself to Rich and Eunice at next month's meeting.

Figure 3-15   Article3's text

create three empty linked text frames first, then insert the text you typed in the other application into the text frames in your ClarisWorks document.

To create the first empty linked frame:

1 **Scroll down your newsletter document until the top of the second page is visible, and click in the empty area to deselect any selected objects.** Notice that the graphics ruler along the left edge of the window does not start at 0 inches at the top of the second page. Instead, it starts at 9 inches. ClarisWorks measures multipage graphics documents as one long page.

2 **Choose Frame Links (Ctrl+L) from the Options menu to turn it on.**

3 **Select the text tool, and click and drag to create the article's first linked frame at the top of the document.** Begin the text frame at the 9.75-inch mark down the left margin, and drag across to 3.5 inches and down to 12 inches.

4 **Release the mouse and press Enter on the numeric keypad to select the frame.** The frame shows selection handles and link indicators.

Now, start to create the second empty linked text frame by clicking the continuation indicator at the bottom of the first. Notice that as soon as you click the continuation indicator, the outline of the first frame becomes invisible; you cannot discern where it is on the page or how large it is. Figure 3-16 illustrates the problem. This occurs because text frames are preset to not show any border (that is, the line width of a text frame is preset to None).

To make it easier to see the empty frame, change its line width so it shows a border:

1   **Select the graphics tool in the tool palette.**

2   **Click in the empty frame you just created to select it.**

3   **From the line width menu, choose 1 pt.**

Now when you click on the continuation indicator to create the next linked frame, the empty frame is visible by its border. Create the remaining two empty, linked text frames:

1   **Click the continuation indicator at the bottom of the first frame.**

2   **Click and drag to create the second linked frame to the right of the first.** Begin the second frame 4 inches across and down at the 10-inch mark, and drag across to the right edge of the document and down to 12 inches.

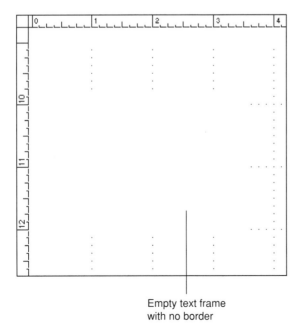

Empty text frame
with no border

Figure 3-16   The first linked text frame appears to be invisible on the page

3   **Release the mouse.** As soon as you release the mouse, the frame shows selection handles and link indicators. Also, the frame has the same line width setting (1 point) that you set for the first frame.

4   **Click the continuation indicator at the bottom of the second frame.**

5   **Click and drag to create the last linked frame below the second one.** This time, begin the last frame 4.75 inches across and down at the 12.25-inch mark, and drag across to the right edge of the document and down to 15 inches.

6   **Release the mouse.**

The three empty text frames are complete, as shown in Figure 3-17.

If you frequently use a certain page layout, you can create a document template that contains a series of empty linked text frames. Simply draw the linked frames and position them as you desire in the document. Then save the page layout as ClarisWorks stationery, with a .CWS file extension. See Chapter 2 if you want to review the discussion about creating stationery.

TIP

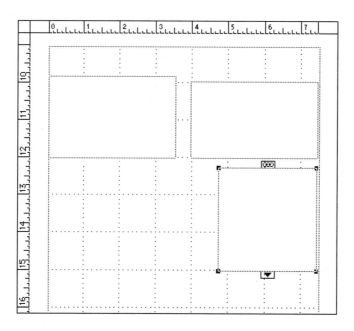

Figure 3-17   The empty text frames for the third article

Now you are ready to insert text from the document you created earlier in this section. The process of inserting text from a document created in another application differs from simply copying and pasting it. Both methods yield the same result. However, when you use the insert method, you insert the whole document. Furthermore, inserting a document saves you time because you don't need to launch the other application, open the other document, copy the text, start ClarisWorks (if necessary), or paste the text into a ClarisWorks document.

To insert a Microsoft Word for Windows document into the text frames you created for Article3:

1   **Scroll your document until the first linked frame on the second page is visible.**

2   **Double-click the first linked frame.** The text insertion point appears in the upper-left corner inside the frame.

3   **Choose Insert from the File menu.** The Insert dialog box opens.

4   **In the dialog box, click to the right of the List Files of Type box to open the drop-down menu (see Figure 3-18).** The menu lists some document formats you can insert into a ClarisWorks text frame or document.

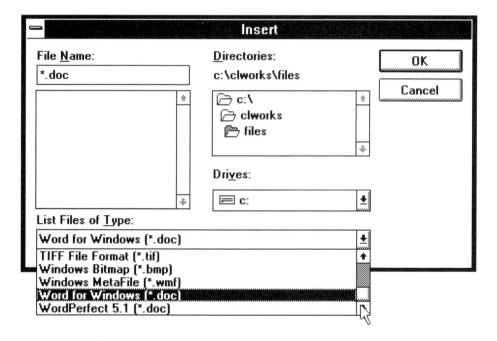

Figure 3-18   The List Files of Type drop-down menu in the Insert dialog box

5   Scroll in the list if necessary, and choose "Word for Windows (*.doc)" (or the format appropriate for your document) from the drop-down menu (see Figure 3-18).

6   Locate the document you want to insert, and select it from the file list.

7   Click OK.

ClarisWorks inserts the text document into the linked text frames, beginning at the text insertion point, and continuing through the remaining frames. After the text is inserted, the text insertion point is positioned at the end of the text in the last frame.

Note   *If you get the overflow indicator in the third frame, you may need to adjust either the size of your frame(s) or the line spacing within frames.*

With Article3 laid out in your newsletter document, you can now format the text of all the articles.

Formatting article text

In this section, you change the format of the paragraphs within each article as follows:

- The first paragraph of each article aligns with the left edge of the text frame
- The first line of subsequent paragraphs indents by 0.25 inches

To make these format changes, use the text ruler. You can use the text ruler to format text inside frames just as you used the text ruler in Chapter 2 to format a text document.

Before you begin, make sure your newsletter document is open and active. To format Article1:

1   Scroll in your document until the first linked frame of Article1 is visible.

2   Click inside the first frame to position the text insertion point at the beginning of the second paragraph, as shown in Figure 3-19.

3   Press Delete or Backspace to delete the blank line separating the first line *(Happy Holidays to...)* from the second paragraph. The second paragraph should still be active.

4   Switch to the text ruler using the Rulers dialog box.

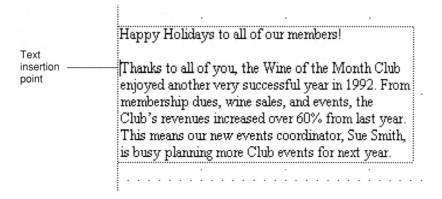

Text
insertion
point

Happy Holidays to all of our members!

Thanks to all of you, the Wine of the Month Club enjoyed another very successful year in 1992. From membership dues, wine sales, and events, the Club's revenues increased over 60% from last year. This means our new events coordinator, Sue Smith, is busy planning more Club events for next year.

Figure 3-19   Positioning the text insertion point in the first frame

5   In the text ruler, drag the first line marker to the right until it is 0.25 inches from the left indent marker. The paragraph now has the first line indented properly. (If you don't know how to identify the first line indent marker in the text ruler, see "Tab Markers" section in Chapter 1.)

6   To copy the new ruler settings, choose Copy Ruler from the Format menu.

7   Click in the second text frame to position the text insertion point at the beginning of the next paragraph, which begins *Speaking of events*. . . .

8   Choose Apply Ruler from the Format menu to apply the ruler settings to the current paragraph.

9   Click in the third text frame to position the text insertion point at the beginning of the next paragraph, which begins *Last month was our*. . . .

10 Press Delete or Backspace to delete the blank line above the paragraph.

11 Repeat step 8 to apply the ruler settings to this paragraph.

Article1 is now properly formatted. Follow these steps to format the other two articles until all paragraphs, except the first of each article, are indented by 0.25 inches. Your newsletter articles should now be formatted as shown in Figure 3-1.

Before you move on to add the remaining text frames to the newsletter, you need to make a couple of modifications to the articles. Specifically, you need to add cues for your readers so they know when an article begins and ends. In the sample newsletter, the beginning of each article is indicated by the first character in the article, which has a different font size and style (Times New Roman Bold 24 point) from the rest of the text. The end of each article is denoted by a dingbat, which is a small solid diamond shape. The following steps describe how to make these modifications to Article1. When you are finished with Article1, repeat the steps for the other two articles.

TIP

The dingbat used in this procedure is actually a character from the Wingdings font family. If you don't have Wingdings fonts installed in your system, select any font type and hold down the Alt key as you type any four-digit number between 0129 and 0255 on the numeric keypad. Doing so generates unusual characters from the font's extended character set. For example, with Times New Roman selected, press Alt+0182 to type a paragraph symbol (¶). You can use the Windows Character Map to help you select a special character for your chosen font.

To make the modifications:

1 **Select the first character in the first linked frame of Article1, the *H* in *Happy Holidays*. . . .**

2 **Choose 24 Point from the Size menu, and choose Bold (Ctrl+B) from the Style menu.**

3 **To add a dingbat to the end of the article, position the text insertion point after the last word in the third frame.** In this case, the last word is *feast*.

4 **Press the spacebar once.**

5 **Choose Wingdings from the Font menu, and choose 10 Point from the Size menu.**

6 **Type u (a lowercase U) to insert the dingbat character ◆ at the end of the article.** If you don't have the Wingdings font, refer to the previous tip for an alternative suggestion.

TIP

To save yourself some time in applying the above modifications to each article, you can create a macro that makes the changes for you throughout the entire document. Briefly, you choose Record Macro from the Macros cascading menu in the File menu, to begin recording, follow steps 1 through 6 previously listed, and choose Stop Recording from the Macros cascading menu when you are done.

Figure 3-20 shows how these changes affect Article2.

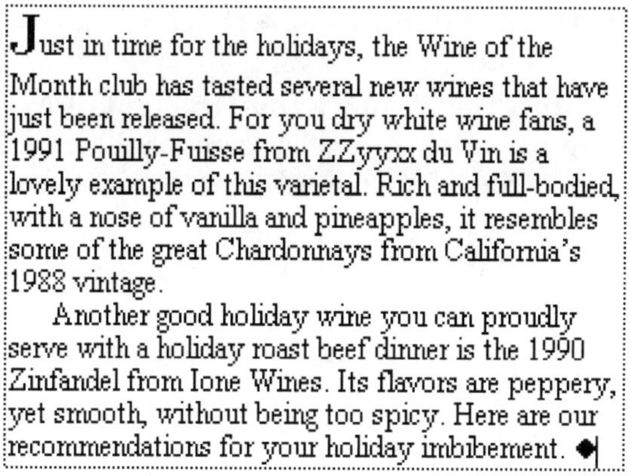

Just in time for the holidays, the Wine of the Month club has tasted several new wines that have just been released. For you dry white wine fans, a 1991 Pouilly-Fuisse from ZZyyxx du Vin is a lovely example of this varietal. Rich and full-bodied, with a nose of vanilla and pineapples, it resembles some of the great Chardonnays from California's 1988 vintage.

Another good holiday wine you can proudly serve with a holiday roast beef dinner is the 1990 Zinfandel from Ione Wines. Its flavors are peppery, yet smooth, without being too spicy. Here are our recommendations for your holiday imbibement. ◄

Figure 3-20   Article2 with formatting changes

Before moving on, you can lock all of the elements of your newsletter in place so you don't accidentally move them or otherwise alter them. To do this, with the graphics tool selected, choose Select All from the Edit menu, and choose Lock (Ctrl+H) from the Arrange menu. The selection handles dim around all objects to indicate they are locked in position.

Adding remaining text frames

In this section, you add three text frames for the remaining text elements. Specifically, the remaining text frames contain

- Headline for Article2
- Banner for page 2
- Closing message at the bottom of page 2

Begin by opening your newsletter document, if it isn't already open. Make sure that the rulers, tool palette, and graphics grid are visible. If necessary, scroll to the first page of the newsletter so the middle of the second column is visible. You will add the text frames in the order listed previously. All of the frames are unlinked and independent from one another. So the first step you need to take is to turn off Frame Links.

To add the headline for Article 2:

1 **Select the graphics tool, if necessary.** If any of the objects are selected in the document, click anywhere in the document to deselect them before you disable Frame Links.

2 **Choose Frame Links from the Options menu to turn it off.**

3 **Select the text tool.**

4   Switch from the text ruler to the graphics ruler using the Rulers dialog box.

5   Click and drag to create a text frame above the text of Article 2. Begin the text frame approximately 4.5 inches across and approximately 4 inches down, drag across to the 6.5-inch mark, then down to the 4.5-inch mark.

6   With the text insertion point blinking in the frame, type the following text, pressing ↵ after the first line:

> New Releases
> for the Holidays

7   Press Enter on the numeric keypad to select the frame.

8   Choose Center from the Alignment cascading menu in the Format menu.

9   Choose Times New Roman from the Font cascading menu and 18 Point from the Size cascading menu in the Format menu.

If you don't like the position of the frame, you can move it or resize it, as you would any other graphics object.

Now scroll to the top of the second page so you can add a banner. The banner, sometimes called a *folio*, identifies the newsletter, its date of issue, and the page number. To add the banner:

1   Switch to the graphics ruler using the Rulers dialog box.

2   Select the text tool.

3   Position the I-beam pointer above the first frame of Article 3, and click once. ClarisWorks creates a small text frame (see Figure 3-21).

4   Type the following text. (In step 8 you'll change the lowercase *L* to a bullet character.)

> Wine of the Month Club<space><lowercase L><space>Holiday
> Edition<space><lowercase L><space>page 2

The frame expands as you type to accommodate the text (see Figure 3-22).

5   Press Enter on the numeric keypad to select the frame.

6   Move the frame until its upper-left corner is flush with the upper-left corner of the page, and resize it to approximately 5.25 inches wide and 0.25 inches long.

7   Click inside the frame to switch to the text environment and to activate the frame.

8   Change the font size and style of each banner part, as follows:

Wine of the Month Club	Times New Roman Bold 14 point
<space>lowercase L<space>	Wingdings Plain 12 point
Holiday Edition	Times New Roman Plain 14 point
<space>lowercase L<space>	Wingdings Plain 12 point
page 2	Times New Roman Plain 12 point

9   When you are finished, click anywhere outside the frame.

The last text frame contains the closing message at the bottom of page 2. This time, create a different effect by changing the frame's fill color and text color.

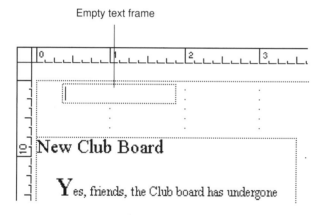

Figure 3-21   Empty text frame for the banner

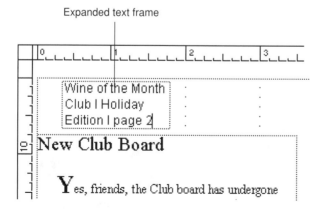

Figure 3-22   The text frame expands to accommodate the text

1   **Scroll to the bottom of the second page.**

2   **Select the text tool.**

3   **Click and drag to create a text frame at the bottom of the page.** Begin the text frame at 1.5 inches across and 16.25 inches down the document and drag across to 6 inches and down to 17 inches.

4   **Change the font type and size to Roman 18 point or any other font you want.**

5   **In the frame, type the following uppercase text, pressing ↵ after each line (except the last one):**

> WISHING YOU A VERY HAPPY
> HOLIDAY SEASON
> AND A PROSPEROUS NEW YEAR!

6   **Press Enter on the numeric keypad to select the frame.** The graphics tool becomes active and selection handles appear around the frame.

7   **Press Ctrl+\ to align the text in the center of the frame.** Ctrl+\ is the keyboard shortcut for the Center menu command from the Alignment cascading menu (Format menu).

8   **To change the fill color, click the fill color tool, and select Black from the fill color palette.** The text momentarily disappears.

9   **To change the text color, leave the frame selected, choose Text Color from the Format menu, and select White in the color palette.**

Figure 3-23 shows what your text frame should look like.

In this example, the fill color is black and the text color is white. If you have a color monitor and a color printer, you can create more lively combinations of fill and text colors. For example, to keep with the holiday theme of the newsletter, you can fill the frame with a light green color and change the text color to red.

TIP

> WISHING YOU A VERY HAPPY
> HOLIDAY SEASON
> AND A PROSPEROUS NEW YEAR!

Figure 3-23   The last text frame with fill and text color changed

You have just finished adding all of the text elements to your newsletter. Now you can move on to add the graphic elements.

TIP

At any time, you can spell-check the text within your frames. You don't even have to switch environments by selecting another tool to do so. Simply choose Check Document (Ctrl+=) from the Spelling cascading menu in the Edit menu. The Spelling dialog box appears. The spelling checker begins in the first frame and proceeds through each frame sequentially, whether or not the frames are linked, unlinked, locked, or unlocked, until the entire document is checked.

Adding graphics

The graphic elements that need to be added to the newsletter include clip art, design elements, and a diagram.

Before you continue, open the newsletter document, if it isn't already open, and make sure the tools, ruler, and graphics grid are visible. (If necessary, switch from the text ruler to the graphics ruler.)

Importing clip art

This section presents several different methods you can use to import clip art into your ClarisWorks documents.

There are three pieces of clip art used in the newsletter. The first, a picture of a champagne bottle popping open, appears to the right of the masthead at the top of the newsletter. The second, a picture of a wine glass and wine bottle, appears to the left of Article2's headline. Finally, the last piece of clip art is a design element that appears twice in the masthead, on either side of the word *Club*.

Clip art is available from many different sources. Users groups usually offer several different collections, or you can download clip art from bulletin board systems or online services. Some Windows applications, such as Corel Draw, include clip art libraries. You can also purchase clip art from commercial software companies. For example, the clip art used in this book comes from two commercial software sources: ClickArt Business Images from T/Maker and the Potpourri Kwikee InHouse PAL (Professional Art Library) from Multi-Ad Services, Inc. The ClickArt Business Images collection comes as separate PC Paintbrush (.PCX) files. The Kwikee InHouse PAL clip art files come on CD-ROM in encapsulated PostScript (.EPS) file format.

Most clip art comes in a .PCX, .BMP, or .EPS file format, which makes it very easy to use with any Windows application. Through the Claris XTND technology, ClarisWorks can easily import these and other graphics file formats.

(See the Appendix for information on XTND and importing files.) In addition to importing clip art into a ClarisWorks document, you can copy the art from within another application and paste it into the document.

The champagne bottle

In this section, you import the clip art image of a champagne bottle into the newsletter. In this case, the champagne bottle is a Windows MetaFile (.WMF) located on CD-ROM. The steps you follow give you a general idea of how to import clip art into your newsletter document from another disk, either CD-ROM, another external disk drive, or a floppy.

To import the clip art, use the Insert command in the File menu, as you did earlier in this chapter to insert the contents of a Microsoft Word document into the text frames for Article3. After importing the clip art, you reduce its scale, and position it in the masthead area next to the newsletter title.

If you have another disk drive, or a CD-ROM drive, make sure that the disk drive is properly connected to your PC, and that the power is on. Insert the disk containing your clip art into the drive, and follow these steps:

1   **With your newsletter document open and active, scroll to the upper-right corner of the first page.**

2   **Select the graphics tool from the tool palette and click once in the upper-right corner of the document to set the insertion point.**

3   **Choose Insert from the File menu.**

4   **In the Insert dialog box, choose "Windows MetaFile (*.wmf)" from the List Files of Type drop-down menu.** If your clip art is a different file format, make the appropriate choice from the drop-down menu.

5   **Locate the clip art file you want to insert by navigating to the appropriate disk and directory.**

6   **Select the file from the file list, and click OK.**

ClarisWorks inserts the clip art where you last clicked in the document. The clip art is selected, indicated by selection handles, and can now be manipulated as any graphics object. If necessary, drag the picture into the document so you can see it entirely.

If you import clip art or any other graphics file as .CGM, .PCT, or .WMF, the Ungroup Picture command becomes available in the Arrange menu. After selecting the imported graphic, choose Ungroup Picture to work with each element of the picture as a separate graphic. The Ungroup Picture command is not available for graphics imported as .EPS, .PCX, .BMP, or .TIF.

TIP

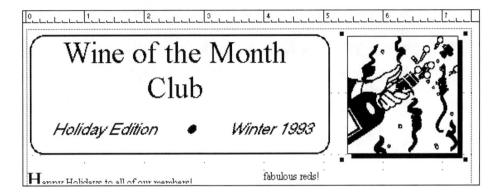

Figure 3-24   Champagne bottle clip art in position

The clip art may be too big to fit in its position next to the masthead. To scale the picture and move it into its proper position:

1   With the picture selected, choose Scale Selection from the Options menu. The Scale Selection dialog box opens.

2   Type 50 **in both boxes to set the horizontal and vertical scales to 50% respectively, and click OK.** The picture is reduced to half of its original size.

3   With the picture still selected, drag it to the upper-right corner of the document, just to the right of the masthead.

When the picture is properly scaled and positioned, the top of your document looks like Figure 3-24.

If you want to align both the masthead and clip art objects so their bottom edges are precisely lined up, use the Align Objects dialog box. Before you do, be sure to unlock the masthead object by selecting it and choosing Unlock (Shift+Ctrl+H) from the Arrange menu. You cannot align, or otherwise modify, objects that are locked.

The wine glass and wine bottle

The process of importing the clip art picture of a wine glass and wine bottle is very similar to importing the champagne bottle picture. However, this time, the clip art comes from the ClickArt Business Images collection in .PCX file format on disk. The example gives you a general idea of how to import clip art from a file on your hard disk into the newsletter document.

As before, use the Insert command to import this clip art. After importing it, reduce the picture's scale, and position it in the second column of the newsletter, to the left of Article2's headline.

To import the picture of the wine glass and wine bottle:

1   **With your newsletter document open and active, scroll to the middle of the first page so you can see the second column.**

2   **Select the graphics tool from the tool palette, and click once to the left of Article2's headline to set the insertion point.**

3   **Choose Insert from the File menu.**

4   **In the Insert dialog box, choose "PC Paint Brush Bitmap (*.pcx)" from the List Files of Type drop-down menu.**

5   **Locate the clip art file you want to insert by navigating to the appropriate disk and directory.**

6   **Select the file from the file list, and click OK.** ClarisWorks inserts the clip art where you last clicked in the document.

Figure 3-25 shows the clip art just inserted into the newsletter document.
As before, the clip art is too big to fit into position. Follow the steps you used to scale the champagne bottle picture to reduce this picture by 50% horizontally and vertically. When the picture is scaled, move it into position just to the left of the headline text. Figure 3-26 shows the picture properly positioned in the document.

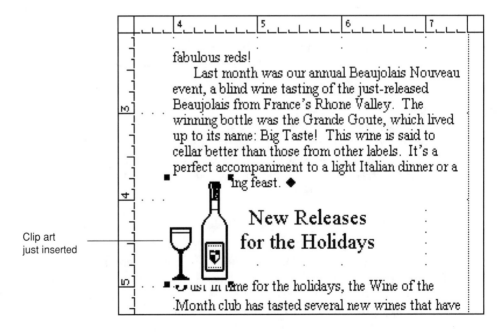

Clip art
just inserted

Figure 3-25   Wine glass and wine bottle clip art inserted into the newsletter document

Figure 3-26 Wine glass and wine bottle clip art in position

The masthead design elements

In this section, you add a clip art image of a design element to your document. The element appears twice in the masthead. After importing it, you duplicate the graphic and move both of them into proper position.

In this case, let's assume the design element is an individual clip art file that you are viewing in another Windows graphics application (such as PC Paintbrush or Corel Draw). This example gives you a general idea of how to copy clip art from another Windows application to the Clipboard and paste it into a ClarisWorks document. (Clipboard is an application that comes with Windows. It is in the Main program group.)

Before you begin, you should have both applications (your graphics program and ClarisWorks) running. To copy clip art from another graphics program into the newsletter document:

1 **With the newsletter document open and active, scroll to the top of the first page so the masthead is visible.**

2 **Select the graphics tool, and click once in the masthead to set the insertion point.**

3 **Press Alt+Tab to switch to the other application (such as PC Paintbrush).**

4 **With the design element visible in the application window, select it and choose Copy from the Edit menu.** The design element is copied to the Clipboard. Figure 3-27 shows the design element in the Clipboard Viewer.

5 **Press Alt+Tab to switch to ClarisWorks.**

6 **Make your newsletter document active, if necessary, and choose Paste (Ctrl+V) from the Edit menu.** The design element is pasted from the Clipboard at the place you last clicked the mouse. Selection handles appear around the pasted image. With the clip art image selected, drag it to the left of the word *Club,* and position it as shown in Figure 3-28.

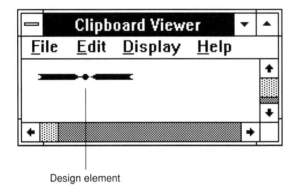

Design element

Figure 3-27   Clipboard Viewer showing masthead design element

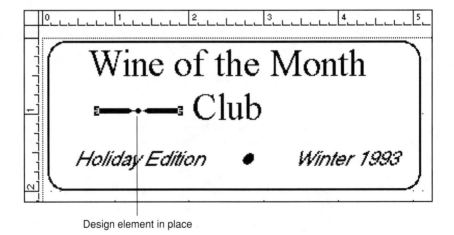

Design element in place

Figure 3-28   First design element in place in masthead

Since the design element appears twice in the final masthead, you need to duplicate the image. Do so now by choosing Duplicate (Ctrl+D) from the Edit menu, by copying and pasting the image, or by simply choosing Paste from the Edit menu (if the image is still in the Clipboard).

Note   *The Duplicate command does not use the Clipboard; the Copy command does.*

With the duplicate image selected, drag it to the right of the word *Club* to move it into position. To line up both design elements:

1 **Select them both by Shift-clicking them.**
2 **Choose Align Objects (Shift+Ctrl+K) from the Arrange menu.**
3 **In the Align Objects dialog box, select "Align bottom edges" from the "Top to Bottom" options, and click OK.**

Figure 3-29 shows both design elements properly aligned and in place in the masthead.

In addition to these clip art design elements, the newsletter includes another design element: dotted lines, which you create using the drawing tools.

Figure 3-29   Both design elements in place in the masthead

Drawing dotted lines

The process of drawing dotted lines involves changing line width and pen pattern, and drawing the lines with the line tool.

In this section, you draw two dotted lines in the newsletter. The first appears between the masthead area and the text on the first page. The second appears before the closing message on the last page. To draw the first line:

1   **Select the line tool in the tool palette.**

2   **Position the drawing pointer between the masthead and the text and against the left margin of the first page.**

3   **Holding down the Shift key, click and drag across the document to draw a straight line from the left margin to the right margin.**

4   **With the line selected, choose 2 pt. from the line width menu (in the tool palette) to make the line thicker.**

5   **With the line still selected, choose the pen pattern shown in Figure 3-30.**

Choosing any pen pattern that is comprised of vertical lines produces a dotted line. If you want the dots in the line to be smaller, choose the pen pattern to the right of the one shown in Figure 3-30. If you want the dots to be smaller and closer together, choose the pen pattern below the one shown in Figure 3-30.

With the first dotted line completed, copy and paste it onto the second page so it divides the text from the closing message on the bottom of the page. Figure 3-31 shows both dotted lines in position.

To see dotted lines more clearly in your document, choose Hide Graphics Grid from the Options menu to hide the graphics grid, as shown in Figure 3-31.

TIP

Pen pattern

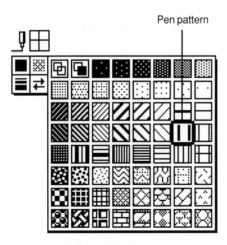

Figure 3-30   The selected pen pattern produces a dotted line

Figure 3-31   Both dotted lines in position (first page—top—and second page—bottom)

Creating a diagram

The last graphic element in the newsletter is a diagram that illustrates the organization of the club board members (see Figure 3-32).

You can use the techniques in this section to create other types of diagrams such as

- Business organization charts
- Genealogical family trees
- Floor plans
- Process flow diagrams
- Flow charts

The newsletter organization chart appears on the second page and supplements the text of Article3. It is composed of several different objects: a rectangle, five rounded rectangles, four lines, and six small text frames. The rectangle serves as a border for the other diagram elements. The five rounded rectangles correspond to each of the five board positions illustrated in the diagram. The

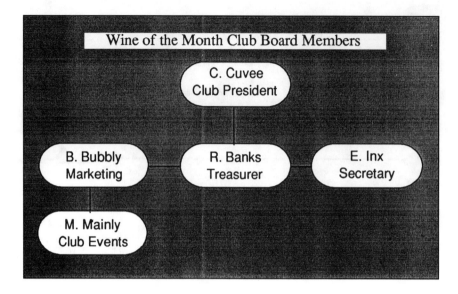

Figure 3-32   Newsletter organization chart

four lines show the relationship between and reporting structure of the five positions. Small text frames are used to add the board member names and their positions inside of the rounded rectangles. Finally, a text frame at the top of the diagram shows its title.

Begin with the left half of the second page visible. The diagram goes below Article3's first frame and to the left of the third frame. Make sure the graphics grid, tools, and graphics ruler are showing on the screen. Now you are ready to create the rectangles.

1   **Select the rectangle tool.**

2   **Click and drag to draw the rectangle.** Begin the rectangle against the left margin at approximately 12.25 inches down, and drag across to 4.5 inches and down to 15 inches.

3   **If necessary, choose Show Graphics Grid from the Options menu to turn on the grid, and choose the transparent fill pattern from the fill pattern palette (see Figure 3-33).**

4   **Now select the rounded rectangle tool, and click and drag to draw the first rounded rectangle anywhere on top of the rectangle you just drew.** Make the rounded rectangle 1.25 inches wide and 0.5 inches long.

5   **Release the mouse, and drag the selected object to the position shown in Figure 3-34.**

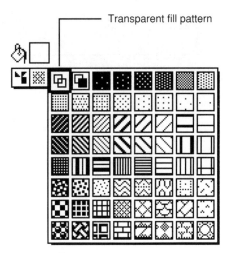

Figure 3-33   Transparent fill pattern

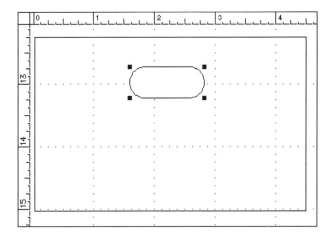

Figure 3-34   First rounded rectangle in position

Now you are going to duplicate this rounded rectangle four times to create the remaining rounded rectangles. With the object still selected, press Ctrl+D four times. Your screen shows five rounded rectangles of equal size layered and staggered one on top of the other.

One by one, click and drag each rounded rectangle to the positions shown in Figure 3-35. Use the "Align centers" option in the Align Objects dialog box to precisely align the objects with one another along their centers.

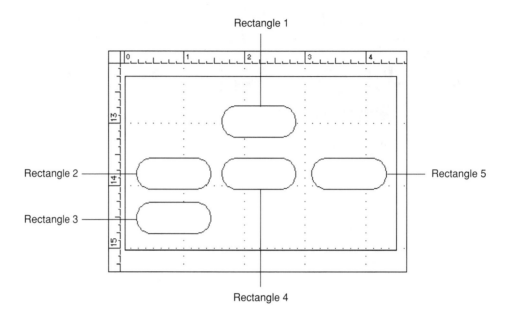

Figure 3-35   The five rounded rectangles in place

To draw the four lines, double-click the line tool to lock it, and hold down the Shift key as you draw a straight line between each of the rounded rectangles. Use the finished diagram shown in Figure 3-32 as a guide for line placement.

Now, add the names and titles of the board members to the diagram using the text tool. Before doing, you need to change some of the preset text settings. The diagram text, except for the diagram title, appears in Arial 10 point. Select the graphics tool, and use the Font and Size cascading menus of the Format menu to change the font type and size to Arial 10 point. Also, notice that each text element in the diagram appears centered in the rectangles. So, choose Center (Ctrl+\) from the Alignment cascading menu in the Format menu.

Because you are going to use the text tool repeatedly, double-click it in the tool palette to lock it. Now begin to add the text frames.

1   **Click in the top rounded rectangle.** A small text frame appears with the text insertion point blinking in the center of it.

2   **Type the following, pressing ↵ after the first line:**

> C. Cuvee
> Club President

3   **Repeat steps 1 and 2 to enter the following text inside each rectangle:**

Rectangle 2:	B. Bubbly
	Marketing
Rectangle 3:	M. Mainly
	Club Events
Rectangle 4:	R. Banks
	Treasurer
Rectangle 5:	E. Inx
	Secretary

4   When you are finished, press Enter on the numeric keypad to select the last text frame and select the graphics tool.

The text frames need to be repositioned and sized so they each fit neatly inside the rounded rectangles. With the graphics tool selected, click each text frame in succession, and drag and resize them so they are in the positions shown in Figure 3-36.

You are nearly finished with the diagram. You only need to add the diagram title and apply a different fill pattern to the large rectangle around the diagram. Select the text tool now. Before adding the title, change the font type and size to Times New Roman 12 point using the Font and Size cascading menus in the Format menu. Then, click and drag to create a text frame at the top of the diagram that is approximately 3.5 inches wide and 0.25 inches long. Type the title of the diagram (*Wine of the Month Club Board Members*) and press Enter on the numeric keypad to finish. (You may need to move the text frame so it is centered between the left and right edges of the outside rectangle.)

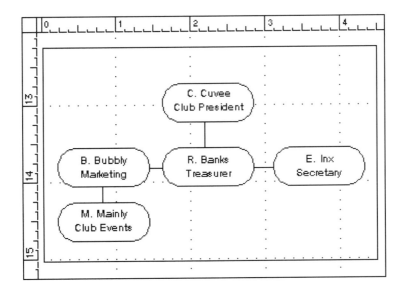

Figure 3-36   Text frames in position within rounded rectangles

Now click the large outside rectangle to select it and choose a fill pattern from the fill pattern palette. Notice that the rounded rectangles and the text frames inside the diagram are not affected by the new fill pattern. This is because the large outside rectangle is *behind* the other objects in the diagram, since you drew it first. If you had drawn the large rectangle last, or if you moved it to the front, filling it with a pattern would have covered up the other objects.

Before moving on, you should group the elements of your diagram. Hold down the Ctrl key as you drag the arrow pointer around the diagram. By holding down the Ctrl key, you select all of the objects that intersect the selection rectangle. Choose Group (Ctrl+G) from the Arrange menu.

With all of your graphic elements in place in the newsletter, the next section describes how to add the spreadsheet elements and complete your newsletter.

Adding spreadsheet elements

In this section you will add the two spreadsheet elements to the newsletter: a table derived from a spreadsheet frame and a chart based on financial data in a spreadsheet frame. Because the chart is based on spreadsheet data, you must create a spreadsheet in order to produce the chart. When you are finished adding these elements, your newsletter will be complete.

Both of the spreadsheet elements appear on the first page of the newsletter. Open your newsletter document if it isn't already open, and scroll until the bottom of the first page is visible.

Creating the table

Figure 3-37 shows the table you create in this section. The table supplements the text of Article2, which discusses new wine releases for the holidays.

You create the table by creating an empty spreadsheet frame and entering information in it. Then you format and sort the information as you want it to appear in the table. Finally, you change a few display options so the spreadsheet looks more like a table than a spreadsheet.

Vintner	Year	Varietal	Retail Price
Bubbles	1991	Champagne	$10.00
Grand Goute	1992	Beaujolais	$15.00
Ione Wines	1990	Zinfandel	$7.00
Temptation	1990	Cabernet	$20.00
ZZyxx du Vin	1991	Pouilly-Fuisse	$18.50

Figure 3-37   Newsletter table

Creating the first spreadsheet frame

To create the first spreadsheet frame for your table:

1   **Select the spreadsheet tool in the tool palette.**

2   **Click and drag to create a spreadsheet frame in the lower-right corner of the first page.** The frame should include column headings A through D, and row headings 1 through 8 (see Figure 3-38). Don't worry if the frame overlaps the text; you will correct that later when you change column widths and display options.

3   **Release the mouse.** Cell A1 is selected and ClarisWorks switches to the spreadsheet environment. Above the graphics ruler at the top of the window is the entry bar area, as shown in Figure 3-38.

4   **In order to work with a larger view of the spreadsheet frame, choose Open Frame from the Window menu.**

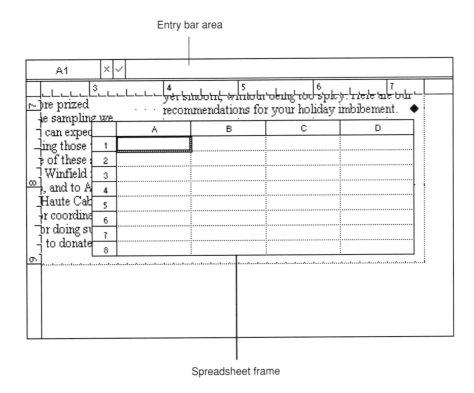

Figure 3-38   Drawing the spreadsheet frame for the table

The spreadsheet frame opens in full view in a separate window on the screen. Now, with cell A1 selected, add the information shown in Figure 3-39. You can either enter data in each cell a column at a time or a row at a time. If you enter data in a column at a time (that is, enter column A's data, then column B's, and so on), press ↵ after each entry to move one cell down. If you enter data in a row at a time (that is, enter row 1's data, then row 2's data, and so on), press Tab after each entry to move to the next cell to the right.

Now, change the font type and size of the data in the spreadsheet frame. To change the font, press Ctrl+A to select all of the cells, and use the Font and Size cascading menus in the Format menu to change the font type and size, respectively. In the final table, the data appears in MS Sans Serif 10 point. If you want, you can choose another font that distinguishes the table data from the rest of the newsletter. When you are finished, click anywhere in the spreadsheet to deselect the cell range.

As you can see in Figure 3-39, columns B and D are wider than they need to be. You should resize columns B and D so they are just wide enough to display the column titles. To narrow column B, position the cursor in the column heading area on the line dividing columns B and C. Notice that the cursor changes to the resize pointer. Click and drag to the left until column B is the

	A	B	C	D
1	Vintner	Year	Varietal	Retail Price
2				
3	Grand Goute	1992	Beaujolais	15
4	Bubbles	1991	Champagne	10
5	Temptation	1990	Cabernet	20
6	Zzyxx du Vin	1991	Pouilly-Fuisse	18.5
7	Ione Wines	1990	Zinfandel	7

Figure 3-39   The table's data

	A	B	C	D	E
1	Vintner	Year	Varietal	Retail Price	
2					
3	Grand Goute	1992	Beaujolais	15	
4	Bubbles	1991	Champagne	10	
5	Temptation	1990	Cabernet	20	
6	Zzyxx du Vin	1991	Pouilly-Fuisse	18.5	
7	Ione Wines	1990	Zinfandel	7	
8					
9					
10					

Figure 3-40   Spreadsheet columns resized to proper widths

width you want. Center the data in column B by selecting the column and pressing Ctrl+\. Now narrow column D; this time, position the cursor in the column heading area on the line dividing columns D and E. When you are finished resizing the columns, your spreadsheet should look similar to Figure 3-40.

Formatting the spreadsheet data

You need to make two formatting changes to the spreadsheet frame data. First, you need to change the format of the data in the Retail Price column so it appears as currency. Second, you need to add a border underneath the first row to make the titles of each column stand out from the rest of the table.

To change format of the numbers in column D (Retail Price):

1   **With the crossbar pointer positioned over column heading D, click once to select the entire column.**

2   **Choose Number from the Format menu, or press Shift+Ctrl+N.** The Numeric dialog box opens (see Figure 3-41).

3   **Click Currency in the Number area of the dialog box, as shown in Figure 3-41, and click OK.**

All of the numbers in column D now appear in currency format, with a dollar sign ($) preceding the number, and two decimal places showing.

To add a border underneath the titles of each column of information:

1   **With the crossbar pointer positioned over row heading 1, click once to select the entire row.**

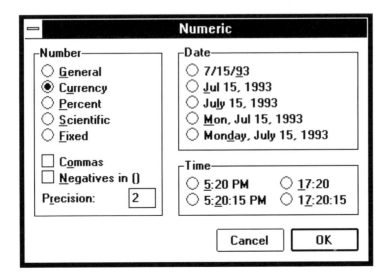

Figure 3-41   Setting numbers to appear in currency format

2 **Choose Borders from the Format menu.** The Borders dialog box opens.

3 **In the dialog box, click Bottom to select that option, and click OK.**

A solid line delineates the text in row 1 (the column titles). With the formatting changes completed, your spreadsheet should now look like the one shown in Figure 3-42.

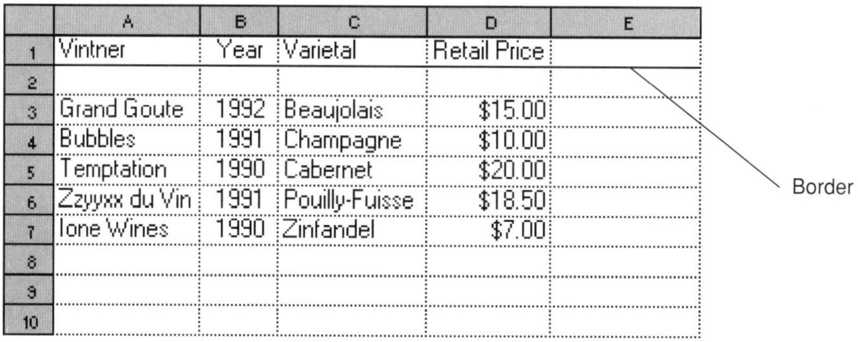

	A	B	C	D	E
1	Vintner	Year	Varietal	Retail Price	
2					
3	Grand Goute	1992	Beaujolais	$15.00	
4	Bubbles	1991	Champagne	$10.00	
5	Temptation	1990	Cabernet	$20.00	
6	Zzyyxx du Vin	1991	Pouilly-Fuisse	$18.50	
7	Ione Wines	1990	Zinfandel	$7.00	
8					
9					
10					

Figure 3-42 Formatting changes complete

Sorting the spreadsheet data

Now you need to sort the information in the table so the vintners are listed in ascending alphabetical order, from A to Z. To do this, you use the Sort dialog box to specify

- Range of cells to sort
- Order key
- Sort order
- Sort direction

In this case, the desired sort range is from A3 to D7. If you select a range of only A3 to A7 instead, the names of the five vintners will sort alphabetically, but the associated data—year, varietal, and retail price—will not sort with them. Always make sure that you include all of the associated data in the sort range.

The *order key* determines the cell address to begin the sort. In this case, the order key is cell A3. Only one order key needs to be specified, because you are only going to do a first order sort. It is possible to do second and third order sorts in ClarisWorks by specifying second and third order keys in the dialog box, but this is only necessary if the first order key contains like values. In other words, second and third order sorts let you sort up to three categories of information. For example, if your table showed Bubbles the vintner listed twice in column A, and column B showed two different years for Bubbles, you could specify a second order key to sort first by vintner, and then by year. If this discussion doesn't make sense to you, experiment with different sort order keys in your spreadsheet. Sorting spreadsheet cells, like sorting database records, is much easier to do than to explain.

The sort order used in your spreadsheet is ascending, as opposed to descending, which sorts in reverse alphabetical order, from Z to A. The sort direction determines the direction to sort from the order key, either vertically or horizontally. In this case, the sort direction is vertical and the information will sort from cell A3 down. (With a horizontal direction, the information sorts from cell A3 across.)

To sort the information in your table:

1   **Click in cell A3, and drag across to select the range A3 through D7.**

2   **Choose Sort (Ctrl+J) from the Calculate menu.** The Sort dialog box opens (see Figure 3-43).

The dialog box shows the correct cell range, order key, sort order, and sort direction selected. This is because ClarisWorks is preset to use the range of cells you select before opening the dialog box. It is also preset to specify the first cell in the range as the order key and to sort in ascending order and in a vertical direction.

3   **Because the preset settings are correct for the sort, click OK to sort the spreadsheet information.** When you are finished, column A information is sorted correctly, and the information associated with each vintner rearranges accordingly.

Now you are ready to change display options and complete your table. Before doing so, press Ctrl+W to close the open spreadsheet frame and return to the newsletter document.

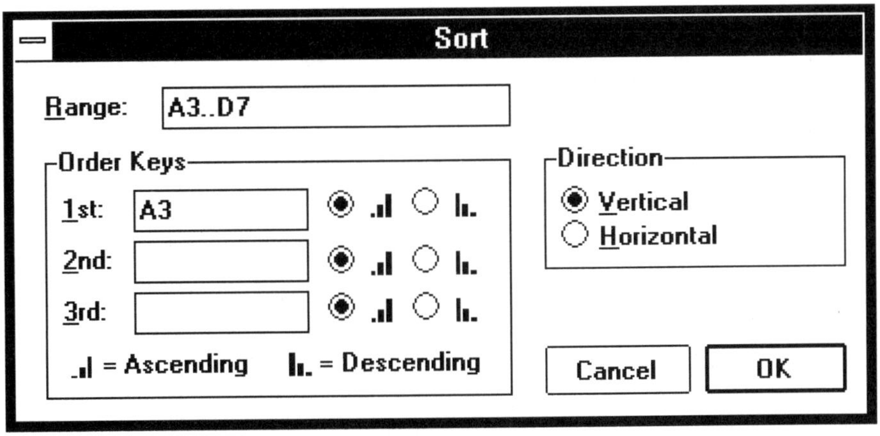

Figure 3-43   Sort dialog box

Changing display options

To change some of the spreadsheet frame's display options:

1 Press Enter on the numeric keypad to select the spreadsheet frame.

2 Open the Display dialog box by choosing Modify Frame (Shift+Ctrl+I) from the Options menu.

3 In the dialog box, click the following options to uncheck them: Grid Lines, Column Headers, Row Headers.

4 Click OK for your changes to take effect.

You can also open the Display dialog box by holding down the Ctrl key as you double-click the selected spreadsheet frame.

TIP

These display changes remove the grid lines that form to show each cell. The column and row headers also disappear. Your finished table should look like the one shown in Figure 3-44. You may need to move and resize your spreadsheet frame/table so it is properly positioned in the second column below Article2's text frame.

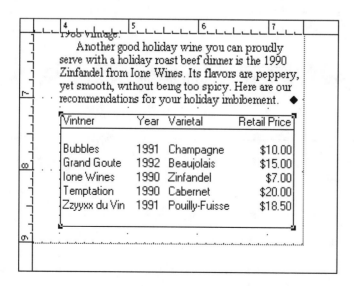

Figure 3-44   The spreadsheet frame/table in position

Making the chart

The other spreadsheet element that appears in the newsletter is a chart. You can create a spreadsheet chart in any ClarisWorks document type using a spreadsheet frame.

The chart (see Figure 3-45) supplements the text of Article1, which discusses the club's revenue increases over the previous year. It appears in the middle of the first column on page 1, between the first two text frames of Article1.

To make the chart, you create an empty spreadsheet frame and enter information in it. Then you select the data to chart and make a three-dimensional stacked bar chart. Finally, you move the chart into position and make a few modifications to it.

The spreadsheet frame itself will not be visible in the newsletter; when you are finished, you will move the chart over the frame so the chart hides it.

Before moving on, make sure your newsletter document is open and the rulers, tools, and graphics grid are visible.

TIP

Instead of creating a spreadsheet frame and charting its data, you can make a chart within a spreadsheet document and copy and paste it into the newsletter document. However, doing so breaks the link between the spreadsheet data and the chart. That is, if you changed the data in the spreadsheet, the changes will not be updated in the chart after you paste it into the newsletter. You can also create a chart in a spreadsheet frame opened in full view, then resize the frame to show only the chart.

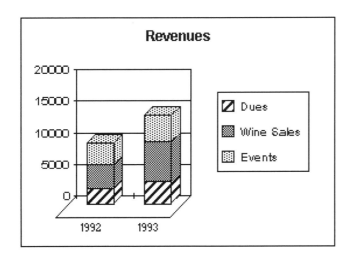

Figure 3-45   Chart appearing in the newsletter

Creating the second spreadsheet frame

To create the second spreadsheet frame for your chart:

1   **Select the spreadsheet tool in the tool palette.**

2   **Click and drag to create a spreadsheet frame between the two text frames in the first column on the first page (see Figure 3-46).** The frame should include column headings A through C, and row headings 1 through 6.

3   **Release the mouse.** Cell A1 is selected and ClarisWorks switches to the spreadsheet environment (see Figure 3-46).

4   **Enter the data into the frame, as shown in Figure 3-47. Press Tab to move across the spreadsheet one cell at a time; press ◄┘ to move down one cell at a time.**

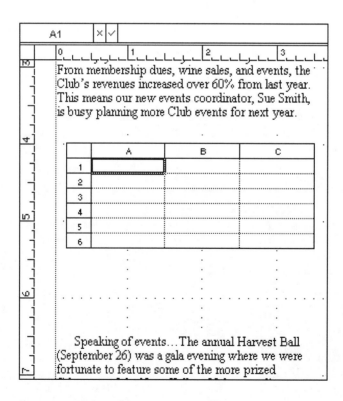

Figure 3-46   Drawing the second spreadsheet frame for the chart

	A	B	C
1	Funding	1992	1993
2			
3	Dues	2500	3750
4	Wine Sales	3885	6061
5	Events	3250	4250

Figure 3-47   Chart data

Since the frame itself does not appear in the newsletter, you don't need to resize any columns or make any other changes to it.

Charting the spreadsheet data

The process of making a chart in ClarisWorks is simple: select the data you want to chart, and use the Make Chart dialog box to choose a chart type and set options. To chart the data you just entered in the frame:

1   **Click in cell A3, and drag down and across to select cells A3 through C5.** You include the row titles (Dues, Wine Sales, and Events) in the selection so the chart's legend includes them to identify the sources of funding.

2   **Choose Make Chart from the Options menu, or press Ctrl+M.** The Make Chart dialog box opens and lists options for a pie chart (the preset chart type).

3   **In the dialog box, click the stacked bar chart icon in the Categories area, as shown in Figure 3-48.** The Options area of the dialog box changes to show those options that apply to stacked bar charts.

4   **Check the 3-Dimensional option to select it.** If you have a color monitor, leave the Color option checked. Otherwise, uncheck the Color option.

5   **Leave the other options as is, and click OK.**

ClarisWorks draws the chart, places it in its own frame in the document, and switches to the graphics environment. The chart is automatically selected. You can immediately modify it as you would any other graphics object.

At this point, you can change any of the chart's options, or change the chart type to a line chart, for example. To do this, open the Make Chart dialog box by double-clicking the chart, by choosing Modify Chart from the Options menu, or by pressing Shift+Ctrl+I.

Stacked bar chart

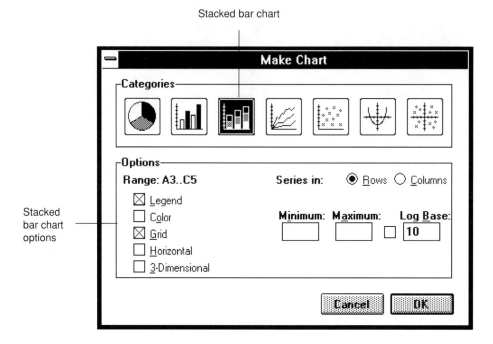

Stacked bar chart options

Figure 3-48   The Make Chart dialog box with stacked bar chart selected

Any text or number formatting changes you make in a spreadsheet frame affects the way text and numbers appear in the chart.

TIP

Modifying the chart

ClarisWorks automatically places a chart in a frame that has a preset size. In this case, the chart is too big to fit in the space between the two text frames. The first modification you need to make is to resize the chart. Since the chart is already selected, click the lower-right selection handle, and drag it into the chart until the chart is approximately 3.5 inches wide and 2.5 inches long.

Now move the chart into position: drag it so it hides the spreadsheet frame and is centered between the two text frames in the first column. Figure 3-49 shows the chart's proper size and position.

If you want to change any of the data in the spreadsheet frame, you need to move the chart behind the spreadsheet. To do this, select the chart, and choose

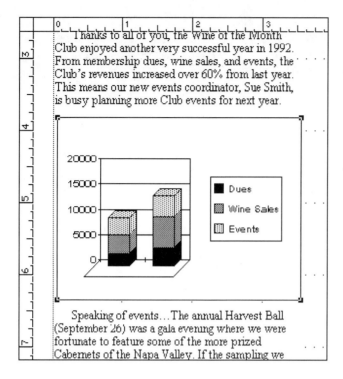

Figure 3-49   Chart in position

Move Backward from the Arrange menu. The chart moves to the back layer so you can view the spreadsheet frame. Any changes you make in the spreadsheet frame are immediately reflected in the chart.

The other modifications to the chart include adding text labels to the X (horizontal) axis and a chart title and changing the pattern of one of the chart elements. X-axis labels identify which stacked bar corresponds with which series of data (in this case, 1992 and 1993). The chart title appears inside the chart's frame, just above the chart's grid. The X-axis labels and the title are actually text frames. To add them to the chart:

1   If the spreadsheet frame is in front of the chart, select it and choose Move To Back from the Arrange menu.

2   Select the text tool.

3   Change the font type, size, and style using the cascading menus in the Format menu. For example, change the font to Arial Bold 12 point.

4   To add the chart's title, click in the upper region of the chart. An empty text frame appears.

If you type **Revenues** *in cell A2 and include the cell in your selection to make the chart, the title Revenues will automatically appear in the chart.*

TIP

5   Type Revenues **and press Enter on the numeric keypad to select the title's text frame.**

6   **Drag the text frame containing the title until it is in the position you want.**

7   **To add text labels on the X-axis, double-click the text tool to select and lock it.**

8   **Change the font to Arial Plain 10 point, or any other font you choose.**

9   **Click in the chart below the left stacked bar, and type** 1992; **click below the right stacked bar, and type** 1993.

10 **Select the graphics tool, resize the labels' text frames, and drag them into position.**

Your chart should look like the one shown in Figure 3-50.

Now you are ready to change the pattern of one of the chart's elements. To do this, you use the pattern boxes in the chart's legend in conjunction with the fill pattern palette in the tool palette. In this sequence of steps, you change the pattern of the Dues chart element in both stacked bars.

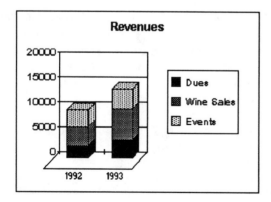

Figure 3-50 Chart with X-axis labels and chart title in position

Figure 3-51 Chart legend with the Dues chart element selected

1 **In the legend, click once inside the small box to the left of the word *Dues*.** A tiny white circle appears inside the Dues legend box indicating that it is the selected chart element. Figure 3-51 shows the chart's legend at 200% magnification with the Dues chart element selected.

2 **Click the fill pattern tool, and drag to tear the fill pattern palette off of the tool palette.**

3 **Select a different pattern by clicking it in the fill pattern palette.**

4 **When you are finished, click the fill pattern palette's close box.**

Experiment with different patterns until you find the one you want. Each time you select a different pattern, the chart element box in the legend and each of the chart elements in the chart itself change to reflect the new pattern.

You can also change the color of any chart's pie slice, bar, line, or scatter point using the same technique. In the legend, simply click the box of the chart element you want to change, and choose a new color from the fill color palette.

TIP

You don't have to tear off the pattern palette to change a chart element. However, having the palette open on the screen makes it easier to experiment with different choices. Don't forget that you can tear off any of the fill and pen palettes and drag them wherever you want on the screen.

You can also change the chart's border, background color, or fill pattern by selecting the chart and using the fill and pen tools in the tool palette. For the newsletter chart, however, just use the preset settings: black hairline border, white fill color, and opaque fill pattern.

Summary

Your newsletter is now complete and ready to print or save for later use. You can print your newsletter on two separate pages; if your printer supports it, you can use the Manual Feed option in the Print Setup dialog box to print the newsletter on one double-sided page by manually turning the page over.

You can merge your newsletter document with names and addresses from a database document. By printing your newsletter double-sided on one page and merging it with a database document, you can make your newsletter a self-mailing document. For example, instead of the closing message text frame at the bottom of page 2, you can create a text frame to contain names and addresses merged from a database document. The next chapter describes how to create database documents and how to merge the data with other documents, such as your newsletter.

Chapter Four

Managing Personal Records

About this chapter

This chapter focuses on using the database environment to manage personal records. The techniques used in this chapter are also appropriate for business applications.

In this chapter, you create a database document for storing and retrieving names, addresses, and birthdays of personal friends. After creating the database document, you use a database layout to modify the arrangement of information and generate a list. You will also learn how to create mailing labels, enhanced by the use of graphics. The final section of the chapter describes how to merge database information with text documents and text frames.

Creating the personal database

In this section, you will create a ClarisWorks database document for personal or home use. The structure of the document—that is, the field names and field types—and the techniques you use to work with the document can be used for storing and retrieving any type of information. For example, other personal database documents can contain

- Phone numbers
- Home inventory

- Checkbook tracking
- Books, CDs, or software
- Account payments
- Wine cellar management

The sample database document, which is called Friends.CWK, contains the names, addresses, and birthdays of ten people. In database terminology, the document contains ten records, each of which contains fields to store the name, address, and birthday information. As you remember, a field is a category of information. A *field type* determines the type of information a field can contain, such as text, numbers, dates, or times.

The sample database document contains fictitious names, addresses, and birthdays. Instead of using the sample data, you can enter real names, addresses, and birthdays of your own friends.

To begin, you create a new database document and define the database structure (field names and field types). Then, with your fields defined, you enter data into records. Start now by launching ClarisWorks for Windows and create a new database document by choosing Database in the New dialog box.

Defining the fields

As soon as you create a new database document, you see the Define Fields dialog box shown in Figure 4-1. This is where you define the structure of your database

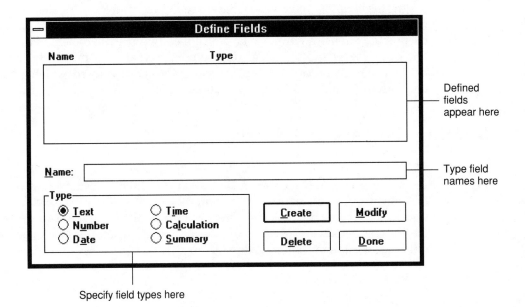

Figure 4-1   Define Fields dialog box

by giving each field a name and specifying the type of information the field should contain.

With the Define Fields dialog box open on your screen, follow these steps to define the fields listed in Table 4-1.

1   In the Name area of the dialog box, type Name.

2   The preset field type is Text, the correct type for the Name field, so click Create, or press ↵, to create the Name field.

3   Repeat steps 1 and 2 to create the Street, City, State, and Zip fields, which are also text fields, using the field names listed in Table 4-1. The top region of the dialog box lists the field names and types you've defined so far.

4   In the Name area of the dialog box, type Birthdate.

5   In the Type area, click Date (or press Alt+a), then click Create.

6   When you are finished, click Done to close the dialog box.

Table 4-1   Friends.CWK Database Structure

Field Name	*Field Type*
Name	Text
Street	Text
City	Text
State	Text
Zip	Text
Birthdate	Date

The new database document shows the first blank record, which consists of the fields you just defined, and positions the text insertion point in the first field (Name, in this case). The *selection bar,* a solid vertical line running along the left edge of the document, indicates that the record is active, or current. Figure 4-2 shows what your screen should look like.

The document is preset to show in Browse view (Browse is checked in the Layout menu). Browse, one of three database views available in ClarisWorks, is where you enter and edit data in records and view the records. (See "Database Documents" section in Chapter 1 for details on viewing database documents.)

The document is also preset to show in List View (which is also checked in the Layout menu). List View, an option of viewing your data in Browse, enables you to see all of the records as a list in the document window. When List View and Page View (Window menu) are turned off, only one record appears in the window at a time. The difference between turning List View on or off is not apparent until you enter data and add more records.

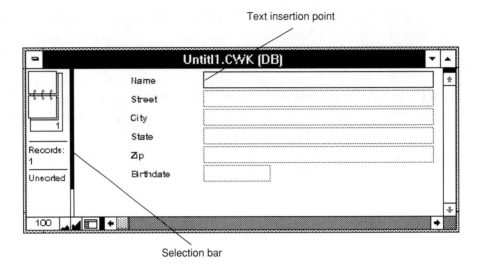

Figure 4-2   The first blank record appears in the document

Entering data

With your fields defined and the first blank record appearing in the window, you are ready to enter data. In the sample database, you enter a combination of alphanumeric characters into the text fields and dates into the date field.

Entering the first record's data

If the text insertion point is not blinking in the first field, click anywhere in the Name field to activate the field and set the insertion point. If the record is selected (highlighted), press Tab to activate the first field. To type the data in the fields of the first record:

1 **With the text insertion point blinking in the Name field, type** Nelson Barrister.

2 **To move to the next field, press Tab, or click in the Street field.**

3 **Type** 767 Madison **in the Street field.**

4 **Press Tab, or click in the City field.**

5 **Type** New York, **and press Tab.**

6 **Type** NY **in the State field, and press Tab.**

7 **Type** 10011 **in the Zip field, and press Tab.**

8 **In the Birthdate field, type** 4/15/50. You must enter the date in the Birthdate field in a format that ClarisWorks supports. (See Table 1-2 in Chapter 1 for a list of supported date formats.) Date fields are preset to show dates as mm/dd/yy.

9   When you are finished, press Enter on the numeric keypad to select the record, or leave the text insertion point blinking at the end of the Birthdate field.

As you enter the data, all of the standard text editing capabilities are available to you, including Cut, Copy, Paste, and Clear. If you make a mistake in one of the fields, press Shift+Tab to move up through the fields one at a time, or press Tab to move down one field at a time. To move to the end of a line in a field, press Ctrl+Down arrow; to move to the beginning of a line, press Ctrl+Up arrow.

If you press ↵ in a field, ClarisWorks inserts a new line in the field and expands the field entry area accordingly. In this way, you can enter multiple lines of data, or even paragraphs, in one field.

Note   *You can enter up to 510 characters in one text field. However, changing the font type or style in a field takes 20 characters off of this limit for each change.*

Now you are ready to add more records to your database document and enter the remaining data.

Adding the remaining records

To add a new blank record to the database document, choose New Record from the Edit menu, or press Ctrl+R. The next blank record appears in the window below the first one. The new record is selected and has the insertion point blinking in its first field. If you turn List View off in the Layout menu, the new record appears by itself at the top of the document in the window.

Notice that the status panel, located in the panel area to the left of the document, updates to reflect the additional record (see Figure 4-3).

Specifically, the database book at the top of the panel shows that record 2 (the new record) is the active record. The status area also indicates that the document now has two records. As you add more records, the database book and status information update to indicate the currently selected record and the total number of records in the document.

With the insertion point blinking in the Name field of record 2, continue to enter data, add a new record, enter data, and so on, until you have entered all of the records. Table 4-2 lists the remaining data for the Friends database. Remember to press Tab to move to the next field in a record (or press Shift+Tab to move to a previous field) and to choose New Record (Ctrl+R) from the Edit menu to add a new record. When you are finished, the status panel should indicate that you have ten total records.

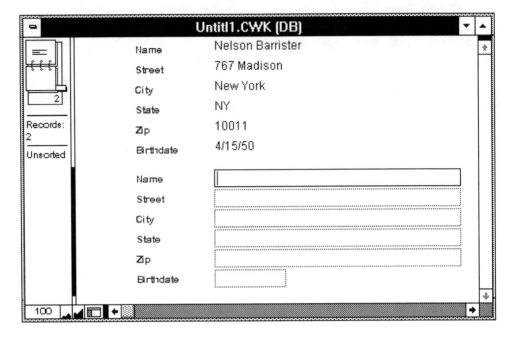

Figure 4-3   Adding the second record

Table 4-2   Remaining Data for Friends.CWK Database Document

Name	Street	City	State	Zip	Birthdate
Jackie Jolley	12121 Winter Springs	Minneapolis	MN	55789	6/8/36
T. Miller	12345 Newell	Mobile	AL	23332	11/6/35
Kelly Smith	145 Prairie's Edge	Prairieville	MN	55665	3/21/60
Emma Jones	1234 Main Street	Lincoln	NE	63332	2/11/65
Mimi Mere	80 Cajun Drive	New Orleans	LA	22002	7/14/63
Audrey O'Brien	9090 Historical Road	Minetown	CA	95999	10/27/18
Susie Adams	10 Forked Road	Majorville	TN	34343	8/4/80
Sheri Millerface	150 Fleahart Lane	Los Angeles	CA	93111	10/28/61
Elizabeth Spuller	54321 Turquoise Ave	Lake City	MI	44334	9/13/15

Save your document, and name it Friends.CWK.

In the next section, you will use a macro to modify the sample database by splitting the contents of one field into a new field. You'll also add calculation fields to the structure for sorting by birthday and for calculating age.

Modifying the database

If you look at the structure of the sample database document, you notice that the Name field contains both first and last names. Ordinarily, you define two fields—one for the first name and one for the last—when defining database fields for documents that contain names.

Defining two fields for first and last names gives you several advantages over using just one name field. For example, using the last name field, you can sort the records in the document by last name, or select a set of records by last name. You can also use only the last name or only the first name during a mail merge. Later in this chapter, when you merge the sample database document with a text document, you will need only the first name.

Splitting fields

To split the name field into two fields, you must define another field and move part of the data from the Name field into the new field. Of course, with only ten records in the database, it would be simple to manually retype the last names into the new field. However, splitting the field would be a very time-consuming effort if you had thousands of records in the database.

Using macros

Splitting the Name field can easily be automated with a macro. A *macro* is a recording of keystrokes and mouse clicks that you can play back at the press of a key to handle repetitive tasks (such as splitting the Name field). ClarisWorks lets you record and play back macros in any of the four application environments. For example, you can create a macro that types your name in a text frame or document. In the spreadsheet environment, a macro can sort a selection of cells, then print the document. You may also use a macro in any environment to automate the process of applying formatting changes to text, numbers, and objects.

Before recording the macro, you need to make a few modifications to the sample database. The modifications include

- adding a new field
- renaming an existing field
- changing the tab order (the order in which you move through fields when pressing the Tab key)

After making these changes, you then record and play back a macro to handle the task of splitting the Name field. The macro cuts the last name from the Name field and pastes it into the new field. (See "Recording the Macro" later in this chapter.)

Changing field definitions

Before recording the macro, you need to define a new field to hold the last name and rename the Name field to First Name. To do so:

1   **Choose Define Fields (Shift+Ctrl+D) from the Layout menu.** The Define Fields dialog box opens.

2   **Type** Last Name **in the Name area of the dialog box, click Text in the Type area, and click Create.** The Last Name field is created and added to the bottom of the field list in the dialog box.

3   **To rename the Name field to First Name, scroll in the dialog box until the Name field appears in the field list.**

4   **Click once on the Name field.** The field is selected in the field list and appears highlighted in the Name area of the dialog box.

5   **With the field highlighted in the Name area, type** First Name, **as shown in Figure 4-4.**

6   **Click Modify to change the name of the field.** The Name field now appears in the field list as First Name.

7   **Click Done to return to the database document.**

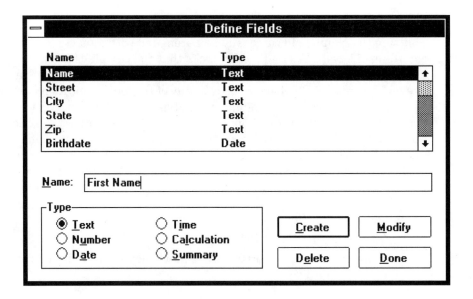

Figure 4-4   Renaming the Name field to First Name

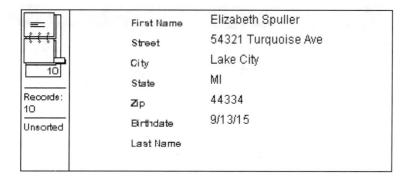

Figure 4-5   The Last Name field is added to the bottom of the record

Your database document now reflects your changes. What was originally the Name field is changed to First Name. The new Last Name field appears below the Birthdate field (see Figure 4-5). Anytime you define additional fields in a database document, ClarisWorks appends, or adds, the new fields to the existing ones in the order in which you define them.

To move from the First Name field to the Last Name, you have to press Tab several times to move through the entire record. This is because the tab order is preset to match the order in which the fields are defined.

Changing tab order

You can change the tab order to move through fields in any way you want. In this document, you want to move directly from the First Name to the Last Name field when you press Tab. This will save you time and keystrokes in recording and playing back the macro. To change the tab order:

1   **Choose Tab Order from the Layout menu.** The Tab Order dialog box opens (see Figure 4-6). The Field List area lists the fields in the order in which they were defined. The Tab Order area lists the current tab order in effect. In Figure 4-6, the Field List and the Tab Order list the fields in the same order because ClarisWorks presets tab order to the order in which you defined fields. If you change the vertical placement of fields in Layout, the preset Tab Order reflects the new vertical placement.

2   **Click Clear.** This clears all of the field names from the Tab Order area so you can set the tab order from scratch.

3   **Click First Name in the Field List area, and click Move.** As soon as you select a field name in the Field List, the Move button becomes available and shows directional arrows to indicate the direction in which you can move the

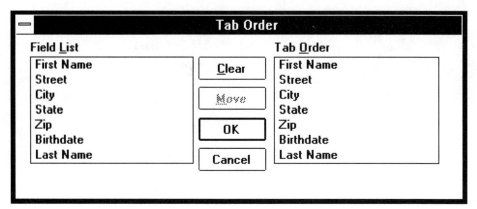

Figure 4-6   Tab Order dialog box

field: either from the Field List to the Tab Order area (as in this case) or from the Tab Order to the Field List area.

The First Name field appears highlighted at the top of the Tab Order area and the directional arrows (<<) change in the Move button. At this point, if you decide you do not want First Name to be the first field in tab order, you can click Move to move it back into the Field List.

4   Click Last Name in the Field List area, and click Move. Last Name appears below First Name in the Tab Order area.

5   Click Street in the Field List area, and hold down the Shift key as you click the remaining fields in the following order: City, State, Zip, and Birthdate. You can also hold down the Shift key as you drag through the field names to select or deselect them.

6   Click Move. The fields move from the Field List to the Tab Order area in the order in which you selected them.

7   When you are finished, click OK.

Note   *The order you specify in the Tab Order dialog box affects the tab order in Browse and Find.*

Now, when you press Tab in one of the records, you move directly from the First Name to the Last Name field at the bottom of the record. Pressing Tab from the Last Name field moves up to the Street field, and so on, following the tab order you specified.

If you do not want to be able to Tab into a given field in Browse or Find, remove the field or don't include it in the Tab Order area of the dialog box. This does not prevent you from accessing the field for data entry or editing; you can still click on the field to add or edit data. Removing a field from the tab order simply prevents you from being able to Tab into it.

Changing tab order does not change the order in which the fields appear in the document. Field arrangements are affected by layouts. Later in this chapter and in the next chapter, you will create different layouts to change the way fields appear in the document. For now, use the preset layout (also called *standard layout*), which lists fields in the order in which you define them.

With your fields and tab order properly set up, you are ready to record the macro to split names into two fields.

Recording the macro

The process of recording a macro is straightforward:

- Assign a name and key combination to your macro
- Initiate the macro recording mode
- Execute the series of steps you want to automate
- Stop recording

To record the macro correctly, you must turn off List View by choosing it from the Layout menu. When List View is off (unchecked in the Layout menu), you can only view and work with one record in the window at a time. This is necessary for recording your macro because your macro contains a mouse click to activate the First Name field. When ClarisWorks records mouse clicks, it records the position of the pointer in the window when you click; it does not record the field in which you click. This means that when you click in the First Name field to activate it, ClarisWorks records the click in the first field at the top of the window. If you record the macro with List View on, the macro only works on the first record because it is the one at the top of the window.

Next, select the first record in the database document. To do this, click the database bookmark and drag it up until the database book indicates that record 1 is the current record. In Figure 4-7, the current record is record 10 (as indicated in the status panel) and the bookmark is dragged to record 1 (the number 1 shows in the database book). When the mouse is released, record 1 becomes the current record and appears in the window.

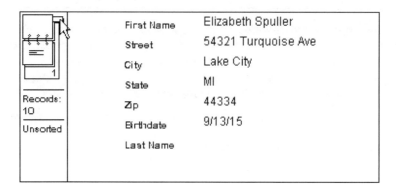

First Name	Elizabeth Spuller
Street	54321 Turquoise Ave
City	Lake City
State	MI
Zip	44334
Birthdate	9/13/15
Last Name	

Figure 4-7   Dragging the database bookmark up to select the first record

The steps you are going to record for the name split macro are as follows:

- Make the First Name field active
- Select the last name
- Cut the last name to the Clipboard
- Move to the Last Name field
- Paste the last name from the Clipboard
- Move to the next record

Once you record these steps and assign them to a macro key combination, you press the key combination to play the macro through each of the records in the database document. To record your macro:

1   **Choose Record Macro from the Macros cascading menu in the File menu, or press Shift+Ctrl+J.** The Record Macro dialog box opens, as shown in Figure 4-8, prompting you to assign a name and key combination to your macro. ClarisWorks automatically assigns an Untitled name to the macro, followed by a number, which represents the number of macros you have recorded during the current ClarisWorks session. The insertion point is set for you to assign the macro to a Ctrl+Alt+Key combination.

2   **In the Ctrl+Alt+Key box, type a letter, such as** n. This is the key combination you use to invoke the macro, such as Ctrl+Alt+n. If you prefer to assign the macro to a function key, click Function Key, and press the function key you want to use, such as F9, or simply press the function key without clicking Function Key in the dialog box. (The preset function key to use is F5, which appears in the box when you click Function Key.)

3   **Press Tab to move the insertion point to the Name box, and type a new macro name, such as** Split Field.

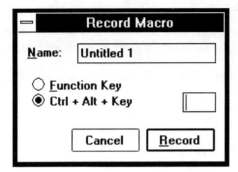

Figure 4-8   Record Macro dialog box

4   **When you are ready to begin recording, click Record.** The dialog box disappears and a microphone icon appears in the upper-left corner of the application's title bar, indicating that ClarisWorks is in macro recording mode. All mouse clicks, keystrokes, menu selections, or dialog box selections you perform are recorded into the macro until you choose Stop Recording from the Macros cascading menu.

5   **Click in the First Name field of record 1 to make the field active.**

6   **Press Ctrl+Down arrow to position the blinking insertion point at the end of the line of text.**

7   **Press Shift+Ctrl+Left arrow to select the last name.** By using these keyboard shortcuts within the field, you can be sure to navigate to the correct position and select only the text you want each time.

8   **Choose Cut (Ctrl+X) from the Edit menu, and press Backspace to remove the space that follows the first name.** The last name is cut to the Clipboard from the end of the First Name field.

9   **Press Tab once to move to the Last Name field.** This is where changing the tab order comes into play. You press Tab once to move to Last Name.

10 **Choose Paste (Ctrl+V) from the Edit menu.** The last name is pasted into the Last Name field from the Clipboard.

11 **Click once on the bottom page of the database book in the status panel or press Ctrl+↵ to move to the next record.** When the macro plays back, it automatically moves to the next record after splitting the field in the current record.

12 **When you are finished recording the macro, choose Stop Recording (Shift+Ctrl+J) from the Macros cascading menu.**

The previous steps include keyboard shortcuts you can use within fields. Table 4-3 is a complete list of the keyboard shortcuts available for navigating within fields.

TIP

Table 4-3 Keyboard Shortcuts

Key Combination	Result
Ctrl+Up arrow	Moves insertion point to beginning of line
Ctrl+Down arrow	Moves insertion point to end of line (or next end of line if already at end of a line)
Ctrl+Right arrow	Moves insertion point to end of the next word to the right
Ctrl+Left arrow	Moves insertion point to beginning of next word to the left
Shift+Right arrow	Selects/deselects one character to the right
Shift+Left arrow	Selects/deselects one character to the left
Shift+Up arrow	Selects/deselects from current position to same position on previous line
Shift+Down arrow	Selects/deselects from current position to end of same position on next line
Shift+Ctrl+Right arrow	Selects/deselects one word right of current position
Shift+Ctrl+Left arrow	Selects/deselects one word left of current position
Shift+Ctrl+Up arrow	Selectss/deselects from current position to beginning of line
Shift+Ctrl+Down arrow	Selects/deselects from current position to end of line

You are finished recording the macro. Now, with record 2 currently active, you can play back the macro to split the field through the remaining records. To play back the macro, press the key combination you assigned to it in the Record Macro dialog box. Or, choose Play Macro (Shift+Ctrl+X) from the Macros cascading menu, select your macro from the list in the dialog box, and click Play. Figure 4-9 shows the Play Macro dialog box with the Split Field macro selected.

The macro splits the name into two fields, moves to the next record, and leaves the insertion point blinking in the Last Name field. Continue pressing the macro key combination to play back the macro for each record until you have reached the end of the document and all of the fields are split.

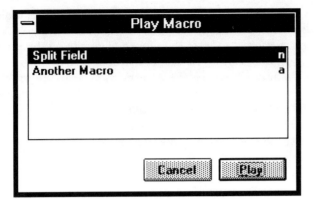

Figure 4-9   Selecting the Split Field macro from the Play Macro dialog box

TIP

A macro can end with another macro, thereby allowing you to chain macros together. To do this while the macro is still in record mode and after you have recorded the steps you want in the macro, press an Ctrl+Alt+Key combination, such as Ctrl+Alt+a. Then, stop recording, and edit the macro to assign Ctrl+Alt+a (the same key combination you pressed during macro recording) as the macro key combination. This way, the macro plays back recursively until you press Esc to stop it. You can use this technique to split the name field across all records in the document with one keystroke.

To save your macro, choose Save Macros from the Macros cascading menu, give your macro file a name (such as MyMacros.MAC), and click OK. (ClarisWorks macro files have the .MAC file extension.) All of the macros you record during the current ClarisWorks session are saved to the macro file. Each time you launch ClarisWorks and want to be able to use your macros, you must load them into memory; if you do not, the macros are not available, and pressing the macro key combination has no effect. To load your macros, choose Load Macros from the Macros cascading menu to select and make available your macro file.

Note   *If you want your macros to automatically load into memory when you launch ClarisWorks, name the macro file CWMACROS.MAC.*

Adding calculation fields

Recall from Chapter 1 that calculation fields contain formulas and functions to compute a resulting value. In other words, you use calculation fields to compute a result, rather than manually typing in data.

In this section, you add two calculation fields to your personal database. The first calculation field contains a formula that uses the Birthdate field and a ClarisWorks built-in function to extract the month from Birthdate and convert it to a number. This procedure allows you to sort the database by the month of people's birthdays. (If you don't extract the month from the birthday, ClarisWorks sorts by year first, then by months, then by days.) The second calculation field also uses the Birthdate field, along with functions, operators, and constants, to calculate the age of each person in the database. Later in this chapter, you will use these calculation fields to generate a list of ages and birthdays, sorted by month.

Extracting the birthday month

To create the calculation field, choose Define Fields from the Layout menu. In the name area of the dialog box, type **Birth Month** as the field name, and click Calculation (or press Alt+l) to specify a calculation field. When you click Create to add the field, the Calculation dialog box opens (see Figure 4-10). You use the Calculation dialog box to enter a formula for the field. The formula can contain other fields, operators (such as +, –, and so on), constants (text or numbers you type), and functions.

The Birth Month formula uses the MONTH function and the Birthdate field. The MONTH function extracts the month from a date and converts it to a number.

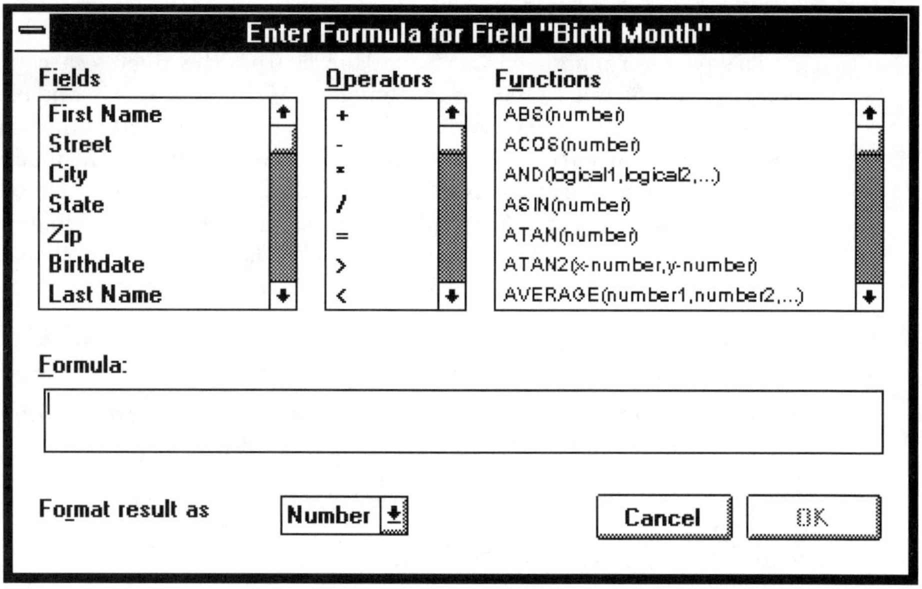

Figure 4-10   Calculation dialog box

Note *ClarisWorks stores dates and times as serial numbers by calculating the number of days since January 1, 1904. For example, the date 12/4/93 is stored as 32845, which is the number of days between 1/1/04 and 12/4/93. Some date and time functions accept serial numbers as arguments. Don't let this terminology confuse you. When a function syntax includes a serial number, simply supply a date field or time field, and it will be treated as a serial number.*

Also, ClarisWorks assumes the twentieth century (the 1900s) for dates that you enter with a year of 11 through 99. That is, 1/1/11 through 12/31/99 are stored as January 1, 1911 through December 31, 1999. For dates that are entered as 1/1/00 through 1/1/10, ClarisWorks assumes the twenty-first century (the 2000s); 1/1/00 is stored as January 1, 2000, and 1/1/10 is stored as January 1, 2010.

To build the Birth Month formula:

1 **In the Functions area of the Calculation dialog box, scroll down the list of functions until you see the MONTH function.**

2 **Click MONTH(serial-number) to select the function.** When you click the function name, it appears in the Formula area of the dialog box in its proper syntax (see Figure 4-11). The arguments required by the function appear as a list, separated by commas, between parentheses.

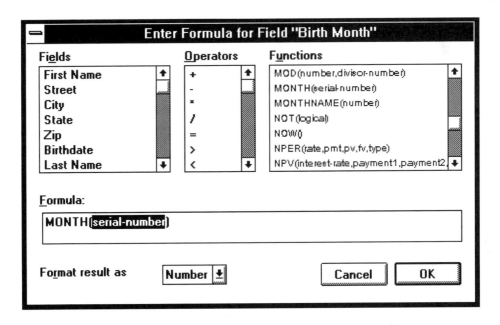

Figure 4-11   The MONTH function appears in the Formula area

3   **Select the serial-number argument, as shown in Figure 4-11.** You are going to replace serial-number with the Birthdate field.

4   **In the Fields area of the dialog box, click Birthdate once to select it.** ClarisWorks replaces *serial-number* with *Birthdate*.

NOTE   *Birthdate is enclosed in single quotes. In calculation field formulas, field names must be enclosed in single quotes, and text constants must be enclosed in double quotes.*

---

5   **Click OK to complete the formula.**

6   **Click Done in the Define Fields dialog box to return to the document.**

The new field is added to the bottom of the existing fields in the standard layout, and the result of the calculation appears in the new field. Notice that the number in Birth Month is the same as the month number in the Birthdate field. Your screen should look like the one shown in Figure 4-12.

TIP

If you have more than one friend who has a birthday during a given month, you can define another calculation field to extract the day number from the Birthdate field. The formula for this field is

```
DAY('Birthdate')
```

When you sort the database document, you can sort on both the Birth Month and Birth Day fields. See "Sorting Records" later in this chapter for more information on sorting.

First Name	Nelson
Street	767 Madison
City	New York
State	NY
Zip	10011
Birthdate	4/15/50
Last Name	Barrister
Birth Month	4

Figure 4-12   A record from the Friends database showing the new calculation field

Calculating age

To calculate the age of each person in the database, you need to create another calculation field. Follow the same steps you took in creating the Birth Month field to create a new calculation field with the field name Age. In the Calculation dialog box, enter the following formula for the Age field:

```
TRUNC((NOW()-'Birthdate')/365.25)
```

Let's examine this formula. The parentheses determine the order of precedence during calculation. Calculations within the innermost pair of parentheses are performed first. In this case, if the NOW function included an argument in its parentheses, the argument would be evaluated first. Since it doesn't, the first part of the formula that ClarisWorks evaluates is

```
NOW()-'Birthdate'
```

The NOW function returns the current date, using the date and time set in your system. (Our example assumes that the year is 1992.) Subtracting the date in Birthdate from the current (NOW) date results in a serial number, which represents the difference as number of days. Because we are more interested in how many years old a person is, rather than number of days, the result must be divided by 365, the number of days in one year, to convert the days to years. However, 365 does not account for leap years, so use 365.25 as the divisor. The NOW()-'Birthdate' part of the formula is enclosed in parentheses so it is evaluated first before the division takes place:

```
(NOW()-'Birthdate')/365.25
```

If you were to leave the formula as it stands now, the result would be a number with eight decimal places. Instead, use the TRUNC function in the formula to truncate the resulting number; in other words, TRUNC returns a whole number by simply leaving off decimal points and places. (TRUNC is different from the ROUND function, which rounds off the given number to a specified number of digits.)

With the Age field defined and the formula entered in the Calculation dialog box, your screen should look similar to the one shown in Figure 4-13.

There is more to using a database than for just storing information. The real power of a database comes in retrieving information. One way of retrieving information is to create a report or a list that arranges the information in a certain way. The next section describes how to do just that. (Another way of retrieving information—searching for information based on specific criteria—is described in Chapter 5.

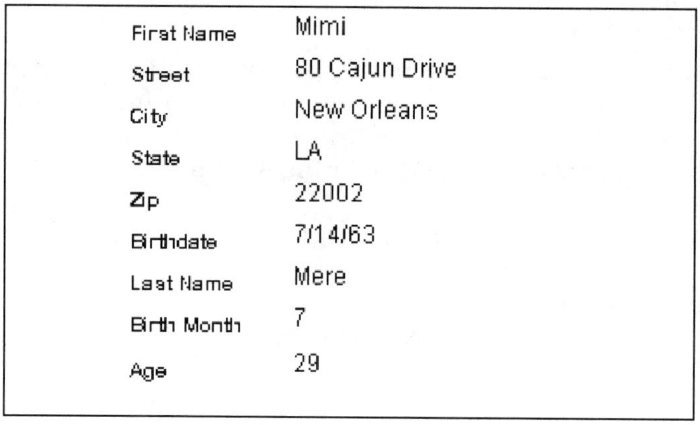

First Name	Mimi
Street	80 Cajun Drive
City	New Orleans
State	LA
Zip	22002
Birthdate	7/14/63
Last Name	Mere
Birth Month	7
Age	29

Figure 4-13   A record from the Friends database showing both calculation fields defined (Birth Month and Age)

Generating a list

In this section, you use the sample database document to generate a list of birthdays. The list is in the form of a columnar report, as shown in Figure 4-14. As you can see, the birthday list, or report, includes the Birthdate, First Name, Last Name, and Age fields, and is sorted by month using the Birth Month field.

The process of generating this report is as follows:

- Create a new layout
- Modify the layout
- Sort the document
- Print or preview the report

If it isn't already open, open your personal database, and turn List View on in the Layout menu.

Creating the layout

Before creating a new layout, switch to Layout view by choosing Layout (Shift+Ctrl+L) from the Layout menu. Figure 4-15 shows the standard layout of the sample database document.

The status panel is replaced by the tool palette and the graphics tool is selected. When viewing a database document in Layout, you are actually in the graphics environment. Each field and field name is considered a text object. The graphics menus and commands and the tool palette are available. You use the Layout view as you would use the graphics environment—to manipulate objects within the document.

Birthday Report

Birthdate	First Name	Last Name	Age
Feb 11, 1965	Emma	Jones	27
Mar 21, 1960	Kelly	Smith	32
Apr 15, 1950	Nelson	Barrister	42
Jun 8, 1936	Jackie	Jolley	56
Jul 14, 1963	Mimi	Mere	29
Aug 4, 1980	Susie	Adams	12
Sep 13, 1915	Elizabeth	Spuller	77
Oct 27, 1918	Audrey	O'Brien	74
Oct 28, 1961	Sheri	Millerface	31
Nov 6, 1935	T.	Miller	57

Revised: 1/4/93

Figure 4-14   Birthday Report

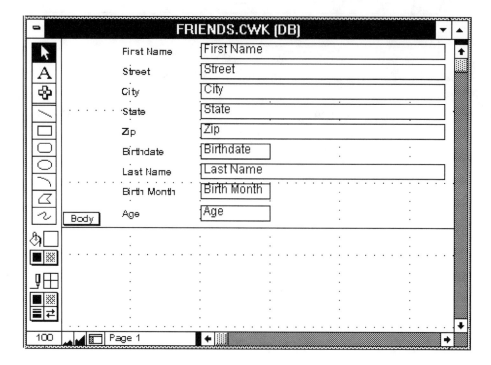

Figure 4-15   The sample database document in Layout view

Layout view is the only database view that allows you to access other ClarisWorks environments. This is because Layout is the only database view where you can use the tools in the tool palette to switch to the graphics, text, or spreadsheet environments.

TIP

Also notice the horizontal line running below the fields and field names. This is a *layout part boundary*. In this case, the line is denoting the boundary of the layout's body part. Later on in this chapter, you will have the opportunity to work with the other layout parts.

You can create a new layout with your document in either of the three database views (Browse, Find, or Layout). ClarisWorks offers five different types of layouts—standard (preset), columnar report, labels, blank, and duplicate. Up to this point, you have been working in the standard layout. To use the columnar report layout for your birthday report:

1   **Choose New Layout from the Layout menu.** The New Layout dialog box opens (see Figure 4-16).

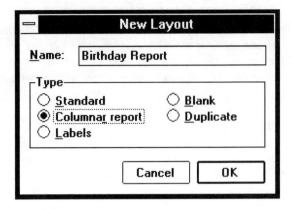

Figure 4-16   Defining a new layout for the Birthday Report

2   Click Columnar report to select that layout type.

3   In the Name box, type Birthday Report, **as shown in Figure 4-16.**

4   Click OK when you are done.

So that you may define the order in which fields should appear in the columns of your report, the Set Field Order dialog box opens. This dialog box is similar to the Tab Order dialog box you used earlier. It lists the fields in the order you defined them in the Field List area and lists the order in which you want fields to appear in the report in the Field Order area. Set the field order now to match the Field Order area of the dialog box shown in Figure 4-17. Be sure to select each field in the order in which it should appear. When you are finished, click OK.

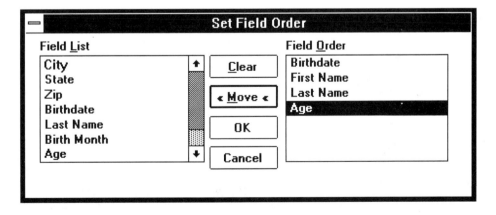

Figure 4-17   Setting the field order for the Birthday Report

CAUTION   *Selecting too many fields in the Set Field Order dialog box may cause the headings and data in your columnar report to wrap to the next line, rendering the report difficult to read. If you anticipate more columns than the width of a page can accommodate, use the Print Setup dialog box to set your page orientation to landscape (horizontal) mode.*

The new layout appears in the document window. Switch to Browse to see how different this new layout looks from the standard layout. The contents of each field in all records appear in a distinct column. ClarisWorks automatically positions the columns of field information in the document and arranges the data accordingly. The field names automatically appear in Bold and Underline style. In the columnar report layout, the columns (down) are fields, and the rows (across) are records. Clicking in a row selects the record in that row, allowing you to enter or edit data in the new layout.

Switch to Layout now. Your screen should look like the one in Figure 4-18. Notice that the columnar report layout automatically places field names in a header layout part and places the fields themselves in the body layout part.

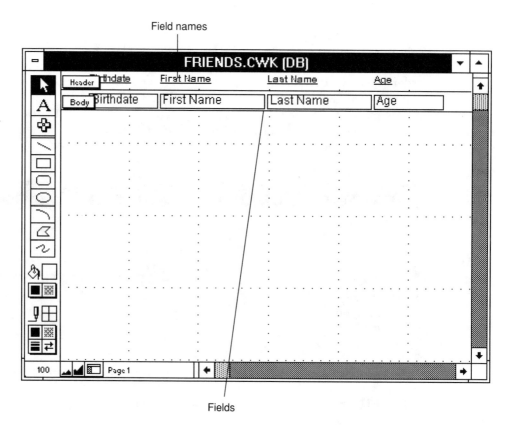

Figure 4-18   Columnar report in Layout view

Modifying the layout

When viewing your document in Layout, you can make modifications or additions to the database layout. You can draw graphics, import graphics, add a text or spreadsheet frame, change fill or color patterns or colors, and so on. You can also add other layout parts, such as a footer. The idea is that, when you use one of the five layout types, ClarisWorks provides the framework for the layout, and you customize it in any way that suits you.

In this section, you work in Layout view to make the following modifications to your layout:

- Change the position of text objects
- Change font and alignment of text objects
- Add a title to the report in the header part
- Add the current date to the layout in the footer part

Before you begin, make sure your database document is open in Layout and the tool palette is visible.

Note   *You should know about the Layout Info dialog box, even though you won't use it in this section. By choosing Layout Info from the Layout menu, you can change certain aspects of the current layout, such as the layout name, the number of columns in the layout, the print order of columnar data, and the way extra space between objects is handled when you print. Figure 4-19 shows the Layout Info dialog box for the Birthday Report.*

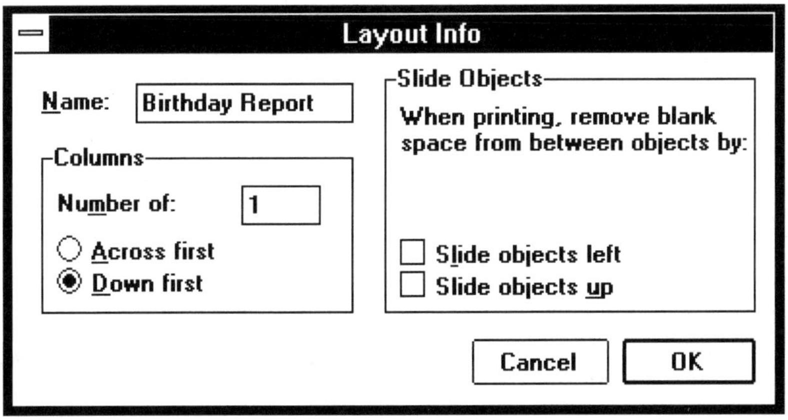

Figure 4-19   Layout information for the Birthday Report

Formatting the text objects

The field names and fields in the layout are treated as text objects (in fact, field names are actually text frames). If you click one of these objects to select it, selection handles appear. You can resize or move the text object anywhere you want on the layout, just as you would move or resize a text frame in any other document type.

The first change you make to the layout is to move the text objects so they are centered in the document. To do this, turn on the graphics ruler (Show Rulers in the Window menu), which will aid you in positioning the frames. Then, select all of the frames by choosing Select All from the Edit menu. Position the graphics pointer over one of the selected frames, then click and drag to the right until the first field and field name is at about the 1-inch mark on the top ruler (see Figure 4-20).

Note   *As you move the graphics pointer over the layout, you may see it change to the resize pointer. (This is the same pointer you see in a spreadsheet frame or document when you resize a row or column.) When you move the pointer over one of the layout part boundaries, it changes to the resize pointer, allowing you to change the size of the associated layout part. In "Adding the Report Title" later in this chapter, you will use the resize pointer to change the size of the body layout part.*

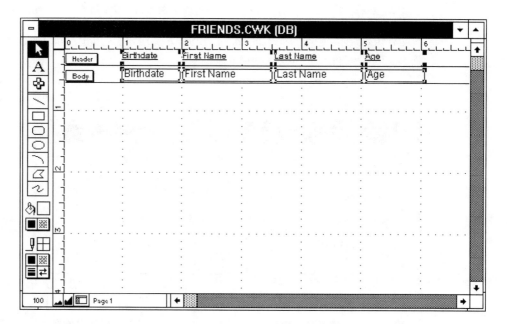

Figure 4-20   Positioning the text objects in the center of the document

The next modification is to change the font used in all of the text objects. With all of the text objects still selected, choose a new font (such as Times New Roman) from the Font cascading menu. The field names still appear in Bold and Underline style in the new font type, but they are 2 points smaller than the text in the body. To change the font size of the field names, click anywhere in a blank area of the layout to deselect all of the objects, Shift-click to select the field names (in the header part), and choose 12 Point from the Size cascading menu.

Aside from changing attributes such as font size, type, style, or color, you can also edit the text itself inside of text frames in the layout. This only applies to the text frames containing the field names, not to the frames containing the field data. In this way, you can change a field name in one layout without permanently changing it in the database structure.

TIP

Currently, all of the text is set to align with the left margin of each column, as indicated by the position of text in the frames on the layout. You are going to change the alignment of text by centering the Age data underneath the column's heading. To do so:

1   **Click anywhere in the layout to deselect all of the objects.**

2   **Click once on the Age field in the Body layout part, as shown in Figure 4-21.** Selection handles appear around the Age field frame.

3   **Choose Center (Ctrl+\) from the Alignment cascading menu in the Format menu.**

The word *Age* in the field's frame is centered within the frame. With a few of your changes done, switch to Browse to see how changes in the layout are affecting the way your document looks.

Figure 4-21   Selecting the field to change alignment of data

When you are working in Layout and want to see how your layout changes affect your document, you can set up two different views of your document and view them both on the screen at the same time. One view can show the document in Layout and the other can show it in Browse. To do this, with your document in Layout (or Browse), choose New View from the Window menu. This opens another window, identical to the original, with :2 added to the document name. With this new view active, switch to Browse (or Layout, whichever view the original is not in). Finally, pull down the Window menu, and press Ctrl as you choose Tile Windows. One window now appears above the other so you can see the contents of both. Any changes you make in the Layout window immediately appear in the Browse window, and vice versa.

Follow the preceding tip and open two views of your document: one in Browse and one in Layout. In the Browse view window, you can see that the column heading *Age* is off-center from the data (see Figure 4-22). This occurs because you centered the data but not the Age heading, which leaves the heading left justified (preset). To center the heading, make the Layout view window active, select the Age field name frame, and drag it until it is in the desired position. (Watch the Browse view window to see your changes.)

Birthdate	First Name	Last Name	Age
4/15/50	Nelson	Barrister	42
6/8/36	Jackie	Jolley	56
11/6/35	T.	Miller	57
3/21/60	Kelly	Smith	32
2/11/65	Emma	Jones	27
7/14/63	Mimi	Mere	29
10/27/18	Audrey	O'Brien	74
8/4/80	Susie	Adams	12
10/28/61	Sheri	Millerface	31
9/13/15	Elizabeth	Spuller	77

Figure 4-22   Viewing your changes in Browse

One final change is left to make on the text objects. Suppose you decide to show the dates in the Birthdate field in the Jul 15, 1993 format rather than the preset 7/15/93. To do so:

1 **In Layout, double-click the Birthdate field, or click once to select the field, and choose Field Format (Shift+Ctrl+I) from the Options menu.** The Field Format dialog box opens (see Figure 4-23). Because the selected field is a date field, the dialog box shows date field options. (If you had selected a number field, the Field Format dialog box would show number field options.)

2 **Click the second option to select it, and click OK to return to the layout.**

3 **View your changes in the Browse view window.**

Note   *In Layout, you use the Field Format dialog box to change formatting options for number, date, or time fields. If you double-click on a text field in Layout, or select a text field and choose Field Format from the Options menu, nothing happens. You cannot use the Field Format dialog box to change text options. Instead, use the cascading menus in the Format menu to change font type, size, alignment, and so on.*

You may notice that the birthdays appear to crowd the first names in the report. To adjust this, work in Layout, select both the Birthdate field name and field data frames, and drag them to the left until they are in the desired position.

Figure 4-23   Use the Date Format dialog box to change the display of date data in a layout

Another way you can arrange objects is to use the Align Objects dialog box. For example, if you accidentally move one of the text frames out of position, you can select it along with another object and realign them with one another using the options in the Align Objects dialog box.

TIP

Adding the report title

To add a title to a report or any other document, you generally use a header so the title can repeat on each page of the document. In the ClarisWorks database environment, there are two ways you can use a header to add a title to your report: you can add the title in the layout header part or add it in the document's header region.

The difference between these methods is that the contents of a layout's header only appears in the current layout, whereas the contents of a document's header appear in all layouts. If you use both a layout header part and a document header, the document header appears above the layout header in the document; Figure 4-24 illustrates this. The same is true of layout footers and document footers. If you use both a layout footer part and a document footer, the document footer appears below the layout footer in the document.

Note *You must switch to Page View in Browse to see a document's header or footer. On the other hand, you can view layout header or footer parts with Page View turned on or off.*

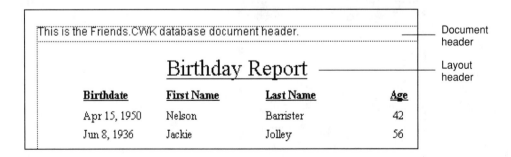

Birthdate	First Name	Last Name	Age
Apr 15, 1950	Nelson	Barrister	42
Jun 8, 1936	Jackie	Jolley	56

This is the Friends.CWK database document header. — Document header

Birthday Report — Layout header

Figure 4-24   A document header and a layout header, with document set to Browse and Page View

The bottom line is that anything you add, modify, or set in Layout only affects the current layout. It does not affect any of the other layouts associated with the current database document. There is only one exception to this rule:

If you change any options in the Document dialog box from Layout view, your changes are reflected in all of the document's layouts. For example, if you are in Layout and you change margin settings in the Document dialog box, all other layouts inherit these same margin settings.

In the case of your report title, you only want the title to appear in the document when you are using the Birthday Report layout. If you decide to switch to the standard layout you originally used to enter data, you don't want the Birthday Report title to appear at the top of the document. So, you add the title to your report using the header part in the Birthday Report layout.

To adjust the header part to make room for the title and add the report title by creating a text frame in the layout:

1   **Work in Layout and turn on the graphics rulers, if they aren't already visible.**

2   **Move the pointer over the header part boundary line until it changes to the resize pointer.**

3   **With the resize pointer, click and drag the header part boundary down to the 1-inch mark on the left ruler and release the mouse.**
    This makes the header area large enough to contain both the field names and the report title. When you release the mouse, the header boundary is repositioned 1 inch down the page, and the body part moves down, retaining its relative position to the header part. The field names in the header part stay in their original position.

4   **To move the field names down so there is room for the title, hold down the Ctrl key, and drag through the field name frames to select them.**

5   **With the field name frames selected, start to drag them down; hold down the Shift key as you continue dragging. When the frames are just above the header part boundary line, release the mouse and Shift key.** Holding down the Shift key allows you to move the frames down in a straight line. Now you are ready to add the text frame for your title.

6   **Select the text tool in the tool palette.**

7   **Click and drag to create a text frame in the header part above the field names.** Begin the text frame approximately 2 inches across and approximately .25 inch down, then drag across to the 4.75-inch mark and down to the 0.5-inch mark.

8   **Using the Font and Size menus, change the font to the same one used in the document and choose a font size larger than 12 point (such as Times New Roman 24 Point).** Because this is a title, you should choose a larger font than the rest of the report. Leave Underline selected in the Style menu. (If Underline is not selected, choose it now from the Style menu.)

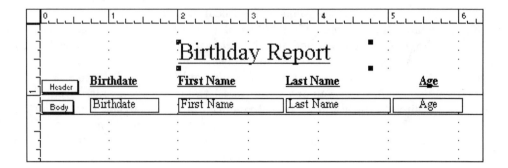

Figure 4-25   Adding the report title in Layout

9   **Type** Birthday Report, **and press Enter on the numeric keypad when you are finished.**

Your layout should look like Figure 4-25. Look in the Browse view window to see your changes.

The final modification you are going to make to this layout is to add a footer part to display the date of the report.

Adding the footer part

Adding the report date to the footer part in your layout is very much like adding a title to the header part. In this case, however, there is no footer part on the layout yet. So, you must insert a footer part before you can add a text frame to contain the current date. Begin by making the Layout view window active, if necessary, and turning on the graphics rulers.

Note   *Rulers are only visible in Layout, or in Browse with Page View turned on. Rulers are not visible in Find.*

To insert the footer part, choose Insert Part from the Layout menu. The Insert Part dialog box appears, as shown in Figure 4-26. Click Footer to select the part type, and click OK.

When you return to the layout, you see that ClarisWorks has added the footer part below the body part. To add the text frame for the report date:

1   **Select the text tool.**

2   **Click once in the footer part to create a text frame in the lower-right corner of the part.**

3   **Reduce the font size to 10 Point by choosing it from the Size menu. If necessary, choose Plain Text (Ctrl+T) from the Style menu.**

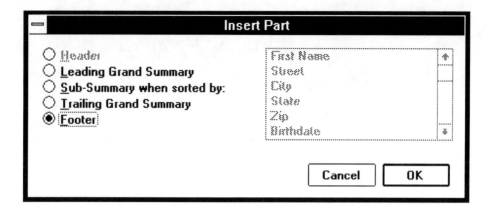

Figure 4-26   Inserting a footer part into the layout

4   Type Revised: . Be sure to type two spaces after the colon. Now you are going to insert the current date.

5   Choose Insert Date from the Edit menu. The current date appears in the text frame. By using Insert Date, the date will always be updated.

6   Press Enter on the numeric keypad to select the text frame, and drag it into the desired position in the footer part.

7   As you look in the Browse view window, drag the selected text frame in the Layout view window until it is in the desired position.

If you want the date in your footer to appear in a different format, use the Preferences dialog box (Edit menu) to change it. Now, any date you insert (even in another layout) will appear in the new format. You can set Preferences at any time, in either Browse, Layout, or Find.

TIP

Your report should now look like the one in Figure 4-27. You may notice horizontal lines marking the body of the report. The position of these lines depends on the size of your document window. The shorter the window, the narrower the body of the report appears in the window. The longer the window, the more of the report you can see. The size of the header and footer parts remains fixed, while the size of the body part changes to accommodate the size of the document window.

Birthday Report

Birthdate	First Name	Last Name	Age
Apr 15, 1950	Nelson	Barrister	42
Jun 8, 1936	Jackie	Jolley	56
Nov 6, 1935	T.	Miller	57

Revised: 1/4/93

Figure 4-27   Report with header and footer, viewed in Browse

If you want to add more space between the rows in your report, you can lengthen the body part in the layout. In Layout, position the resize pointer on the body part boundary, and click and drag the body part down to the desired position. In the Browse view window, you see that each row of data has more space.

TIP

You are finished modifying your report layout. Close the Layout view window now, and press Ctrl+S to save your document. Now, move on to sort the data in the document and prepare it for printing.

You can turn on Page View in Browse at any time to preview what your document will look like when it prints. You can even work in Page View when you are in Browse, if you prefer. Turning on Page View also causes the part boundary lines to disappear from the document in Browse. However, Page View does not show sliding objects.

TIP

Sorting the data and preparing to print

Once you have created and modified your report layout, the next step to take before printing it is to sort the information in the way you want it to appear in the report.

Sorting records

You can sort the records in your database document on any field, or on a combination of fields. For example, if your personal database has several records containing the same birthday, you can sort first on Birthdate, then on Last name, then on First Name, and so on. Additionally, you can specify a different sort order for each sort field. For example, you can specify an ascending (0 to 9) sort on Birthdate, and a descending (Z to A) sort on Last Name.

For your report, you use the Birth Month field you defined earlier in this chapter to sort the records in the database based on the month of a person's birthday, in ascending order. To sort the information:

1   **With your document in Browse, choose Sort Records from the Organize menu, or press Ctrl+J.** The Sort Records dialog box appears (see Figure 4-28). Like the Tab Order and Set Field Order dialog box, the Sort Records dialog box lists the fields on the left, in the order you defined them, and lists the sort order on the right.

2   **To sort by month of birthday, scroll to the Birth Month field in the Field List, and click once to select the field.**

3   **Click Move to move the Birth Month field to the Sort Order area.** The Birth Month field is selected in the Sort Order area. (Double-clicking the field in the Field List also moves it to the Sort Order area.)

If you want to add more fields to the sort order to further narrow down the sort, you can continue moving fields from the Field List to the Sort Order. For example, if you created the Birth Day field mentioned in an earlier tip, double-click it in the Field List to move it to the Sort Order after Birth Month.

4   **Leave the "Ascending order" option selected at the bottom of the dialog box for the Birth Month field.**

5   **Click OK to sort the data.**

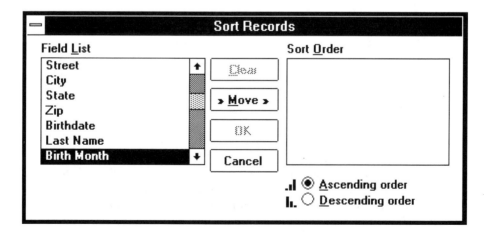

Figure 4-28   Sort Records dialog box

Birthday Report

Birthdate	First Name	Last Name	Age
Feb 11, 1965	Emma	Jones	27
Mar 21, 1960	Kelly	Smith	32
Apr 15, 1950	Nelson	Barrister	42
Jun 8, 1936	Jackie	Jolley	56
Jul 14, 1963	Mimi	Mere	29
Aug 4, 1980	Susie	Adams	12
Sep 13, 1915	Elizabeth	Spuller	77
Oct 27, 1918	Audrey	O'Brien	74
Oct 28, 1961	Sheri	Millerface	31
Nov 6, 1935	T.	Miller	57

Revised: 1/4/93

Figure 4-29   Birthday Report, sorted by Birth Month

ClarisWorks rearranges the data in the report so the earliest month in a year appears first and the latest month in a year appears last (see Figure 4-29). Press Ctrl+S to save your document.

Now you are ready to preview and print your report.

Printing the report

While in Browse, turn on Page View to preview your document. To see the entire report in the document window, you may have to reduce the document's view by either using the zoom controls or choosing View Scale from the Window menu. Viewing your document in Page View is an important first step to take before printing, because you can see how your report will look when it prints.

In previewing your report, you see page guides, marking the document margins, and the footer part at the bottom of the document. You may also see elements of your report that you don't like and want to change.

For example, the report seems to have a great deal of white space for the number of records in the database. One way to adjust this is to change the document margins. Choose Document from the Format menu now. In the Document dialog box, set all four margin options (Top, Bottom, Left, and Right) to 1 inch. (Remember, any settings you change in the Document dialog box affects all layouts, not just the current one.)

Another important step to take before you print your report is to determine whether or not you want to remove the extra spaces between fields and objects in the report. ClarisWorks is preset to leave the extra spaces between objects in a columnar report layout; that is, the Slide Objects options in the Layout Info dialog box are not selected. This makes sense because you want to maintain the space between the columns of data in a columnar report. If you want to close up space between columns, select the "Slide objects left" option; if you want to close up space between the rows of data, select the "Slide objects up" option; or select both options to close up all spaces between fields.

Note   *You cannot see the effects of changing the Slide Objects options until you print your document.*

Once you are satisfied with the way your report looks in Page View, print it by choosing Print (Ctrl+P) from the File menu. The Print dialog box is a little different in the database environment than in the other environments. Specifically, the dialog box gives you the option of printing either the current record or all visible records (see Figure 4-30).

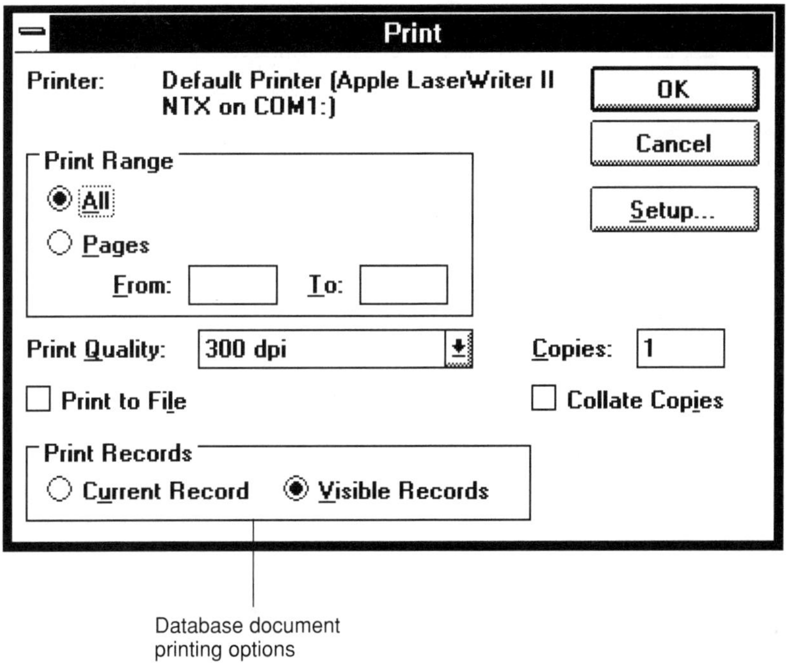

Database document
printing options

Figure 4-30   Print dialog box showing database document printing options

The Current Record option refers to the record that is active when you open the Print dialog box. The Visible Records option refers to the current set of records. In this case, the visible records are all records in the database document. Hidden records (those you remove from the set using Hide Selected or Hide Unselected from the Organize menu) do not print, nor do records you have omitted using a Find request. Hiding records and using Find requests is described more fully in Chapter 5. For now, you only need to be aware of the database document printing options available.

TIP

ClarisWorks is preset to print data in a columnar report, like the Birthday Report, down first. This means that the data in the first (leftmost) column prints first, then the data in the second column, and so on. If you are using a dot-matrix printer, you should change the setting so the data prints across first. Click the "Across first" option in the Columns area of the Layout Info dialog box to make the change.

In the next section, you use a different type of layout for your personal database—the label layout.

Creating mailing labels

One of the database layouts available in ClarisWorks is the label layout, which is specifically intended for producing mailing labels from database documents. To produce mailing labels, you create a new layout, set label size, and specify the field order in the layout.

In this section, you create a set of mailing labels using the Friends database document. (If you created your own database, feel free to use it for the labels.) The mailing labels will include the following fields:

- First Name
- Last Name
- Street
- City
- State
- Zip

To begin, you set up the document so its size matches the size of your sheet of labels. You then create the new layout, specify the dimensions of the labels, and set the field order. Finally, to add some visual interest to your labels, you add some graphics to the layout so that each label includes the graphic.

Setting up the document

The first step to creating mailing labels is to measure the labels you plan to use. There are many different sizes and kinds of mailing labels available for use with computers. Some come as 1-up labels, where you only print one label across at a time. Some come as 4-up labels, where you can print four labels across the page at a time. Aside from the number of labels across the page, the actual size of the labels varies greatly. Finally, some labels come on sheets of paper that you can feed into a laser printer like regular paper, while others come in a continuous form that feeds into a dot-matrix printer. For example, in Figure 4-31, 14 labels come 2-up on a standard size sheet of paper (8.5 by 11). Each label is 4 inches wide and 1.5 inches long.

The procedures in this section use the label and page dimensions illustrated in Figure 4-31. Whichever type or size of label you are using, take a sample sheet of your labels in hand now along with a ruler, and take the following measurements.

First you need to determine the size of the label sheet. Measure the following:

A. Width and height of the sheet of paper that contains the labels

B. Distance between the top of the sheet and top of the first label or labels

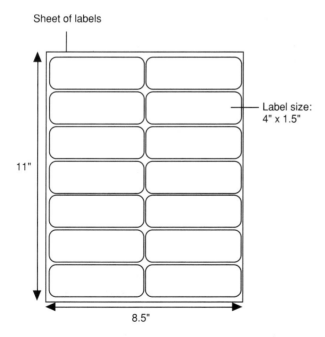

Figure 4-31   Diagram of a set of labels on a sheet of paper

C. Distance between the bottom of the sheet and the bottom of the last label or labels

D. Distance from the left edge of the paper to the left edge of the leftmost label

E. Distance from the right edge of the rightmost label to the right edge of the paper

These measurements determine the document margin settings you need to specify in the Document dialog box. Measurement A determines whether or not you need to change the size of the document. In Figure 4-31, this measurement is 8.5 inches by 11 inches; no change is necessary. Measurements B and C correspond to the top and bottom margins of the document, respectively; measurements D and E correspond to the left and right margins, respectively.

TIP

When changing document size, use the same logic described in Chapter 2, in which you created the envelope template. You must imagine your label sheet glued in the center of a standard 8.5 by 11 piece of paper. If the label sheet does not match a standard piece of paper, you have to set the document size by changing document margins. For example, if you are using continuous, 1-up pin-feed type labels and each sheet is 4.75 inches wide, set both the left and right margins to 1.875 inches, plus any additional space you want on either side of the labels. Why 1.875 inches? Subtract the width of your label sheet from 8.5 (8.5 – 4.75 = 3.75), and divide the difference by 2 (3.75 / 2 = 1.875). The result is the setting for both the left and right margins (assuming you are feeding pages through the middle of the printer).

Now set the document margins using your measurements. Make sure your personal database is active, and choose Document from the Format menu. In the Document dialog box, set the document margins so your document is the same size as the sheet of paper containing the labels. For the sample label sheet, the document margins are

Top	.25
Bottom	.25
Left	.5
Right	.5

After setting the document margins, turn on Page View, and turn on the graphic rulers to verify that the size of your document matches the size of your label sheet.

Now you need to determine the size of the label's printing area. You do this by measuring the distance between labels on the sheet. For 1-up labels, you measure the distance between the top edge of the first label and the top edge of

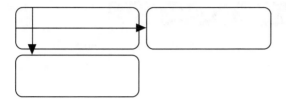

Figure 4-32   How to measure your labels

the label below it. For 2-up or more labels, you measure the same distance, plus the distance from the left edge of the leftmost label to the left edge of the next label to the right. Figure 4-32 illustrates how to measure your labels. You use these measurements in the Label Layout dialog box when you create the layout.

Note   *You must include the distance between labels in your measurements to ensure that printing begins on the next label in the correct place. If you don't measure these distances, the label contents may creep up or over the page and text won't print correctly in the label area.*

With your labels properly measured, you are ready to create the label layout and define the label dimensions.

Creating the layout

To create a label layout:

1   **Choose New Layout from the Layout menu.**

2   **In the Name area of the New Layout dialog box, type a layout name, such as** Mailing Labels**.**

3   **Click Labels in the Type area to select the label layout type, and click OK.** The Label Layout dialog box opens (see Figure 4-33), showing the preset number of labels across and label dimensions.

4   **In the dialog box, set the number of labels across the page, the label width, and label height (see Figure 4-33).** Press Tab to move among the entry areas in the dialog box. The settings shown in Figure 4-33 correspond to the label measurements taken in the previous section. The labels are 2-up (2 across the page). The distance between the left edge of the leftmost label and the left edge of the next label to the right is 4.25 inches; and the distance between the top of one label to the top of the next label is 1.5 inches.

5   **When your dimensions are set correctly, click OK.** The Set Field Order dialog box opens. This is the same dialog box that appears when you create a columnar report layout (see Figure 4-17).

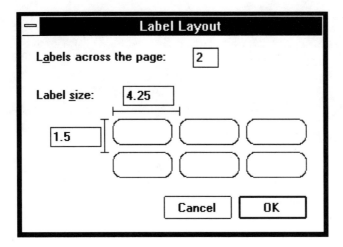

Figure 4-33   Label Layout dialog box

Note   You may see an alert message that says you must reduce the page margin size for all labels to fit across the page. Ignore this message, and click OK. The labels will fit properly, given the dimensions you specified in the Label Layout dialog box and the margin settings you specified in the Document dialog box. The only problem you may have is if you have extremely long fields that stretch the entire width of the 4.25-inch label.

6   Set the field order now as follows, selecting each field in the order in which you want it to appear in the labels:

First Name
Last Name
Street
City
State
Zip

7   When the Field Order list matches the above list, click OK.

ClarisWorks creates the label layout. Switch to Layout view, if necessary. Only the fields appear in the layout, which only contains a body part; field names do not appear in label layouts. You can turn on the graphics ruler to verify that the body part in the layout is the size you specified in the Label Layout dialog box. Figure 4-34 shows that the label size is correct: 4.25 by 1.5.

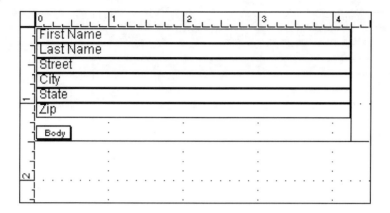

Figure 4-34   A new label layout

Note   *If the body part correctly matches the size of your label, it is extremely important that you do not alter its size in the layout. If you do, the data in your document will not fit properly in the labels. If the body part is not sized correctly for the label, you can adjust it in the layout.*

The fields appear in a stack in the layout, in the order you specified in the Set Field Order dialog box.

Modifying the label layout

So that your labels appear in proper mailing address form, you need to resize and move a few of the fields. The First Name and Last Name should appear on the first line together. To make this change:

1   **Click the First Name object once to select it.**

2   **Hold down the Shift key as you drag the lower-right selection handle to the left.** Shift-dragging the selection handle constrains your movements to straight lines.

3   **When the field object is approximately 1.5 inches wide, release the mouse.**

Now you have room for the Last Name field. Repeat these same three steps, resizing the Last Name field object to approximately 1.5 inches. With the Last Name field still selected, drag it next to the First Name field on the first line in the layout. Then, select both First Name and Last Name field objects, choose Align Objects from the Arrange menu, select the "Align bottom edges" option, and click OK. Your layout should look like the one shown in Figure 4-35.

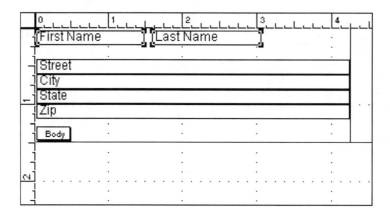

Figure 4-35   The First Name and Last Name fields are in proper position

If you have trouble lining up the Last Name and First Name field objects, select all of the objects in the layout by pressing Ctrl+A and choose Align To Grid (Ctrl+K) from the Arrange menu. This adjusts each object so it is aligned with the autogrid. Instead, you can disable the autogrid by choosing Turn Autogrid Off (Ctrl+Y) from the Options menu. This enables you to more freely position the objects in the layout.

When you are resizing fields in a layout, keep in mind the amount of data each field contains. For example, if only one record in the document contains a very lengthy Last Name field, be sure to make the field large enough to display or print that data. On the other hand, if a field always contains just a few characters, such as the State field, you can resize it to be quite small on the layout. To see how changes in Layout affect your document, open another view in Browse.

TIP

Next, you need to revise the layout so the City, State, and Zip data all appear on the same line. You may want to display or print a comma between the City and State data. Follow the steps you just finished to resize the City, State, and Zip field objects. This time, the City field should be approximately 1.25 inches; the State field can be as small as 0.25 inches; and the Zip field should be approximately 1 inch.

With the fields resized, drag the State and Zip fields one by one up to the same line as City. Leave room between City and State for the comma. To make sure the three fields are properly lined up, select them and choose Align Objects from the Format menu. In the dialog box, select the "Align bottom edges" option, and click OK.

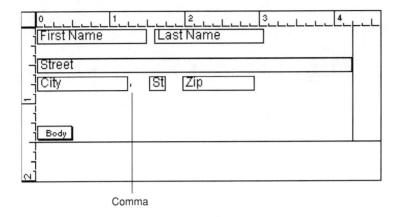

Comma

Figure 4-36   Adding a comma to the label layout

To add a comma between City and State, you place it in a text frame in the layout. Select the text tool from the tool palette. Click once anywhere in the layout, type a comma in the text frame, and press Enter on the numeric keypad. Although it may be difficult to see the comma in the text frame as Figure 4-36 illustrates, resize and move the selected text frame so it fits in the space between City and State. Select the City, State, and Zip fields and the text frame, and use the Align Objects dialog box to align their bottom edges.

Choose Hide Graphics Grid from the Options menu so you can better see the comma in the layout.

TIP

You need to make three more adjustments to complete your layout. First, shorten the length of the Street field so it is approximately 3 inches long. Second, select the First Name and Last Name fields, and hold down the Shift key as you drag them down so they are positioned close to the Street field. Third, to make room for the graphic that you add in the next section, you need to position all of the objects in the center of the body part. Press Ctrl+A to select all of the objects, and move them until they are in the center of the body part, as shown in Figure 4-37. When you are finished with these changes, press Ctrl+S to save your document.

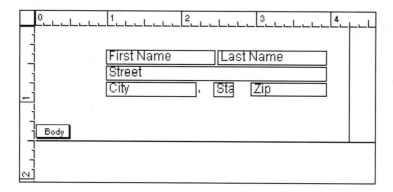

Figure 4-37   All objects are in proper position

Previewing the labels

Before moving on to add the graphics to your labels, switch to Browse and turn on Page View to see your document so far. Notice that extra space appears between fields within each label. ClarisWorks is preset to close up that extra space when you print the labels.

To check that the Slide Objects options in the Layout Info dialog box are selected, choose Layout Info from the Layout menu. If the Slide Objects options are not selected, click them now. (Remember that you must print your labels to see the effect of the Slide Objects options. Objects do not slide in Page View.)

Note   *If field objects are touching each other in the layout, they do not slide together when you print. Make sure there is a small amount of space between field objects. Also, a field will not slide left if the field to the left is taller; nor will a field slide up toward a wider field.*

If you look in the Layout Info dialog box shown in Figure 4-38, you see that the number of columns shown in the dialog box matches the number of labels across the page you specified in the Label Layout dialog box earlier. You also see that ClarisWorks is preset to print labels across the page first. If you want to print the first column of labels first, then the second, click the "Down first" option in the dialog box.

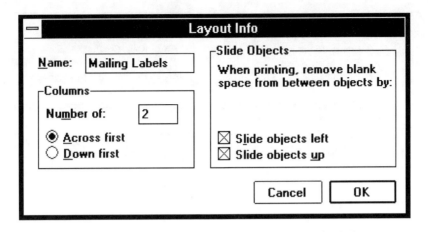

Figure 4-38   Layout Info dialog box showing label layout options

Adding art to the labels

Because you are in the graphics environment when you are viewing a database document in Layout view, you can add any kind of graphics to it. You can add design elements, draw your own creation using the drawing tools, or even insert graphics from other documents into the layout, if you wish. The possibilities are only limited by your imagination.

In this book, however, the possibilities are limited by the amount of space available. Therefore, this section describes how to add a clip art image to the label layout. (See Chapter 3 if you need a refresher on clip art.) Just as you added clip art to the Wine of the Month Club newsletter in Chapter 3, you can add clip art to a database document by pasting it into the layout. This simple addition gives your labels a more interesting look and lets you customize the labels for a particular purpose.

In keeping with the birthday theme, the sample clip art image used in this section is a balloon with confetti surrounding it. The graphic is part of the ClickArt Business Images clip art collection and is stored on disk as a .PCX file. For the following steps, suppose this file (or any clip art file you want to use) is on your hard disk. To add the clip art to your label layout from disk:

1   **With your database document active, switch to Layout, if necessary.**
    You should still be using the Mailing Labels layout.

2   **Click once to the left of the objects in the layout to set the insertion point.**

3   **Choose Insert from the File menu.** The Insert dialog box opens.

4   **Navigate to the disk and directory containing the .PCX file (or the file you want to use).**

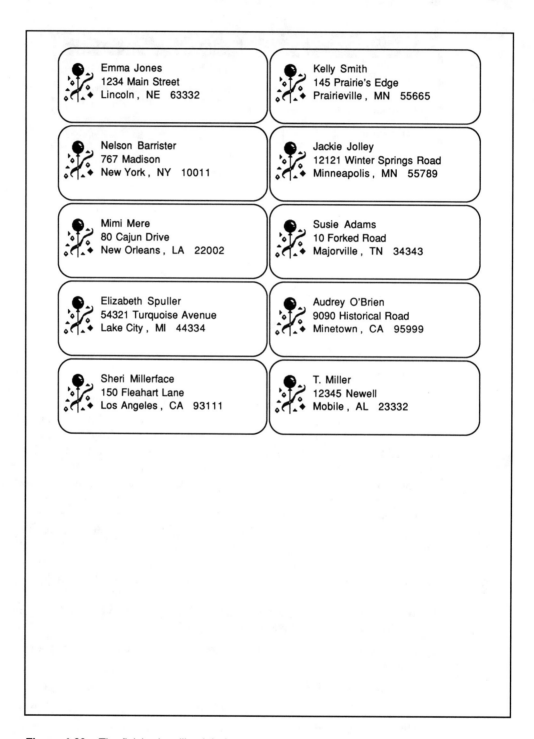

Figure 4-39   The finished mailing labels

5 In the List Files of Type drop-down box, select "PC Paint Brush (*.pcx") (or the format appropriate to your file).

6 Select the .PCX (or other type) file to insert from the file list, and click OK.

The graphic appears in the layout where you clicked. If necessary, move it into the desired position in the layout. Switch to Browse to see the graphic in position in each label.

Figure 4-39 on page 242 shows what the labels look like when they print out.

If it seems that the comma is not being handled properly in your printout, it could be that you do not have the Style set to Plain Text in the text frame containing the comma. Remember that the preset text style for field names in Layout is Underline. Try selecting the text frame and choosing Plain Text from the Style cascading menu.

TIP

Merging database information with text

One of the greatest joys in using a database is the ability to automate merging your stored information with text, often called *mail merge*. Mail merge is commonly used for producing form letters, in which you merge names and other information from a database document with a text document.

In this section, not only will you merge your personal database with a text document, but you will also merge it with text in a text frame. This ability to merge database information with text frames is one of the most powerful, yet little known, features of ClarisWorks; it enables you to merge database information with graphics or spreadsheet documents.

To merge data with text, you need a database document and a text document (or frame), both of which must be open in ClarisWorks. The database document you use for both types of mail merge is the Friends database. First, you will merge this data with a text document, which is a birthday greeting, then you will merge it with the envelope template you created in Chapter 2. Each time, you use different fields from the database.

Mail merge with text documents

Assume you want to send a birthday greeting to each person in your database on his or her birthday. First, you create a text document for the birthday greeting, then you merge certain information from your database with the birthday greeting. Figure 4-40 shows an example of what your birthday greeting might look like.

Happy Birthday, Emma!

February 11, 1965

As you turn 27, we wish for you the successes you seek, the happiness you deserve, and the fulfillment you desire!

Best Wishes,
Joe and Jane Doe

Figure 4-40   A birthday greeting merge document

In this example, you see that data from the First Name, Birthdate, and Age fields in the Friends database is merged with the birthday greeting text document. In the following steps, it is assumed that your text document is already created. If you want to use the example birthday greeting, create a new text document now, and type the text shown in Figure 4-40, leaving the first name, birth date, and age information blank for now. Save this document as Greeting.CWK.

Before you begin, open the text document (Greeting) and the database document (Friends), if they aren't already open. Make the text document active by choosing it from the Window menu. To do the mail merge:

1 **Click once in the text document below *Happy Birthday* and before the exclamation point to set the insertion point.** You must position the insertion point in the text document where you want the field's data to appear. Set the insertion point for the First Name field data.

2 **Choose Mail Merge from the File menu or press Shift+Ctrl+M.** The Select Data dialog box opens (see Figure 4-41). This is where you select the database document you want to use for the mail merge. If you have more than one database document open, they are listed alphabetically in the directory area. In this case, only one database is open, Friends.CWK.

3 **Double-click Friends.CWK (or your own personal database) to select it for the mail merge, or click once to select it, then click OK.** This opens the Mail Merge dialog box shown in Figure 4-42 for you to select the merge fields from the database document.

Unlike other dialog boxes in ClarisWorks, this dialog box is *modeless,* which means you can perform other tasks outside of the dialog box while it is still open. For example, you can switch between open documents, choose any command from the menus, open other dialog boxes, and so on.

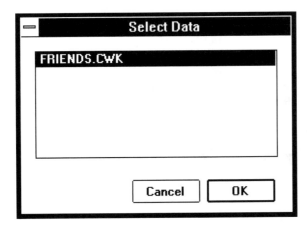

Figure 4-41   The Select Data dialog box asks you to select a database document for the mail merge

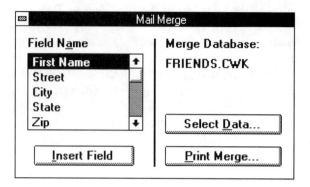

Figure 4-42   The Mail Merge dialog box listing the fields from the Friends.CWK database

4   In the Field Name area of the dialog box, click First Name once to select it, then click Insert Field.

The First Name field appears in the document at the insertion point, surrounded by the « and » delimiters (see Figure 4-43). The insertion point appears after the name of the field you insert. You have successfully inserted your first merge field in the text document.

If the Mail Merge dialog box is blocking the view of your document, you can move it elsewhere on the screen at any time.

TIP

Now you are going to insert the Birthdate field in the text document. You want the birthday date to appear between *Happy Birthday, «First Name»!* and the second paragraph. Leaving the Mail Merge dialog box open, click in the text document where you want the birthday to appear. This sets the insertion point for the next merge field. In the dialog box, select Birthdate from the Field Name area, and click Insert Field. This time, *«Birthdate»* appears in the text document.

Happy Birthday,
«First Name»!

Figure 4-43   The First Name field is inserted in the text document

To insert the final merge field, Age, position the insertion point after *As you turn* in the text document. In the dialog box, select Age from the Field Name area, and click Insert Field. Figure 4-44 shows what your text document should look like.

You won't be able to see what your document looks like when the data merges with it until you print it. That is, you cannot preview a mail merge document. In addition, you must print your document by clicking Print Merge in the Mail Merge dialog box. If you choose Print from the File menu instead, ClarisWorks prints your document with the delimited field names instead of with the data from the database document.

To complete your mail merge, click Print Merge in the Mail Merge dialog box. This opens the Print dialog box (the same one that opens when you choose Print from the File menu). Click OK in the Print dialog box to print your documents. ClarisWorks prints a separate text document for each visible record in the database document. (Visible records are either those you have not hidden by using one of the Hide commands in the Organize menu or those you have not omitted from a Find.) The First Name, Birthdate, and Age data from the first record appears in the first printed document, the second record's data appears in the second printed document, and so on.

If you want to use a different database document to merge with the text document, click Select Data in the Mail Merge dialog box. This opens the Select Data dialog box (see Figure 4-41), where you select another database document. Again, the database document must be open for you to merge it with the text document. You cannot merge a text document with data from more than one database document at a time. Switching database documents simply allows you to merge a different set of data with the text document.

Happy Birthday, «First Name»!

«Birthdate»

As you turn «Age», we wish for you the successes you seek, the happiness you deserve, and the fulfillment you desire!

Best Wishes,
Joe and Jane Doe

Figure 4-44   Text document with merge fields inserted

When you are finished with your mail merge, click the close box of the Mail Merge dialog box.

Mail merge with text frames

Using text frames, you can perform a mail merge with any ClarisWorks document type. For example, you can merge data from a database document containing a history of sales performance for individual sales people with a spreadsheet document containing a report of unit sales for a given quarter. You may also merge a database document containing a list of Wine of the Month Club members with the newsletter you created in Chapter 3, which is a graphics document.

In this section, you use the envelope template you created in Chapter 2 as your merge document. If you recall, the envelope template is a graphics document containing the Surfcity Sailboats logo and return address. Using a text frame in the envelope template, you merge names and addresses from the Friends database with the envelope template, resulting in a printed envelope that looks like the one shown in Figure 4-45. (If you have created an envelope template for your own personal use, you can use that instead.)

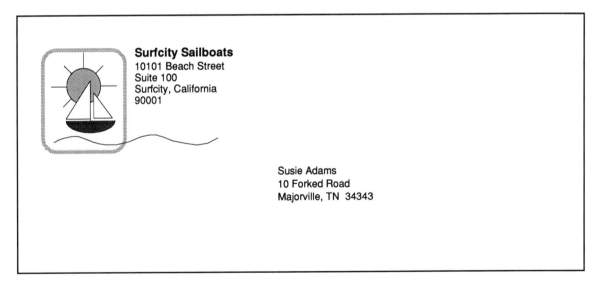

Surfcity Sailboats
10101 Beach Street
Suite 100
Surfcity, California
90001

Susie Adams
10 Forked Road
Majorville, TN 34343

Figure 4-45   The envelope template created in Chapter 2 merged with data from the Friends database

The fields you use for this mail merge are

- First Name
- Last Name
- Street
- City
- State
- Zip

Begin by opening your envelope template document (Envelope.CWS) and your personal database document. As in the previous section, both the database document and the document to contain the text frame must be open. In the database document, select the layout you want to be active for the merge, such as the Mailing Labels layout. Keep in mind that mail merge uses any text attributes or data formats set in the current (active) layout. Make the graphics document containing your envelope template active. If necessary, turn on the graphics grid and the graphics ruler so you can properly position the text frame in the envelope, and make the tool palette visible.

1 **In the graphics document, select the text tool.**

2 **Click and drag to create a text frame in the center of the envelope template.** Begin the frame 4 inches from the left margin, at 2 inches down, and drag across to approximately 6.5 inches and down to the 3-inch mark.

   When you release the mouse, the text insertion point appears in the frame. At this point, you can make any font changes you want or wait until the merge fields are inserted, and then change font type, size, style, or color.

3 **With the text insertion point in the frame, choose Mail Merge from the File menu.** The Select Data dialog box opens, prompting you for the name of the database document.

4 **In the dialog box, click once to select Friends.CWK (or the name of your own database), and click OK.** The Mail Merge dialog box opens.

5 **Select the First Name field and click Insert Field.** *«First Name»* appears in the upper-left corner of the text frame and the Mail Merge dialog box remains open.

6 **To insert a space between the first and last names on the first line, press the spacebar.**

7 **In the Mail Merge dialog box, select the Last Name field, and click Insert Field.** *«Last Name»* appears next to *«First Name»* (see Figure 4-46).

8 **Press ↵ to begin the next line in the text frame.**

9 **Select Street in the Mail Merge dialog box and click Insert Field.** *«Street»* appears on the second line.

Graphics document   Mail Merge dialog box

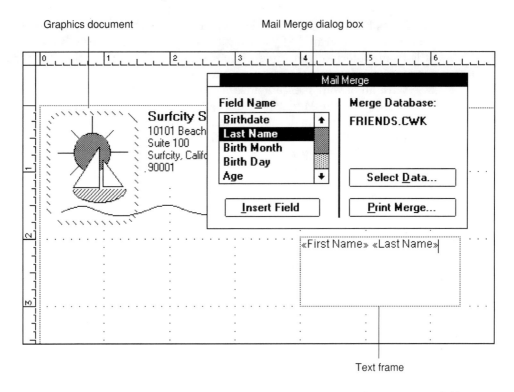

Figure 4-46   Text frame in the graphics document containing the first two merge fields

10 **Press ↵ to begin a new line.** In this last line of the text frame, you insert the City, State, and Zip fields.

11 **Select City in the dialog box, and click Insert Field.**

12 **Type a comma (,) and a space, and insert the State field.**

13 **Press the spacebar twice to insert two spaces, and insert the Zip field.**

Your text frame should look like the one shown in Figure 4-47.

«First Name» «Last Name»
«Street»
«City», «State» «Zip»

Figure 4-47   The text frame containing all of the merge fields

Press Enter on the numeric keypad to select the frame, or leave the insertion point inside the frame. If you want to change text attributes, do so now. With the frame selected, you can even move it to a different location in the document; the merge relationship remains intact.

With all of your merge fields inserted into the text frame, you can now click Print Merge in the Mail Merge dialog box. ClarisWorks prints a new envelope for each person in the database, replacing the field names in the text frame with a name and address. When you are finished, close the Mail Merge dialog box.

Summary

In this chapter, you applied some of the features of the database environment to manage personal information. In doing so, you learned how to use a macro to split data into two fields and how to use calculation fields. This chapter also described how to use two types of database layouts—columnar report and labels—for retrieving information from your database in a certain format.

The next chapter presents more advanced techniques in describing how to use the database environment to create business reports and forms. Whereas this chapter focused on using database documents for personal purposes, the next chapter focuses on small business uses.

Chapter Five

Creating Business Reports and Forms

About this chapter

This chapter expands upon the previous chapter by describing how to use the ClarisWorks database environment to create business reports and forms. In creating reports and forms, you will also use the text, graphics, and spreadsheet environments.

The chapter uses two database documents to demonstrate how to design an order entry form, generate a customer invoice, and create a sales report. You will also use the ClarisWorks macro feature to relate the two database documents to each other. In creating the reports and forms, you use some of the more advanced features of the database environment, such as finding information based on multiple criteria, using functions and formulas in calculation fields, using layout summary parts, and including spreadsheet data.

Setting up the database documents

Most businesses, small or large, sell something to potential customers and attempt to make a profit from the sales. When a business sets up a database management system, it needs to consider its way of doing business. What kind of information is important to store in the system? How will different kinds of information be used together for reports, invoices, and so on? What types of information should be stored together in a file? How does the customer purchase the product or service from the business? Is it a retail operation? Mail order?

Phone order? In short, when you set up a business database on the computer, always keep in mind what kind of information you want to be able to retrieve from it.

When you think about automating your business, you may think of using spreadsheets. Spreadsheets easily lend themselves to managing and analyzing financial data (Chapter 6 describes how to do just that). Yet, a database is a more natural information retrieval vehicle than a spreadsheet. A database system, which is generally a set of different files that you use together to automate your business, gives you many more options and more flexibility than a spreadsheet does for retrieving and presenting your data. For example, unlike a spreadsheet, a database lets you set up reports and forms that are customized for your way of doing business; information can appear anywhere you want on any size page. In addition, you cannot do a multiple-criteria search in a spreadsheet, or work with part of the data while hiding or omitting the rest. In fact, a database's information retrieval capabilities is one of the most important advantages of using it over a spreadsheet.

There are probably as many ways to set up a database system as there are businesses. This chapter uses a database system for a fictitious hardware retail business that is set up to track point-of-sale transactions and inventory. The database system consists of two database documents: an inventory price list and a sales file. The inventory price list contains a list of each item in inventory and its price; the sales file stores records of each sales transaction. Your system may also include a customer file containing names, addresses, and customer account information. You may even set up an accounts receivable file to track customer payments. You could monitor when payments are due as well as which customer payments are past due. What you include in your business system depends entirely on what you want to be able to retrieve from it.

Assume for the time being that you are the manager of a small hardware store. Your objectives are to

- store transaction information for each sale
- provide a way of looking up prices
- automate the process of generating an invoice at point of sale
- determine which salespeople are performing best

The techniques presented in this chapter address each of these objectives using the two database documents mentioned earlier.

Note   *The terms* database document, database file, *and* database *are used interchangeably in this chapter to refer to a single database document you create in ClarisWorks. The terms* database management system, database system, *or* business system *refer to a set of database documents and their layouts used together for a particular business solution.*

The inventory price list

The first database document you set up is the inventory price list. You use this file to keep track of the store's inventory and to look up prices of items. Although you won't do so in this chapter, you can also use it to create an inventory report to determine which items need to be reordered or which items sell the best.

The file contains the following information:

- Item number
- Name of each item in the store
- Item price
- Quantity on hand

To set up the inventory price list, start ClarisWorks. In the New dialog box, select Database as the document type, and click OK. When the Define Fields dialog box opens, use the database structure shown in Table 5-1 to define the fields.

Table 5-1   Inventory Price File Structure

Field Name	Field Type	Purpose
Item #	Text	Assign a number to item
Item Name	Text	Description of item
Item Price	Number	Retail price of item
Quantity	Number	Number of units in stock

The sample inventory price list contains eight records, shown in Figure 5-1. With the first blank record selected and its first field active, enter the data shown in the figure. See Table 4-3 in Chapter 4 if you need help navigating in the fields. See "Database Documents" in Chapter 1 if you need help navigating between records.

To view the data in two columns as shown in Figure 5-1, choose Layout Info from the Layout menu. In the Columns area, set the number of columns to 2, and click "Across first." You must turn Page View on in Browse to see the two columns.

TIP

Switch to Layout to make any changes to the font used for field names and data or to change the format used to display the numbers. For example, the Item Price data shown in Figure 5-1 is set to a Fixed number format. The Fixed option uses the Precision setting (preset to 2) to display numbers with a fixed

Item #	10011		Item #	10012
Item Name	15" hammer		Item Name	8" Philips screwdriver
Item Price	25.00		Item Price	5.95
Quantity	3		Quantity	10
Item #	10013		Item #	10014
Item Name	wire cutters		Item Name	shovel
Item Price	10.00		Item Price	5.95
Quantity	5		Quantity	3
Item #	10015		Item #	10016
Item Name	6' garden hose		Item Name	box of 1" nails (100 ct.)
Item Price	7.50		Item Price	2.50
Quantity	10		Quantity	25
Item #	10017		Item #	10018
Item Name	needle nose pliers		Item Name	power drill
Item Price	8.25		Item Price	30.00
Quantity	15		Quantity	4

Figure 5-1   Data for the inventory price list

number of decimal points. To change the display of the Item Price data, in Layout, double-click the Item Price field. The Number Format dialog box opens (see Figure 5-2). Click Fixed, leave Precision set to 2, and click OK. You can also open the Number Format dialog box by selecting the desired field and choosing Field Format from the Options menu.

The database Number Format dialog box is similar to the Numeric dialog box available in the spreadsheet environment, except that the Number Format dialog box only displays options for numeric data. If you double-click a date field, the dialog box only shows options for date data. Similarly, if you double-click a time field, the dialog box only shows time data options. In the spreadsheet environment, it displays all options for numeric, date, and time data.

Save your document now, and name it Inventry.CWK. Now you are ready to set up the second database document, the sales file.

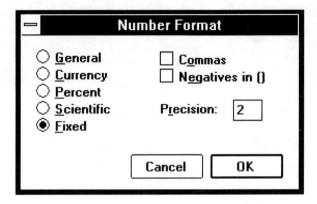

Figure 5-2   The Number Format dialog box in the database environment

The sales file

The sales file keeps track of each sales transaction as it occurs. You use this file to enter orders, produce invoices, and generate sales reports. This will become the main database document in your database system.

The file contains the following information:

- Customer number
- Customer name
- Date of sale
- Item sold
- Price of item
- Quantity sold
- Total of sale
- Salesperson

Create another database document now by choosing New from the File menu. Select Database as the document type, and click OK. When the Define Fields dialog box opens, use the database structure shown in Table 5-2 to define the fields.

The Item Total field is a calculation field that computes total amount of the sale. When you click Create in the Define Fields dialog box to create the field, the Calculation dialog box opens. To define this field, enter the following formula in the Formula area of the Calculation dialog box:

```
'Price'*'Quantity'
```

Table 5-2　Sales File Structure

Field Name	Field Type	Purpose
Customer #	Text	Identify customer by number
Sold To	Text	Customer/company name
Date	Date	Date of sale
Item #	Text	Number of sold item
Price	Number	Price of item sold
Quantity	Number	Quantity of sold item
Item Total	Calculation	Price times Quantity
Salesperson	Text	Name of salesperson

During data entry, ClarisWorks automatically computes the total amount of the sale by computing the product of the item's price and the quantity sold. The result appears in the Item Total field.

When you are finished defining the fields, do not enter any data at this time. In the next section, after you design the order entry form, you will enter data into the sales order file. Before you move on, save your document, and name it Sales.CWK.

TIP

When you are entering data, or after data is entered, you can choose Check Document from the Spelling cascading menu to check the spelling of words across all fields and records in your database document. In Browse and Find, the spelling checker checks the words in those text fields placed in the body part; it does not check data in other field types.

In Layout, the spelling checker checks all text objects (field names and other text frames) in the layout, including those in summary parts; it doesn't check the spelling of field objects, regardless of which layout part contains them.

Using an order entry form

In this section you design and use a form for entering data into the Sales file. You can apply the techniques presented in this section to any type of form you want to create in ClarisWorks.

You begin with a standard layout type and customize it for the order entry process. After you design the order entry form, you use it to add data to the file. In addition, you use the database's searching capabilities to find records that match a given criteria.

During data entry, you use a macro to look up the price of an item in the inventory price list. The last part of the section describes how to use your macro in a calculation field to fully automate the task of looking up a price. By using the macro, you relate the two database files, and give ClarisWorks the power similar to a relational database system. (A *relational database system* allows data to be accessed based on relationships between several database files.)

Designing the form

Figure 5-3 shows what the order entry form will look like when you are finished with this section.

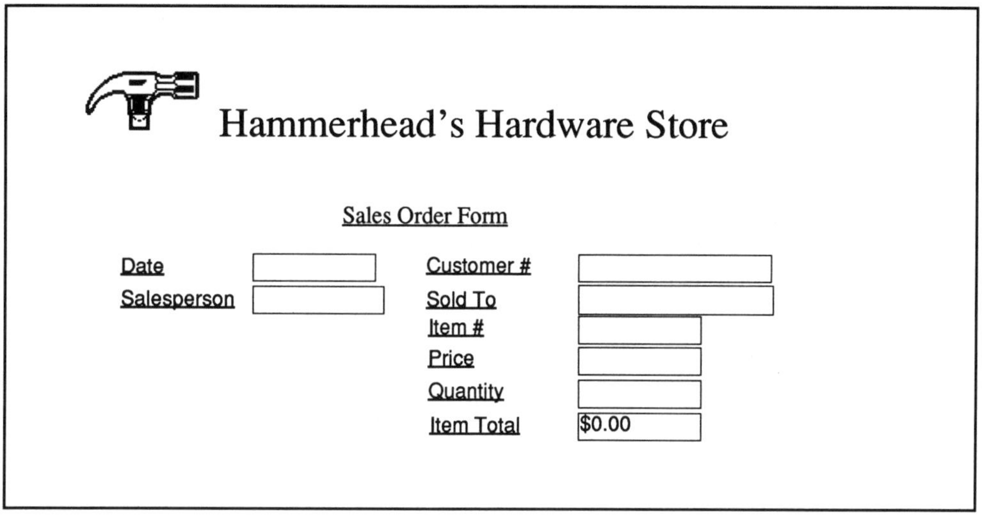

Figure 5-3   The order entry form

The form is based on a standard layout type and is customized to include graphics and text. This relatively simple design demonstrates how easy it is to create a form in ClarisWorks. In designing your own business forms, experiment with field placement, use of graphic elements and text, or use of various object attributes (such as color, patterns, line widths, and so on). Remember, the database layout lets you arrange information in any way you want.

Creating the layout

Make the Sales file the active document. You should still be viewing your empty Sales file in Browse.

You are going to create a new layout based on the current (standard) layout. There are two ways to approach this: you can modify the existing layout, or you can create a duplicate layout. In this case, you want to create a duplicate layout so you can leave the current layout intact. To do so:

1   Choose New Layout from the Layout menu.

2   In the New Layout dialog box, type a name for the layout, such as Order Form.

3   Click Duplicate to select that layout type, and click OK.

ClarisWorks returns you to Browse (or the view you were in when you created the layout). An exact duplicate of the standard layout appears on the screen and becomes the active layout. To verify that Order Form is the current layout, see that it is checked at the bottom of the Layout menu.

Modifying the layout

Now you are going to customize the standard layout by making a few modifications, including

- Repositioning the fields and field names
- Changing the font size and style of the field names
- Adding a border around fields
- Adding a header
- Inserting text and graphics in the header

Create two views of the document so you can watch how changes in Layout affect your document. Choose New View from the Window menu. When the new window opens (which is an exact copy of the original window), choose Layout from the Layout menu. The original view is in Browse, the new view is in Layout. Tile the windows horizontally by pressing Ctrl as you choose Tile Windows from the Window menu. Make the Layout view active, if it isn't already, and turn on the graphics rulers (Shift+Ctrl+U).

Repositioning layout objects   First, move the fields and field names into position. All of the fields and field names except Date and Salesperson need to move to the right; Date and Salesperson need to move to the left. To move the fields and field names into position:

1   Hold down the Shift key as you click to select each field and field name (except Date and Salesperson).

2   Drag the selected objects to the right until the left edges of the frames containing the field names are aligned with the 3-inch mark in the top ruler.

3   Click once on the Date field name frame to select it. This also deselects the other objects.

4   Hold down the Shift key as you click to select the Date field, the Salesperson field, and the Salesperson field name frame.

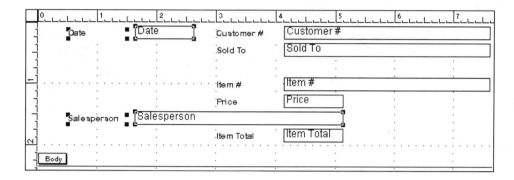

Figure 5-4   Moving the fields and field names into position

5   Drag the selected objects up and to the left, until the left edges of the frames containing the field names are in the position shown in Figure 5-4.

Notice that the Salesperson field is blocking the Quantity field and field name. Some of the other fields in the right column are also a bit too long for the information they will contain. Change the length of the Salesperson field now so it is about the same size as the Date field. Similarly, shorten the length of the Customer # and Sold To fields so they are each about 1.5 inches long, and shorten the Item # field to be 1 inch long. To reposition the objects to close up the space between them in each column:

1   Select the Salesperson field and field name. Drag them up so they are below the Date objects and in line with the Sold To objects. Click anywhere to deselect these objects.

2   Hold down the Shift key as you select the Item #, Price, Quantity, and Item Total objects. Drag them up so they are below the Sold To objects.

Figure 5-5 shows how the resized and repositioned objects look in the layout. To make sure that the left and bottom edges of the objects in each column are lined up straight, use the Align Objects dialog box. Select the field name frames in the first column first, and select the "Align left edges" option in the dialog box. Next, select the Date and Salesperson fields, and do the same thing. Continue this procedure, selecting one column of objects at a time until the left edges are aligned, then repeat it to align the bottom edges of each line of objects.

Changing object attributes   With your layout objects properly sized and positioned, you are going to change their attributes. First, change the number format to currency. Next, change the font style and size of the field name frames. Finally, add a border around the field objects.

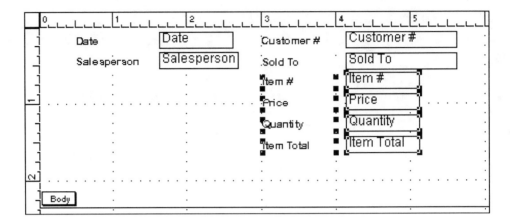

Figure 5-5   Order Form layout with objects resized and repositioned

To change the number format of the Price and Item Total fields to currency, double-click the Price field object (not the field name) to open the Number Format dialog box (see Figure 5-2). In the dialog box, click Currency, and click OK. Do the same thing for the Item Total field object. Now, after you enter the data in Browse, the item's price and total will be preceded by a dollar sign and show two decimal places. To change the font style and size of the field name frames:

1   **Shift-click to select each of the field name frames.**

2   **To change the font style to underline choose Underline (Ctrl+U) from the Style cascading menu in the Format menu.** The text now appears in bold and underline.

3   **Turn off the bold style by choosing Bold (Ctrl+B) from the Style cascading menu (in the Format menu).**

4   **With the field name frames still selected, change the font size to 12 Point by choosing the new size from the Size cascading menu.**

If an object slips out of alignment when you click it to select it, choose Undo Move from the Edit menu, or press Ctrl+Z.

TIP

Date		Customer #	
Salesperson		Sold To	
		Item #	
		Price	
		Quantity	
		Item Total	$0.00

Figure 5-6   Browse view of the Sales file showing object attribute changes

Now you are going to add borders to each of the field objects. This way, the on screen order form looks like an order form you might fill out on paper, with the borders denoting areas where you enter information. If you wanted to you can also add borders to the field name frames. Recalling that fields and field names are actually frames in a layout, and that frames are preset to have a line width of None, you can add borders to the fields by using the line width menu in the tool palette. Before you begin, make sure your layout window is larger than half the screen size so you can access the pen tools. To add borders:

1 **Click anywhere in the layout to deselect the field name frames.**

2 **One by one, select the field objects or drag the selection marquee to select them.**

3 **Choose Hairline from the line width menu in the tool palette.**

Look at the Browse view of your document to see the changes. Your order form should look like Figure 5-6.

Adding the header   The order form's header contains the name of the hardware store and its logo. You want the store name and logo at the top of each layout for this document (not just the Order Form layout). For example, later on when you create an invoice and a sales report, you want the name and logo to appear at the top of the page. You accomplish this by adding the name and logo in a document header, rather than a layout header part. (See "Adding the Report Title" in Chapter 4 for a discussion of the differences between these two types of headers.)

With the Browse view of your document active, choose Insert Header from the Format menu. ClarisWorks switches you to Page View and opens the header region at the top of the document. First, add the graphic (the hardware store's logo), then type the name of the hardware store in the header region.

The graphic used for the hardware store is a clip art image located in the Business Images package from ClickArt; you can use any clip art or other graphic that you want. Since you can't use the Insert command (File menu) in a database document header or footer, use the following method to insert the graphic from a file into the database's header:

1   **Create a new graphics document.**

2   **In the graphics document, choose Insert from the File menu.**

3   **Select the correct file format, locate the graphic file you want to use, and click OK.** The graphic is inserted into the graphics document, and it is selected.

4   **Press Ctrl+C to copy the graphic to the Clipboard.**

5   **Save and close the graphics document.**

6   **Make the Sales file active in Browse. Make sure the insertion point is blinking in the header region.**

7   **Press Ctrl+V to paste the graphic from the Clipboard into the header.** Figure 5-7 shows what your document should look like.

Before you add the store's name, change the font to Times New Roman 24 Point. Insert a couple of spaces and type **Hammerhead's Hardware Store** next to the clip art in the header region. To create some space between the header region and the main body of your order form, you need to change the line spacing in the header:

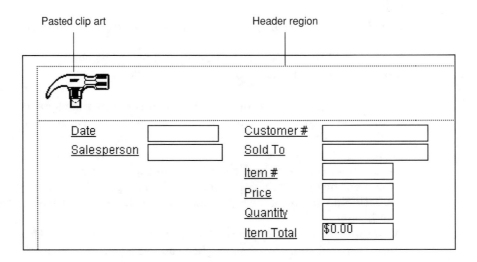

Figure 5-7   Clip art pasted in the document header region

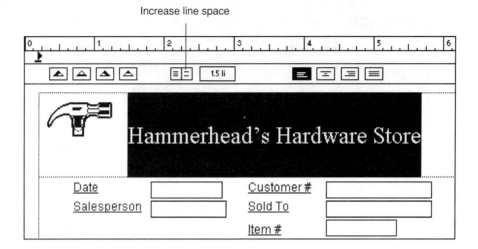

Figure 5-8   Increasing line spacing in the header

1   **Choose Show Rulers (Shift+Ctrl+U) from the Window menu.** The text ruler appears along the top of the document window.

2   **In the text ruler, click the Increase Line Space icon once.** This increases the line space to 1.5 lines, as shown in Figure 5-8.

3   **When you are finished, choose Hide Rulers from the Window menu to turn off the text ruler.**

Now the current layout and each subsequent layout you create has the store name and logo in the header region. Remember that you must turn on Page View in Browse to see the header. You cannot see the header in Layout or Find.

You are almost finished with the order form. To complete it, add a text frame to the top of the body part identifying this as the sales order form:

1   **Switch to Layout (or click in the layout window) and turn on the graphics ruler.**

2   **Select all of the objects in the layout by pressing Ctrl+A.**

3   **To make room for the text frame, hold down the Shift key as you drag the objects down in the body part about 0.5 inch.**

4   **Select the text tool from the tool palette.**

5   **Click once above the other objects in the layout.**

6   **Change the font type, size, and style to Times New Roman 14 Point Underline.**

7   **In the text frame, type** Sales Order Form.

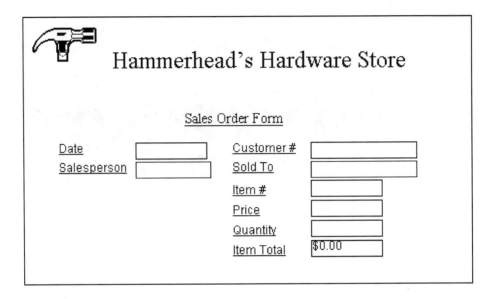

Figure 5-9   Order form with all modifications complete

8   Press Enter on the numeric keypad when you are finished to select the text frame.

9   Drag the text frame in the layout until it is centered in the area above the other objects.

Switch to the Browse view (or click in the Browse window) to see your changes. Your screen should look like Figure 5-9.

You can hide the page guides and margins in the Sales document so you can see more of your document in the window, as shown in Figure 5-9. To do this, choose Document from the Format menu, deselect the Show Page Guides and Show Margins options, and click OK. This also hides the line that separates the header region from the main part of the document.

TIP

The sales order form is complete. Now you or the hardware store employees can use it to enter the required information at the time of a sale, thereby recording each sales transaction.

Using the form to enter data

With your Sales file open in Browse, make sure Order Form is the active layout. You won't need the layout window, so close it now.

Since the fields are in a different order in the current layout than the order in which you defined them, you must change the tab order for the layout. To illustrate, press Tab to move through the fields of the blank record. Notice that you do not move sequentially through the fields; rather, you move down the layout, tabbing from left to right for fields that are horizontally aligned. So you can move from top to bottom through each column of fields, use the Tab Order dialog box now to set the following order:

Date

Salesperson

Customer #

Sold To

Item #

Price

Quantity

Item Total

Now, when you press Tab, you move through the fields in the order in which they appear in the layout, tabbing down in columns.

Turn Page View off, if necessary, and enter the data shown in Figure 5-10 into the Sales file. Choose New Record (Ctrl+R) from the Edit menu to add new records until you have six records. Since the Item Total data is automatically computed, you don't need to type data into that field.

ClarisWorks offers a keyboard shortcut, Ctrl+ − (minus sign), that allows you to quickly enter date, time, and record number data into fields. Press Ctrl+ − to enter the current date in a date field. Press Ctrl+ − to enter the current time in a time field. In a number type field, pressing Ctrl+ − enters the current record number.

TIP

If you have one or more consecutive records that contain the same or some of the same data, you can use the Duplicate Record command in the Edit menu to create an exact copy of the current record. In the duplicate record(s), you can then just edit any of the data that differs from the original. For example, the first four fields of the first three records in the Sales file contain the same information. You can enter the data in the first record, create two duplicate records, and edit the data in the last four fields.

Date	11/26/93		Date	11/26/93
Salesperson	Rob		Salesperson	Rob
Customer #	001		Customer #	001
Sold To	Rodney's Roofing		Sold To	Rodney's Roofing
Item #	10012		Item #	10013
Price	$5.95		Price	$10.00
Quantity	3		Quantity	1
Item Total	$17.85		Item Total	$10.00
Date	11/26/93		Date	11/26/93
Salesperson	Rob		Salesperson	Tom
Customer #	001		Customer #	002
Sold To	Rodney's Roofing		Sold To	Greg's Landscaping
Item #	10011		Item #	10014
Price	$25.00		Price	$3.95
Quantity	2		Quantity	1
Item Total	$50.00		Item Total	$3.95
Date	11/26/93		Date	11/27/93
Salesperson	Tom		Salesperson	Yogi
Customer #	002		Customer #	003
Sold To	Greg's Landscaping		Sold To	Local Construction
Item #	10015		Item #	10011
Price	$7.50		Price	$25.00
Quantity	2		Quantity	1
Item Total	$15.00		Item Total	$25.00

Figure 5-10   The first six records of the Sales file

Using macros to relate files

What if the hardware store salespeople don't know the price of an item and need to look it up? With both the Inventry and Sales files open, they could manually switch from the sales order form to the inventory price list, locate the price for the appropriate item number, and copy the price from the inventory price list to the sales order form.

Instead, you can record a macro to automate this process of looking up an item's price. In doing so, you relate the two database documents on the Item # field. That is, you use the data in the Item # field of the Sales file to find the same data in the Item # field of the Inventry file. If you had created another database document to contain customer information, such as names, addresses, and account balances, you could similarly relate the Sales file to the customer file on the Customer # field. There are numerous examples of how this technique can be applied. The bottom line is that, although the ClarisWorks database environment is a *flat file* rather than a relational system, you can use macros to make it act like a relational system.

This section describes how to record a price lookup macro and play it back during data entry to find an item's price. The last part of this section describes how to use the macro in a calculation field formula to automatically fill in the price.

Because the most important step in the macro is using a find request to search the Inventry file, you need to know how to use a find request before you record the macro.

Finding records

A find request is an arrangement of fields in the Find view. When you choose Find from the Layout menu, ClarisWorks uses the currently active layout to display what looks like a blank record on your screen. This blank record is called the *find request*. The "fields" in the find request are search fields in which you enter data to specify the search criteria for finding a group of records that contain the same data.

Before you record your price lookup macro, which includes a find request, practice creating a find request now. To search the Sales file for all records containing 002 in the Customer # field:

1 With the Sales file open and the Order Form layout active, choose Find (Shift+Ctrl+F) from the Layout menu. You can be in either Browse or Layout view when you choose Find.

A new find request opens on your screen (see Figure 5-11). Notice that the status panel area changes to show status information about the find request and options to select for the search.

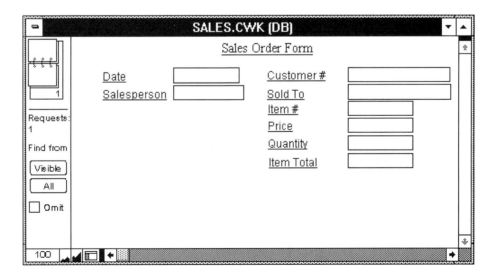

Figure 5-11   A blank find request

2   Press Tab twice to move the insertion point to the Customer # field.

3   Type 002.

4   Click All in the status panel area or press ↵ to find all of the records matching the request.

ClarisWorks finds two records that match the find request and switches to Browse to display them. The remaining records are put away, or hidden. The status panel now indicates that two out of six records are in the found set (that is, the two found records are the only visible records in the file). Figure 5-12 shows the status panel with this information.

If you create a find request with only some of the records visible, you can use the Visible option in the Find status panel to limit your search to the visible records; or you can use the All option to search through all records, visible or hidden.

Another option in the Find status panel is Omit. Check the Omit box before clicking Visible or All to omit the found records from the visible set. Omitting records is the same as hiding them.

Figure 5-12   Status panel indicating results of the find request

TIP

You can create more than one find request. Multiple find requests appear the same as records in Find, and the database book indicates the number of find requests you've created. Creating multiple find requests allows you to do "logical or" searches.

*For example, create one find request, and type **002** in Customer #. Choose New Request (Ctrl+R) from the Edit menu. In the next find request, type **Greg's Landscaping** in the Sold To field. When you click All to do the search, ClarisWorks finds those records that either have 002 in Customer # or Greg's Landscaping in Sold To. This way, if any records containing Greg's Landscaping do not have the correct customer number (002), you can still find the desired records.*

Another way of finding records is to use the Match Records command from the Organize menu. Matching records is different from using find requests. (See "Using the Match Records Command" later in this chapter for more information.) When you match records, the unfound records are not hidden; rather, the found records are selected, leaving the unfound records unselected. Matching records also allows you to specify more complex search criteria.

Now that you know about finding records, you can proceed to record your price lookup macro.

Recording the price lookup macro

The price lookup macro includes these steps:

- Copying the Item # of the price to look up from the current record in the Sales file
- Making the Inventry file active
- Pasting the Item # in the Item # search field in a find request
- Finding the matching record in the Inventry file
- Copying the Price data from the found record to the Price field in the Sales file

To begin, open both the Sales and Inventory files, and make the Sales file active. Make all of the records in Sales visible by choosing Show All Records (Shift+Ctrl+A) from the Organize menu.

Make sure the Sales document is in Browse view and Page View and List View are turned *off* in the Layout menu. The macro will not work if you have List View turned on. (Chapter 4 explains the importance of turning off List View.)

Add a new record to the Sales file (press Ctrl+R), and enter the data shown in Figure 5-13. Be sure to skip the Price field.

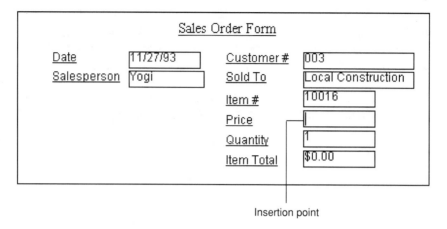

Insertion point

Figure 5-13   Data for record 7

Begin recording the macro by choosing Record Macro (Shift+Ctrl+J) from the Macros cascading menu in the File menu. In the Record Macro dialog box, assign Ctrl+Alt+p as the macro key combination for the macro, and name the macro Price Lookup. When you are ready to record the macro, click Record in the dialog box, and follow these steps:

1 **Click to set the insertion point in the Price field (see Figure 5-13).**

2 **Press Shift+Tab to move to the previous field, which is the Item # field.**

3 **Press Shift+Ctrl+Left arrow to select the item number.**

4 **Press Ctrl+C to copy the item number to the Clipboard.**

5 **Choose Inventry.CWK from the Window menu to make that the active file.**

6 **Press Shift+Ctrl+F to create a new find request.** A new find request opens with the insertion point blinking in the Item # field.

7 **Press Ctrl+V to paste the item number from the Clipboard into the Item # field in the find request.**

8 **Press ↵ to search all of the records in the Inventry file for the matching item number.** (Pressing ↵ in a find request is the same as clicking All in the status panel.) After pressing ↵, or clicking All, the found record appears in Browse.

9 **Press Tab three times to move to the Price field in the found record.**

10 **Press Shift+Ctrl+Left arrow in the Price field to select the price data.**

11 **Press Ctrl+C to copy the selection to the Clipboard.**

12 Choose Sales.CWK from the Window menu to switch to that file.

13 Click once in the Price field.

14 Press Ctrl+V to paste the item's price from the Clipboard into the Price field.

You have successfully looked up the price of the item in the other file and copied the price into the current record. Choose Stop Recording from the Macros cascading menu. Your macro is complete.

Using keystrokes to navigate and choose commands from menus is safer than using mouse clicks when you are recording a macro. When you record keystrokes, you can be sure that the correct sequence of events is being recorded.

TIP

To play back your macro, add another record to the Sales file and enter the data shown in Figure 5-14. Again, skip the Price field, but leave the insertion point blinking in the Price field so you can play back the macro from that point.

With the insertion point blinking in the Price field, press Ctrl+Alt+p (the key combination assigned to your macro) to play back the macro. If your macro is successful, a price of $30.00 appears in the Price field of record 8.

Note   *When you press Tab to move out of the Price field, the Item Total field updates automatically. Until both the Price and Quantity fields contain data, Item Total = $0.00.*

Sales Order Form

Date	12/5/93	Customer # 003
Salesperson	Rob	Sold To Local Construction
		Item # 10018
		Price
		Quantity 1
		Item Total $0.00

Figure 5-14   Data for record 8

Be sure to save your macro by choosing Save Macros from the Macros cascading menu. Remember that you must load your macro file into memory to make the macros in the file available. To do this, choose Load Macros from the Macros cascading menu.

Using the macro in a calculation field

If you really want to automate the process of looking up an item's price, you can create a calculation field in the Sales file that uses the MACRO function. This way the macro can automatically play back without your having to invoke it with its key combination.

To effectively use this technique, you need to create two new fields. One field is a text field that you place on the order form to ask if the person entering data wants to look up a price. The other field is a calculation field that uses the response in the text field to determine whether or not the macro should be played to look up the price. After creating the new fields, you place the text field on the layout—but you do not place the calculation field there. The calculation field simply exists as a vehicle for playing back the macro.

Open the Define Fields dialog box now. Create the first field by typing the field name Lookup, selecting Text as the field type, and clicking Create. You will use this field in the layout to ask for a Y (yes) or N (no) response to the question, "Do you want to look up the price?"

To create the calculation field, name the field Price Macro, select Calculation as the field type, and click Create. The Calculation dialog box opens for you to enter the formula for the Price Macro field. Type the following formula, or use the Fields, Operators, and Functions areas of the Calculation dialog box to build the formula:

```
IF('Lookup'="Y",MACRO("Price Lookup"))
```

When you are finished, click OK in the Calculation field, and click Done in the Define Fields dialog box.

The formula contains two functions: MACRO and IF. The MACRO function plays a previously recorded macro and requires one text argument, which is the name of the macro to play back. Be sure to type the macro name exactly as you entered it in the Record Macro dialog box and enclose the name in double quotation marks.

The IF function accepts three arguments: a logical expression, an if-true result, and an if-false result. A logical expression might be

```
Today=TEXTTODATE("12/11/93")
```

IF evaluates the logical expression. If true, it returns the if-true result; if false, it returns the if-false result. The third (if-false result) argument is not required. If you omit it and the logical expression evaluates as false, nothing happens. This way you force IF to do something or do nothing.

In this case, the IF function evaluates the expression

`'Lookup'="Y"`

as "if the Lookup field has Y as its data." If the result is true (Y is in the Lookup field), the MACRO function plays the Price Lookup macro. If Y is not in the Lookup field, nothing happens.

Your screen shows the two new fields added to the document. (When you define a field, ClarisWorks automatically places it on the current layout.) You want the Lookup field in the layout, but not the Price Macro calculation field. Switch to Layout now, select the Price Macro field name and field object, and press Delete to remove them. To change the Lookup field name to a prompt, double-click the field name's frame, and edit the text so it reads as follows:

Do you want to look up a price (Y or N)?

Press Enter on the numeric keypad to select the frame. Move and resize the frame and the Lookup field object until they appear in the layout as shown in Figure 5-15.

You can add the Lookup field to the bottom of the Tab Order list in the Tab Order dialog box in order to tab into the field in Browse. Then, when you press Tab from the Quantity field, you move to the Lookup field. If you don't add Lookup to the Tab Order list, you can click the field in Browse to access it.

TIP

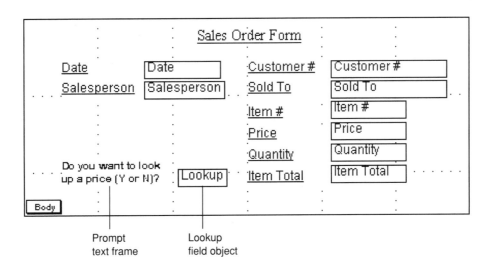

Figure 5-15   The Lookup field object and prompt are in position in the layout

Now try out your new creation. With both the Inventry and Sales files open and the Sales file active in Browse with List View off, move to one of the records in the Sales file, and delete the Price data so you can see if the process works. Tab to or click in the area next to the prompt to activate the Lookup field. Type **Y** (make sure it is an uppercase Y) and press Tab or Enter on the numeric keypad. The macro plays back by looking up the price in the other file and placing the price in the Price field of the current record in the Sales file.

If you want to force an uppercase response in the Lookup field, you can do so by including the UPPER function in the Price Macro calculation field formula, as follows:

```
IF(UPPER('Lookup')="Y",MACRO("Price Lookup"))
```

TIP

Now you need to change the response in the Lookup field from Y (or y) to N (or n). If you do not make this change and you subsequently define a new field, the Price Lookup macro automatically executes after you leave the Define Fields dialog box. To prevent the macro from automatically executing, Type **N** in the Lookup field after correctly running the macro. Or, include this step in the Price Lookup macro.

Generating an invoice

In this section, you use the data entered in the Sales file to generate an invoice for each customer's order on a given day. If you look at the way the Sales file is set up, you see that a record can only store the sale of one item. What if a customer purchases several items at once? For example, Rodney's Roofing bought three items from the hardware store on 11/26/93. The techniques in this section describe how to produce an invoice to accommodate single or multiple purchases.

You begin by creating a blank layout type for the invoice. You then insert the appropriate fields into the blank layout and arrange them in the body and header parts. To include the total amount of the sale for all items sold, you add a new summary field to the file and add a grand summary part to the layout.

After your layout is complete, use multiple search criteria to locate the appropriate records and produce the invoice. Figure 5-16 gives you an example of what the final invoice will look like.

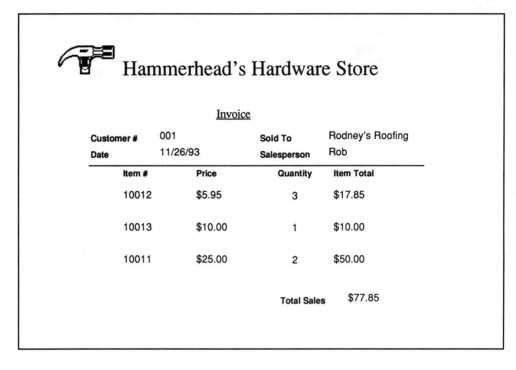

Figure 5-16   The invoice showing the three layout parts (body, header, and grand summary)

Using a blank layout

Before you create the new layout, make sure the Sales file is the active document. Since none of the preset layout types can accommodate the design of the invoice, you are going to use a blank layout type to insert only the fields and layout parts you need. (You could use one of the preset layout types but this would require more effort because you would have to rearrange all of the fields.)

Create a new, blank layout now by choosing New Layout from the Layout menu. In the New Layout dialog box, click Blank to select that layout type, name the layout Invoices, and click OK. Switch to Layout. The new layout only contains an empty body part; it does not contain any fields. One by one, you must manually insert the fields you want in the layout.

Including fields in a header part

The invoice includes all of the fields in the Sales file. However, some of the fields appear in the body part, and some are located in the header part, which you must add to the layout. The body part only contains the field data for Item #, Price, Quantity, and Item Total. The field names for these fields, as well as the

Hammerhead's Hardware Store

Invoice

| **Customer #** | 001 | | **Sold To** | Rodney's Roofing |
| **Date** | 11/26/93 | | **Salesperson** | Rob |

Item #	**Price**	**Quantity**	**Item Total**
10012	$5.95	3	$17.85

Invoice

| **Customer #** | 001 | | **Sold To** | Rodney's Roofing |
| **Date** | 11/26/93 | | **Salesperson** | Rob |

Item #	**Price**	**Quantity**	**Item Total**
10013	$10.00	1	$10.00

Invoice

| **Customer #** | 001 | | **Sold To** | Rodney's Roofing |
| **Date** | 11/26/93 | | **Salesperson** | Rob |

Item #	**Price**	**Quantity**	**Item Total**
10011	$25.00	2	$50.00

Total Sales $77.85

Figure 5-17   Result of placing all fields in the body part

remaining fields and field names in the file, are placed in the header part. If you insert all of the fields in the body part instead and do not use the header part, the information repeats for each item sold in the invoice. Figure 5-17 illustrates this.

In other words, whatever you place in the body part repeats for each record in the file or, in the case of your invoice, for each record matching the Customer # and Date you specify. By including some fields and their field names in a header part, you can ensure that data does not repeat for each record.

Insert a header part in your layout now. Choose Insert Part from the Layout menu. In the Insert Part dialog box, click Header, and click OK. Your layout contains an empty body and an empty header; now you are ready to insert fields.

Inserting fields

Begin by resizing the header part; it is a little too small to accommodate the objects. To do this, position the resize pointer over the header part boundary and drag down to the 1.25-inch mark on the vertical ruler.

Now you can insert fields in the header part. Turn on the graphics ruler so you can more precisely place fields in the layout. Choose Insert Field from the Layout menu. In the Insert Field dialog box, Ctrl-click to select the Customer #, Sold To, Date, and Salesperson fields, then click OK. ClarisWorks automatically places the four fields and their field names in the body part. Select all of the objects by pressing Ctrl+A, and drag them into the header part.

Shorten the length of the field objects and position all of the objects in the header part so they are arranged as shown in Figure 5-18. (Use the Align Objects dialog box to align the objects in the header part with each other.)

Insert the remaining fields—Item #, Price, Quantity, and Item Total—into the body part. These fields get a little different treatment. Because you don't want the field names to repeat in the body of the invoice, but you do want the data in the fields to repeat, move the field names into the header part, leaving the field objects in the body part. The field names will appear as column headers for the data that appears in the body of the invoice. Move and resize the objects so your layout looks like the one shown in Figure 5-19.

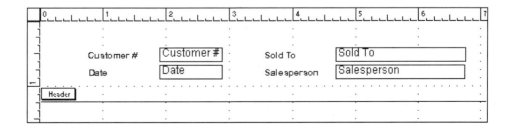

Figure 5-18   Arrangement of field names and field objects in the header part

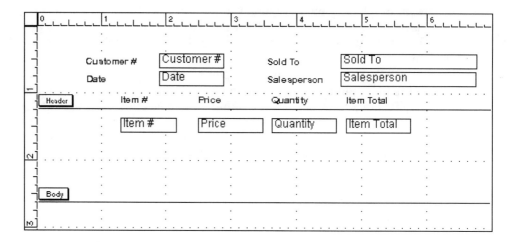

Figure 5-19   Fields in place in the Invoices layout

The size of the body part determines how much room each record occupies in your document. You can think of the body part boundary as a *section break;* another record's data begins after the body part boundary. In the Invoices layout, you see that there is about 1 inch of blank space between each record's data. (If you switch to Browse, you can see this effect better.) To close up the space between each record's data, resize the body part by positioning the resize pointer over the body part boundary and dragging up to about the 1.75-inch mark on the vertical graphics ruler. Switch to Browse to see your changes.

Note   *In Browse, you notice that the header part contains customer, date, and salesperson data from the current record, but the body part lists sales information from all records in the document. Later in this section, when you use Match Records, you will limit the sales information in the body part to those records that pertain to the current customer.*

Before you move on to add text and graphics to the invoice, you need to make two object attribute changes. Specifically, you need to change the number format of the Price and Item Total fields and change the alignment of the Quantity field data.

Switch to Layout, and double-click the Price field object to open the Number Format dialog box. Click the Currency option, then click OK. Do the same thing for the Item Total field object.

Now change the alignment of the data in the Quantity field so it is centered below the Quantity field name in the document. In Layout, select the Quantity field name and field object, and choose Center (Ctrl+\) from the Alignment cascading menu in the Format menu. Switch to Browse to see your changes.

Adding text and graphics

Earlier in this chapter, when you defined the Order Form layout, you added a header to the Sales database document and placed the store's name and logo in it. Because this header was defined at the document level rather than at the layout level, the Invoices layout inherits it. So you don't need to add this to the layout; it is already in place. To verify that this is true, switch to Browse and turn on Page View.

The text and graphics objects that remain to be added to the Invoices layout include text to identify this form as an invoice and a line to divide the header information from the body.

Switch to Layout, and select the text tool. Click once in the header part above the existing objects. In the text frame, type **Invoice**. Change the font type, size, and style if you want. For example, the final invoice shown in Figure 5-16 uses Times New Roman 14 Point Underline. Move the text frame so it is centered between the left and right edges of the layout.

To add the line in the header part, select the line tool from the tool palette. Begin the line approximately 0.75 inches across and 1 inch down. Hold down the Shift key as you drag across the layout to draw a straight line. When the line is about 5.5 inches long, release the mouse. Figure 5-20 shows what your layout should look like now.

Your invoice is nearly complete. In the next section, you add a grand summary part to the layout to show the sum of the Item Total fields in the invoice.

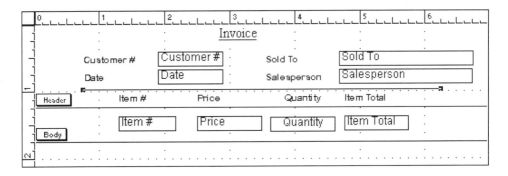

Figure 5-20   Text and graphics in place in the Invoices layout

Adding a grand summary part

You use a grand summary part to summarize, or total, data over all visible records in a document. In the case of your invoice, you want to summarize the Item Total field data for all of the items sold to a particular customer on a given day. The result is the total sales amount on the invoice.

There are two types of grand summary parts: leading or trailing. A *leading summary part* displays the summarized information before the body part; conversely, a *trailing grand summary* appears after the information it summarizes. Your invoice will use a trailing grand summary part.

To attain a summary total, you need to add a summary field to your database structure. The summary field uses a formula to add the values in a given field for all visible records. In this case, the summary field formula totals the information in the Item Total field. This summary field is then inserted into the grand summary part in the layout. The important thing to remember is that a summary field and a grand summary part work together to summarize data in a layout. To define the summary field:

1   **Choose Define Fields from the Layout menu.**

2   **In the Define Fields dialog box, type the field name** Total Sales, **click Summary (or press Alt+S) to select that field type, then click Create.** The Calculation dialog box opens for you to enter the formula for the Total Sales summary field.

3   **Type the formula shown in the formula area of the dialog box in Figure 5-21.** Be sure to enclose the Item Total field name in single quotation marks.

4   **When you are finished, click OK in the Calculation dialog box, and click Done in the Define Fields dialog box.**

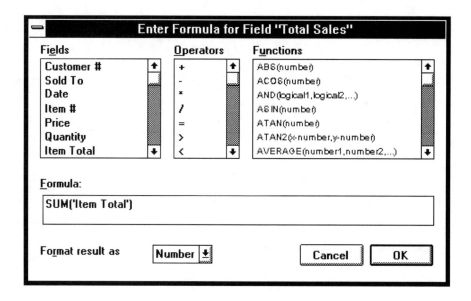

Figure 5-21   Formula for the Total Sales summary field

Now, add the grand summary part to the layout. In Layout, choose Insert Part from the Layout menu. In the Insert Part dialog box, click Trailing Grand Summary, and click OK. The layout updates to show the grand summary part below the body part in the layout. With the summary field defined and the grand summary part inserted into the layout, you are ready to add the summary field to the grand summary part. To do so:

1   **In Layout, choose Insert Field from the Layout menu.**

2   **In the Insert Field dialog box, click Total Sales, and then click OK.**
    The Total Sales field and its field name appear at the bottom of the body part, which expands to accommodate it.

3   **To move the summary field into proper position, select the Total Sales field and field name, then drag the objects into the grand summary part until they are in the position shown in Figure 5-22.**

Slide the body part up so it is in line with the 1.75-inch mark in the vertical ruler, and change the format of the Total Sales field so its contents appear in Currency format.

Note   *You won't be able to see the effect of the grand summary part until you switch to Browse and turn on Page View. Summary part information is only visible in Page View.*

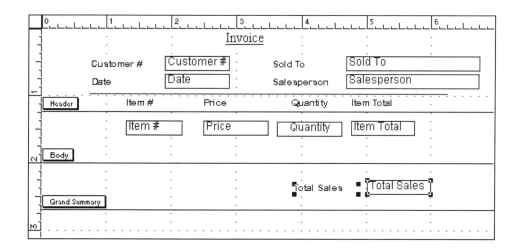

Figure 5-22   The summary field in position in the grand summary part

Your invoice layout is complete. In the next section you limit the data shown in the invoice to that pertaining to a given customer on a particular date. Before you move on, press Ctrl+S to save your changes to the Sales file.

Searching for invoice data

Before you can print or view a customer's invoice, you need to locate all of the records for the given customer on the given date. You can do this in one of two ways: by using a find request or by choosing Match Records from the Organize menu. Either way, you need to specify two search criteria—the customer's identifying number and the date of the sale.

If you use a find request, you must switch to a different layout to type the search criteria in the search fields, then switch back to the Invoices layout to view the found set. This is necessary because you cannot access the Customer # and Date fields in the header part of the Invoices layout. Try it. Choose Find from the Layout menu and try to click in the Customer # field. ClarisWorks doesn't let you. The same is true in Browse—you cannot edit or enter data in the fields located in the header part. Only the fields in the body part are accessible in Find and Browse.

Using the Match Records command

You can use the Match Records command instead of using a find request to locate records. The Match Records command does not use any layout to conduct a search. Instead, when you match records, you specify a search criteria as a formula using a dialog box that closely resembles the Calculation dialog box. The Match Records feature also lets you specify a more complex search criteria than a find request does.

In the following steps, you use Match Records to search for all of the records in the Sales file that contain a customer number of 001 and a date of 11/26/93. The result of the search becomes the data for an invoice for Customer 001 on the specified day. To do the search:

1   **With the Invoices layout active, switch from Layout to Browse.** You must switch to Browse, because the Organize menu is not available in Layout.

2   **Choose Match Records (Ctrl+M) from the Organize menu.** The Match Records dialog box opens. Notice that it is similar to the Calculation dialog box (see Figure 5-23). The only difference is that it does not contain the "Format result as" option.

3   **In the Formula area of the dialog box, type the following formula, or use the Fields, Operators, and Functions areas to build the formula:**

```
AND('Customer #'="001",'Date'=TEXTTODATE("11/26/93"))
```

```
┌─────────────────────────────────────────────────────────────────┐
│ ─            Enter Match Records Condition                        │
├─────────────────────────────────────────────────────────────────┤
│ Fields              Operators        Functions                    │
│ ┌─────────────┬─┐  ┌─────┬─┐  ┌──────────────────────────┬─┐      │
│ │ Customer #  │▲│  │ +   │▲│  │ ABS(number)              │▲│      │
│ │ Sold To     │ │  │ -   │ │  │ ACOS(number)             │ │      │
│ │ Date        │ │  │ x   │ │  │ AND(logical1,logical2,...)│ │      │
│ │ Item #      │ │  │ /   │ │  │ ASIN(number)             │ │      │
│ │ Price       │ │  │ =   │ │  │ ATAN(number)             │ │      │
│ │ Quantity    │ │  │ >   │ │  │ ATAN2(x-number,y-number) │ │      │
│ │ Item Total  │▼│  │ <   │▼│  │ AVERAGE(number1,number2,...)│▼│   │
│ └─────────────┴─┘  └─────┴─┘  └──────────────────────────┴─┘      │
│                                                                   │
│ Formula:                                                          │
│ ┌───────────────────────────────────────────────────────────┐   │
│ │ │                                                           │   │
│ │                                                             │   │
│ └───────────────────────────────────────────────────────────┘   │
│                                                                   │
│                              ┌──────────┐  ┌──────────┐          │
│                              │  Cancel  │  │    OK    │          │
│                              └──────────┘  └──────────┘          │
└─────────────────────────────────────────────────────────────────┘
```

Figure 5-23   Match Records dialog box

The AND function requires two logical expressions and results in true if both expressions are true, or false if one of the expressions is false. In this case, you use the AND function to tell ClarisWorks to match records in which both logical expressions are true. The TEXTTODATE function is used to convert the date entered as text to a date data type.

If you want to be able to use this search formula again, select it in the dialog box, and press Ctrl+C to copy it to the Clipboard before you leave the dialog box. This way, when you choose Match Records again, you can paste the formula into the dialog box instead of retyping it.

TIP

4   Click OK in the Match Records dialog box.

ClarisWorks returns to Browse and highlights (selects) the records that match the search criteria (see Figure 5-24).

Because you only want to work with the found set, choose Hide Unselected [Ctrl+)] from the Organize menu to hide the records not matching the search criteria. The unselected records are temporarily put away. This step is important because your summary field only summarizes visible records. If you

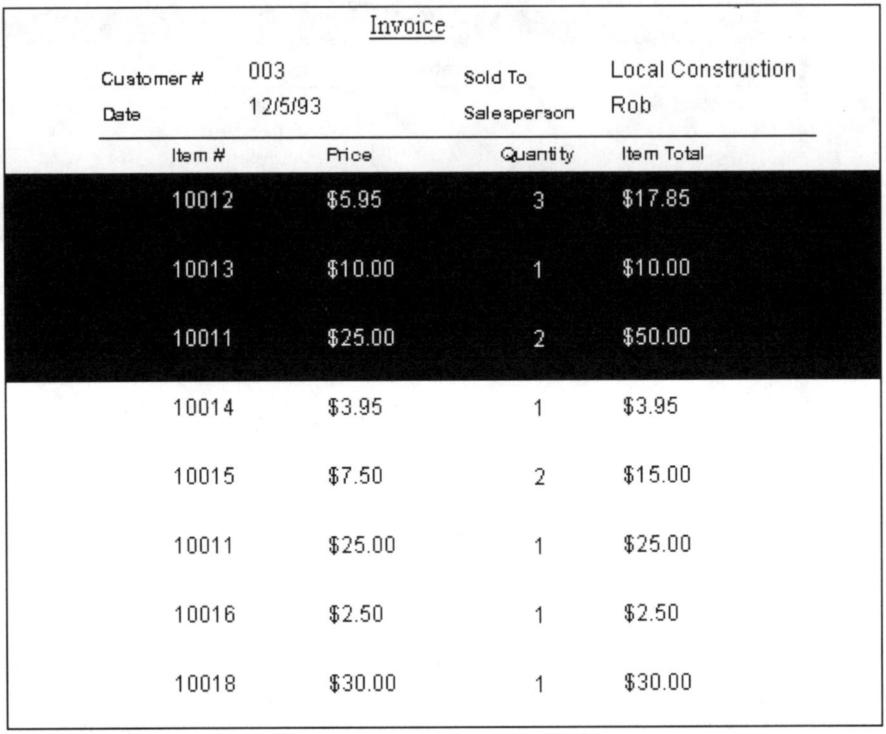

Invoice			
Customer # 003		**Sold To**	Local Construction
Date 12/5/93		**Salesperson**	Rob
Item #	Price	Quantity	Item Total
10012	$5.95	3	$17.85
10013	$10.00	1	$10.00
10011	$25.00	2	$50.00
10014	$3.95	1	$3.95
10015	$7.50	2	$15.00
10011	$25.00	1	$25.00
10016	$2.50	1	$2.50
10018	$30.00	1	$30.00

Figure 5-24   The matching records are selected in the current layout

do not hide the unselected records, they are included in the invoice and in the Total Sales summary data in the grand summary part.

The data appearing in the header part of your invoice may not match the data in the found set of records nor that shown in Figure 5-24. Again, field data in the header part is treated differently than field data in the body part. ClarisWorks uses the Customer #, Date, Sold To, and Salesperson data from the record that was selected before you performed the search. However, when you turn on Page View (Shift+Ctrl+P), the correct data appears in the header part.

In Browse, turn on Page View, and you'll see the invoice for Customer # 001's purchases on November 26, 1993. Figure 5-16 shows the resulting invoice. Use the previous steps to search for each customer number and date in your Sales file to generate an invoice for each sale.

When printing your invoice or any other database document, you have the option of printing the layout with either the currently selected record or the visible records. These options appear in the Print dialog box when you choose

Print from the File menu. To make these options available in the dialog box, you must choose Print from Browse. If you choose Print from Layout, these options are not available.

Note   The ClarisWorks Find/Change feature provides another way of searching for information. Find/Change does not search for records matching criteria. Instead, it finds or replaces a word or phrase in your document. Find/Change is available in all ClarisWorks environments.

In the database environment, you can use Find/Change in Browse and Find views to find or replace a character, word, or phrase in text, number, date, and time fields. Find/Change does not search in calculation or summary fields for the specified text. In Layout, you can use Find/Change to find or replace a character, word, or phrase in any text frame, including field names. Find/Change does not search in field objects in Layout view.

Creating a sales report

In this section, you use the Sales file to create a report that subtotals sales by salesperson and totals overall sales. The report is based on the columnar report layout and is modified to include the following elements:

- Sub-summary part to contain each salesperson's total amount sold
- Trailing grand summary part to contain total overall sales
- A spreadsheet frame to contain the summary data
- A chart derived from the spreadsheet frame showing each salesperson's percent of overall sales

First, you will create a new layout for the Sales file, then you will add the necessary summary fields to the database structure and summary parts to the layout. Finally, you will include a spreadsheet in the report to chart the summary data. Figure 5-25 shows what your report will look like when you are finished with this section.

Hammerhead's Hardware Store

Salesperson	Date	Item #	Price	Quantity	Item Total
Rob	11/26/93	10011	$25.00	2	$50.00
Rob	11/26/93	10013	$10.00	1	$10.00
Rob	11/26/93	10012	$5.95	3	$17.85
Rob	12/5/93	10018	$30.00	1	$30.00
			Salesperson Total:		$107.85
Tom	11/26/93	10015	$7.50	2	$15.00
Tom	11/26/93	10014	$3.95	1	$3.95
			Salesperson Total:		$18.95
Yogi	11/27/93	10016	$2.50	1	$2.50
Yogi	11/27/93	10011	$25.00	1	$25.00
			Salesperson Total:		$27.50

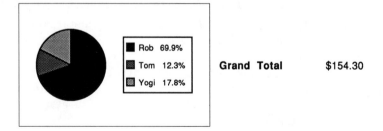

Grand Total $154.30

Figure 5-25   Finished sales report

Creating the layout

Begin with the Sales file open and active. Create a new layout by choosing New Layout from the Layout menu. In the dialog box, click "Columnar report" to select that layout type, name the layout Sales Report, and click OK.

The Set Field Order dialog box opens for you to specify the fields to include in the report and the order in which they should appear across the document. One by one, select the following fields, and click Move to move them to the field order list in the order shown:

Salesperson

Date

Item #

Price

Quantity

Item Total

When you are finished in the dialog box, click OK. Switch to Layout. The preset columnar report layout displays on your screen, with field names in the header part, and field objects in the body part.

The modifications you need to make to the layout include resizing and moving the field names and field objects, specifying different alignment options for field data, and changing the number format of two of the fields.

As you did earlier in this chapter, resize and move the field names and field objects in the layout so they are sized and positioned as shown in Figure 5-26.

Turn on the graphics ruler so you can position the objects more exactly. Use the Align Objects dialog box to align the objects with one another. If you want, create two views of your document—one in Layout, one in Browse—to track how layout changes affect the overall look of your report.

The position and size of the objects in the layout shown in Figure 5-26 allow for changes in alignment of some of the data. For example, the Price field data

Figure 5-26   Proper size and position of the report layout objects

will appear right-aligned in the Price column. If you don't arrange the Price field name frame and the field object as shown in the figure, the data and column name will not look right in the report.

Now change the alignment of some of the field objects so the data appears lined up in the report. Specifically, the Price and Item Total field data need to be aligned against the right edge of the field so the numbers align properly along their decimal points. The Quantity field data needs to be centered within the Quantity column.

In Layout, Shift-click to select the Price and Item Total field objects in the body part. Choose Right (Ctrl+]) from the Alignment cascading menu in the Format menu. Notice that the field names inside of the objects shift to the right to indicate that they are now right-aligned. To change the alignment of the Quantity field data, click its field object, and choose Center (Ctrl+\) from the Alignment cascading menu. Look at the Browse view and decide whether or not you are satisfied with your layout changes. You may need to make further adjustments in the position of field names or field objects.

Now change the format of the Price and Item Total field objects to currency using the Number Format dialog box.

You are finished with your layout modifications and can move on to add the summary parts to your layout. If you want, you can also change font attributes for the field names and field data. For example, in the final sales report shown in Figure 5-25, the field names appear in Arial 12 Point Underline instead of the preset Arial 10 Point Bold and Underline.

Adding summary parts

When you created the invoice earlier in this chapter, you used a trailing grand summary part to display Item Total summary information. Your sales report includes a grand summary part again as well as a sub-summary part.

You use a sub-summary part to calculate and display subtotals across a group of sorted records. In the case of the sales report, you are going to use a sub-summary report to subtotal the Item Total field for each salesperson. Like grand summary parts, sub-summary parts work with a summary field. You must have a summary field defined in order to use a sub-summary part. (Recall that a summary field uses a formula to summarize data in a given field across all visible records.) The summary field used in the report sums the data in Item Total. Unlike grand summary parts, which summarize data for all visible records, sub-summary parts summarize data for records in a sorted group. That is, after using a summary field to calculate your subtotals and inserting a sub-summary part to display the summary field data, you sort your document using the field by which you want the data summarized. In the case of the sales report, you sort the data by salesperson, because you want subtotals by salesperson.

You can place a sub-summary part above or below the data that it summarizes. You can also insert more than one sub-summary part in a layout. For example, your sales report could have a sub-summary part to show subtotal sales by salesperson for a given day and another sub-summary part to show subtotal sales by salesperson for all days.

Like grand summary parts, you can only view the data in sub-summary parts when you are in Browse with Page View turned on or when you print the document. Additionally, sub-summary parts do not appear until records are sorted.

Adding the sub-summary part

The first step in adding a sub-summary part is to define a summary field. For the report, you want a summary field that contains a formula to sum all of the data in the Item Total field for a particular salesperson. The formula for this summary field is

```
SUM('Item Total')
```

Notice that this is the same formula in the Total Sales summary field you defined earlier for your invoice. You have two options: you can use the Total Sales summary field in your sub-summary part, or you can define another summary field that contains the exact same formula as the Total Sales summary field. You can use the Total Sales summary field because, when you insert it in the sub-summary part, it only summarizes the data in each group of sorted records (such as each salesperson) and will not apply to all of the records as it did in the invoice. Therefore, since you can use an existing summary field here, you don't need to define a new one.

The second step to adding a sub-summary part is to insert the part in the layout. To insert the part:

1   **In Layout, choose Insert Part from the Layout menu.** The Insert Part dialog box opens, with the "Sub-Summary when sorted by:" option already selected for you (see Figure 5-27).

    You use the field list in the right area of the dialog box to specify the field to which the sub-summary information will apply.

2   **Click Salesperson in the field list to specify it as the sort field for the sub-summary part.**

3   **Click OK.** A message box opens for you to specify whether the sub-summary should appear above or below the data it summarizes.

4   **Click Below.**

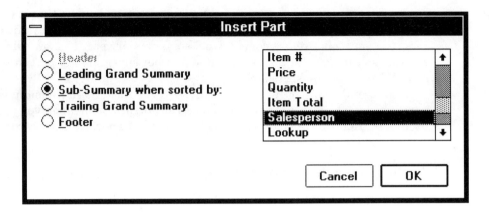

Figure 5-27   The Insert Part dialog box with "Sub-Summary when sorted by:" selected

The sub-summary part appears below the body part in the layout and is labeled "Sub-summary by Salesperson." If you select Above in the message box, the sub-summary part appears between the header and body parts or between a leading grand summary part and the body part.

Now you are going to insert the summary field into the new part. Choose Insert Field from the Layout menu. In the dialog box, double-click the Total Sales summary field. It appears in the body part of the layout. Select the field and its field name, and drag it into the sub-summary part (see Figure 5-28). Then resize the body part back to its original size.

With your summary field in position, you need to rename the field name frame to Salesperson Total, change the number format of the Total Sales field to Currency, and set the field to align against the right edge of the field. Click in the field name frame to switch to the text environment, and edit the text so it

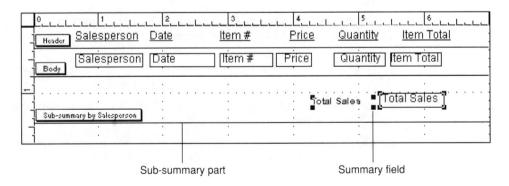

Figure 5-28   The summary field in the sub-summary part

reads "Salesperson Total:". If you want, you can change the text attributes at this point as well. Resize and move the frame as needed to accommodate the text change.

Select the Total Sales field object, and change the number format to Currency in the Number Format dialog box. To change the field's alignment so it is in line with the Item Total data in the report, leave the object selected, choose Right from the Alignment cascading menu in the Format menu, and use the Align Objects dialog box to align the right edges of the Total Sales and Item Total field objects in the layout.

Before you can see the sub-summary data, you must sort the file on the same field you specified when you inserted the part (Salesperson, in this case). To sort the file:

1   **Switch to Browse.**

2   **Choose Sort Records (Ctrl+J) from the Organize menu.**

3   **In the Sort Records dialog box, click Clear to remove the existing sort order, if one is in effect.**

4   **Select the Salesperson field from the Field List.**

5   **Click Move to move it to the Sort Order list, then click OK.** Your document is now sorted alphabetically by Salesperson.

If you want your sales report sorted by Salesperson and Date, specify both fields, in that order, in the Sort Order list of the Sort Records dialog box. This way the report sorts first by Salesperson, then by Date.

TIP

To view the sub-summary data, turn on Page View. Figure 5-29 shows part of the data in the Sales file in the Sales Report layout with subtotals for each salesperson. Now you are ready to add the grand summary part to your layout.

Note   *The store logo and name are still in place in this new layout because you placed them in a header at the document level earlier in this chapter.*

Hammerhead's Hardware Store

Salesperson	Date	Item #	Price	Quantity	Item Total
Rob	11/26/93	10012	$5.95	3	$17.85
Rob	11/26/93	10013	$10.00	1	$10.00
Rob	11/26/93	10011	$25.00	2	$50.00
Rob	12/5/93	10018	$30.00	1	$30.00
			Salesperson Total:		$107.85
Tom	11/26/93	10014	$3.95	1	$3.95
Tom	11/26/93	10015	$7.50	2	$15.00
			Salesperson Total:		$18.95

Figure 5-29   Part of the data in the Sales Report layout with data sorted by salesperson and with subtotal data in place

Adding the grand summary part

In your report, you want to display a grand total that is the total amount sold for all salespeople. You use a grand summary part and a summary field to do this.

The summary field formula needs to add up the Item Total field across all records. So the formula is exactly the same as the Total Sales summary field you used in the grand summary part for your invoices:

```
SUM('Item Total')
```

Although you can use the Total Sales summary field for this grand summary part, you already inserted the Total Sales summary field into the sub-summary part. ClarisWorks only allows you to insert a field into a layout once. So, this time you need to define a new summary field that has the exact same formula as the Total Sales summary field.

Use the Define Fields dialog box now to create a new field named Grand Total and select Summary as the field type. Enter the previous formula in the Formula area of the Calculation dialog box, click OK, and click Done. Your new summary field is now defined. To place it in the layout in a grand summary part:

1 **Switch to Layout.**

2 **Choose Insert Part from the Layout menu.**

3 **In the dialog box, select Trailing Grand Summary, and click OK.** The grand summary part appears in the layout below the sub-summary part.

4 **Choose Insert Field from the Layout menu.**

5 **In the dialog box, select the Grand Total summary field you just defined, and click OK.**

The Grand Total field and its field name appear in the body part of the layout. Drag them down into the grand summary part until they are in the position shown in Figure 5-30, and resize the body part to its original size.

As you did with the sub-summary field object, you need to change the number format of the Grand Total field to Currency and set the field to align against the right edge of the field. Select the Grand Total field object, and change the number format to Currency in the Number Format dialog box. To align the field data with the rest of the data in this column of the report, leave the object selected, choose Right from the Alignment cascading menu in the Format menu, and use the Align Objects dialog box to align the right edges of the Grand Total, Total Sales, and Item Total field objects in the layout. If you want, change the font size of the Grand Total field name to 12 point. To see your changes, switch to Browse view, and turn on Page View. The Grand Total data appears at the bottom of the page, below the last salesperson's subtotal.

In the next section, you add a spreadsheet frame to your database document to make a chart based on the summary data.

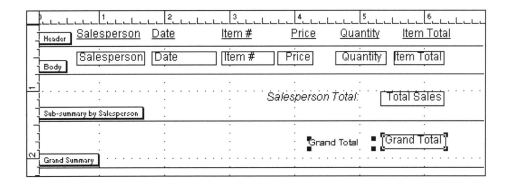

Figure 5-30   The Grand Total summary field in position in the grand summary part

Including a spreadsheet frame

To jazz up your sales report and to emphasize each salesperson's performance in the report, you can include a pie chart. This way, at a glance, you can determine the percentage of sales each salesperson is achieving.

In Chapter 3, you created a chart based on spreadsheet frame data in a graphics document. In this case, you use a spreadsheet frame in a database document. You can add spreadsheet frames to a database document in Layout view, where the tool palette is available.

The ability to add spreadsheet frames to a database document has many useful applications. For example, you can include a spreadsheet in a sales report to show historical data, such as past sales performance for each salesperson. Or you can paste data from one database document into a spreadsheet frame in another database document to show related information. In this section, you are going to use the spreadsheet frame to extract the summary data from the report and chart it.

Copying summaries

ClarisWorks gives you the ability to copy summary data from a database document to the Clipboard. Switch to Browse now, make sure Page View is on, and pull down the Edit menu. Notice that the Copy command has become Copy Summaries.

The Copy Summaries command becomes available in the Edit menu when you are in Browse with Page View on, with no records selected, and with at least one summary part in the current layout. When you choose Copy Summaries, the summary data appearing in your document is copied to the Clipboard, where it remains available for you to use in any way you want. Any type of summary data is copied, including leading and trailing grand summary data and sub-summary data. You can paste the summaries into any document type or paste them into fields in a database. The idea behind Copy Summaries is to give you a method of collecting and using summary information.

For your report, you use Copy Summaries to copy the summary information from the sales report to a spreadsheet frame that appears in the same document. In Browse, choose Copy Summaries now to copy the sub-summary and grand summary data from your report to the Clipboard. The summaries remain in the Clipboard until you perform another Copy or Cut operation, or until you quit ClarisWorks.

Adding the spreadsheet frame

You can add a spreadsheet frame anywhere in the layout that you want, as long as you place it inside of a layout part. However, keep in mind the way in which ClarisWorks treats objects in different layout parts. For example, if you place the spreadsheet frame in the body part, it repeats for each record in your document; if you place it in the header part, it repeats at the top of each page of your document; in the footer part, it repeats at the bottom of each page. The logical choice of layout part to contain the spreadsheet frame is the grand summary part. This way, the spreadsheet data only appears once in the document, at the end of the data (trailing grand summary) or at the beginning of the data (leading grand summary).

To create your spreadsheet frame, switch to Layout now, make sure the tool palette is visible, and turn on the graphics ruler. So you have room in the grand summary part, resize it so it is approximately 2.5 inches high—that is, the distance from the sub-summary part boundary and the grand summary part boundary is 2.5 inches.

Select the spreadsheet tool from the tool palette and, in the grand summary part, click and drag to create a spreadsheet frame that is two columns wide and four rows long, as shown in Figure 5-31. When you release the mouse, ClarisWorks switches to the spreadsheet environment, activates the spreadsheet menus, and selects cell A1 in the frame.

To make sure the summaries are still in the Clipboard, switch to the Program Manager and double-click the Clipboard icon in the Main program group to open the Clipboard. If the summaries are not in the Clipboard, switch back to your Sales document in ClarisWorks, make sure you are in Browse and Page View, and choose Copy Summaries (Ctrl+C) from the Edit menu. Figure 5-32 shows the Clipboard containing the sales report summaries. The first three numbers are each salesperson's subtotal and the last number is the grand total.

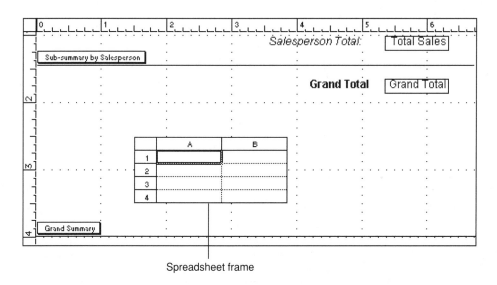

Spreadsheet frame

Figure 5-31   Creating a spreadsheet frame in the layout

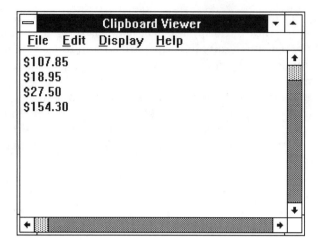

Figure 5-32   Summaries in the Clipboard

Since you want to be able to identify which summary belongs to which sales-person, you need to type the names of the salespersons in the order in which they appear in the report. Then you can paste in the summaries. To enter the data:

1   **Switch to Layout.**

2   **In the spreadsheet frame, click in cell A1.**

3   **In cell A1, type** Rob; **in cell A2, type** Tom; **and in cell A3, type** Yogi. Press ↵ to move down the spreadsheet one row at a time.

4   **In cell A4, type** Total.

5   **Click in cell B1 to make it active.**

6   **With cell B1 active, choose Paste (Ctrl+V) from the Edit menu.** The summaries appear in cells B1 through B4 and these cells are selected in the frame (see Figure 5-33).

Notice that the number formats you specified for the summary data are dropped when you copy and paste the summaries. If you want to retain the same number formatting in the frame, leave the range B1 through B4 selected, choose Number from the Format menu, and click Currency in the Numeric dialog box.

Note   *If the summary data changes in the database document, it is not automati-cally updated in the spreadsheet frame. That is, once summaries are copied and pasted, they do not remain linked to the data in the database document. You must copy and paste summaries into the spreadsheet frame manually if you change any of the data.*

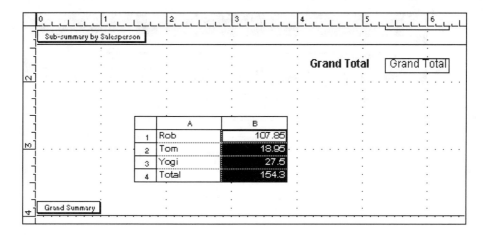

Figure 5-33   The report summaries pasted in the spreadsheet frame

Making the chart

Now you are ready to chart the summary information from the spreadsheet frame so that the chart appears at the bottom of the report in the grand summary part. You are going to chart each salesperson's sub-summary. To create the chart:

1   In the spreadsheet frame, select cells A1 through B3. This selects the names of the salespeople and their subtotals. The selected names are included in the chart's legend when the Legend option is selected in the Make Chart dialog box.

2   Choose Make Chart (Ctrl+M) from the Options menu. The Make Chart dialog box opens, showing the pie chart type and its options selected (see Figure 5-34).

3   Leave the pie chart type selected in the Categories area of the dialog box. Select the Show Percentages option, and deselect Color. Show Percentages displays numbers as a percent of the total in the chart's legend (preset) or in each pie slice. You deselect Color so you can print the chart on a black-and-white printer. If you have a color printer, leave Color selected.

4   Leave all other options as is, and click OK.

A large pie chart appears in the window on top of the current layout and the legend shows each salesperson's name and his or her respective percent of overall sales. Selection handles appear around the chart and the graphics tool is selected in the tool palette. Use the selection handles to resize the chart so it is small enough to fit in the grand summary layout part, and drag the chart so it appears to the left of Grand Total and covers the spreadsheet frame, as shown in Figure 5-35.

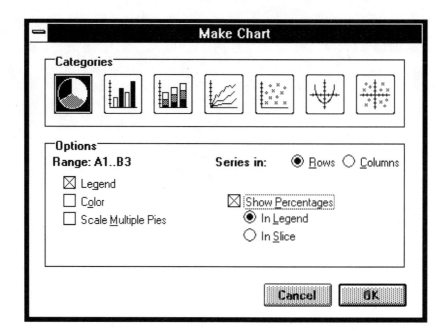

Figure 5-34   The Make Chart dialog box with pie chart selected

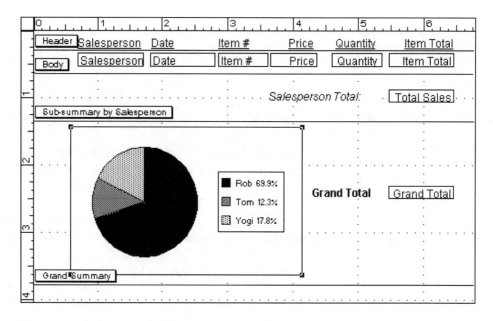

Figure 5-35   The pie chart in position in the grand summary part

With your chart in position in the layout, switch to Browse, and turn on Page View to see how your report looks. Your report should look like the final sales report shown in Figure 5-25. Press Ctrl+S to save your document.

At this point, if you want to print your sales report, choose Print from the File menu, select either the Current Record or Visible Records option in the Print dialog box, and click OK. See "Printing the Report" in Chapter 4 for more information on printing reports and forms.

Summary

In this section, you used the features of the database, text, graphics, and spreadsheet environments together to create a sales order entry form, an invoice, and a sales report from data in two database documents. Of course, there are many other types of reports and forms you can create in ClarisWorks using the same techniques presented here.

The next chapter focuses on using the spreadsheet environment to manage home and business financial information.

Chapter Six

Managing Financial Information

About this chapter

This chapter focuses on how to use the spreadsheet environment most effectively for home or business needs. You will learn how to use the spreadsheet, graphics, and text environments together to create a household budget and an installment payment table for amortizing loans.

In creating the different spreadsheets presented in this chapter, you will use a variety of formulas and functions to perform both simple and complex computations. The chapter also describes how to annotate spreadsheet data with text frames and enhance spreadsheets with graphics and charts.

Creating a household budget

Spreadsheets easily lend themselves to managing and analyzing financial data. A spreadsheet is an electronic worksheet where you enter data—primarily numeric data—and perform calculations on the data. The spreadsheet's grid is similar to ledger paper that an accountant might use for managing financial information. The beauty of a spreadsheet is that you can perform what-if analyses, automate computations by specifying formulas and using the functions built into ClarisWorks, and format the data for presentation purposes. (You may want to refresh yourself on spreadsheet basics by referring to the following sections of Chapter 1 before continuing: "The Spreadsheet Environment," "Spreadsheet Documents," and "Spreadsheet Tool.")

In this section, you create an annual budget for a typical household. The budget shows various categories of expenses by month for a given year. The steps for creating the budget are as follows:

- Creating and setting up a new spreadsheet document
- Entering data
- Using formulas
- Formatting the spreadsheet and its data
- Adding text frames and graphics
- Charting the budget data
- Printing the budget

Figure 6-1 on pages 306 and 307 shows what the household budget and its associated chart will look like when you complete this section.

Setting up the document

Begin by starting ClarisWorks and create a new spreadsheet document. In the New dialog box, click Spreadsheet to select that document type, and click OK. A new, untitled spreadsheet appears on the screen.

Before entering data into the new spreadsheet, you can make several changes to the document to customize your work area. (If you prefer, you can make these changes later after entering your data.) The setup options you change in this section include the document margins and spreadsheet size. You change these options using the Document dialog box (which is also available for other document types) and the Display dialog box (which is available only for spreadsheet documents and frames). Other options you can change for spreadsheet documents are available in the Display dialog box, which you use later in this chapter to turn off the grid lines, column headers, and row headers.

In addition to changing document options, you can also add a header or footer to your spreadsheet before entering data. Inserting headers and footers in spreadsheet documents works the same as adding them to other document types.

Changing margins

With your new spreadsheet document open and active, choose Document from the Format menu to open the Document dialog box. Figure 6-2 shows the Document dialog box with the preset spreadsheet options.

Notice that the dialog box offers slightly different options than the Document dialog box that opens for other document types. In addition to margins, starting page number, and display settings (which are always included in this dialog box regardless of document type), this dialog box also offers spreadsheet size options (explained in the next section). The Display area of the dialog box shows the Show Margins and Show Page Guides options dimmed, although the Show

Margins option is checked. When you view your document in Page View, these options become available in the dialog box. In Page View, spreadsheet documents are preset to show the page margins and hide the page guides.

To change the margin settings for a spreadsheet document, enter a number in the Top, Bottom, Left, or Right boxes in the Document dialog box. For your household budget, set all of the margins to 0.45 inches, which gives you a little more room for displaying data on each page. Leave the dialog box open for now.

Note   *The minimum margin sizes you can set depends on the type of printer you are using. For example, you can set margins to a very narrow size, such as .0125 inches. However, when you choose Print from the File menu to print the spreadsheet, you may see a message warning you that the document will be clipped when it prints.*

Margin settings are preset to measure in inches (in the U.S. version). This preset unit of measurement is determined by the Ruler dialog box. You can change the margins to measure in picas, points, millimeters, or centimeters by using the Ruler dialog box.

Changing the margins in a spreadsheet document does not at first appear to have any effect. In order to see the margins, you must turn on Page View in the Window menu. Also, make sure the Show Margins option is checked in the Document dialog box so the margins are visible in Page View.

Changing spreadsheet size

The size of a spreadsheet is determined by the number of rows and columns you have set in the Document dialog box. ClarisWorks is preset to create a new spreadsheet with 40 columns across and 500 rows down. By changing the Columns Across and Rows Down options in the Document dialog box, you change the size of the spreadsheet and thus the size of your available work area.

You can set the spreadsheet size up to 256 columns and 16,384 rows, which makes 4.2 million cells available to you. Most of the spreadsheet work you do with ClarisWorks, however, will not require a work area that is so large. In fact, you should change the Columns Across and Rows Down options so your spreadsheet does not contain many extraneous cells. Working with a spreadsheet grid that is larger than you need occupies unnecessary RAM (memory). Moreover, when you print a spreadsheet document, all of the cells beyond those that contain data or formatting information are also printed. Consequently, you may end up printing extra pages that only contain blank cells. To reduce the spreadsheet size for your budget:

1   **With the Document dialog box open, click in the Columns Across box and type** 15.

2   **Press Tab to move to the Rows Down box and type** 55.

3   **Click OK to return to the document.**

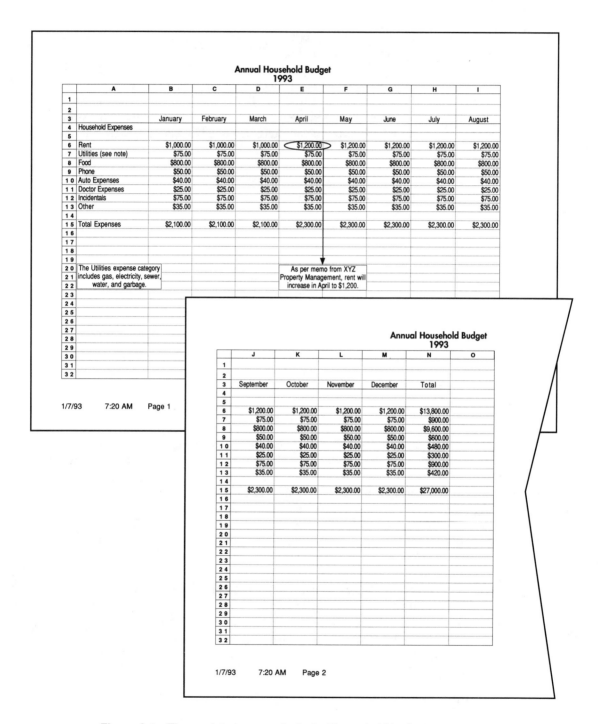

Figure 6-1   Three printed pages of a typical household budget

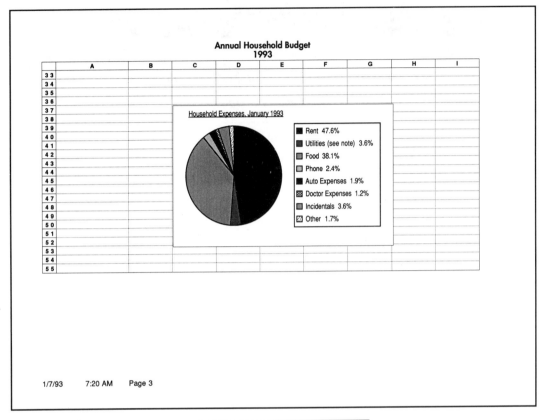

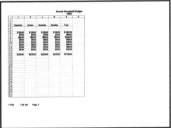

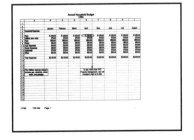

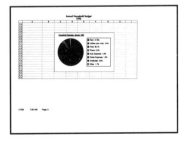

Figure 6-1   Three printed pages of a typical household budget (continued)

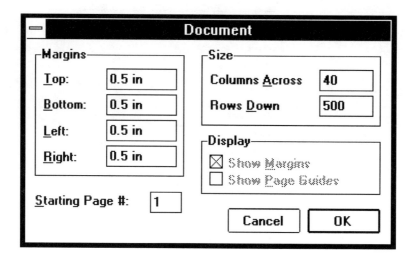

Figure 6-2   The Document dialog box with spreadsheet options

To see that your changes take effect, scroll across and down the document. Your spreadsheet should include columns A through O and rows 1 through 55.

You can set the number of columns or rows as low as 1, provided that you do not have any data in rows below 1 or in columns to the right of A. In other words, if you have data in your spreadsheet, the minimum number of rows down or columns across you can set in the Document dialog box is the last row or column containing data. For example, if you have data in row 250, you cannot set Rows Down below 250; if you have data in column AA, you cannot set Columns Across below 27.

You can also reduce the size of your spreadsheet by deleting cells. When you delete cells by choosing Delete Cells from the Calculate menu, you remove them from the spreadsheet grid. The remaining cells shift up (for row deletion) or left (for column deletion). As a result, the size of the spreadsheet is reduced by the number of rows and/or columns you delete; this reduction is reflected in the Document dialog box. For example, if you select rows 1 through 10 and choose Delete Cells from the Calculate menu, those rows are removed from the spreadsheet; the remaining rows then shift up, and the Rows Down setting in the Document dialog box is reduced by 10. If you select one cell at a time to remove, a dialog box appears prompting you to specify the direction in which the remaining cells should shift: up or left.

Similarly, you can increase spreadsheet size either by increasing the Columns Across and Rows Down settings in the Document dialog box or by inserting cells. To insert cells, select one or more rows in the spreadsheet and choose Insert Cells from the Calculate menu to add more rows; or select one or more columns and choose Insert Cells to add more columns. The number of rows or columns you select determines the number of rows or columns added to your spreadsheet. The remaining cells shift down (for row addition) or right (for column addition). To add one cell at a time, select the cell where you want the new one to be positioned, and choose Insert Cells from the Calculate menu. The Insert Cells dialog box appears and you specify the direction in which the current cell should shift: down or right. You can also select a range of cells and specify the insert direction.

When you first set up a spreadsheet document, you may not know exactly how many rows and columns you will need. If you prefer, you can adjust the spreadsheet size after entering data. If you specify the spreadsheet size before entering data and find the size is not large enough to accommodate your data, you can add columns and rows as needed.

Adding a header and footer

The process of adding a header and footer to a spreadsheet document is the same as adding them to any other document type. (See "Adding Headers, Footers, and Footnotes" in Chapter 2 for a complete description of headers and footers.) To add a header and footer to your budget document:

1   **Choose Insert Header from the Format menu.** ClarisWorks switches to Page View, activates text-related menus, and opens the header region of the document. Notice that, in Page View, you can see the size of the margins you set in the Document dialog box.

2   **In the header region, type** Annual Household Budget **and press ↵ to begin a second line in the header region.**

3   **Type** 1993.

4   **Press Ctrl+A to select the header text, and change the font style to Bold.**

5   **Choose Show Rulers from the Window menu.** The text ruler opens. When the I-beam pointer is active, choosing Show Rulers automatically displays the text ruler. When the crossbar pointer is active, choosing Show Rulers displays the graphics ruler.

6   **Click the center alignment icon to center the text in the header region.**

7   **Press Shift+Ctrl+U to hide the text ruler.**

8   **Press Enter on the numeric keypad to access the spreadsheet document and activate the previously selected cell.**

When you leave the header region and return to the spreadsheet document, ClarisWorks leaves you in Page View and activates the spreadsheet-related menus. Your document should resemble Figure 6-3.

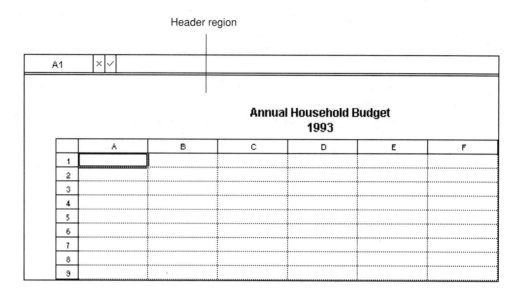

Figure 6-3   Header added to the budget spreadsheet

To add a footer, choose Insert Footer from the Format menu. ClarisWorks opens the footer region, activates text-related menus, and switches to Page View. To insert the date, time, and page number in the footer region:

1   **Choose Insert Date from the Edit menu.**

2   **Press Tab twice.**

3   **Choose Insert Time from the Edit menu.**

4   **Press Tab.**

5   **Type Page (be sure to include a space after the word), and choose Insert Page # from the Edit menu.** Your document should resemble Figure 6-4.

6   **Press Enter on the numeric keypad to access the spreadsheet document and activate the previously selected cell.**

The footer shown in Figure 6-4 uses the preset font, Arial 12 point. You can change text attributes in the footer region just as you can in the header region.

Remember that headers and footers are visible only in Page View in spreadsheet documents. When you turn Page View off, your header and footer temporarily disappear, as do the page margins and page guides (if you have them set to show). Throughout most of your work in spreadsheets, it is best to turn off Page View. This gives you slightly better performance—calculations complete more quickly, scrolling moves faster, and so on. Choose Page View from the Window menu to turn it off now.

With your document set up, you are ready to enter data into the budget spreadsheet.

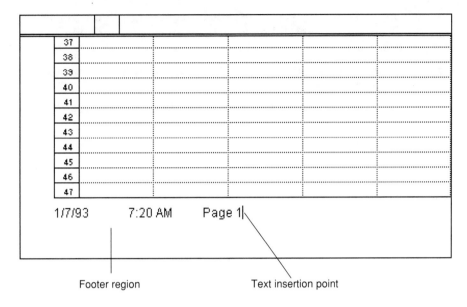

Footer region   Text insertion point

Figure 6-4   Footer added to the budget spreadsheet

Entering data

Before entering data into your spreadsheet, it is important to consider the type
of information you will be working with and how that information should best
be arranged in the grid. Typically, elements of time (such as weeks, months,
quarters, years, and so on) are grouped by column, while categories of data
within each time element are grouped by row. That is, you arrange a spreadsheet to show how various types of information change across time.

For example, in your budget, the elements of time are months of the year,
and each month appears in a separate column. The different types of information that change across time are categories of household expenses, and each
expense category appears in a separate row. The intersection of a row and
column reveals the amount of money spent in a particular expense category
during a given month.

To identify the various expense categories and the months of the year, enter
column and row labels into your spreadsheet first. To enter the row labels:

1 **Click in cell A4, and type** Household Expenses. This label actually serves
   as a title for the row labels to follow. Don't worry that the column is too
   narrow to contain the text you just typed; you will fix that later.

2 **Press ↵ twice to enter the Household Expenses label in the spreadsheet and to move down two cells.** Cell A6 should now be active.

3 Using Table 6-1, type the text in the designated cells, and press ↵ after typing each label to enter it in the spreadsheet and to move down one cell.

4 Click in cell A15, type Total Expenses, and press Enter on the numeric keypad.

5 Save your document by pressing Ctrl+S, and name it Budget.CWK.

Table 6-1   Budget Row Labels

In cell...	Type...
A6	Rent
A7	Utilities
A8	Food
A9	Phone
A10	Auto Expenses
A11	Doctor Expenses
A12	Incidentals
A13	Other

When you are finished typing the row labels and saving the document, your screen should look like the one in Figure 6-5.

Notice that some of the row labels are too long to fit in the cell properly. Later in this chapter when you format the spreadsheet, you will change the size of the cells to accommodate the text.

Now enter the column labels across the spreadsheet, using Table 6-2 as a guide. Be sure to press Tab after typing each label to enter the text and move to the next cell to the right.

Table 6-2   Budget Column Labels

In cell...	Type...
B3	January
C3	February
D3	March
E3	April
F3	May
G3	June
H3	July
I3	August
J3	September
K3	October
L3	November
M3	December
N3	Total

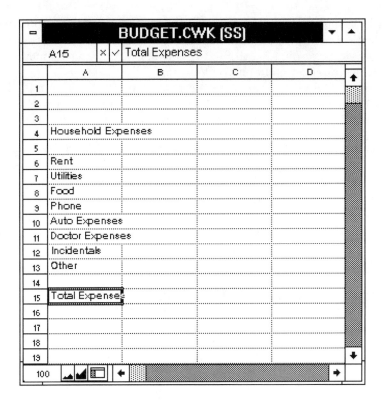

Figure 6-5   Budget spreadsheet with row labels entered

Rows 1 and 2 are blank in the budget spreadsheet. You can type row and column labels or data in these cells if you wish, or you can use these first few rows for the document title and date rather than placing them in a header or footer. Leaving them blank in the budget creates white space that makes the main body of the budget easier to read when it's printed.

TIP

With your row and column labels entered, you can use the spelling checker to make sure there are no spelling errors. Recall that the spelling checker is available in all ClarisWorks environments. To spell-check your budget, choose Check Document from the Spelling cascading menu in the Edit menu, or press Ctrl+=. The Spelling dialog box opens and spell-checking begins immediately. Correct any misspelled words by typing the correct spelling in the Word box or by selecting an alternate word from the suggestion list, and click Replace. ClarisWorks corrects the spelling in the appropriate cell and continues checking the document. When you are finished, click Done in the dialog box.

Now that your row and column labels are entered and checked for spelling, you can enter the budget data. Using Figure 6-6 as a guide, enter data in column B now, beginning in cell B6. Press ↵ after typing each amount to enter it into the spreadsheet and to move down one cell.

Column B's data is exactly the same as that in columns C and D. You have three different options for entering the next two columns of data. First, you could manually enter the data, just as you did for column B, but this is not very efficient. Second, you could select cells B6 through B13, copy the data to the Clipboard, make cell C6 active, paste the data into column C, and repeat the copy-and-paste method for column D. A much better alternative is to *fill* cells. With this method, you use the data in column B to fill cells in columns C and D. Filling is a shortcut to the copy-and-paste method. When you choose Fill Right or Fill Down from the Calculate menu, ClarisWorks copies and pastes data in one step. In order to fill, you first select the cells containing the data to be copied along with the cells to be filled.

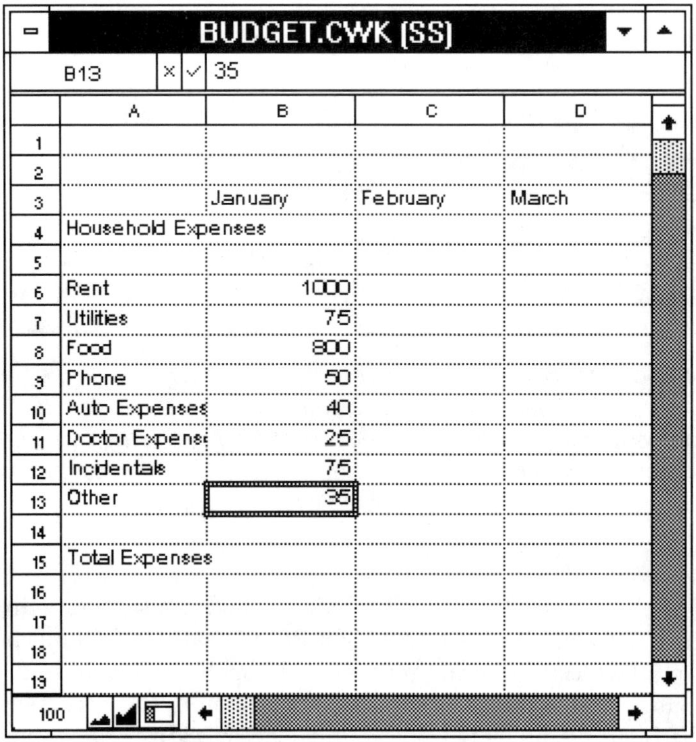

	A	B	C	D
1				
2				
3		January	February	March
4	Household Expenses			
5				
6	Rent	1000		
7	Utilities	75		
8	Food	800		
9	Phone	50		
10	Auto Expenses	40		
11	Doctor Expense	25		
12	Incidentals	75		
13	Other	35		
14				
15	Total Expenses			
16				
17				
18				
19				

BUDGET.CWK (SS)

B13   × ✓ 35

Figure 6-6   Budget data entered in column B

To copy the contents of cells B6 through B13 into the adjacent cells in columns C and D using the Fill Right command:

1   Click in cell B6, and drag to select the cell range B6 through D13.

2   Choose Fill Right from the Calculate menu, or press Ctrl+R.

The contents of each cell selected in column B is copied to the adjacent cells in columns C and D. Your budget document should resemble Figure 6-7.

When you fill cells, ClarisWorks copies the contents of cells. That is, if a cell contains a formula, the formula and not just the result of the formula is copied. Thus, filling cells is useful for copying existing formulas to blank cells.

TIP

Another way of filling cells is to fill them down the spreadsheet grid. You use the Fill Down command (Calculate menu) to apply the contents of cells in a given row (or selection of rows) down the spreadsheet grid into rows below the

	A	B	C	D
		B6	×✓ 1000	
3		January	February	March
4	Household Expenses			
6	Rent	1000	1000	1000
7	Utilities	75	75	75
8	Food	800	800	800
9	Phone	50	50	50
10	Auto Expenses	40	40	40
11	Doctor Expens	25	25	25
12	Incidentals	75	75	75
13	Other	35	35	35
15	Total Expenses			

Figure 6-7   Filling cells in columns C and D

upper-left anchor point in the selection. In other words, filling cells right works to copy cell contents into columns, and filling cells down works to copy them into rows.

The remaining household expense data is almost exactly the same for the rest of the months in the year in your budget. The only difference between January to March data and April to December data is that rent increases to $1,200 in April. To finish entering the data:

1   **Click in cell E6 to make it active.**

2   **Type** 1200**, and press ⏎ to enter the data into the cell and move down one cell.**

3   **Select cells D7 through E13.**

4   **Choose Fill Right from the Calculate menu.** This step copies the contents of cells D7 through D13 into cells E7 through E13.

5   **To fill the remaining cells in the budget with data, select cells E6 through M13.**

6   **Choose Fill Right from the Calculate menu.**

You are finished entering data into your budget document. In the next section, you use a formula to calculate total expenses by month and by expense category. Before you move on, save your spreadsheet by choosing Save from the File menu.

TIP

To see your row and column labels as you scroll across and down your spreadsheet, you can split the window into panes using the pane tools. For example, scroll in the document so columns A and B are visible, click the vertical pane tool (to the left of the scroll bar below the document), and drag to create a split between columns A and B in the budget document. Now, when you scroll across the document, the row labels stay in position in the left pane as you view data in columns of data in the right. You can also keep your column labels in view by dragging the horizontal pane tool down to create a split between rows 3 and 4. Figure 6-8 illustrates this technique. See "Viewing Documents" in Chapter 1 for more information on using the pane tools.

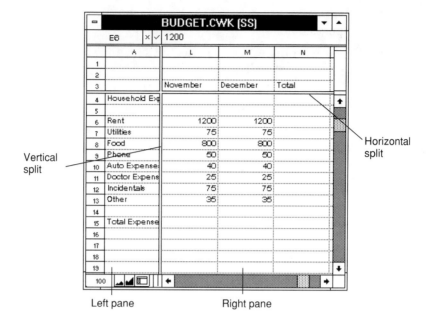

Figure 6-8   The document window split into four panes

Using formulas

The real power of a spreadsheet is its ability to automate calculations with formulas. A formula can be as simple as adding two values together or complex enough to include several ClarisWorks built-in functions. In this section you use formulas in your budget to calculate total monthly expenses and the total expense amount for each category. You will use two formulas, each of which uses SUM, one of the built-in ClarisWorks functions.

One of the most commonly used functions, SUM automatically adds a series of values. The syntax of the SUM function is as follows:

```
SUM(number1, number2,...)
```

Most functions require arguments that are listed inside parentheses and separated by commas. The SUM function can take no arguments, only one argument, or up to fourteen arguments. The arguments must be numeric values or expressions resulting in numeric values. The values can be specified as a cell range, as non-contiguous cells, as constants, or as a combination of these.

Using the SUM function is similar to using the simple addition feature of ClarisWorks. With simple addition, you can quickly add values by clicking in the cells whose values you want to add. For example, let's say you want to add up the auto, doctor, and incidental expenses for January, and you want the result to appear in cell B14. To add the expenses:

1   **Select cell B14.** This is the cell where you want the result of your addition to appear.

2   **Type an equal sign** (=). The equal sign appears in the entry bar area and tells ClarisWorks that you are entering a formula.

3   **One at a time, click in cells B10, B11, and B12.** ClarisWorks automatically places a plus sign (+) between the cell references.

4   **Press Enter on the numeric keypad, or click the Accept Entry icon in the entry bar, to enter the formula into cell B14.**

The result of your addition appears in B14. With this technique, you do not have to manually type a plus sign between the values in the formula's expression.

You won't be using the formula just entered in cell B14. Delete it now: make cell B14 active, and choose Clear or Cut from the Edit menu, or press Delete.

Formula rules

Before you enter your formulas in the budget, it is important to keep certain rules in mind that apply to using formulas in spreadsheet documents.

- Begin a formula by selecting the cell in which you want the result to appear.
- You can only enter a formula in one cell at time. If you have a cell range selected, the formula is entered into the active cell in the range and the result appears in that cell.
- Always type an equal sign (=) to begin a formula in the entry bar. The equal sign tells ClarisWorks that a formula follows. If you don't type an equal sign, whatever you type in the entry bar is considered a literal value and appears in the selected cell.
- Be sure to use correct syntax for functions in formulas. If you are in doubt, choose Paste Function from the Edit menu to place the function with its syntax in the entry bar, then replace the arguments with the values you want to use. Pasting a function is described more fully later in this section.

In addition to the rules just stated, note the following:

- You can use either upper- or lowercase letters when you enter formulas and functions.
- If you use functions in a formula and do not use the correct arguments, the message "Bad Formula" appears.

- Some functions do not require any arguments, and some arguments are optional.
- If a formula does not evaluate correctly, an error code appears as the result in the cell. Table 6-3 lists the error codes you may encounter and what may have caused the error.

Table 6-3 Formula Error Codes

Error	Probable Cause
#ARG!	Invalid number of or data type of argument(s)
#DATE!	Invalid date value
#DIV/0!	Divide-by-zero error (you can't divide by zero)
#ERROR!	Nonspecific error message
#N/A!	Data not available
#NUM!	Invalid numeric value
#PRECISION!	Insufficient precision for displaying value
#REF!	Invalid cell reference
#TIME!	Invalid time value
#USER!	User-defined error
#VALUE!	Invalid value

Results of formulas appear in cells. When a formula is evaluated, it results in one of the following types of data:

- Text
- Number
- Date
- Time
- Boolean (logical TRUE or logical FALSE)

Entering the formulas

You enter the first formula in cell B15 to calculate total expenses by month. Then, by filling cells C15 through N15, you copy the formula for all months. Next, you enter the second formula in cell N6 to calculate total annual expenses by category and fill cells N7 through N13 with the second formula. To enter the first formula:

1   **Select cell B15.**

2   **Type an equal sign to begin the formula.**

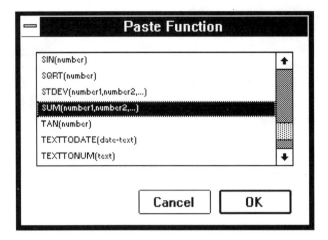

Figure 6-9   Paste Function dialog box

3   **Choose Paste Function from the Edit menu.** The Paste Function dialog box opens (see Figure 6-9).

4   **Scroll down the list of functions until the SUM function is visible.**

To move more quickly in the Paste Function dialog box, type the first character of the function you want, such as **s** *for SUM. This takes you to the beginning of the list of functions for that letter of the alphabet. (If you are really fast, you can type the whole function name to move directly to it.)*

TIP

5   **Click SUM to select that function, and click OK, or double-click the SUM function.** The syntax of the SUM function appears in the entry bar to the right of the equal sign. (If you forget to type the equal sign, it is automatically entered for you so it precedes the function.) The first argument (*number1*, in this case) is highlighted, reminding you that you need to replace it with a valid number.

6   **Leave *number1* highlighted, and click in cell B6 to replace *number1* with the B6 cell reference.** *B6* appears as the first argument in the function and the insertion point is blinking just to the right of *B6* in the formula.

7   **From the insertion point, drag to select the remaining characters in the function, up to but not including the closing parenthesis.**

8   Type two periods (..), and click in cell B13. This step replaces the second argument with a cell range reference, where B6 and B13 are anchor points. The two periods indicate a cell range.

9   Click the Accept Entry icon to enter the result of the formula in cell B15.

Your budget document should look like the one in Figure 6-10.

Note   *The window shown in Figure 6-10 is no longer split into panes, as described earlier in this chapter. To remove a split, drag the horizontal or vertical pane tool up or to the left, respectively, until the split disappears.*

	A	B	C	D
		BUDGET.CWK [SS]		
B15		=SUM(B6..B13)		
1				
2				
3		January	February	March
4	Household Expenses			
5				
6	Rent	1000	1000	1000
7	Utilities	75	75	75
8	Food	800	800	800
9	Phone	50	50	50
10	Auto Expenses	40	40	40
11	Doctor Expense	25	25	25
12	Incidentals	75	75	75
13	Other	35	35	35
14				
15	Total Expense	2100		
16				
17				
18				
19				

Figure 6-10   Cell B15 shows the result of the formula you just entered

Instead of clicking in each anchor point and typing two periods between them, you can specify a cell range in a formula by clicking in the first anchor point and dragging to the last one. ClarisWorks automatically inserts the two periods between the anchor points.

TIP

Copy the first formula into cells C15 through N15 by filling the cells. Click in cell B15, and drag across to cell N15. Choose Fill Right (Ctrl+R) from the Calculate menu. The SUM formula is copied across the cells and the cell range reference changes in each formula relative to the column it is in. The next section provides information on relative references.

The next step is to enter the second formula in cell N6 and copy it to cells N7 through N13. This time, instead of using the Paste Function dialog box, type the SUM function into the entry bar.

	BUDGET.CWK [SS]			▼ ▲
N6	× ✓	=SUM(B6..M6)		
	L	M	N	O
1				
2				
3	November	December	Total	
4				
5				
6	1200	1200	13800	
7	75	75		
8	800	800		
9	50	50		
10	40	40		
11	25	25		
12	75	75		
13	35	35		
14				
15	2300	2300	13800	
16				
17				
18				
19				
100				

Figure 6-11   The second formula—SUM(B6..M6)—entered in the budget spreadsheet

To enter the second formula:

1 **Click in cell N6 to make it active.**

2 **Type an equal sign to begin the formula and type** SUM(.

3 **Click in cell B6, and drag across to cell M6.** The anchor points (B6 and M6) appear as the SUM function argument, with two periods between them.

4 **Type the closing parenthesis), and click the Accept Entry icon to enter the formula and its result in cell N6.**

Your document should look like the one shown in Figure 6-11.

Copy the second formula into cells N7 through N13 by filling the cells. Click in cell N6, and drag down to cell N13. Choose Fill Down (Ctrl+D) from the Calculate menu. The SUM formula is copied down the cells and the cell range reference changes in each formula relative to the row it is in.

Referencing cells

You can use three different types of cell references in ClarisWorks:

- Relative
- Absolute
- Mixed

When you type a cell reference in a formula or click in a cell to reference it, you are using a *relative reference,* which identifies the location of a cell relative to other cells. Thus, if you copy a formula containing a relative reference, the reference changes to reflect the relative position from the new cell. In the previous section, you used relative cell references in the two formulas.

Absolute references, on the other hand, do not change when you copy a formula. The reference is to a specific cell, identified by its cell address (such as C5). To specify an absolute cell reference, enter a dollar sign ($) preceding the column and row in the address of the cell you want to remain absolute. For example, $C$5 specifies an absolute reference to cell C5.

When you are clicking a cell to reference it in a formula, press Ctrl+Alt as you click to automatically establish an absolute cell reference.

TIP

A *mixed reference* contains a combination of absolute and relative references. You use mixed references in formulas when you want one part of the cell address to remain fixed (absolute) and the other part to change (relative). For example, typing $C5 in a formula specifies an absolute column reference and a relative row reference. Similarly, C$5 specifies a relative column reference and an absolute row reference. In either of these examples, the absolute reference remains fixed and the relative reference changes when you move or copy the formula to other cells. When you develop a payment table later in this chapter, you will use absolute references. See "Entering Data and Formulas" later in this chapter for more information about absolute references.

Now, with the data and formulas entered into your budget document, you are ready to make formatting changes to it. Before you move on, be sure to save your document by pressing Ctrl+S.

Formatting the spreadsheet

You have many options available for changing the format of elements in your spreadsheet. All of these formatting options are conveniently located in the Format menu. You can

- specify that numeric, date, and time data appear in a different format
- change the attributes of text and data, including font type, size, style, color, and alignment
- add one of five types of borders to a selection of cells
- specify the exact width of one or more columns, or the exact height of one or more rows

In this section, you will make the following format changes to your budget spreadsheet:

- Change the format of data to currency
- Change the font type and size in the entire document
- Resize the cells
- Format the column labels

Changing data formats

You change the way data is displayed in spreadsheets by first selecting the cell or cell range you want to change, then using the Numeric dialog box (or double-clicking a cell to open the Numeric dialog box).

Begin with your budget open and active. To display your budget data in currency format with comma separators:

1 **Click in the row header area, and drag down to select all of rows 6 through 15.**

2 **Choose Number from the Format menu or press Shift+Ctrl+N.** The Numeric dialog box opens (see Figure 6-12).

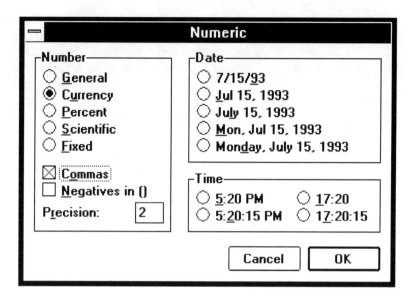

Figure 6-12   Numeric dialog box

3   In the dialog box, select the Currency and Commas options, and click OK.

The currency symbol appears before each numeric value in the selected range, and commas separate hundreds, thousands, and so on. You don't have to make data format changes by row; instead, you can make the changes by cell, by column, by range, or across the entire spreadsheet.

TIP

You can record a macro for formatting changes you make frequently. Changing data to currency format, for example, is a common task in spreadsheet work. By recording a macro, you can save time in making the change. To create a macro for changing data to currency:

1   *Select the cell(s) to change and choose Record Macro (Shift+Ctrl+J) from the Macros cascading menu in the File menu.*

2   *Assign a key combination (such as Ctrl+Alt+c) and a name (such as Currency) to your macro in the Record Macro dialog box.*

3   *Follow steps 2 and 3 in the previous list to display your budget data in currency format with comma separators.*

4   *When you are finished, choose Stop Recording (Shift+Ctrl+J) from the Macros cascading menu.*

The next time you want to change the data format to currency, simply select the cell(s) to change, and press Ctrl+Alt+c (the macro key combination).

If you want to save this macro so you can use it in subsequent ClarisWorks sessions, choose Save Macros from the Macros cascading menu, name your macro file (such as SSMacros.MAC), and click OK in the dialog box. The next time you launch ClarisWorks, use the Load Macros command to load the macro file into memory. If you want your macros to automatically load into memory when you launch ClarisWorks, name the macro file CWMACROS.MAC.

Changing text attributes

You change text attributes in spreadsheet documents by first selecting the cell(s) to change, then making a choice from the Font, Size, Style, or Text Color cascading menus in the Format menu.

In the following steps, you change the font type and size for the entire spreadsheet. These changes affect the contents of all cells, whether they contain text, numbers, dates, or times.

1 **To select the entire spreadsheet document, click in the upper-left corner of the document, where the row and column headers intersect (see Figure 6-13).**

2 **Choose a new font (such as MS Sans Serif) from the Font cascading menu in the Format menu.**

3 **Choose a bigger font size (such as 12 Point) from the Size cascading menu.**

The contents of all cells display in the new font and size.

TIP

The contents of cells in spreadsheet documents and frames are preset to display in Arial 9 point. Following the steps just described changes the preset font type and size for the current document. You can also change the preset font type and size by using the Default Font dialog box. To do so, choose Default Font from the Options menu, set a new preset font and size in the Default Font dialog box (see Figure 6-14), and click OK.

If you select a cell or range that has a different font than the default, the new font and size are automatically selected when you open the Default Font dialog box (see Figure 6-14).

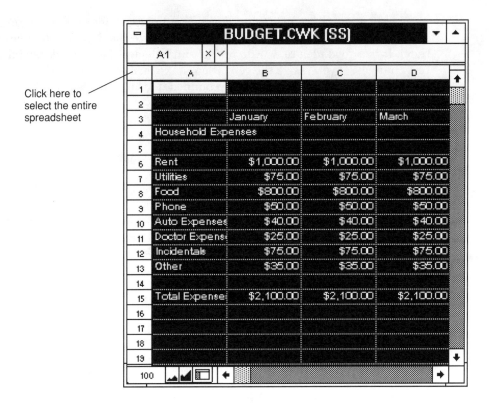

Click here to select the entire spreadsheet

Figure 6-13   Selecting the entire spreadsheet

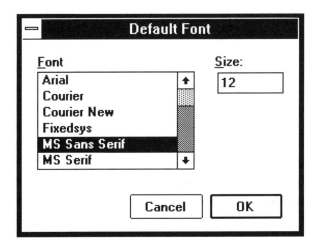

Figure 6-14   Default Font dialog box

Now that you have made data format and text attribute changes, you can move on to set the size of the cells to accommodate the data and text within them. It is a good idea to wait to resize your cells until after making data and text changes. If you resize the cells then make formatting changes to them, you may have to resize them again to accommodate the changes.

Resizing cells

Column A is not wide enough to contain the row labels. In addition, if you changed the font for the document to 12 point or more, the rows are probably not high enough to contain the data.

You can use two different methods to resize cells. The first method involves using the resize pointer to increase or decrease the size of columns or rows. (See "Modifying a Spreadsheet's Appearance" in Chapter 1 for more information on using the resize pointer.) The second method involves specifying an exact column width or row height in points. To change the width of column A and the height of rows 3 through 13 by this method:

1   **Click in the column A header to select the entire column.**

2   **Choose Column Width from the Format menu.**

3   **In the Column Width dialog box, type 115, as shown in Figure 6-15, and click OK.** Column width (preset to 72 points) can be set in the 0 to 510 range, inclusive.

4   **Click the 3 in the row header area, and drag down to select rows 3 through 15.**

5   **Choose Row Height from the Format menu.**

6   **In the Row Height dialog box, type 17, and click OK.** Row height (preset to 15 points) can be set in the range 0 to 256, inclusive.

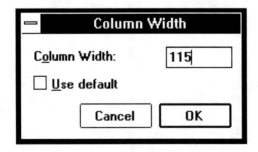

Figure 6-15   Using the Column Width dialog box to change cell size

Figure 6-16 shows part of the budget spreadsheet with the cell size changes in effect.

	A	B	C	D
1				
2				
3		January	February	March
4	Household Expenses			
5				
6	Rent	$1,000.00	$1,000.00	$1,000.00
7	Utilities	$75.00	$75.00	$75.00
8	Food	$800.00	$800.00	$800.00
9	Phone	$50.00	$50.00	$50.00
10	Auto Expenses	$40.00	$40.00	$40.00
11	Doctor Expenses	$25.00	$25.00	$25.00
12	Incidentals	$75.00	$75.00	$75.00
13	Other	$35.00	$35.00	$35.00
14				
15	Total Expenses	$2,100.00	$2,100.00	$2,100.00
16				
17				
18				
19				

(Window title: BUDGET.CWK [SS]; cell reference A3)

Figure 6-16   Part of the budget spreadsheet with cells resized

When changing row height, you should make the row height at least 2 points greater than the size of the font used in the cells. This enables you to better read the text and data in those cells.

TIP

Formatting column labels

The final formatting change you need to make to your budget is to format the column labels. Specifically, to make the display more appealing, center the column labels within the cells and add a border beneath them.

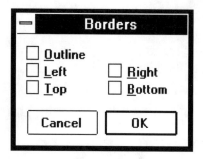

Figure 6-17   Borders dialog box

To center the column label text, select row 3, which contains the column labels, and choose Center (Ctrl+\) from the Alignment cascading menu in the Format menu. The alignment change applies to the contents of all cells in the selection.

To add a border beneath the column labels, leave row 3 selected, choose Borders from the Format menu, click Bottom, and click OK. The Bottom border option places a solid line along the bottom of all cells in the selection. In addition to Bottom, the Borders dialog box provides you with four other options (see Figure 6-17).

The Outline option places a border around the periphery of the entire selection. The Left, Top, and Right options place a border around either the left, top, or right edge of each cell in the selection. You can select a combination of borders, except Outline, which is mutually exclusive from the other options. If you select Left, Right, Top, and Bottom, a border appears around each individual cell in the range. You can add borders to a single cell, a row, a column, or a range of cells to highlight them as you wish. To remove a border, select the cells that have the border, choose Borders from the Format menu, and click OK. Because the Borders dialog box always opens with no border options selected, clicking OK restores the selection to the preset (no border) status.

Enhancing the spreadsheet

Now that your budget spreadsheet is formatted, you can add special effects to enhance and emphasize the data within it. In this section, you will

- use text frames to annotate cell data
- add graphics to the budget to liven it up
- make a chart to see trends in your data

Annotating cell data

One way of enhancing your spreadsheet data is to use text frames as cell notes. This procedure is called *annotation*. By adding text frames to your document, you can explain differences in expenses between months, or describe what an expense category includes.

In this section, you add two text frames that act as cell notes. The first cell note explains why the rent expense category changes in April. The second one describes what expenses are included in the Utilities category.

Begin with your spreadsheet document open and active. To create the text frames, you need to show the tool palette. Press Shift+Ctrl+T, or click the panel icon in the window to open the tool palette now. When you open the tool palette in a spreadsheet document, the spreadsheet tool is the preselected tool.

The first cell note pertains to cell E6, the April rent expense. If you look at the budget data, you see that rent increases from $1,000 to $1,200 in April. If this were your own personal budget and you were the only person using the document, you would probably know why this expense category increased. However, to clarify the increase for others looking at the budget, you can add a note explaining the increase.

ClarisWorks gives you the flexibility of adding text frames anywhere in a spreadsheet document. For easy readability, you want to add the text frame in a place that does not obscure the data in the budget. The most obvious place to add the text frame is in the area below the data. To add a text frame to contain a note for cell E6:

1   **Scroll the budget so the range E20 through F25 is visible in the window.** It may be helpful for you to use the pane tools to "lock" the column labels. This way you can identify the columns when you scroll in the document.

2   **With the tool palette visible, select the text tool.** The cursor changes to the I-beam pointer, indicating the text tool is active.

3   **Click and drag to create an empty text frame across cells E20 to F25, as shown in Figure 6-18.**

4   **In the text frame, type the following:**

    As per memo from XYZ Property Management, rent will increase in April to $1,200.

5   **When you are finished, press Enter on the numeric keypad to select the frame.**

Selection handles appear around the frame and the graphics tool is selected in the tool palette. The size of the frame shrinks so it is just large enough to contain the text.

Now you are going to change some of the attributes of text in the frame and of the frame itself. Specifically, change the font to MS Sans Serif (or the font you used for the main document), change the alignment of text so it is centered in the frame, and add a border around the frame.

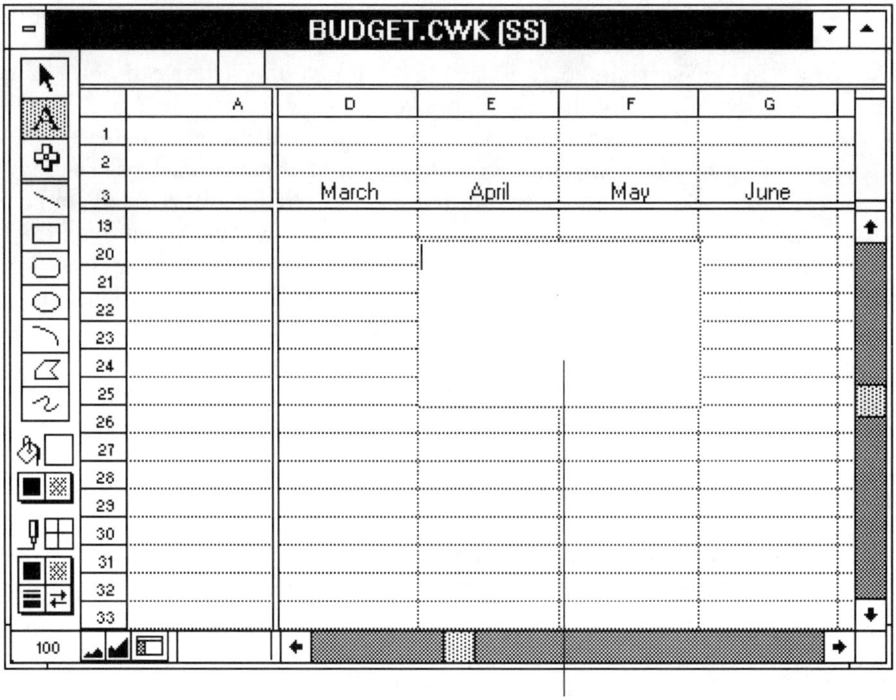

Empty text frame

Figure 6-18   First empty text frame in the budget spreadsheet

1   With the text frame selected, choose MS Sans Serif from the Font cascading menu. The text inside the frame changes to the new font type and the frame remains selected. If you don't have MS Sans Serif installed in your system, choose another font to match the one used in the main document.

2   Choose Center (Ctrl+\) from the Alignment cascading menu. Each line of text in the frame aligns in the center, between the left and right edges of the frame.

3   With the frame still selected, add a border around the frame by choosing Hairline from the line width menu in the tool palette.

If you have a color system, you can also change the fill and line color of the frame or the color of text inside the frame. (You can change these colors on a black and white system as well, but you won't be able to see the changes until you view the document on a color monitor or print it on a color printer.)

Your first text frame is complete. Your document should resemble Figure 6-19.

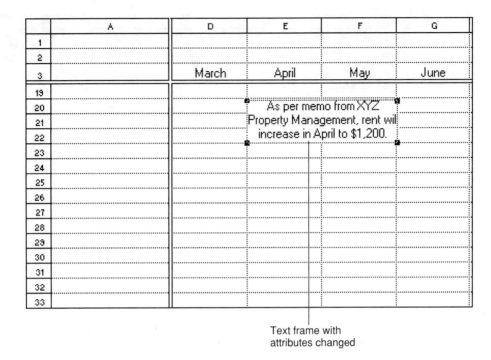

	A	D	E	F	G
1					
2					
3		March	April	May	June
19					
20			As per memo from XYZ		
21			Property Management, rent will		
22			increase in April to $1,200.		
23					
24					
25					
26					
27					
28					
29					
30					
31					
32					
33					

Text frame with
attributes changed

Figure 6-19   First text frame with attributes changed

Now you are going to add the second text frame for another cell note. This frame annotates cell A7 and details what expenses are included in the Utilities category. Again, you add the text frame in the document so it is below the data. Make sure the tool palette is visible and that the cell range A20 to A27 is visible in the window. You can remove the splits in the window now if you want. To add the second text frame:

1   Select the text tool.

2   Click and drag to create an empty text frame across cells A20 to A27.

3   In the text frame, type the following:

The Utilities expense category includes gas, electricity, sewer, water, and garbage.

4   When you are finished, press Enter on the numeric keypad.

Selection handles appear around the text frame and the graphics tool is selected in the tool palette. The size of the frame shrinks so it is just large enough to contain the text. If you want, change the same attributes for the text and the frame itself as you did for the first text frame.

Figure 6-20 shows both of the text frames in the spreadsheet document.

	A	B	C	D	E	F
12	Incidentals	$75.00	$75.00	$75.00	$75.00	$75.00
13	Other	$35.00	$35.00	$35.00	$35.00	$35.00
14						
15	Total Expenses	$2,100.00	$2,100.00	$2,100.00	$2,300.00	$2,300.00
16						
17						
18						
19						
20	The Utilities expense				As per memo from XYZ	
21	category includes gas,				Property Management, rent will	
22	electricity, sewer,				increase in April to $1,200.	
23	water, and garbage.					
24						
25						
26						
27						
28						

Second text frame   First text frame

Figure 6-20   Both text frames in position in the budget spreadsheet

There is no real way to electronically link the text frames to the cells with which they are associated. So, if you want to "relate" the frame to a cell, you must refer to the note in the cell. For example, to refer to the second text frame in cell A7, edit the contents of cell A7 so it reads *Utilities* (see note).

1   Click in cell A7.

2   In the entry bar, position the insertion point after the word *Utilities*, and type (see note).

3   When you are finished, click the Accept Entry icon.

You can also add a graphic element (such as a line or an arrow) to visually represent the relationship between the cell and its note. The next section describes how to do this.

You can also add text frames to spreadsheet documents for other uses. For example, you can use a text frame to contain the name of the spreadsheet document. Instead of putting this information in the header, as you did earlier in this chapter, you can use a text frame for it.

Adding graphics

In addition to text frames, graphics provide another way for you to enhance your spreadsheet data. Using the drawing tools, you can add a wide variety of graphics. You can even import other graphics, add your own logo, or paste clip art into the spreadsheet document. In this section, you will use the line and oval tools to emphasize the data in cell E6 (April rent) and connect the data with its cell note. Feel free to experiment with other drawing tools to create other graphic effects.

Begin with your budget document open and active, and make sure the tool palette is visible. To draw a circle around the number in cell E6:

1   **Select the oval tool in the tool palette.**

2   **Using the drawing pointer, click and drag to draw an oval around the data in cell E6.**

3   **Release the mouse.** When you release the mouse, selection handles appear around the oval and the graphics tool is selected in the tool palette. The oval appears to be on top of the data so as to obscure it (see Figure 6-21). To correct this so you can see the data, you need to change the fill pattern of the oval.

4   **With the oval object still selected, select the transparent fill pattern from the fill pattern palette (see Figure 6-22).**

Changing the oval to the transparent fill pattern allows you to see through the oval to the data. Figure 6-23 illustrates this.

Now you are going to draw a line from the oval you just drew around cell E6 to the cell note you created earlier. To draw the line:

1   **Select the line tool in the tool palette.**

2   **Choose Arrow At End from the arrowhead menu in the tool palette.** Recall from Chapter 1 that the arrowhead menu is one of the line tools, and it lets you turn lines into arrows. This option places an arrowhead at the end of the line when you release the mouse.

	A	B	C	D	E	
3		January	February	March	April	
4	Household Expenses					
5						
6	Rent	$1,000.00	$1,000.00	$1,000.00		
7	Utilities	$75.00	$75.00	$75.00	$75.00	
8	Food	$800.00	$800.00	$800.00	$800.00	
9	Phone	$50.00	$50.00	$50.00	$50.00	

Figure 6-21   Oval with the preset opaque fill pattern obscures the data

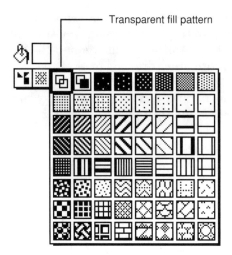

Transparent fill pattern

Figure 6-22   Fill pattern palette

	A	B	C	D	E	
3		January	February	March	April	
4	Household Expenses					
5						
6	Rent	$1,000.00	$1,000.00	$1,000.00	$1,200.00	
7	Utilities	$75.00	$75.00	$75.00	$75.00	
8	Food	$800.00	$800.00	$800.00	$800.00	
9	Phone	$50.00	$50.00	$50.00	$50.00	

Figure 6-23   Transparent oval emphasizes data in cell E6

3 Hold down the Shift key as you click and drag to draw a straight line from the oval object to the first text frame. Draw the line along the grid line between columns E and F.

4 Release the mouse.

The line is selected and the arrowhead at the end of the line points to the top of the text frame. Your document should resemble Figure 6-24.

To better view the graphics you just added, turn off the grid lines in the document. To do so, select the spreadsheet tool (or click in a cell to activate spreadsheet-related menus), and choose Display from the Options menu. In the Display dialog box, deselect the Grid Lines option, and click OK.

TIP

March	April	May
$1,000.00	$1,200.00	$1,200.00
$75.00	$75.00	$75.00
$800.00	$800.00	$800.00
$50.00	$50.00	$50.00
$40.00	$40.00	$40.00
$25.00	$25.00	$25.00
$75.00	$75.00	$75.00
$35.00	$35.00	$35.00
$2,100.00	$2,300.00	$2,300.00

As per memo from XYZ Property Management, rent will increase in April to $1,200.

Figure 6-24   Drawing a line in the budget document

Charting monthly expenses

One of the best ways to emphasize a spreadsheet document is to make a chart that shows trends in the data. You can create seven different types of spreadsheet charts in ClarisWorks.

- *Pie chart* (preset chart type) charts each value in a row or column as a pie slice relative to the whole pie. Selecting one row or column of data creates a single pie chart; selecting more than one row or column of data creates a chart showing a separate pie for each row or column of data. Pie charts are most useful for showing the relative contribution of each value to the whole series of data.

- *Bar chart* presents each column or row of data as a vertical (preset) or horizontal bar; multiple columns or rows of data appear as side-by-side bars. Bar charts are best used for comparing relationships between numeric data.

- *Stacked bar chart,* similar to bar chart, shows each value in a row or column as a segment within one bar, causing the bars to appear stacked one on top of the other. Stacked bar charts are most useful for comparing relationships among numeric values in two or more rows and columns.

- *Line chart* illustrates how values change over time. The data series containing values usually appears along the Y-axis, while time appears along the X-axis. Line charts are best for showing trends, especially in financial applications. (In Chapter 7, you will use a line chart to show fluctuations in the stock market.)

- *Scatter chart* shows discrete points of data at the appropriate intersection between the X-axis and Y-axis. Scatter charts do not show relationships among the points. These charts are most useful for showing grouping of values when the actual values are of less interest than the overall pattern.

- *X-Y chart* plots one set of data against another and is most useful for showing how one set of values changes as another set changes. To use an X-Y chart, you must select two or more rows or columns of data (not including row or column labels). The first column's data is plotted along the X-axis, and the remaining data is plotted along the Y-axis.

- *Scattered X-Y chart,* a cross between an X-Y and a scatter chart, plots discrete points of data without showing any relationship among the points and plots one set of data against another.

In this section, you create a pie chart that shows the expenses for the month of January. Each pie slice, or chart element, represents one expense category. The chart legend also shows percentages for each category. Both the size of the chart elements and the percentage information indicate your spending trends by category during the month. Figure 6-1 illustrates the completed pie chart.

A pie chart is the best chart to use in this case because it can effectively show relationships between data in one column of the spreadsheet (column B, in this case). Each chart element appears relative to the whole pie. Although you could also use a bar chart, it is not as effective because of the range of numbers in column B. With a bar chart the bars representing data for the rent and food categories would be significantly larger than the rest of the bars in the chart, making it difficult to see accurate trends. Figure 6-25 illustrates this.

TIP

If you want to use a bar chart for January expenses or other data that spans a wide numeric range, select the Log Base option for bar charts in the Make Chart dialog box. (Open the Make Chart dialog box by choosing Make Chart from the Options menu.) This option changes the Y-axis scale from a linear to logarithmic orientation and is preset to log base 10. The log base Y-axis scale is useful for charting data that does not easily lend itself to a linear scale. Figure 6-26 shows the same bar chart in Figure 6-25, but with the Y-axis scale set to log base 10. Notice that the chart's grid lines now correspond to the logarithmic scale. If you find these lines distracting, deselect the Grid option in the Make Chart dialog box.

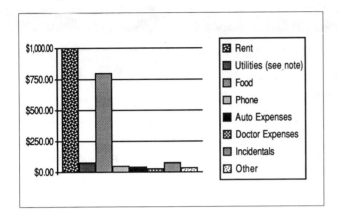

Figure 6-25   A bar chart can sometimes make it difficult to see accurate relationships

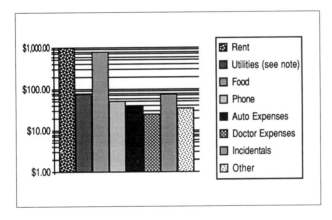

Figure 6-26   Bar chart displayed with log base 10 Y-axis scale

To create a pie chart showing January expenses:

1   **With the budget document open and active, select cells A6 through B13.** Be sure to include the row labels so the chart elements can be properly identified in the chart's legend.

2   **Choose Make Chart (Ctrl+M) from the Options menu.**

3   **In the Make Chart dialog box, select Show Percentages, and leave all other preset options as is (see Figure 6-27).** If you are using a color system, the Color option in the Chart dialog box is preset to be selected; otherwise it is deselected.

4   **Click OK.**

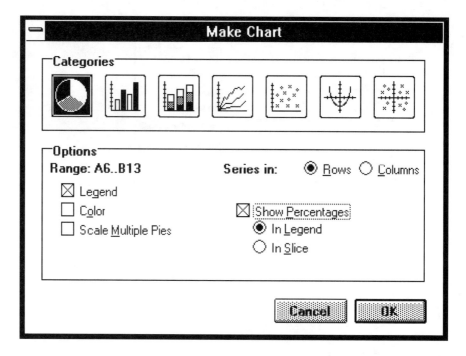

Figure 6-27   Make Chart dialog box showing options for pie charts

ClarisWorks creates the pie chart on top of the spreadsheet grid and places selection handles around it. The chart uses the row labels in the legend and shows each expense category as a percentage of all expenses during the month. Figure 6-28 shows the resulting pie chart.

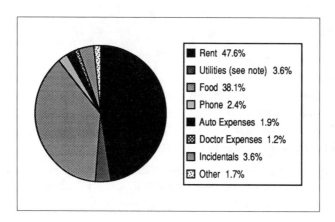

Figure 6-28   The budget pie chart

Now you can make modifications to your chart. To add a title to the chart, select the text tool from the tool palette, click in the chart above the pie, create an empty text frame, and type the title **Household Expenses, January 1993**. With the text frame selected, move and resize it until it is in the desired position inside the chart. If you want to change any text attributes in the frame, use the cascading menus in the Format menu.

Remember that you can also modify the chart by changing the patterns used in the chart elements. To do so, click once on one of the chart elements in the legend, and choose a new pattern from the fill pattern palette in the tool palette. Similarly, using the fill color palette, you can change a chart element's color (if you are using a color system). You can also change the attributes of the border around the chart, such as the line width, color, or pattern. Experiment with these tools until you are satisfied with your chart.

TIP

After adding a text frame for a title to your chart, you should group the text frame with the chart itself. Select the chart and the frame, and choose Group from the Arrange menu. If you don't group them, the objects behave separately. For example, if you move or copy the chart, the title does not move or copy with it if the objects are not grouped. Be sure to group the text frame with the chart after modifying the chart elements. You cannot modify chart elements if the chart is grouped.

If you want to emphasize a particular slice in a pie chart, you can explode it. To do so, hold down the Alt key as you click in the small box to the left of the chart element in the legend box. For example, to emphasize the phone expense in your pie chart, Alt-click the box to the left of the word *Phone* in the legend. To unexplode a pie slice, Alt-click the legend box again.

With your chart modified and grouped, you should move it to an empty area in the document so you can still see your data. Select the chart now and drag it down in the document so it is positioned across cells C37 to G52.

Note *Do not copy and paste the chart to move it to the new position. If you do so, the link between the chart and the data will be broken, and any changes in the data will not be reflected in the chart.*

You have many options available for charting your data. For example, you could chart total expenses for all months using the data in column N. Or, instead of charting only one column of data, you can chart data across multiple columns. Using the budget data, you can chart expenses across two or more months.

It is possible to chart the data in the entire budget (that is, the data in the cell range A6 through M13). However, you must make the size of the chart quite large so you can see the correct proportions of data in each chart element. If you want to chart all of the data, use a stacked bar chart instead of a pie chart. With a stacked bar chart (see Figure 6-29), each section of each bar represents an expense category, and each bar represents a month. Make sure the chart is using the rows for the data series. When the chart appears in the window, enlarge the chart so you can better view the details within it. Choose Scale Selection from the Options menu, and use 150% for both horizontal and vertical scale percentages. Figure 6-29 shows what this chart looks like.

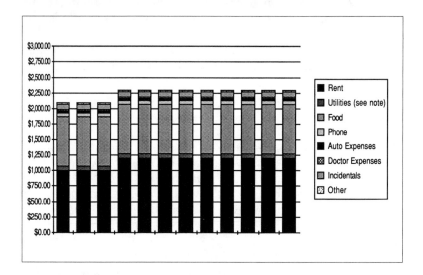

Figure 6-29   Stacked bar chart of all budget data

Printing tips

Your budget document is complete and you are ready to print it out. This section offers some tips for printing spreadsheet documents.

Preview your document

Printing spreadsheets to the point of satisfaction can be a trial-and-error process. This is true of any other ClarisWorks document type or any application. The most important step you can take before printing is to preview your document by turning on Page View. Page View shows the margins and page guides (if these options are checked in the Document dialog box). You also can view and make changes to the document's header and footer. Perhaps most importantly, Page View allows you to see how the document pages are going to break when they print. When you are satisfied with the way your document looks in Page View, print the document by choosing Print from the File menu.

Adjust margin settings

In spreadsheet documents, ClarisWorks automatically breaks pages at the row (horizontal break) and column (vertical break) nearest to margins specified in the Document dialog box. If ClarisWorks can't fit an entire row or column on the current page, the row or column moves to the next page. In short, the margin settings you specify in the Document dialog box determine how ClarisWorks automatically breaks pages in your spreadsheet document.

One way to fit spreadsheet documents satisfactorily on one or more pages is to experiment with various margin settings. In fact, the margin settings you specified at the beginning of this chapter were derived through experimentation.

Adjust page breaks

In addition to changing margin settings, you can adjust page breaks by setting them manually. To set page breaks in a specific place in the document, select the column, row, or cell where you want the break, and choose Add Page Break from the Options menu. To set a vertical page break, select the column to the left of where you want the page to break. To set a horizontal page break, select the row above where you want the break. If you select a cell and choose Add Page Break, page breaks are inserted along the right and bottom borders of the selected cell (see Figure 6-30). Manual page breaks are indicated by dashed lines when you view the spreadsheet document with Page View turned off.

To remove a manual page break, select the cell or range of cells bordering the break, and choose Remove Page Break from the Options menu. To remove all of the page breaks in the spreadsheet document (except those that ClarisWorks inserts automatically), choose Remove All Breaks (Options menu) from anywhere in the document.

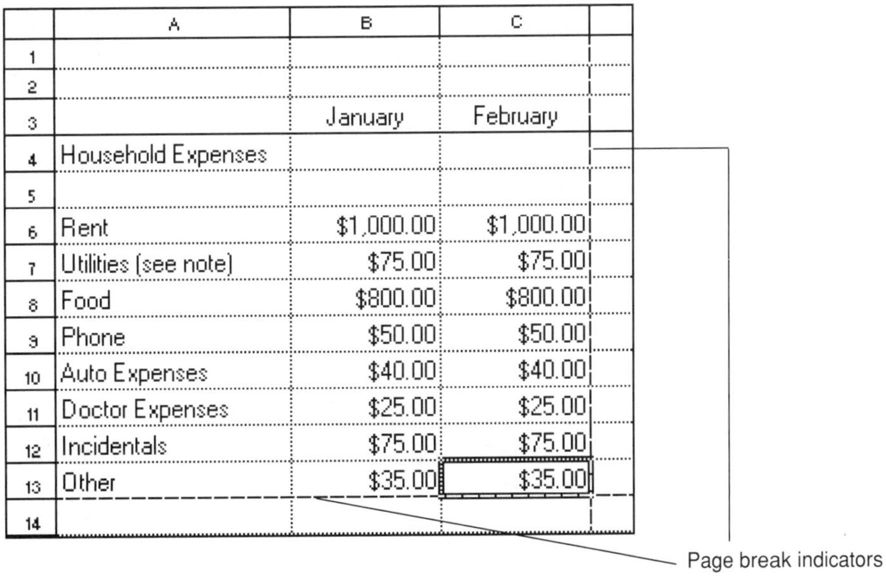

	A	B	C	
1				
2				
3		January	February	
4	Household Expenses			
5				
6	Rent	$1,000.00	$1,000.00	
7	Utilities (see note)	$75.00	$75.00	
8	Food	$800.00	$800.00	
9	Phone	$50.00	$50.00	
10	Auto Expenses	$40.00	$40.00	
11	Doctor Expenses	$25.00	$25.00	
12	Incidentals	$75.00	$75.00	
13	Other	$35.00	$35.00	
14				

Page break indicators

Figure 6-30 Page breaks inserted to the right of and below cell C13

Reduce the document view

To see the elements of a spreadsheet page better, reduce the document view. Click the left zoom control or set an exact scale percentage by choosing View Scale from the Window menu. To return to 100% magnification, click the zoom percentage box. (Clicking this box toggles between 100% and the most recent zoom percentage you specified.) Reducing the view during Page View is particularly useful for documents that span more than one page because it enables you to get an overall view of the page breaks.

Print in landscape mode

Your budget is a good example of a spreadsheet document that is more horizontally than vertically oriented. That is, the document is wider than it is long. For these types of spreadsheet documents, where data spans more columns than can fit in one page, it is best to print them in landscape mode. Landscape mode refers to the horizontal page orientation printing option. When set, landscape mode prints your document lengthwise across the page.

With your budget in Page View, scroll in the document. Your document should span six pages. Notice that the chart you created earlier is cut in half by a page break. Also, notice that pages 3 through 6 do not contain much of the spreadsheet. By setting your document to landscape orientation, you can reduce the number of pages to four. This change also allows all of the columns to fit on pages 1 and 2; the pie chart fits on page 3. To set the document for landscape printing:

1   **Choose Print Setup from the File menu.** The Print Setup dialog box opens. The dialog box and its options vary depending on the printer you have connected to your PC and the default printer specified in the Print Manager.

2   **In the orientation area of the dialog box, select the Landscape option.**

3   **Click OK to return to the document.**

4   **Turn on Page View to see how the change affects your document.**

5   **Reduce the document view so you can see the new page breaks.**

Limit pages to print

In spreadsheet documents like the budget, where the grid spans more pages than is required to display all of the data, you can limit the number of pages to print in the Print dialog box.

If you follow the previous tip and set the budget document to landscape orientation, you may notice that page 4 does not contain any data. If you were to print the budget now, you would waste a sheet of paper by printing this page. To limit the number of pages printed:

1   **Choose Print (Ctrl+P) from the File menu.** The Print dialog box opens. The dialog box you see depends on the printer currently connected to your PC.

2   **In the Print dialog box, set the Print Range from 1 to 3.**

3   **Click OK to print the first three pages of your document.**

Set a print range

Another way you can limit printed output is to set a print range using the Print Range dialog box (Options menu). This technique differs from the previous tip in that it allows you to print a specified cell range, not a page range. Setting a print range is useful for printing selected parts of the spreadsheet. To print the budget data for January, February, and March:

1   **With your budget document open and active, select the cell range A1 through D31.**

2   **Choose Print Range from the Options menu.** The Print Range dialog box opens. When you select a cell range before opening the dialog box, the Cell Range option is preset, as shown in Figure 6-31.

    You can set a different cell range by typing it in the dialog box. If you want to print all of the cells with data, regardless of what cell range you have selected, select the All Cells With Data option.

3   **Click OK to return to the document.**

When you click OK in the Print Range dialog box, ClarisWorks does not print the document. It simply stores the print range settings until you are ready to print. The next time you choose Print from the File menu, ClarisWorks prints the document using the current cell print range. Switch to Page View to see the

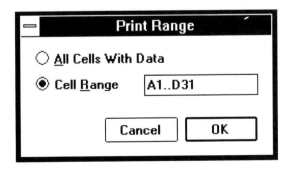

Figure 6-31   The Print Range dialog box showing the selected cell range

selected print range. To see the entire document in Page View again, select the All Cells With Data option in the Print Range dialog box.

TIP

When you click the All Cells With Data option in the Print Range dialog box, any empty cells containing formatting instructions (such as number formats, text attribute changes, alignment, or border information) are treated as if they contain data. For example, if the number format of cell O55 has been changed to Currency but cell O55 does not contain data, all of the cells up to and including cell O55 are included in the selected cell print range. To work around this condition, before you choose Print Range from the Options menu, hold down the Alt key as you click in the intersection of the row and column headers in the upper-left corner of the spreadsheet. This selects only those cells that contain actual data. Now, when you select the All Cells With Data option in the Print Range dialog box, empty cells with formatting information are disregarded.

Collapse unused columns or rows

Yet another method of limiting the data that appears in printed output is to collapse columns and/or rows that don't contain any data; you may also collapse those containing data that you don't want to print.

For example, suppose you just wanted to print a summary of household expenses by category for 1993. Rather than print a document containing expense details for each month, you are only interested in the totals for each expense category. By collapsing columns B through M, you can print the summary you want. Turn Page View off, if necessary. To collapse columns B through M:

1   **Click in the column B header, and drag across the document to select all of columns B through M.**

2   **Choose Column Width from the Format menu.**

3   **In the Column Width dialog box, type 0, and click OK.**

Figure 6-32 shows the result.

Although the collapsed columns and their data remain intact, they do not appear in the spreadsheet. To reinstate them in the document, select the columns on either side of the collapsed range (columns A and N, in this case), and set the column width back to its previous setting using the Column Width dialog box.

	A	N	O
1			
2			
3		Total	
4	Household Expenses		
5			
6	Rent	$13,800.00	
7	Utilities (see note)	$900.00	
8	Food	$9,600.00	
9	Phone	$600.00	
10	Auto Expenses	$480.00	
11	Doctor Expenses	$300.00	
12	Incidentals	$900.00	
13	Other	$420.00	
14			
15	Total Expenses	$27,000.00	
16			
17			
18			
19			
20	The Utilities expense		
21	category includes gas,		
22	electricity, sewer,		
23	water, and garbage.		
24			

Figure 6-32   Budget spreadsheet with columns B through M collapsed

Change display options

If you want your spreadsheet to print without the grid lines or the column or row headers, you can change these options in the Display dialog box. Choose Display from the Options menu, deselect the options you want to turn off, and click OK. Turning off these options is useful for presentation purposes. With them off, your output looks cleaner, and is easier to read.

You can also use this dialog box to show or print solid grid lines instead of dashed grid lines or to show or print formulas instead of their results in cells. Another display option, Mark Circular Refs, allows you to disable the display of bullet characters (•) around a number resulting from a circular reference in a formula.

Note   *You cannot change display options for a selected cell range. Display options affect the entire spreadsheet document or a set of linked spreadsheet frames.*

Section summary

In this section, you used many of the spreadsheet environment's features to create and modify a household budget. See how closely your resulting document resembles the one in Figure 6-1. In the next section, you will create a payment table to track installment payments and amortize a loan.

Creating a payment table

Most of us are plagued with making installment payments of some kind every month. These payments may be towards one or two credit cards, a mortgage, a car loan, and so on. Using a ClarisWorks spreadsheet, you can set up a table that tracks each of your monthly installment payments. A payment or amortization table helps you determine the monthly payments you need to make towards your accounts, given an account balance, an interest rate, and the number of months in which you want to pay the account off.

The payment table you create in this section assumes you have five installment accounts, including three credit card accounts, a credit union loan, and a car loan. In lieu of the sample data presented here, feel free to use data from your own personal or business installment accounts.

In the first part of this section, you create a table to determine the monthly payments needed to pay off the balances for each account. Figure 6-33 shows what your finished payment table will look like.

Later, using the car loan, you add a payment activity area to the payment table. This information lets you see how much of your monthly payments goes toward the loan principal and how much goes towards paying interest. It also calculates a new monthly balance for the term of the loan.

In creating the payment table, you will build formulas that use several ClarisWorks financial functions. Some formulas contain relative cell references, and others contain absolute cell references. By using cell references rather than constant values, you can change the values in the referenced cells to calculate different payments.

Installment Payments

Creditor	Interest Rate	Balance	Term	Monthly Payment
ABC Dept Store Card	15.0%	$3000.00	24	$145.46
Credit Union Loan	19.8%	$5000.00	36	$185.31
Easy Credit Card	13.0%	$2000.00	12	$178.63
Main Street Bank Can	18.5%	$500.00	12	$45.96
My Car Loan	17.0%	$15000.00	60	$372.79

Figure 6-33   Payment table for five installment accounts

Determining installment payments

In this section, you create a spreadsheet document to determine the monthly payments needed to pay off five installment accounts. The steps you take are as follows:

- Set up the document
- Enter the data
- Use a formula with the PMT financial function
- Sort the cells

The end of this section provides several other examples of how you can use ClarisWorks financial functions to solve other real-world financial problems.

Setting up the document

Begin by opening a new, untitled spreadsheet document. Choose New from the File menu, select Spreadsheet, and click OK. Before entering any of the install-ment payment information, set up the document by setting the default font, changing column width and row height, and specifying the spreadsheet size. To set up the document:

1 **Choose Default Font from the Options menu.**

2 **In the dialog box, leave Arial as the font, change the font size to 12 Point, and click OK.** From now on, everything you enter into the new spreadsheet appears in the new default font size.

3 **To accommodate the larger default font size, select the entire spreadsheet by clicking in the intersection of column and row headers, and set the row height to 17 points using the Row Height dialog box (Format menu).**

4 **Using the Column Width dialog box (Format menu) one at a time, select the following columns and set these column widths:**

Column A	128 points
Column B	74
Column E	96

5 **To set the spreadsheet document size, choose Document from the Format menu.**

6 **In the dialog box, set Columns Across to 6 and Rows Down to 82. Leave all other options as is, and click OK.**

Entering row and column labels

Your spreadsheet is now properly set up. To type the row and column labels that identify data in the payment table and to format the label text:

1 **In cell A1, type** Installment Payments, **and press Enter on the numeric keypad.** This label acts as a title for your document. If you prefer, you can put the title in the document header or place it in a text frame.

2 **Type** Creditor, Interest Rate, Balance, Term, **and** Monthly Payment **in cells A3, B3, C3, D3, and E3, respectively, pressing Tab to enter the text and to move to the next cell to the right.**

3 **In cells A5, A6, A7, A8, and A9, type** Main Street Bank Card, Easy Credit Card, ABC Dept Store Card, Credit Union Loan, **and** My Car Loan, **respectively, pressing ↵ to enter the text and to move down to the next cell.**

4 **Select cells A3 through E3, and press Ctrl+U to underline the text in the cells.**

5 **Select cells B3 through E3, and press Ctrl+\ to center the text in each cell.**

Your document should look like Figure 6-34. Your table is now ready for data. Before adding the data, save your new document by pressing Ctrl+S, and name the document Payments.CWK.

	A	B	C	D	E
			A9 × ✓ My Car Loan		
1	Installment Payments				
2					
3	Creditor	Interest Rate	Balance	Term	Monthly Payment
4					
5	Main Street Bank Card				
6	Easy Credit Card				
7	ABC Dept Store Card				
8	Credit Union Loan				
9	My Car Loan				
10					
11					

Figure 6-34   Payment table formatted with row and column labels

Entering the data

The data in your payment table is composed of constant values (in columns B, C, and D) and a formula (in column E). Constant values or *literals* are those you type, rather than values that result from formulas. Using the data shown in Figure 6-35, type the constant values into your payment table now.

	A	B	C	D
1	Installment Payments			
2				
3	Creditor	Interest Rate	Balance	Term
4				
5	Main Street Bank Card	0.185	500	12
6	Easy Credit Card	0.13	2000	12
7	ABC Dept Store Card	0.15	3000	24
8	Credit Union Loan	0.198	5000	36
9	My Car Loan	0.17	15000	60

Figure 6-35   Constant values in the payment table

Note   When you type the interest rate values, it is not necessary to type a zero (0) before the decimal point. ClarisWorks automatically places the zero in front of the decimal point when you enter a fractional number in a cell.

Now you need to change the format of the data you just entered. To format column B's data as Percent and column C's data as Currency, and to align column D's data in the center of the cells:

1   **Click in the column B header to select the entire column.**

2   **Choose Number (Shift+Ctrl+N) from the Format menu.**

3   **In the Numeric dialog box, select Percent, set Precision to 1, and click OK.**

4   **Click in the column C header to select the entire column.**

5   **Use the Numeric dialog box to format the data as Currency, and leave Precision set to 2.** You can also select Commas to include comma separators in the numbers.

6   **Select cells D5 through D9.**

7   **Press Ctrl+\ to align the data in the center of the cells.**

TIP

Earlier in this chapter you created a macro to format cell data as Currency with comma separators. Instead of setting this format manually in step 5 of the previous instructions, you can play back the currency macro you recorded earlier. To do so, choose Load Macros from the Macros cascading menu in the File menu, locate your macro file, and click OK in the dialog box. With your macros loaded into memory, simply press the macro key combination you used to record the macro (such as Ctrl+Alt+c).

Using the PMT function

You are ready to enter the formula to calculate monthly payments in column E of your payment table. The formula uses PMT, one of ClarisWorks financial functions. The syntax of the PMT function is

```
PMT (rate, nper, pv {,fv} {,type})
```

The PMT (pronounced "payment") function calculates equal payments required to pay off a loan or investment, given a periodic interest rate (rate), a fixed number of periodic payments (nper), and the beginning loan amount (pv—short for present value). The fv and type function arguments are optional. The fv argument refers to "future value." If it is not specified in the function, fv is presumed to be zero. That is, when the loan is paid off, it has a future value of zero. The type argument refers to the type of payment made—0 for payments at the end of periods (preset), or 1 for payments at the start of periods. For your current purposes, you do not need to use the fv or type arguments. To use the PMT function in the formula for cell E5:

1 **Click in cell E5.**

2 **Choose Paste Function from the Edit menu.** The Paste Function dialog box opens. Scroll down the list of functions until you see PMT (see Figure 6-36).

3 **Double-click the PMT function in the dialog box.** The function appears in the entry bar of cell E5, with the rate argument highlighted. ClarisWorks automatically precedes the function with an equal sign (=), which indicates a formula is to follow.

4 **Click in cell B5 to replace the rate argument with the interest rate value.** The interest rates you entered in column B are annual interest rates. To use this value in the PMT function, you must convert the rate to monthly. This is because the interest rate and the term must both be the same, either annual or monthly. In this case, the term is expressed in number of months, thus the reason for the interest rate conversion.

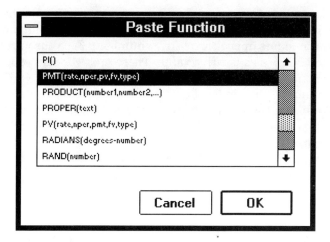

Figure 6-36   Paste Function dialog box showing PMT function

5 **To convert the interest rate from annual to monthly, type** */12*. The */12* tells ClarisWorks to divide the value in B5 by 12 (the number of months in a year).

6 **Select the nper argument and click in cell D5 to replace** *nper* **with the term value.**

7 **Select the pv, fv, and type arguments, and click in cell C5 to specify the loan balance (present value).**

8 **Press Enter on the numeric keypad to enter the formula into cell E5.**

Your document should resemble Figure 6-37.

	A	B	C	D	E
3	Creditor	Interest Rate	Balance	Term	Monthly Payment
4					
5	Main Street Bank Card	18.5%	$500.00	12	-45.9590588187
6	Easy Credit Card	13.0%	$2000.00	12	
7	ABC Dept Store Card	15.0%	$3000.00	24	
8	Credit Union Loan	19.8%	$5000.00	36	
9	My Car Loan	17.0%	$15000.00	60	
10					

PAYMENTS.CWK [SS]

E5   =PMT(B5/12,D5,C5)

Figure 6-37   Payment formula and result in cell E5

Notice that the result of your formula appears as a negative number because, from a financial perspective, payments are considered outgoing debits. Conversely, credit amounts appear as positive numbers. For your purposes, you want the result to appear as a positive value. There are two ways you can alter the formula so the monthly payment amount appears as a positive number. One way is to type a minus (–) sign in front of the cell reference for the balance (pv argument). To do this, in the entry bar area, click in front of the *C* in the cell reference C5, and type a minus sign. When you click the Accept Entry icon, the result becomes a positive value. Another way to alter the formula is to use the ABS function., which evaluates a numeric expression and converts the result to an absolute value. Using this method, your formula looks like this:

```
ABS(PMT(B5/12,D5,C5))
```

Use either one of these methods now to convert the result to positive. The result of the formula is still not formatted correctly for the payment table. Specifically, the result displays with 10 decimal places and is not formatted to display as currency. Because you want all of the monthly payment values appearing in column E to format as currency with two decimal places, change the format of the entire column. Select column E, and use the Numeric dialog box to set the format to Currency and the Precision to 2. Figure 6-38 shows how these changes affect the display in cell E5.

Now you need to copy the formula in cell E5 to cells E6 through E9. To do so, click in cell E5 and drag down to select the range E5 through E9. Choose Fill Down (Ctrl+D) from the Calculate menu. The formula in cell E5 is copied down the selected range. The cell references change in each formula relative to the row it is in because the formula uses relative cell referencing.

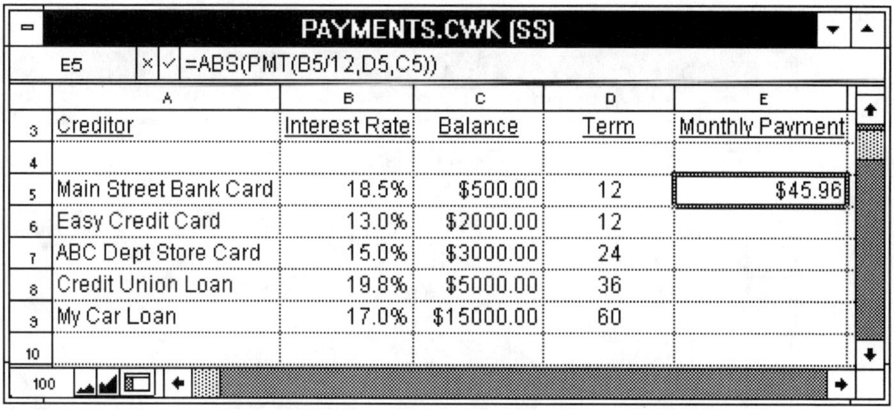

	A	B	C	D	E
	PAYMENTS.CWK [SS]				
E5	=ABS(PMT(B5/12,D5,C5))				
	A	B	C	D	E
3	Creditor	Interest Rate	Balance	Term	Monthly Payment
4					
5	Main Street Bank Card	18.5%	$500.00	12	$45.96
6	Easy Credit Card	13.0%	$2000.00	12	
7	ABC Dept Store Card	15.0%	$3000.00	24	
8	Credit Union Loan	19.8%	$5000.00	36	
9	My Car Loan	17.0%	$15000.00	60	
10					

Figure 6-38   Formatted formula result in cell E5

With the data completely entered into your payment table, you are ready to sort the cells. Before moving on, press Ctrl+S to save your document.

TIP

If you want, you can copy the monthly payments you just calculated and paste them into your household budget. To do this, you need to make room in the budget spreadsheet. With the budget spreadsheet open and active, select row 15, and press Ctrl+Alt as you click in cell A25; this moves the data from row 15 to row 25. Now, with your payment table open and active, select cells A5 through A9, and press Ctrl+C to copy them to the Clipboard. Make the budget spreadsheet active, click in cell A14, and press Ctrl+V to paste the row labels from the payment table. To copy the monthly payment data from the payment table to the budget, select cells E5 through E9 in the payment table, press Ctrl+C, and click in cell B14 in the budget. Because you want to paste only the values (not the formulas) into the budget, choose Paste Special from the Edit menu, select the Values Only option in the dialog box, and click OK. The monthly payment information is pasted into the appropriate cells in column B. Now select cells B14 through M18, and choose Fill Right from the Calculate menu. Copy the formula in cell N13 to cells N14 through N18. Be sure to modify the SUM function formulas in cells B25 through N25 to include the data you just added.

Sorting cells

For easy reference, you decide to sort the data in the payment table so the installment accounts appear in alphabetical order. To do this, you will use the Sort dialog box.

When you sort spreadsheet cells, it is important to think about how the sort affects the data in the document. That is, if you only sort one column (such as column A), you want to make sure the data associated with that column is also sorted. Therefore, before sorting, you must select the range of cells that contains not only the data to sort, but also its associated data. To sort cells:

1 **In the payment table, select cells A5 through E9.**
2 **Choose Sort (Ctrl+J) from the Calculate menu.** The Sort dialog box opens (see Figure 6-39).
3 **Leave all of the preset options as is, and click OK to sort the cells.**

Let's examine the options in the Sort dialog box (see Figure 6-39). Your cell range selection appears in the Range box, and the upper-left anchor point of the selection (A5) becomes the first sort order key. If you want to sort data in columns B and C, beginning with row 5, you enter B5 as the second order key, and C5 as the third. However, it only makes sense to use second and third order keys if the first order key contains like values.

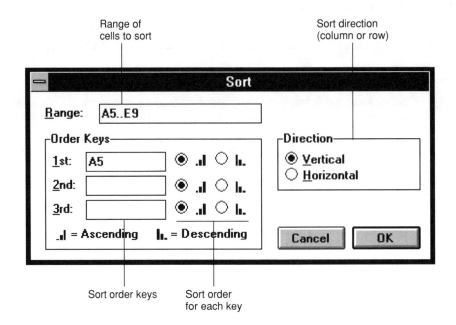

Range of cells to sort

Sort direction (column or row)

Sort order keys

Sort order for each key

Figure 6-39 Sort dialog box for sorting spreadsheet cells

With the Vertical sort direction selected, ClarisWorks sorts in columns beginning with cell A5. If you want to sort the data by row, you select Horizontal.

The Ascending option sorts from A to Z or from lesser to greater values. The Descending option sorts from Z to A or from greater to lesser values.

	A	B	C	D	E
1	Installment Payments				
2					
3	Creditor	Interest Rate	Balance	Term	Monthly Payment
4					
5	ABC Dept Store Card	15.0%	$3000.00	24	$145.46
6	Credit Union Loan	19.8%	$5000.00	36	$185.31
7	Easy Credit Card	13.0%	$2000.00	12	$178.63
8	Main Street Bank Card	18.5%	$500.00	12	$45.96
9	My Car Loan	17.0%	$15000.00	60	$372.79
10					

PAYMENTS.CWK (SS)

A5   ABC Dept Store Card

Figure 6-40 Payment table with cells sorted

Figure 6-40 on page 356 shows how the sort affects the position of data in the payment table, where creditors are listed alphabetically and each row of data remains intact.

The installment payment area of your table is complete. Before moving on, be sure to save your document.

Using other financial functions

In the previous section, you used the PMT function to determine monthly payments toward installment accounts. Let's look at a few more examples of how you can use other financial functions in ClarisWorks spreadsheets to answer other real-world financial questions.

So you don't disturb your payment table data, use a spreadsheet frame for the following examples. This way, you can use the spreadsheet frame like you would use scratch paper and a hand-held calculator to do some quick-and-dirty figuring. To create the frame, make the tool palette visible. Next, as you hold down the Alt key, click and drag to create a small spreadsheet frame in your document (see Figure 6-41).

Note   *When you turn on the tool palette, the spreadsheet tool is already selected because you are working in a spreadsheet document. Therefore, you don't have to take the extra step of selecting it.*

	A	B	C	D	E
1	Installment Payments				
2					
3	Creditor	Interest Rate	Balance	Term	Monthly Payment
4					
5	ABC Dept Store Card				$145.46
6	Credit Union Loan				$185.31
7	Easy Credit Card				$178.63
8	Main Street Bank Card				$45.96
9	My Car Loan				$372.79
10					
11					

Spreadsheet frame

Figure 6-41   Empty spreadsheet frame in the payment table

What if you knew how much to pay towards your accounts but you wanted to determine how long it would take to pay them off? Looking at the values in row 5 in the payment table, assume you want to pay $100 towards your ABC Department Store credit account every month, but you want to determine how many months it will take you to pay it off. If you know the interest rate on the account, the amount of your monthly payments, and the current account balance, you can use the NPER function to determine the number of months required to pay off the account. The NPER function, short for number of periods, uses the following syntax:

```
NPER (rate, pmt, pv {,fv} {,type})
```

As with the PMT function, the fv and type arguments are optional. The fv argument is assumed to be zero, because in the future (that is, at the end of the number of periods), you want your balance to be zero. (If you were making an income investment, you would enter a future value representing the amount of money you expect to earn at the end of the number of periods.) The type argument for NPER is the same as it is for PMT and is assumed to be 0 (payments are made at the end of each period).

In cell A1 of the spreadsheet frame, type an equal sign, and enter the following formula:

```
NPER(.15/12,-100,3000)
```

The formula uses the annual interest rate from cell B5 (15%) and divides it by 12 to convert it to a monthly interest rate. The monthly payment of $100 is expressed as a negative value because it is an outgoing cash flow. The $3,000 value is the present value, or current balance, of the account. When you enter the formula into the cell, it results in 38 (formatted as a Fixed format with Precision set to 0). This tells you that at $100 per month, the account will be paid off in three years and two months (38 months).

Let's take another financial example: Suppose you have a savings account or a money market fund account, into which you deposit $2,000 annually. Your particular account earns 8% interest annually, and your current account balance is $7,000. You want to find out how much money your account will accumulate in five years. You do this using the FV (future value) function. In this case, you know what the present value is ($7,000), but you want to know what it will be worth at the end of the term.

The FV function has the following syntax:

```
FV (rate, nper, pmt {,pv} {,type})
```

This time, the pv and type arguments are optional. The type argument is the same as it is for the PMT, NPER, and PV functions. The pv argument, unless otherwise specified, is assumed to be zero. In your case, your savings account is presently worth more than that ($7,000). To determine what the account will be worth in five years, enter the following formula into a spreadsheet frame cell:

```
FV(8%,5,-2000,-7000)
```

Because each argument is expressed in annual (not monthly) terms, you don't have to divide the interest rate by 12. Also, notice that you can express the interest rate as a percent in the formula rather than as a decimal value. The $2,000 payment is expressed as negative because it is an outgoing cash flow. Similarly, the $7,000 is expressed as a negative value because you have paid that money into your account. This formula results in $22,018.50 (formatted as Currency with Commas selected and Precision set to 2).

You will not need the spreadsheet frame in the rest of this chapter, so select it now using the graphics tool, and delete it. You can also hide the tool palette.

Amortizing a loan

To complete your payment table, you can track the activity of payments made for one or all installment accounts each month. This information provides details on how your loans are amortized over time. By including these details, you can see how much of your monthly installment payment is applied to the principal and the interest, and what the new balance is each month.

In this section you will amortize the My Car Loan payments. You use the payment table created earlier as a data or reference table. In other words, the formulas you add into the amortization area use absolute references to cells in the payment table area.

If you want, you can track the amortization activity for all of the installment accounts listed in your payment table. In fact, by using separate areas of a large spreadsheet grid, you can place several amortization tables within one spreadsheet document.

TIP

Setting up for data entry

So you can focus on the payment table data for My Car Loan, collapse the rows that pertain to the other installment accounts. To do so:

1   **In the payment table, select rows 5 through 8.**

2   **Choose Row Height from the Format menu.**

3   **In the dialog box, type 0 for the row height, and click OK.**

The rows remain collapsed and appear hidden until you restore the row height to its original size. Now use the horizontal pane tool to freeze rows 1 through 9 into view. Click the horizontal pane tool, and drag down until the window splits between rows 9 and 10. Figure 6-42 shows what your document should look like.

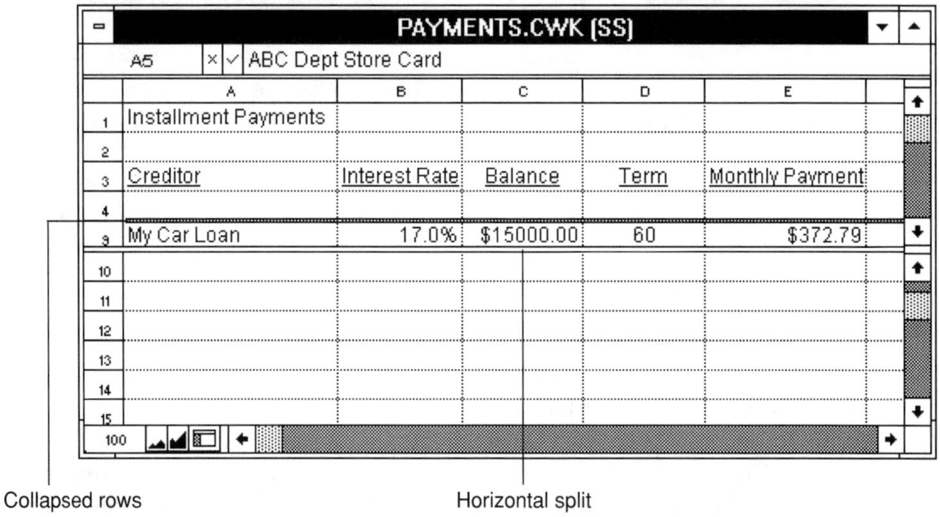

	A	B	C	D	E
1	Installment Payments				
2					
3	Creditor	Interest Rate	Balance	Term	Monthly Payment
4					
9	My Car Loan	17.0%	$15000.00	60	$372.79
10					
11					
12					
13					
14					
15					

PAYMENTS.CWK (SS)

A5   ✕ ✓ ABC Dept Store Card

Collapsed rows   Horizontal split

Figure 6-42   Viewing part of the payment table in a split window

You are ready to add the row and column labels for the amortization table in your document. Because you changed the default font for the payment table earlier in this chapter, the font is already correctly set for the amortization information. Type the following text in the designated cells:

Cell	Text
A11	Amortization Table
A13	My Car Loan
B12	Month
C12	Principal
D12	Interest
E12	Balance

Now select row 12. Change the text style to underline by pressing Ctrl+U and change the alignment to center by pressing Ctrl+\. As shown in Figure 6-43, your document is properly set up for you to enter the amortization data.

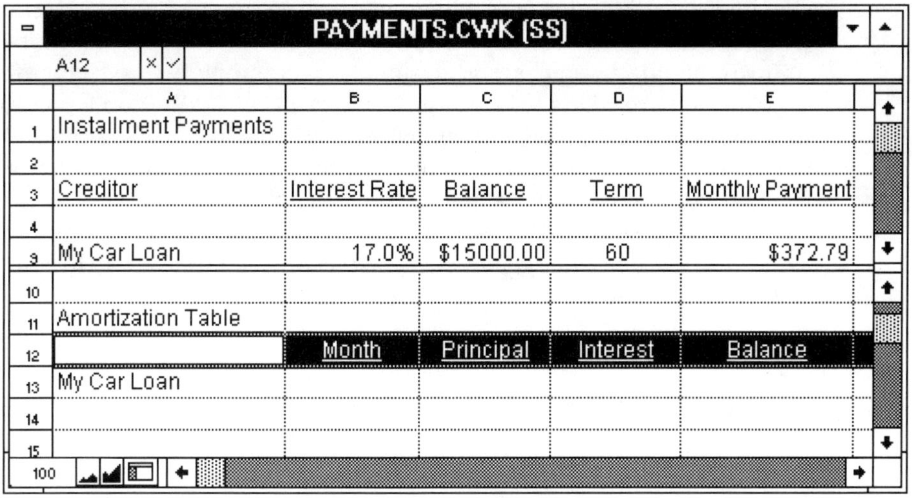

Figure 6-43   Document set up for amortization data

Entering data and formulas

The basic idea behind an amortization table is to determine the principal and interest applied to a loan based on the monthly payment. As a result, you want the amortization table to display each month's data in one row. Looking at cell D9, you can see that this amortization table will require 60 rows of data, one for each period in the term. Earlier you set the spreadsheet size to include 82 rows down, so your document is large enough to contain this data.

The formulas and values you enter in the amortization table can reference the cells in the payment area of the document. This way, if any of the values change in the payment area, the amortization data automatically updates to reflect the changes.

The first value you need to enter into the amortization table is the beginning balance. This amount goes into cell E13 and is the same value that appears in cell C9. Rather than retype the data, you reference the cell itself. To do this, click in cell E13, type an equal sign, and click in cell C9. When you press Enter on the numeric keypad, the value $15000.00 appears in cell E13. If you change the balance in C9, it is automatically changed in E13. The number is properly formatted (Currency with Precision set to 2) because earlier you formatted column E with those settings.

The next step is to label each row in the table by month number. The first month, appearing in row 13, contains the beginning balance. Because you do not make a payment during this month, the month label is zero. Click in cell B13, and type a zero. The number appears as a percentage because you set the column B format to Percent earlier in this chapter. To change the format of column B (from row 13 down) to display round numbers with no decimal places, click in cell B13, and drag down the column to select cells B13 through B82. In the Numeric dialog box, select General, set Precision to 0, and click OK. The first row of data in your amortization table is complete (see Figure 6-44).

Now you are ready to enter data in row 14. Actually, you won't type any more data at all; instead you will enter formulas in cells B14 through E14 and use these formulas to fill the remaining cells in your amortization table. Scroll in the bottom pane of the window, if necessary, to bring row 14 into view.

The first formula you need to create increments the month number down column B. Rather than go down each row, typing numbers 1 through 60, follow these steps to enter a formula in cell B14:

1   **Click in cell B14.**

2   **Type an equal sign to begin the formula.**

3   **Click in cell B13.** This becomes a relative cell reference in the formula.

4   **Type + (a plus sign) and then type 1.**

5   **Press Tab twice to enter the formula into cell B14 and move to cell D14.**

Later, when you copy this formula down column B, the cell reference changes relative to the row in which the formula appears.

The next formula needs to be entered in cell D14. This formula calculates how much of your monthly payment is applied toward the interest you owe on the loan. To determine your monthly interest amount, you multiply the previous

	A	B	C	D	E
1	Installment Payments				
2					
3	Creditor	Interest Rate	Balance	Term	Monthly Payment
4					
9	My Car Loan	17.0%	$15000.00	60	$372.79
10					
11	Amortization Table				
12		Month	Principal	Interest	Balance
13	My Car Loan	0			$15000.00
14					
15					

Figure 6-44   Amortization table with the first row of data entered

month's balance (the beginning balance, in this case) by the monthly interest rate. The formula uses an absolute reference to the interest rate value in cell B9 (17.0%). You use an absolute reference here so that later when you copy the formula down column D, the formula cell reference is always fixed. To enter cell D14's formula:

1   **With cell D14 active, type an equal sign to begin the formula.**
2   **Click in cell B9.**
3   **To make the cell B9 reference absolute, type $ (a dollar sign) before the *B* and before the *9*, as follows:**

$B$9

4   **To convert the interest rate value from annual to monthly, position the insertion point after the *9*, and type** /12.
5   **Type * (an asterisk) to indicate multiplication.**
6   **Click in cell E13.**
7   **Press Enter on the numeric keypad to enter the result of the formula in cell D14.**

To make the formula easier to read, you can place the $B$9/12 part of the formula in parentheses:

($B$9/12)*E13

TIP

The result of the formula is 212.5. Format column D, from row 14 down to row 82, as Currency with Precision set to 2.

With the monthly interest amount calculated, you can now figure how much of your monthly payment applies to the principal. To do so, use a formula that contains an absolute reference to cell E9 (the total monthly payment) and subtract the interest amount you just calculated. To enter the formula in cell C14:

1   **Click in cell C14, and type an equal sign to begin the formula.**
2   **Press Ctrl+Alt as you click in cell E9.** This automatically converts the reference to cell E9 from relative to absolute.
3   **Position the insertion point after *9* in the entry bar and type – (a minus sign).**
4   **Click in cell D14.** Leave this cell reference relative. You want it to change as the formula is copied down the table.

5   Press Enter on the numeric keypad to enter the result of the formula in cell C14. The result of the formula is $160.29. Column C is already properly formatted for currency display, so you don't need to change it.

Once you have determined the monthly interest and monthly principal, you can calculate the new loan balance. This formula simply subtracts the monthly principal from the previous balance. You don't subtract the interest payment from the balance because, unfortunately, interest payments do not go toward reducing your debt. Enter the following formula in cell E14 now (be sure to begin the formula by typing an equal sign):

```
=E13-C14
```

With row 14's formulas entered, your document should look like Figure 6-45.
You are almost finished with your amortization table. You only need to copy the formulas from row 14 down the document. Do so now: select cells B14 through E73 and choose Fill Down (Ctrl+D) from the Calculate menu. The formulas are copied down the document for each of the 60 months. Figure 6-46 shows part of what your final document looks like.

	A	B	C	D	E
	PAYMENTS.CWK [SS]				
	E14 × ✓ =E13-C14				
1	Installment Payments				
2					
3	Creditor	Interest Rate	Balance	Term	Monthly Payment
4					
9	My Car Loan	17.0%	$15000.00	60	$372.79
10					
11	Amortization Table				
12		Month	Principal	Interest	Balance
13	My Car Loan	0			$15000.00
14		1	$160.29	$212.50	$14839.71
15					

Figure 6-45   Amortization table with formulas entered in row 14

	PAYMENTS.CWK [SS]				▼ ▲
E73	× ✓ =E72-C73				

	A	B	C	D	E	
						↑
11	Amortization Table					
12		Month	Principal	Interest	Balance	
13	My Car Loan	0			$15000.00	
14		1	$160.29	$212.50	$14839.71	
15		2	$162.58	$210.23	$14677.15	↓
57		44	$293.50	$79.29	$5303.54	↑
58		45	$297.88	$75.13	$5005.89	
59		46	$301.87	$70.92	$4704.02	
60		47	$306.15	$66.64	$4397.87	
61		48	$310.49	$62.30	$4087.38	
62		49	$314.88	$57.90	$3772.50	
63		50	$319.34	$53.44	$3453.15	
64		51	$323.87	$48.92	$3129.28	
65		52	$328.46	$44.33	$2800.83	
66		53	$333.11	$39.68	$2467.72	
67		54	$337.83	$34.96	$2129.89	
68		55	$342.62	$30.17	$1787.27	
69		56	$347.47	$25.32	$1439.80	
70		57	$352.39	$20.40	$1087.41	
71		58	$357.38	$15.40	$730.03	
72		59	$362.45	$10.34	$367.58	
73		60	$367.58	$5.21	$0.00	
74						↓

| 84 | ◪◪▦ | ← | | | | → |

Figure 6-46   Completed amortization table, shown reduced to 84% view scale

Notice that as the months go by, more of your monthly payments are applied to the principal and less towards your interest due. Be sure to save your payment table by pressing Ctrl+S.

TIP

When you fill a large number of cells with formulas as you just did, it is wise to verify that the formulas copied correctly. You can either click in random cells and examine the entry bar area to spot-check that the formulas are correct, or you can change the document display to show the formulas, rather than their results, in the cells. To take the latter approach, choose Display from the Options menu, select the Formulas display option, and click OK. Selecting this or other display options affects the entire document or frame.

Summary

This chapter described how to use the spreadsheet environment in ClarisWorks for managing financial information. In creating the documents in this chapter, you also used elements of the text and graphics environments.

In addition to budgets and payment tables, there are innumerable types of spreadsheet documents you can create for your own personal or business purposes. For example, you can create a business profit and loss (P&L) statement to record actual income and expense data, and to project future income and expenses. Spreadsheets are fantastic tools for keeping track of your hard-earned money.

The next chapter focuses on using the Windows Terminal program with ClarisWorks. You'll learn how to accomplish a variety of telecommunications tasks, including how to download information into a ClarisWorks spreadsheet for financial analysis.

Chapter Seven

Tele-
communicating

About this chapter

This chapter provides information on how to use the Windows Terminal application with ClarisWorks to do telecommunications tasks. The chapter begins by describing the basics of Windows Terminal, including what the program can do for you and what you need to use it.

The second section of this chapter gives step-by-step instructions for starting Terminal via ClarisWorks, setting up for connection, connecting to another computer, transferring data, and disconnecting.

The third section in the chapter describes how to transfer stock market information from a communications session in Terminal to a ClarisWorks spreadsheet for analysis.

***

Note   *Throughout this chapter, terms such as* other computer *and* remote computer *generally refer to both a computer to which you connect for an online service and a computer to which you connect over a network.*

Windows Terminal basics

This section gives general information about Windows Terminal, a separate application that comes with Microsoft Windows. See Chapter 11 in the Microsoft Windows *User's Guide* for a complete reference.

What is Windows Terminal?

Windows Terminal, or simply Terminal, is a Windows application that lets your computer connect to and exchange information with other computers, and ultimately other computer users.

The process of connecting to other computers and transmitting information between computers is called *telecommunicating*. When you telecommunicate, you can accomplish a wide variety of tasks without ever leaving your computer. For example, you can

- Access informational databases
- Exchange data with mainframe computers
- Get answers to computer-related questions
- Communicate with other computer users
- Make travel reservations and purchase airline tickets
- Check stock quotes
- Go shopping
- Pay your bills and do your banking
- Download shareware programs and utilities

What you need to use Terminal

To use Terminal's communications features with ClarisWorks, you must have

- Windows Terminal installed on your Windows system
- The following statements in your CLARIS.INI file:

```
[ClarisWorks]
Terminal = TERMINAL.EXE
```

- (For external modems) an available serial port on your PC
- Either an internal modem or an external modem with a cable connecting the modem to the serial port

- Either a telephone line to connect the modem to a phone jack or a serial cable to directly connect the modem to another computer in the same room
- (For external modems) a power cord to connect the modem to a power outlet

A *modem* is a device that translates your language into a language that can be transferred across telephone lines and understood by another computer. If you have an external modem, you connect it to the serial port in the back of your PC via a special cable designed specifically for connecting modems to PCs (usually referred to as a *serial cable*). The modem is also connected to a phone jack via a standard telephone cable and to a power source via the power cord that comes with your modem. Figure 7-1 illustrates this configuration.

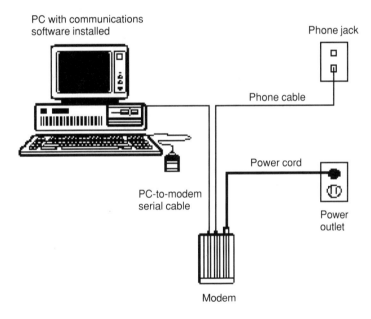

Figure 7-1   External modem configuration

If you have an internal modem, which is a special type of computer card, you insert it into an available expansion slot in your PC. You then connect a phone line from the back of your modem card to a phone jack. (Be sure to follow the manufacturer's instructions that come with your modem to insure proper setup.) Figure 7-2 illustrates an internal modem configuration.

Now that you know some basic information about Terminal and how to properly configure your modem, you are ready to use Terminal with ClarisWorks.

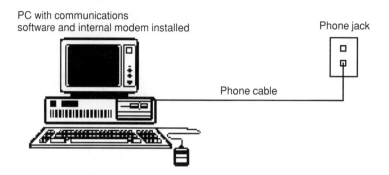

Figure 7-2   Internal modem configuration

Using Terminal with ClarisWorks

You follow this general procedure to use Terminal with ClarisWorks:

- Start Terminal from ClarisWorks.
- Specify settings, preferences, and other options.
- Connect to the other computer.
- Transmit data between computers.
- Disconnect from the other computer.
- Return to ClarisWorks.

Starting Terminal from ClarisWorks

You don't have to switch to the Program Manager to start Terminal while you're working in ClarisWorks. To open Terminal from within ClarisWorks:

1   **Choose New from the File menu.**

2   **In the dialog box, select Communications, and click OK.** ClarisWorks automatically opens Terminal in a separate application window (see Figure 7-3).

The Terminal window consists of a display area where you see and work with data as it comes across the phone lines through your modem onto your screen. Terminal can only accommodate one communications session at a time. A session begins when you initiate, or open, a connection to another computer. A session ends when you disconnect or close a connection. During a communications session, incoming and outgoing text and data appear in the Terminal

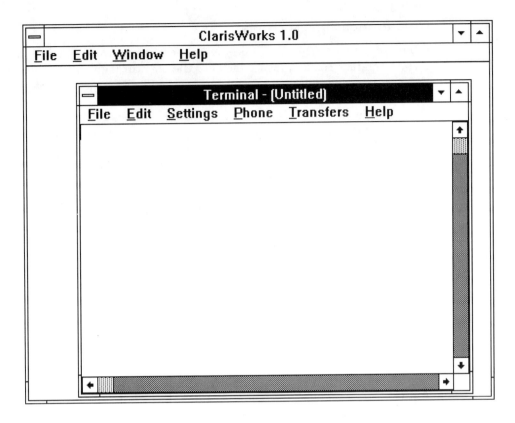

Figure 7-3 Terminal opens in a separate application window

window, scrolling up and off the top of the screen one line at a time. A *buffer* temporarily stores a specified number of lines of text in memory. To view the buffer, scroll in the Terminal window. See "Setting Preferences" later in this chapter for more information about specifying buffer size.

Specifying settings, preferences, and other options

Before conducting a communications session, you need to specify certain settings. There are four types of settings in Terminal:

- Communications settings
- Modem command settings
- Terminal emulation settings
- File transfer settings

These and other options are available in the Settings menu. This section describes how to specify each of these four settings, how to set Terminal preferences, and how to save your settings and preferences for subsequent sessions.

Communications settings

Communications settings include your modem's baud rate, data bits, stop bits, parity, and flow control. It also includes the port through which your modem is connected. Communications settings are required for any type of communications session you plan to conduct.

Communications settings must match the settings expected by your modem and those expected by the other computer or online service. To determine what these settings should be, refer to the manual that came with your modem and your online service manual or instructions for the remote computer. To specify communications settings in Terminal:

1   **Choose Communications from the Settings menu.** The Communications dialog box opens (see Figure 7-4).

2   **In the dialog box, select a Connector first, then select the options required by your modem and by the other computer. Click OK.** Table 7-1 gives a brief description of the options available in the Communications dialog box.

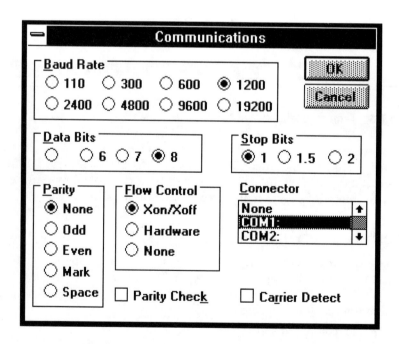

Figure 7-4   Communications dialog box

Table 7-1   Communications dialog box options

Option	Description
Baud Rate	Speed of data transmission
Data Bits	Number of bits per character
Stop Bits	Number of bits used to mark the end of a transmitted character
Parity	Error-checking procedure during data transmission
Flow Control	Method of regulating data flow during transmission; also called handshake
Connector	Port connection used by your modem
Parity Check	Display/don't display the byte where a parity error occurred
Carrier Detect	Use/don't use the modem signal for detecting a carrier signal

Modem command settings

Modem command settings let you tell Terminal which modem you are using (such as Hayes, MultiTech, or TrailBlazer) and whether to use or modify the default command sets for that modem. Terminal sends modem commands to your modem to instruct it to take the appropriate action (such as dialing or hanging up). Modem command settings are required for any type of communications session, and they must match the settings required by your modem. To specify modem command settings in Terminal:

1   Choose Modem Commands from the Settings menu. The Modem Commands dialog box opens (see Figure 7-5).

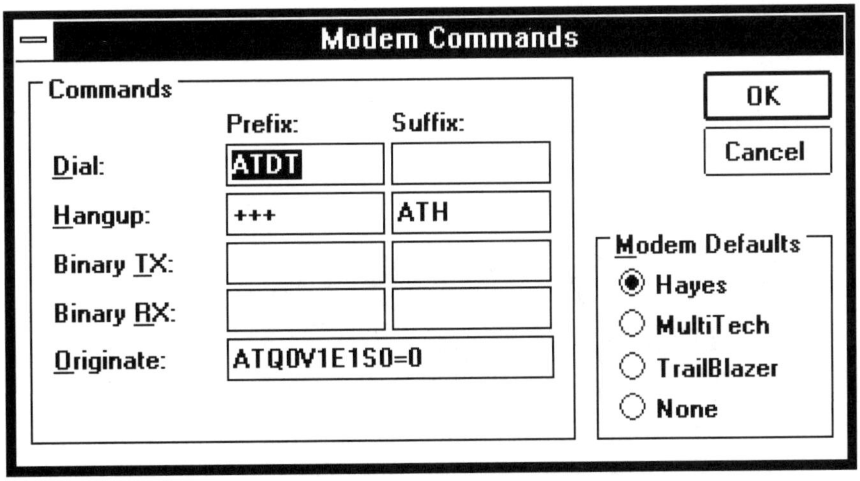

Figure 7-5   Modem Commands dialog box

2 In the Modem Defaults area of the dialog box, select your modem type or the modem most compatible to yours. As you make your selection, the dialog box commands change to reflect the selected modem. If none of the modems listed match yours, select None. When None is selected, the Commands area of the dialog box is blank.

3 In the Commands area, edit the commands as necessary. If you select None, you must type the required commands. Refer to the modem manual for specific commands.

4 When you are finished, click OK.

Terminal emulation settings

Terminal emulation refers to the ability of your computer to emulate, or imitate, a *dumb* terminal. Dumb terminals, which generally consist of a monitor and a keyboard with no CPU, are the type of terminals that connect to a mainframe or minicomputer. If you intend to connect to a mainframe or minicomputer, you must specify terminal settings that match those expected by the host (remote) computer. (Refer to the instructions for your network to obtain this information.) Terminal emulation settings are only required when you need to enable your computer to act like a dumb terminal.

With Terminal, you can set your PC to emulate either of three types of terminals:

- TTY
- DEC VT-100 (preset)
- DEC VT-52

To specify terminal emulation settings:

1 Choose Terminal Emulation from the Settings menu. The Terminal Emulation dialog box opens (see Figure 7-6).

2 Select a terminal emulation type, and click OK.

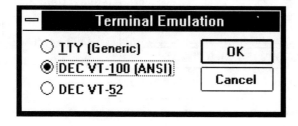

Figure 7-6   Terminal Emulation dialog box

File transfer settings

File transfer settings define the method and protocols used when you send data to or receive data from another computer. These settings are only required when you are planning to transfer data and files across your modem. They are not required for reading or sending electronic mail.

Protocols are electronic instructions or rules that Terminal uses regarding the formatting and transmission of data across the modem. Protocols also automatically check for errors during file transfer and correct them if possible. *File transfer methods,* on the other hand, designate the type of data or file you plan to transfer, either text or binary. Text files are considered straight ASCII text without any font or paragraph formatting. Binary files are any files that contain text and graphics, including formatted ASCII text files and executable program files.

The file transfer protocols supported by Terminal are text, XMODEM/CRC (the most common), and Kermit. Use the text protocol to transfer straight ASCII text without formatting. Use the XMODEM/CRC protocol to send or receive any kind of file—documents with text and graphics, ASCII text files whose formatting you want to retain during transfer, or executable program files. Use the Kermit protocol for mainframe-to-microcomputer file transfers. Both XMODEM and Kermit are error-correcting file transfer protocols; they insure that data arrives in the same condition it was sent. No matter which file transfer settings you specify, they must match the settings required by the remote computer or online service to which you are connecting.

To specify text file transfer settings, choose Text Transfers from the Settings menu, set the options to use for the transfer, and click OK. To specify binary file transfer settings, choose Binary Transfers from the Settings menu, select a protocol (XMODMEM/CRC or Kermit), and click OK. (Refer to the Microsoft Windows *User's Guide* for details on the options available in both the Text Transfers and Binary Transfers dialog boxes.)

See "Transferring Data" later in this chapter for more information on transferring text and binary files.

Setting preferences

Preferences are another set of options you can specify for your communications session. Terminal preferences are optional settings; in general, they affect the display of data in the Terminal window. To specify preferences:

1   **Choose Terminal Preferences from the Settings menu.** The Terminal Preferences dialog box opens (see Figure 7-7).

2   **Select or change any options in the dialog box, and click OK.** Table 7-2 gives a brief description of the options available in the Terminal Preferences dialog box.

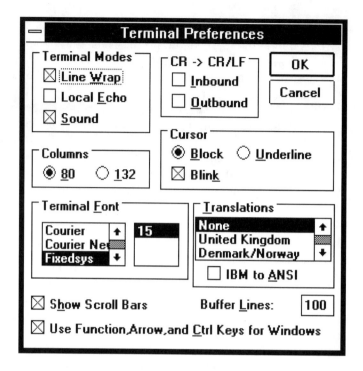

Figure 7-7   Terminal Preferences dialog box

Table 7-2   Terminal Preferences dialog box options

Option	Description
Option	*Description*
Line Wrap	Wrap to next line any characters exceeding screen column width
Local Echo	Echo (show) characters on screen as you type them
Sound	Enable sound of system beep when necessary
>CR -> CR/LF	Convert a carriage return to carriage return/linefeed to incoming or outgoing data
Columns	Set screen column width to 80 or 132 characters
Cursor	Show cursor as block or underline, and blinking
Terminal Font	Set default font and font size for the Terminal window
Translations	Translate incoming or outgoing data to another language
Show Scroll Bars	Enable display of Terminal window scroll bars
Buffer Lines	Specify size of buffer in number of lines (from 25 to 399 for 80-column width, or 25 to 244 for 132-column width)
Use Function, Arrow, and Ctrl keys for Windows	Enable Windows or host computer to recognize function, arrow, and Ctrl keys

Other options

The Settings menu also gives you other options for setting up a communications session:

- Phone Number—Type the phone number to dial
- Function Keys—Assign up to four tasks to each function key
- Printer Echo—Send incoming text to the printer
- Timer Mode—Set a timer on to keep track of your online time

Saving settings

After taking the time to specify your settings and preferences, you should save them to a file so you can use them in future sessions. To do so, choose Save As from the File menu, give the file a name, locate the disk and directory where you want the file saved, and click OK. Terminal files are saved with the .TRM file extension, unless you specify otherwise. Saving Terminal files saves only settings, not data or text you see in the Terminal window.

To use the settings you saved in a Terminal file, choose Open from the File menu, select the file to open, and click OK. The settings saved in the .TRM file replace any default settings in the appropriate dialog boxes.

TIP

You can get ClarisWorks to automatically use a .TRM file for your settings and preferences by adding the following statement to your CLARIS.INI file:

```
C:\<directory\<.TRM file name>
```

For example, if the .TRM file you want to use is called DEFAULT.TRM and is located in the Windows directory, you would add "C:\WINDOWS\DEFAULT.TRM" to the CLARIS.INI file. (Make sure this statement follows the "Terminal = TERMINAL.EXE" statement.)

Now, when you select Communications in the ClarisWorks New dialog box, the new Terminal session automatically uses the settings in the specific .TRM file.

Connecting

Once your settings and preferences are specified, you are ready to begin a communications session. Before you begin, be sure to have your online service or remote network account information accessible. You will need this information to make a proper connection.

Note   *If you are directly connecting two computers in the same room, make sure you are using a null modem cable. Connect one end of the cable to the serial port of one computer and connect the other end to the serial port of the other computer. Also, make sure each computer has its own communications software installed and that the communications settings (such as baud rate, data bits, stops bits, and parity) are identical on both computers.*

The following are general steps for connecting to another computer, to an online service, or to a bulletin board system (BBS) with Terminal:

1   **Turn on your modem, if it isn't already on.**

2   **If necessary, specify settings and preferences, or open a .TRM file with the specified settings.**

3   **Choose Phone Number from the Settings menu, and type the number to dial in the dialog box (see Figure 7-8).** Although they are ignored, you can type parentheses, dashes, or slashes in the phone number string. If you want dialing to pause after an access number (such as 9), type a comma. For Hayes-compatible modems, one comma is equivalent to a 2-second pause.

4   **Set or change any other options in the Phone Number dialog box, and click OK.**

5   **To initiate the connection, choose Dial from the Phone menu.** A status box indicates the number your modem is dialing and counts down the number of seconds specified by the Timeout If Not Connected In option in the Phone Number dialog box.

6   **When the status box disappears, the connection has been successfully made. Press ↵.** By pressing ↵, you tell the other computer that you are ready to respond to a series of prompts. The first prompt is usually one that asks you to identify the host name.

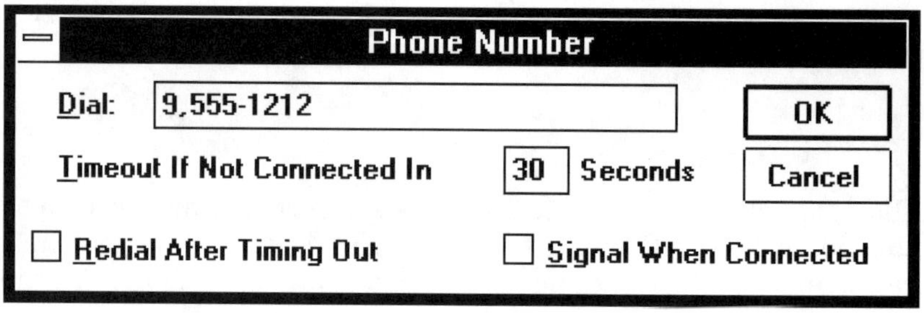

Phone Number	
Dial: `9,555-1212`	**OK**
Timeout If Not Connected In `30` **Seconds**	**Cancel**
☐ **Redial After Timing Out** ☐ **Signal When Connected**	

Figure 7-8   Phone Number dialog box

7 **Using your account information, type an appropriate response after each prompt, pressing the necessary key to send the response, such as ⏎.** Typically, the prompts ask you for your user name or ID number, a password, and other identifying information.

8 **When you see the main menu from the remote computer on your screen, use the commands or keyboard sequences that are appropriate for interacting with the remote computer.** Refer to your online service or BBS user guide or network instructions for the appropriate commands and keyboard sequences.

If you experience any problems during a communications session, follow the suggested solutions in the troubleshooting section of the *Getting Started with Microsoft Windows* manual.

Transferring data

Transferring data across your modem involves either sending files to another computer or receiving files from the other computer. The process of sending a file is commonly called *uploading;* the process of receiving files is called *downloading.* You can upload or download either text or binary files. This section describes how to transfer (upload and download) both types of files.

You can do other work on your computer while you work online. This is especially useful if you are sending or receiving particularly large files.

TIP

Uploading data

You can upload data when you are connected to an online service or BBS, to a remote host computer, or to another computer in the same room. This section describes how to upload ASCII text files first, then describes a similar process for uploading binary files.

Uploading an ASCII text file   Suppose you have a ClarisWorks text document called Memo to Joe that you want to send to Joe via an online service. Joe, who uses the same online service you do, also has a PC, but you don't know if he has ClarisWorks.

Before you set up and connect to the online service, open your text document in ClarisWorks. Press Alt+Tab to switch to ClarisWorks, and choose Open from the File menu to open the document. So Joe can read the document, you need to convert it to DOS (or ASCII) text format, which can be imported into most PC word processing applications. To do so, choose Save As (Shift+Ctrl+S) from the File menu. In the dialog box, click the List Files of Type drop-down menu, and choose "DOS Text File (*.txt)". Give your document a different name (such as Memo2Joe), and be sure to include the .TXT file extension. Click OK in the Save As dialog box to convert the ClarisWorks document to an ASCII text file.

To switch to Terminal, specify the file transfer settings necessary for uploading the text file, and do the upload:

1   **If Terminal is not open, choose New from the File menu in ClarisWorks, select Communications, and click OK.** If Terminal is open, press Alt+Tab to switch to it now.

   To see the contents of the text file in Terminal before sending it, choose View Text File from the Transfers menu, select the file to view, and click OK. The file displays in the Terminal window.

2   **If you have a .TRM file containing the required communications, modem command, and terminal emulation settings, open it now. Otherwise, follow the steps in "Specifying Settings, Preferences, and Other Options" earlier in this chapter to specify these settings.**

3   **Choose Text Transfers from the Settings menu, change any necessary options, and click OK.**

4   **Connect to your online service by following the general procedure in "Connecting" earlier in this chapter.**

5   **Once you are connected, issue the commands necessary to tell your online service that you want to upload a text file.**

6   **When the online service prompts you to begin sending the file, choose Send Text File from the Transfers menu.** The Send Text File dialog box opens (see Figure 7-9).

7   **Navigate to the disk and directory containing the file to upload, and select the file from the File Name area of the dialog box. Change any other options, and click OK.**

As your text file uploads, you see it scroll in the Terminal window. Also, the status area appears along the lower edge of the Terminal window (see Figure 7-10). The status area indicates the progress of the upload. To pause the uploading process, click Pause; to continue, click Resume. To terminate the upload before it's finished, click Stop in the status area. (You can also choose Pause, Resume, or Stop from the Transfers menu.)

When the file has been completely uploaded, issue the command(s) required by your online service to address the file and complete the upload process. When you are finished, log off the online service, and choose Hangup from the Phone menu to disconnect.

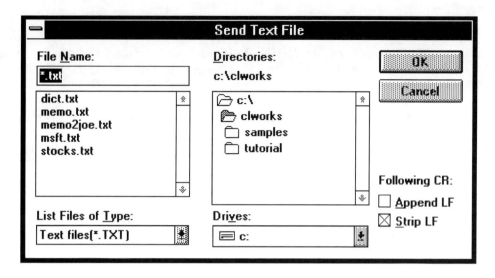

Figure 7-9   Send Text File dialog box

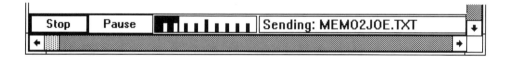

Figure 7-10   Text file transfer status area

Uploading a binary file   Suppose your friend Joe does have ClarisWorks, and you want to send him a ClarisWorks document that contains text and graphics. You can upload the file using a binary transfer.

Begin with Terminal open and your communications, modem command, and terminal emulation settings specified. To do the upload:

1   **Choose Binary Transfers from the Settings menu, select the XMODEM/CRC protocol, and click OK.**

2   **Connect to your online service by following the general procedure in "Connecting" earlier in this chapter.**

3   **Once you are connected, issue the commands necessary to tell your online service that you want to upload a binary file.** Depending on the service, you may have to indicate the protocol you want to use. If so, specify the XMODEM/CRC protocol.

4   **When the online service prompts you to begin sending the file, choose Send Binary File from the Transfers menu.** The Send Binary File dialog box opens. This dialog box is identical to the Send Text File dialog

box (see Figure 7-9), except List Files of Type drop-down menu is preset to the "All Files (*.*)".

5   Navigate to the disk and directory containing the file to upload, select the file from the File Name area of the dialog box, and click OK.

Unlike a text file upload, you don't see the contents of the file scroll in the Terminal window during a binary transfer. As the file is uploaded, the status area shows "Sending: Memo2Joe.CWK" (or the name of your file). To terminate the upload before it's finished, click Stop in the status area. When the status area disappears, the upload is complete.

When the file has been completely uploaded, issue the command(s) required by your online service to address the file and complete the upload process. When you are finished, log off the online service, and choose Hangup from the Phone menu to disconnect.

Downloading data

The process of downloading data from another computer to your computer is similar to uploading data. However, when downloading data, you can specify where you want the received file saved. You can download the file as a new file, or replace an existing file with it. If you are downloading a text file, you also have the option of appending the text to an existing file.

This section describes how to download ASCII text files first, then describes the process for downloading binary files. For more information on downloading data, read "Analyzing Stock Information" later in this chapter. That section contains a step-by-step, practical example of downloading financial information and transferring it into a ClarisWorks spreadsheet for analysis.

Downloading an ASCII text file   Begin with Terminal open, and either specify the appropriate communications, modem commands, and terminal emulation settings, or open a .TRM file containing these settings. To download an ASCII text file:

1   Choose Text Transfers from the Settings menu, change any necessary options, and click OK.

2   Connect to your online service by following the general procedure in "Connecting" earlier in this chapter.

3   Once you are connected, issue the commands necessary to locate the text file you want to download (receive).

4   When the online service prompts you to begin receiving the file, choose Receive Text File from the Transfers menu. This opens the Receive Text File dialog box shown in Figure 7-11.

5   Using the Receive Text File dialog box, follow one of these procedures:

- If you want store the file as a new file, navigate to the desired drive and/or directory, type a name for the received file (be sure to include the .TXT file extension), and click OK.
- If you want to append (add) the received text to an existing file, navigate to the drive and directory containing the existing file, and select its name from the File Name area. Click the Append File option, and click OK. Terminal adds incoming text to the end of the existing text file.
- If you want to replace an existing file with the received text file, navigate to the drive and directory containing the existing file. Select its name from the File Name area, and click OK. Terminal asks you to verify that you want to replace the existing file. If you do, click Yes.

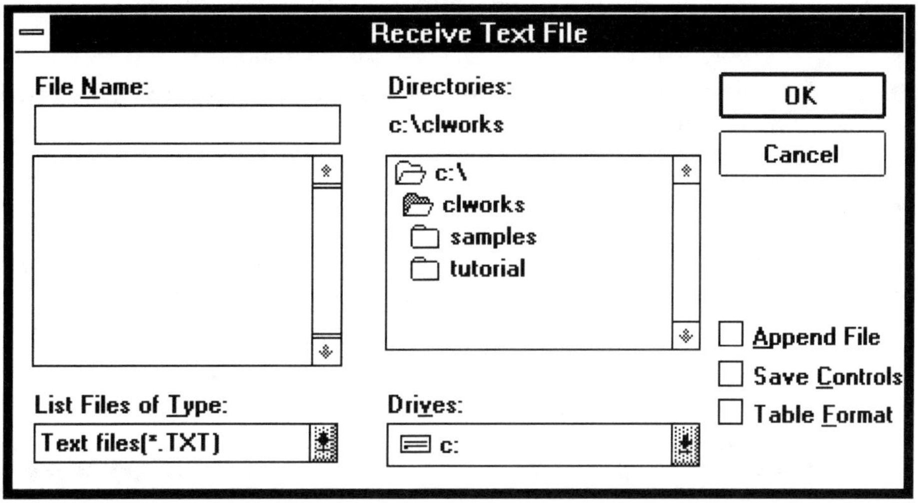

Figure 7-11   Receive Text File dialog box

When the Receive Text File dialog box disappears, the download begins. The status area of the Terminal window shows the name of the receiving file (the file name you gave in the Receive Text File dialog box) and indicates the number of bytes received so far. To pause downloading, click Pause; to continue, click Resume. To terminate the download before it's finished, click Stop in the status area. When the status area disappears, the download is complete.

You can see the contents of the received text file in the Terminal window by choosing View Text File from the Transfers menu.

Downloading a binary file   The process of downloading a binary file from an online service is similar to uploading a binary file. However, unless your online service requires, you don't have to change any file transfer settings. This is because most online services use the XMODEM file transfer protocol, which is the preset protocol in Terminal.

Begin with Terminal open, and either specify the appropriate communications, modem commands, and terminal emulation settings, or open a .TRM file containing these settings. To download a binary file:

1 **If necessary, choose Binary Transfers from the Settings menu, select Kermit or XMODEM/CRC (whichever protocol is required by the online service), and click OK.**

2 **Connect to your online service by following the general procedure in "Connecting" earlier in this chapter.**

3 **Once you are connected, issue the commands necessary to locate the binary file you want to download (receive).**

4 **When the online service prompts you to begin receiving the file, choose Receive Binary File from the Transfers menu.** The Receive Binary File dialog box opens (see Figure 7-12).

5 **Using the Receive Binary File dialog box, follow one of these procedures:**

   • If you want store the file as a new file, navigate to the desired drive and/or directory, type a name for the received file (be sure to include the appropriate file extension, such as .EXE), and click OK.

   • If you want to replace an existing file with the one received, navigate to the drive and directory containing the existing file. Select its name from the File Name area, and click OK. Terminal asks you to verify that you want to replace the existing file. If you do, click Yes.

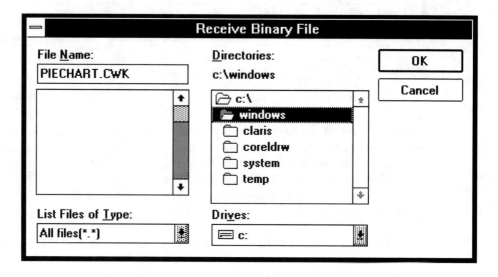

Figure 7-12   Receive Binary File dialog box

When the Receive Binary File dialog box disappears, the download begins. The status area of the Terminal window shows the name of the receiving file (the file name you gave in the Receive Binary File dialog box) and indicates the number of bytes received so far. It also shows the number of dialing retries, which is useful when you have a bad connection. To terminate the download before it's finished, click Stop in the status area. When the status area disappears, the download is complete.

Disconnecting

Breaking a communications connection, or disconnecting, is essentially a two-step process: tell the remote computer you want to disconnect, then tell the modem.

When you are ready to disconnect, issue the appropriate command to tell the remote computer you want to disconnect. Usually, the command is something like bye, off, exit, quit, and so on. Refer to your online service or network manual for the specific command. Following that, choose Hangup from the Phone menu to hang up the phone and reset your modem.

Returning to ClarisWorks

When you are finished telecommunicating, you can close Terminal and return directly to ClarisWorks. To do so, in Terminal, choose Exit from the File menu. If you haven't saved the current settings, Terminal asks if you want to do so. Then, Terminal quits and the Terminal application window closes, returning you to where you were in ClarisWorks when you opened Terminal.

Now you have a general overview of how to use Terminal with ClarisWorks. In the next section, you'll learn how to apply your knowledge of telecommunications and the ClarisWorks spreadsheet environment by analyzing financial information after downloading it from a stock information service.

Analyzing stock information

One of the most common types of information to access online and to download is stock information. Almost all online services have some kind of facility for you to access stock information on every company that is publicly traded. Or, if you are really serious about tracking stock information, you can subscribe to the Dow Jones News/Retrieval network—an online service specifically geared toward locating financial news and information.

Note *Accessing stock information online is usually surcharged, meaning you pay for it in addition to the usual charges you incur online. Refer to your online service for specific pricing information.*

Looking up stock quotes in your daily newspaper is one way of tracking the performance of your favorite company's stock. To gain a full picture of how the stock is performing, you can transfer this information from an online network into a ClarisWorks spreadsheet and analyze its performance over a period of time. This section describes how to do just that.

First, you are going to use Terminal to connect to the online service and download the stock information in tabular format as a text file. Then, you insert the contents of the text file into a ClarisWorks spreadsheet. Finally, assuming you have more than one day's worth of stock information, you plot the data in a line chart so you can analyze it and see trends over time.

Begin by launching ClarisWorks. In the New dialog box, select Communications, and click OK to open Terminal. If you previously saved the settings for connecting to your online service in a .TRM file, open the file now in Terminal. Otherwise, specify the appropriate settings, supply the correct phone number, and choose Dial from the Phone menu to dial your online service.

Once connected, provide your user name or ID, password, and any other information required by the online service to log on. Then, issue the commands necessary to access the stock information area of the service. For example, if you are using CompuServe, the command is GO QQUOTE (for quick quote). When the service asks you to type the stock's ticker symbol, do not type anything yet and move on to the next section.

Transferring stock information into a spreadsheet

Depending on the exchange in which the stock issue is traded, the stock information you can get online includes the name of the company, the number of shares traded, the high price, the low price, the last price, and the price change since the close of the stock market on the previous business day. The date of the stock data is usually also included.

No matter what online service you use, stock prices are generally displayed in tabular form, as shown in Figure 7-13.

In order to transfer stock information to a spreadsheet document, you must receive the data in tabular format. Instead, if you simply copy the data from the Terminal window to the Clipboard, then paste it into a spreadsheet document, the spreadsheet will treat the data as one unit and it will appear in one cell. By

Name	Volume	Hi/Ask	Low/Bid	Last	Change
MICROSOFT CORP COM	14144	87.750	85.500	86.375	-0.750

Figure 7-13   Sample of stock information found online (for Microsoft Corporation, 12/15/92)
(from QQUOTE of the CompuServe Information Service)

downloading the data in tabular format, each column of stock information is treated as a distinct unit of data. When you paste it into the spreadsheet, each column is inserted into a separate spreadsheet column.

When you left off at the end of the previous section, you were still connected to the online service and the service was prompting you to type the stock's ticker symbol. Before you do so, you need to prepare to receive the data as a table. To do so:

1   **Choose Receive Text File from the Transfers menu.**

2   **In the dialog box, type a name for your text file (such as Stocks.TXT), and navigate to the drive and directory where you want it saved.** If you have an existing text file containing stock quotes from previous days, select the file in the File Name area, and select the Append File option to add the current quotes to that file.

3   **To receive the text in tabular form, select the Table Format option in the Receive Text File dialog box, and click OK.** By selecting Table Format, tab characters are inserted between columns of data instead of spaces. Everything appearing in the Terminal window from now until you stop will be downloaded in table format.

4   **Before you type the ticker symbol, click Pause in the status area.** You don't want to capture this entry.

5   **Type the stock's ticker symbol (usually a three- or four-letter abbreviation for the company name).** For example, the ticker symbol for Microsoft is MSFT.

6   **Click Resume, and press ⏎ to display the stock information.** The stock data scrolls across the Terminal window and is captured to the designated text file in table format. For example, if today's date is 2/5/93 and you are looking up the stock price for ABC Company (a fictitious name), you receive the following stock data:

Name	Volume	Hi/Ask	Low/Bid	Last	Change	Date
ABC Company	23576	36.25	35.375	35.875	0.125	2/5/93

7   **After this information displays, click Stop to terminate the capture.**

8   **Log off the online service, and choose Hangup from the Phone menu.**

To verify that the data is in the text file, choose View Text File from the Transfers menu, select the file name, and click OK. This way you can see the contents of the file in the Terminal window. Now choose Exit from the File menu to return to ClarisWorks.

With your stock information saved as a text file, you are ready to transfer it to a ClarisWorks spreadsheet document.

1   **In ClarisWorks, choose Open from the File menu.** The Open dialog box appears.

2   **Click the Import Options switch to expand the dialog box, select the Spreadsheet option, and select "ASCII Text File (*.txt)" from the List Files of Type drop-down menu.**

3   **Select your text file (such as Stocks.TXT) from the File Name area, and click OK.** ClarisWorks converts the text file containing your stock quotes and opens it in a new window.

4   **Select the stock information you want to transfer to the spreadsheet, and press Ctrl+C to copy it to the Clipboard.**

5   **Choose New from the File menu, select Spreadsheet, and click OK to create a new spreadsheet document.** If you already have a spreadsheet document you want to use for the stock information, open it now.

6   **In the spreadsheet document, click in the first cell where you want the data to be pasted.**

7   **Choose Paste from the Edit menu.**

The stock data from the text file is pasted into the spreadsheet document, beginning in the active cell. Figure 7-14 shows an example of how the ABC Company stock data looks in the spreadsheet document after the copy-and-paste operation.

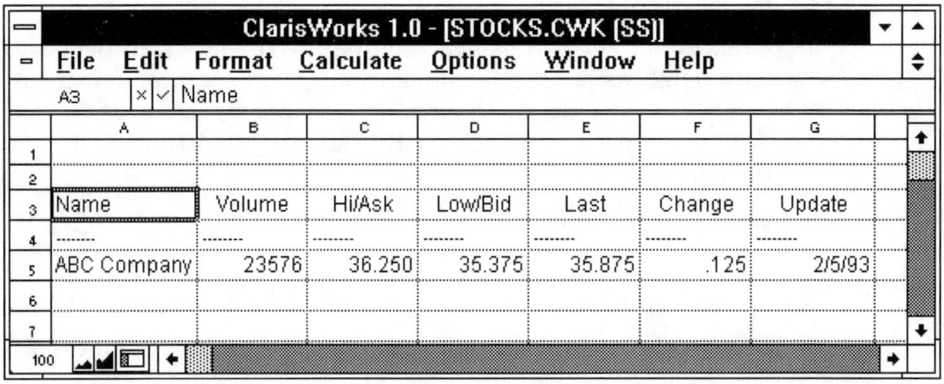

	A	B	C	D	E	F	G
1							
2							
3	Name	Volume	Hi/Ask	Low/Bid	Last	Change	Update
4	--------	--------	--------	--------	--------	--------	--------
5	ABC Company	23576	36.250	35.375	35.875	.125	2/5/93
6							
7							

ClarisWorks 1.0 - [STOCKS.CWK [SS]]
File   Edit   Format   Calculate   Options   Window   Help
A3   Name

Figure 7-14   Stock data for ABC Company from 2/5/93, inserted into a new spreadsheet document from a text file

*You can also copy-and-paste tabular information stored in a text file into a
spreadsheet frame or into a database document.*

TIP

At this point, you can make any modifications you want to the spreadsheet.
Make these two modifications now: select row 4, and choose Delete Cells from the
Calculate menu to remove the dashed lines from the spreadsheet. Then, select
row 3, and choose Underline from the Style cascading menu (Format menu).

You can also change the font type, size, and style, change the alignment of
data within cells, assign a different number format to the data, or resize the
width of the columns. When you've made your changes, press Ctrl+S to save
and name your spreadsheet.

Now you can track fluctuations in the stock's performance, check your stock
price regularly (every day, every other day, or weekly at a minimum), and add
each new table of stock data to your spreadsheet document. For example, Figure
7-15 shows a spreadsheet document containing weekly stock information for
ABC Company over a period of eight weeks.

When you accumulate historical stock information in your spreadsheet, you
can chart the data to see trends and fluctuations at a glance.

	STOCKS.CWK (SS)						
E13							
	A	B	C	D	E	F	G
1							
2							
3	Name	Volume	Hi/Ask	Low/Bid	Last	Change	Update
4	ABC Company	23576	36.250	35.375	35.875	.125	2/5/93
5		22830	37.250	36.000	36.375	.125	2/12/93
6		8515	37.000	36.250	36.750	0.000	2/19/93
7		13527	37.000	36.000	36.000	-.750	2/26/93
8		10350	36.500	35.750	36.500	.500	3/5/93
9		15716	36.750	36.000	36.250	-.250	3/12/93
10		15190	36.750	35.500	36.000	-.250	3/19/93
11		9494	35.500	34.750	34.750	-.500	3/26/93
100							

Figure 7-15   The spreadsheet document with stock data accumulated for eight weeks

Charting stock information

In this section, you use the historical stock information you have accumulated to make a line chart. The line chart is the best choice of chart type because it allows you to see trends over time. In this example, you make a line chart to see the fluctuations of the high, low, and closing price of the ABC Company stock over an eight-week period.

Recall that the first step to making a chart is to select the range of data to include in the chart. If you look at the spreadsheet in Figure 7-15, you see that the data to chart appears in the cell range C4 to E11. You also want to include the column labels so your chart uses them for identification purposes in the legend. Thus, your selection is C3 to E11.

You now need to create the line chart and change the Y-axis scale so your stock data is easier to see in the chart. To do so:

1   **With your data selected, choose Make Chart (Ctrl+M) from the Options menu.** The Make Chart dialog box opens, showing options for a pie chart (the preset chart type).

2   **Click the line chart icon (see Figure 7-16).** When you select the line chart icon, the Make Chart dialog box shows the options for line charts.

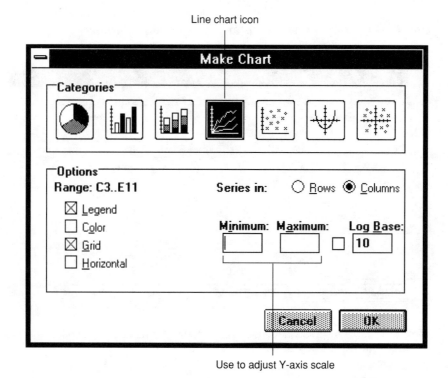

Figure 7-16   The Make Chart dialog box showing options for a line chart

Based on your selection of data, either the Rows or Columns "Series in"
option is preset. The correct setting of this option is very important because
it determines whether each line in the chart represents a row of data or a
column of data. In this case, the preset Columns setting is correct: you want
each chart line to represent a different column of data.

3   **To change the Y-axis scale, type a number in the Minimum box and
a higher number in the Maximum box.** The minimum must be smaller
than the maximum. When you specify a minimum and maximum value, be
sure the values will accommodate the data you are charting. For example,
using the ABC Company stock data, set the minimum Y-axis value to 30 and
the maximum to 40.

4   **If you have a color system, leave the Color option selected.** Line charts
appear better in color than they do in black and white. This is because, on
black-and-white systems, ClarisWorks uses different pen patterns for each
line, and the patterns are often difficult to differentiate in a line chart (see
Figure 7-17).

5   **When you are finished, click OK to close the dialog box and make the
chart.**

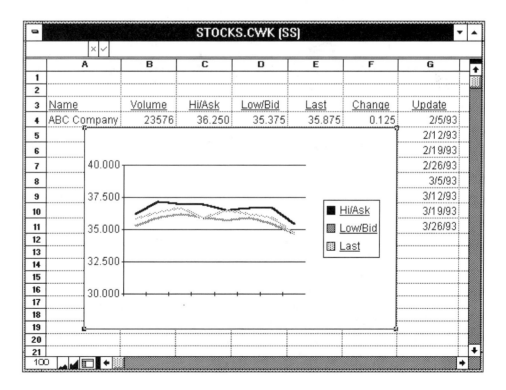

Figure 7-17   Line chart showing stock data for ABC Company

The chart automatically appears on top of the data in the spreadsheet window, as shown in Figure 7-17 on page 391.

At this point, you can make modifications to your chart. To make your chart more understandable, add text labels to the points along the X-axis. These labels are the dates that appear in column G in the sample stock spreadsheet document. At the same time, add a title to your chart. To add text labels and a chart title, make the tool palette visible by choosing Show Tools from the Window menu, and double-click the text tool to select and lock it. Type the text labels from column G at each point along the X-axis, and type the chart title in the area above the chart grid. If you want, you can change the font type, size, and style used for the text labels and title. To align the text labels evenly along the X-axis, select them and use the Align Objects dialog box to align their top or bottom edges. You can also change the pattern or color of the lines in the chart using the pen tool. For example, to change the pen pattern of the "Last" chart line, click its box in the legend, and select another pattern from the pen pattern palette. Figure 7-18 shows how these changes affect the appearance of the chart.

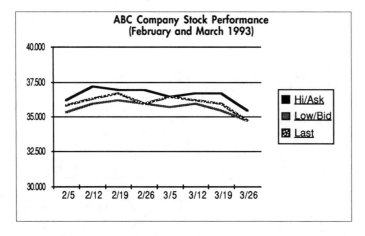

Figure 7-18   Line chart modified to include text labels, chart title, and different "Last" pen pattern

After you add the text labels and title to your chart, it is a good idea to group them with your chart. To do so, select each text object along with the chart, and choose Group from the Arrange menu. This way, if you move, resize, or scale your chart, the text objects will move, resize, and scale with it. If you decide to make further modifications to your chart after grouping the objects together, you must ungroup the objects by selecting them and choosing Ungroup from the Arrange menu. (If you make changes to your data and the chart is grouped, the chart still updates to reflect the changes in data.)

TIP

You can get ClarisWorks to automatically provide the chart title and X-axis labels for you. Doing so requires you to set up your stock spreadsheet document as shown in Figure 7-19.

In this spreadsheet, the Volume data is not included, cell A3 contains ABC Company rather than Name, and the dates from column F are converted to text in column A. You must convert dates to text if you want ClarisWorks to use dates as X-axis labels. To do this, use the formula shown in the entry bar area in Figure 7-19. The DATETOTEXT function converts the dates in column F to text in column A. Now, when you select cells A3 through D11 and create a line chart, the contents of cell A3 becomes the chart title, and the row labels in cells A4 through A11 become the X-axis labels. To see all of the X-axis labels clearly, use the Scale Selection dialog box (Options menu) to enlarge the chart.

A4	×✓ =DATETOTEXT(F4)				
	A	B	C	D	E	F
1						
2						
3	ABC Company	Hi/Ask	Low/Bid	Last	Change	Update
4	2/5/93	36.250	35.375	35.875	.125	2/5/93
5	2/12/93	37.250	36.000	36.375	.125	2/12/93
6	2/19/93	37.000	36.250	36.750	0.000	2/19/93
7	2/26/93	37.000	36.000	36.000	-.750	2/26/93
8	3/5/93	36.500	35.750	36.500	.500	3/5/93
9	3/12/93	36.750	36.000	36.250	-.250	3/12/93
10	3/19/93	36.750	35.500	36.000	-.250	3/19/93
11	3/26/93	35.500	34.750	34.750	-.500	3/26/93

Figure 7-19   The stock spreadsheet document set up for automatic chart labels and title

Summary

This chapter provided you with an overview of the Windows Terminal application and gave you practical instructions for using Terminal with ClarisWorks. If you followed the example for analyzing stock data, you also have some experience with how to integrate data captured during a Terminal session with ClarisWorks. This process is one of many ways to exchange data from other applications with ClarisWorks.

The Appendix that follows provides you with more detailed information on exchanging data so you can use files created in other Windows or Macintosh applications in ClarisWorks, and vice versa.

Exchanging Data with Other Applications

About this appendix

This appendix provides information on using data created by other applications in ClarisWorks and using ClarisWorks data with other applications. It is organized into these topics:

- Claris XTND—a discussion of the Claris XTND System
- Supported file formats—tables listing supported file formats by application area
- Exporting data—how to save ClarisWorks data in another file format
- Importing data—how to open another file format in ClarisWorks
- Importing or exporting user dictionary terms—how to exchange user dictionaries between ClarisWorks and other applications
- Cross-platform tips and hints—useful information for exchanging files between ClarisWorks for Windows and ClarisWorks for the Macintosh

Claris XTND

The ability to use files created in other applications, or write files that can be read by other applications is called *exchanging data*. ClarisWorks makes this ability seamless to you via the Claris XTND system.

The Claris XTND system, which works with text and graphics, is a technology that allows ClarisWorks, or any other Claris product, to read from or write to virtually any other application. Different applications use different *file formats,* which are the internal instructions that describe how data is stored on disk. Using the Claris XTND system, ClarisWorks can *import* (read in) or *export* (write out) all of the most commonly used file formats without you having to make any special changes to your documents.

XTND System files

When you install ClarisWorks, the installation process copies the Claris XTND system's associated files into the Claris subdirectory in your Windows directory (C:\WINDOWS\CLARIS), including

- XTND.DLL, the Claris XTND System engine
- Translator files, one for each file filter, stored on disk as *.XTD
- XTNDTRAN.LST, used internally by ClarisWorks

Claris translators

The translators are file filters, each residing in a separate file in the Claris subdirectory. The translators let you work with more than twenty different file formats in ClarisWorks. Table A-1 lists the Claris translators available for each ClarisWorks application environment. It also gives the name of the translator file associated with each file format supported.

The translators in the Claris subdirectory determine the file formats that are available to you in the List Files of Type drop-down menu of the Open, Insert, and Save As dialog boxes of each application environment.

The Claris XTND system comes with every Claris product. Depending on the type of product, the list of translators may be different. For example, FileMaker Pro for Windows ships with translators that allow you to import or export file formats appropriate to a database. When you install a new Claris product or update to an existing Claris product, the installation procedure replaces existing translators with the new versions.

Table A-1 Claris Translators

Environment	*File Format*	*Translator Name*
Word processing	Text (DOS Text File)	TEXT.XTD
	RTF (Rich Text Format)	RTF.XTD
	Word for Windows	WORDWIN.XTD
	Word for DOS	WORDDOS.XTD
	WordPerfect for Windows	WPERFECT.XTD
	WordPerfect for DOS	WPERFECT.XTD
Graphics	WMF (Windows MetaFile)	WMF.XTD
	EPS (Encapsulated PostScript)	EPS.XTD
	PCX (PC Paintbrush)	PCX.XTD
	CGM (Computer Graphics MetaFile)	CGM.XTD
	BMP (Windows Bitmap)	BMP.XTD
	TIFF (Tagged Image File Format)	TIFF.XTD
	PCT (Macintosh Picture)	PICT.XTD
Database	Text (ASCII)	ASCII.XTD
	DBF (dBASE File)	DBF.XTD
	DIF (Data Interchange Format)	DIF.XTD
	SYLK (Symbolic Link)	SYLK.XTD
Spreadsheet	Text (ASCII)	ASCII.XTD
	DBF (dBASE File)	DBF.XTD
	DIF (Data Interchange Format)	DIF.XTD
	SYLK (Symbolic Link)	SYLK.XTD
	XLS (Excel 3.0)	BIFF.XTD
	WKS, WK1, WK3 (Lotus 1-2-3)	WKS.XTD, WK1.XTD, WK3.XTD

Supported file formats

Through the Claris XTND system, ClarisWorks supports more than twenty different file formats for importing or exporting data. The specific file formats that are available depend upon which document type you are exporting or importing.

The tables in the following sections list the file formats supported for the given document type, the platform on which the file format is most commonly used, and the type of data exchange you can perform with the file format.

Text file formats

Table A-2 lists the file formats that are supported for word processor (text) documents.

Table A-2 Word Processor (Text) File Formats

Format	Platform	Exchange Type
DOS text	IBM PC/compatible	Import, Export, Insert
RTF	IBM PC/compatible, Macintosh	Import, Export, Insert
Word for DOS	IBM PC/compatible	Import, Export, Insert
Word for Windows	IBM PC/compatible	Import, Export, Insert
WordPerfect 5.1/DOS	IBM PC/compatible	Import, Export, Insert
WordPerfect/Windows	IBM PC/compatible	Import, Export, Insert

Except for RTF and DOS text, all of the text file formats supported correspond to their native application. RTF is a Microsoft word processing file format that encodes Microsoft Word formatting instructions (such as ruler settings, font types, and so on) into ASCII so other programs supporting this format (like ClarisWorks) can interpret the document's format. The DOS text format strips the document of any formatting.

Graphics file formats

Table A-3 lists the file formats that are supported for graphics documents.

Table A-3 Graphics File Formats

Format	Platform	Exchange Type
BMP	IBM PC/compatible	Import, Insert
CGM	IBM PC/compatible	Import, Insert
EPS	IBM PC/compatible, Macintosh	Import, Insert
PCT	Macintosh	Import, Export, Insert
PCX	IBM PC/compatible	Import, Insert
TIFF	IBM PC/compatible, Macintosh	Import, Insert
WMF	IBM PC/compatible	Import, Export, Insert

Notice that EPS and TIFF file formats are supported on both Windows and Macintosh platforms. PCT, the Macintosh PICT format, and WMF, the Windows MetaFile format, are the only file formats available for export from ClarisWorks.

Database file formats

Table A-4 lists the file formats that are supported for database documents.

Table A-4 Database File Formats

Format	Platform	Exchange Type
ASCII text	All	Import, Export
DBF	All	Import, Export
DIF	All	Import, Export
SYLK	All	Import, Export

An ASCII text database format is one in which field information is Tab-delimited within each record, records are separated by carriage-return characters, and text is unformatted. DIF, developed for transferring information stored in VisiCalc spreadsheets, is primarily used by ClarisWorks to preserve field names when translating databases created by other applications into a ClarisWorks database document. SYLK, originally developed for transferring information stored in MultiPlan or Excel spreadsheets, works similarly to DIF in translating the data into or out to a database file.

When a ClarisWorks database document is in Browse or Find view, you cannot use the Insert command. In Layout, you can only insert supported text or graphics formats. See "Using the Insert Command" later in this appendix.

Spreadsheet file formats

Table A-5 lists the file formats that are supported for spreadsheet documents.

Table A-5 Spreadsheet File Formats

Format	Platform	Exchange Type
ASCII text	All	Import, Export
DBF	All	Import, Export
DIF	All	Import, Export
SYLK	All	Import, Export
WKS, WK1, WK3	IBM PC/compatible	Import, Export
XLS	IBM PC/compatible, Macintosh	Import, Export

In an ASCII text spreadsheet format, column information is Tab-delimited within each row, rows are separated by carriage-return characters, and text is unformatted.

When you import a DBF database file format into a spreadsheet, fields are translated into spreadsheet columns and records are translated into rows. When you export a ClarisWorks spreadsheet as a DBF file, columns become fields and rows become records.

DIF and SYLK are common spreadsheet file formats supported by most spreadsheet applications across all platforms. For translating spreadsheet information, SYLK is primarily used by ClarisWorks to maintain cell formatting and formulas.

You can only insert supported text or graphics formats into a ClarisWorks spreadsheet. See "Using the Insert Command" later in this appendix.

Exporting data

You export data when you want to save a ClarisWorks file in a format that can be used by another application. You can export text, graphics, spreadsheet, and database documents for use by other programs. The process of exporting a ClarisWorks document is simple and straightforward. To do so:

1 **With the document you want to export open and active in ClarisWorks, choose Save As (Shift+Ctrl+S) from the File menu.** The Save As dialog box opens.

2 **Select a file format from the List Files of Type drop-down menu.** The list of file formats varies depending on the type of document you are saving (text, graphics, database, or spreadsheet).

3 **Rename the document, and locate the disk and directory where you want the exported file stored.**

4 **Click OK to export the file.** A translation status box indicates the progress of the export.

Importing data

You import data into ClarisWorks when you want to use a file created by another application. You can import text, graphics, spreadsheet, and database documents that are saved in a supported file format.

In ClarisWorks, there are three ways for you to import data. You can *open* the foreign document (the document you want to import) as a ClarisWorks document. In this case, the document can be text, graphics, spreadsheet, or database. You can also *insert* a whole foreign document into an existing ClarisWorks document. You can only insert whole text or graphics documents. Finally, you can *embed* a foreign document into a new or existing ClarisWorks document.

Using the Open command

To open a document created by another application in ClarisWorks:

1   **In ClarisWorks, choose Open (Ctrl+O) from the File menu.** The Open dialog box appears.

2   **Click the Import Options switch to expand the dialog box and access supported import formats for a specific document type.** This step is important because it tells ClarisWorks what type of document to open. The bottom of the dialog box displays five document types from which you can choose: ClarisWorks, Word Processing, Graphics, Database, and Spreadsheet.

3   **Select the type of document you want to import, such as Spreadsheet.**

4   **Select a file format from the List Files of Type drop-down menu.** The list of file formats varies depending on the type of document you are importing.

5   **Navigate to the disk and directory containing the file you want to import.**

6   **Select the file and click OK to import the file.**

During the import, ClarisWorks displays a status box that gives the name of the file, the original format of the file, and the status of the import. When the import is complete, the file appears as a ClarisWorks document on your screen, and the title bar shows "Converted," indicating the file was converted into a ClarisWorks document. You can work with the imported document just as you would work with a ClarisWorks document. Be sure to save imported documents in ClarisWorks format using the Save As dialog box.

Using the Insert command

You can insert whole documents created by other applications into existing ClarisWorks text or graphics documents. Spreadsheet documents and database documents in Layout view have the same insert options as a ClarisWorks graphics document.

To insert a foreign document into an existing ClarisWorks document:

1   **Open the ClarisWorks document into which you want to insert the foreign document.**

2   **Position the insertion point (or click the pointer) in the document where you want the contents of the foreign document inserted.**

3   **Choose Insert from the File menu.** The Insert dialog box opens.

4   **Select a file format from the List Files of Type drop-down menu.** The list of file formats vary depending on the type of document you are inserting.

5   **Navigate to the disk and directory containing the file you want to insert.**

6   **Select the file and click OK to insert the file.**

The selected document is inserted in the current ClarisWorks document at the insertion point you set in step 2.

Embedding a document

You can embed a foreign document in a new or existing ClarisWorks document by using the drag-and-drop method from the File Manager. For example, you can embed several text documents created by other word processing applications into a ClarisWorks stationery file (.CWS) that you use as a template for newsletters.

To embed a document created by another application in a ClarisWorks document:

1   **In ClarisWorks, open the document into which you want the foreign file embedded. Or, create a new document.**

2   **Reduce the size of the ClarisWorks document window and reposition it so you will be able to simultaneously see the contents of the File Manager window.**

3   **Press Alt+Tab to switch to the Program Manager.**

4   **Launch the File Manager by double-clicking its icon in the Main program group.**

5   **Navigate to the drive and directory containing the file you want to embed.**

6   **Reduce the size of the File Manager window so you can also see the ClarisWorks document window on the screen.**

7   **From the File Manager, drag the foreign file's icon into the ClarisWorks document window.** The cursor becomes an icon that is a small square with a plus (+) sign inside of it.

8   **Release the mouse to "drop" the file into the ClarisWorks document window.** The contents of the file appear in the ClarisWorks document.

You can use this technique for several files at a time. For example, you can drag five files from the File Manager and drop them into a ClarisWorks document. The files are inserted in the same order you drag and drop them.

For this import method to be successful, the foreign file must have a file format that ClarisWorks supports for the given type of ClarisWorks document. For example, you can't drag and drop a .DBF database file format into a ClarisWorks word processing document. For more information on embedding documents, refer to the Microsoft Windows *User's Guide.*

Importing or exporting user dictionary terms

When you use user dictionaries in ClarisWorks, or any other application, you usually make a significant investment in time customizing the dictionary with special terms. Rather than starting over from scratch by building a new user dictionary, ClarisWorks gives you the option of exporting the ClarisWorks user dictionary for use with other programs. Or, if you have a text file containing dictionary terms, you can import it into the ClarisWorks user dictionary.

You use the User Dictionary dialog box to import or export a user dictionary as a text file. Choose User Dictionary from the Spelling cascading menu (Edit menu) to open the dialog box now. In the dialog box, click the Text File switch. Two new dialog buttons appear: Import and Export.

Note   *If you don't have a user dictionary currently installed, the User Dictionary command is not available in the Spelling cascading menu. To import or export user dictionary terms, you must have a user dictionary installed. See "Installing a Dictionary" in Chapter 2 for information on installing user dictionaries.*

Importing terms into a user dictionary

To import the contents of a text file into the current user dictionary:

1   **With the User Dictionary dialog box open and expanded, click Import.** The Import dialog box appears, and the File Name area automatically lists files with a .TXT extension.

2   **In the Import dialog box, locate the text file whose contents you want to import into the current user dictionary. Click OK.** A message displays to let you know the import is complete.

3   **Click OK to acknowledge the message.** The User Dictionary dialog box is still open. Notice that the list of terms updates to include any new terms from the imported file.

4   **Click OK in the User Dictionary dialog box to return to your document.**

Exporting user dictionary terms to a text file

To export the contents of the current user dictionary to a text file:

1   **With the User Dictionary dialog box open and expanded, click Export.** The Export dialog box opens, and the File Name area automatically assumes you will save the file with a .TXT extension.

2   **In the Export dialog box, type the name for your text file, leave the .TXT file extension, and click OK.** A message displays to let you know the export is complete.

3   **Click OK to acknowledge the message.** The User Dictionary dialog box is still open. The list of terms is unaffected by the export operation.

4   **Click OK in the User Dictionary dialog box to return to your document.**

Cross-platform tips and hints

This section gives you some useful tips and hints for using files that you create with ClarisWorks for Windows with ClarisWorks for the Macintosh. This information applies whether or not you are using a network.

Configuration tips

To exchange data across platforms between ClarisWorks for Windows and ClarisWorks for the Macintosh, you can use one of the following hardware configurations:

- Connect your PC and Macintosh over a network, such as PhoneNet, Novell, AppleTalk, or TOPS.
- On both machines, use a high-density disk drive along with a data-exchange utility.
- Connect your PC directly to a Macintosh using a special cable and exchange files via communications software.

The configuration I used in writing this book includes a PC running Windows 3.1 with an internal 3.5-inch high-density (1.44Mb) floppy disk drive, and a Macintosh running System 7 with an external 3.5-inch high-density floppy disk drive that is capable of reading from or writing to MS-DOS format. On my Macintosh, I'm using Apple's PC Exchange utility program, which lets Macintosh computers work with files stored on 3.5-inch MS-DOS or Windows floppy disks. PC Exchange also lets you format disks in PC or Macintosh format. With this utility program, you can create a PC-format disk from the Macintosh and save files created with ClarisWorks for the Macintosh on the PC-format disk. You can then insert this disk into the high-density floppy disk drive on your PC and open your Mac files directly in ClarisWorks for Windows.

Whichever configuration you choose, it is generally easier to use Mac-created files in ClarisWorks for Windows, rather than using PC-created files in ClarisWorks for the Macintosh.

File naming tips

The best rule of thumb for naming files that you plan to use across platforms is to follow the MS-DOS naming conventions. That is, whether you are saving a ClarisWorks document in Windows or on the Macintosh, name the file with no more than eight characters in the root part of the filename, and optionally add a three-character filename extension. For example, the sample database used in Chapter 4 of this book is named Friends.CWK. *Friends* is the root part of the filename, and *.CWK* is the filename extension.

Versions 1.0v4 and 2.0 of ClarisWorks for the Macintosh can read ClarisWorks for Windows files that are named with a .CWK or .CWS file extension. For example, if you wanted to open Friends.CWK in ClarisWorks on the Macintosh, you would choose Open from the File menu. With the Friends.CWK file appearing in the Open dialog box, select it, and click Open.

On the other hand, if you want to open a ClarisWorks for the Macintosh file in ClarisWorks for Windows and you don't include a file extension, or the filename contains more than eight characters in the root, ClarisWorks for Windows doesn't directly recognize the file in the Open dialog box. To list these files in the Open dialog box, type *.* in the File Name box.

Tips for font compatibility

For best results in maintaining consistency across platforms, use either TrueType fonts or Adobe Type Manager on both Macintosh and Windows machines. If you mix font technologies—the Macintosh uses Adobe Type Manager and the PC uses TrueType fonts, or vice versa—you may notice inconsistent results in word-wrapping at the end of lines, in line spacing, and in the overall look of documents.

In addition to using a similar font technology, you should be aware of how foreign font types are handled in Windows and on the Macintosh. For example, some Macintosh fonts are not available in Windows, and vice versa. The following sections discuss how fonts are substituted on both platforms.

Note *Because ClarisWorks for Windows doesn't support Outline or Shadow font styles (available in ClarisWorks for the Macintosh), you should avoid using them if you are using files across platforms.*

Macintosh-to-PC font substitution

When you use a ClarisWorks file created on the Mac in ClarisWorks for Windows, ClarisWorks for Windows looks at the MACFONT.MAP file (in the CLWORKS directory) to determine which font to substitute for a font you don't have installed.

Table A-6 lists the Macintosh-to-PC font substitutions.

Table A-6 Mac-to-PC Fonts

Macintosh	*PC*
Chicago	Arial
Courier	Courier New
Geneva	Arial
Helvetica	Arial
Monaco	Courier New
New York	Times New Roman
Palatino	Arial
Times	Times New Roman

If the Mac font is not found in the list, Arial is used. If none of the fonts in the list are on this Windows machine, MS Sans Serif is used. You have the option of editing the MACFONT.MAP to add or modify font substitutions.

PC-to-Macintosh font substitution

When you use a ClarisWorks for Windows file in ClarisWorks for the Macintosh, all Windows fonts are displayed in Geneva on the Macintosh.

ASCII character hints

Characters with ASCII decimal values of 0 through 127, inclusive, display and print the same on both Windows and Macintosh computers. However, extended ASCII characters (those with decimal values over 127) are unreliable for consistent results. For example, a Macintosh bullet character (•) is unprintable in Windows. Also, some other extended ASCII Macintosh characters display or print entirely differently in Windows. For this reason, use caution when you are working with extended ASCII characters across platforms.

Index